Western Civilization from 1500

HARPERCOLLINS COLLEGE OUTLINE

Western Civilization from 1500

3rd Edition

Walther Kirchner, Ph.D.
University of Delaware

HarperResource
An Imprint of HarperCollinsPublishers

An American BookWorks Corporation Production

Project Manager: Jonathon E. Brodman
Editor: Robert A. Weinstein

Library of Congress Catalog Card Number 90-56011
ISBN 0-06-467102-X

01   ABW/RRD   20 19 18 17 16 15 14 13 12 11

Contents

1

The Ancient Heritage

The Modern Age begins around 1500. Historians generally date it from the year 1492. By then, Western civilization had undergone an evolution of more than five thousand years. Great empires and civilizations had arisen—and had disappeared. Egyptians, Babylonians, Hittites, Assyrians, Persians, Hebrews, Phoenicians, Etruscans, Greeks, and Romans had passed over the stage of Western history. All of them had flourished in the same comparatively small area, which was restricted to lands surrounding the eastern Mediterranean basin and extended eastward not farther than the valley of the Tigris and Euphrates rivers. Geographic links connected the various peoples: their commercial enterprises, religious beliefs, artistic creations, and political fates were interwoven. The inventions and achievements of each older civilization nourished the thought and the work of civilizations that came after it.

Time has annihilated most of what they produced. Our knowledge of the oldest precursors of Western civilization has, however, increased, owing to the recent work of archaeologists. Yet any direct impact of the Egyptians and Babylonians, Persians and Phoenicians, or Hittites and Etruscans is hard to perceive because of the paucity of surviving monuments. Only indirectly—by affecting Greeks and Romans and, through these, modern Western civilization—has their legacy been preserved. Even the influence of the Hebrews has been limited in its direct effect chiefly to those ethical principles that have come down to us through Christianity.

GREEK CONTRIBUTIONS TO MODERN WESTERN CIVILIZATION

It is different with Greece and Rome. Grecian influence has been felt directly in almost all facets of modern life, and has most powerfully shaped Western civilization.

Language

A first indication of Greece's significance can be derived from the treasure of words the modern world has taken over. Examples are such English terms as philosophy, history, mathematics, aesthetics, mysticism, architecture, poetry, choir, monarchy, democracy, barbarism, theory, paper, and atom. Such words are not important simply for having entered our vocabulary. Rather, their importance lies in the fact that the concepts for which they stand have kept a meaning for modern people; the thought behind them has enriched our thinking; the ideas they represent have retained validity throughout the ages.

Philosophy

Greek thought roamed widely and freely, restrained by clear and logical minds but unimpeded by a written set of values, by an enforced creed, or by a dogma. This was perhaps one of the most important factors that has helped to make the concepts of ancient Greece a permanent, usable tool. The Greeks loved wisdom and sought a path to wise living. They studied the reality that surrounded them and tried first to understand it, then to master it. To achieve such mastery, they looked to noble qualities in human nature, to self-control, fortitude, and temperance. They studied themselves, both as individuals with individual aspirations and as members of a community with a common fate. They searched for a compromise between the ideal state of human beings and the limited status imposed upon them by nature. The Greeks initiated various philosophical schools, including the Sophists, the Epicureans, the Stoics, and the Cynics. Socrates, Plato, and Aristotle (fourth century B.C.) created systems of logic and concepts of ethics that have remained guides ever since. They thought through various ways to direct people in their search for knowledge and drive to action. They recognized that the human mind cannot comprehend everything and that there are limits, within which philosophical investigation could move throughout the history of Western civilization.

Science

With their rational procedures and their reliance upon logical deduction, the Greeks achieved a remarkable insight into the works of nature. They arrived at this insight by speculation rather than by observation and experimentation. This, to be sure, limited their achievement. Since they failed to evolve physical instruments that could have supplemented their methods and measured their results, they came to numerous erroneous conclusions. These, too, contributed to a lasting heritage: as the errors played an important role in the Greek view of the universe, so too, to a large extent, did they dominate Western thought well into the nineteenth century.

Simultaneously, however, the Greeks developed views that modern investigations have, to an astounding degree, proved to be correct. By means of logical deduction, they anticipated many findings acceptable to the modern world, and they prepared the way for fundamental procedures and discoveries. Among such significant achievements were those of Pythagoras, Archimedes, and Euclid in mathematics; of Democritus, who postulated an atomic theory; and of Thales, who taught that the earth is a sphere.

In medicine, views assigned to Asclepiades and principles recognized by Hippocrates and Galen have guided the medical profession into the present. They set forth fundamental concepts of the duties of a doctor, and they recognized the value of sanitariums and healing springs, of hygiene and physical exercise. Moreover, recent psychological trends were anticipated by philosophers like Plato, who insisted on the interconnection of mind and body.

In zoology, data on the animal world were compiled by Aristotle. In geography, on the basis of philosophical speculation and travel accounts, a picture of the globe was drawn which, notwithstanding all its faults, determined the views of geographers well into the Modern Age and has given direction to almost two thousand years of mapmaking. In the field of education, a special contribution was made by Greek philosophers. The Socratic method of teaching by questioning (and demanding logical answers) has become an integral part of modern pedagogy. Invariably, the modern world has been forced to go back to Greek models in its search for a satisfactory path to learning.

Even in military tactics, Greek principles have survived. Though weapons have changed, wedgelike formations for attack and oblique arrangement of battle forces, as used and described by the Greeks, have retained their usefulness.

Art

Greek civilization was marked by devotion to beauty. Their sense of harmony induced the Greeks not only to seek an understandable picture of human beings and the universe, but also to express their thoughts and feelings in a form that would inspire generations to come.

Nowhere is this striving for harmony of form and content more vividly expressed than in their architecture. The Greek temple has remained the best example of serene "classical" beauty. Hardly a town exists in the entire modern Western world where the Greek temple has not been copied outright or has not at least affected the style of public and private buildings. The simplicity and vigor of the Doric column, the grace of the Ionian, and the restrained exuberance of the Corinthian have never ceased to charm and inspire builders and architects. They have imitated Greek friezes, gables, and porticoes, seeking to achieve a similar clarity of line and simplicity of concept. The use of mathematical forms may explain to some degree the marvelous proportions of Greek architecture, but it was the meaningful ideas created by the great masters that have given their work its overwhelming appeal throughout the ages.

As in architecture, so it has been in sculpture, with the statues of Phidias, Praxiteles, and others. Greek sculpture has often been praised for its true-to-life quality. However, it was not this that has given it lasting value; rather, it is the fact that an abstract concept of beauty and a thoughtful approach to life were expressed in such a realistic form.

Unfortunately, we know too little to make similar assertions about Greek painting, music, and dance. Many indications exist, however, that in these arts, too, the Greeks created works of unsurpassed beauty. Some of their instruments, such as the flute and lyre, have been inherited by later ages. But, being more perishable than stone and marble, painting and music could not be passed on to future generations like buildings and sculpture.

Literature

Time has taken a similar toll upon the written works of Greece. Only a small fraction of what the Greeks composed has come down to the Modern Age. Surprising therefore is the unparalleled influence that Greek literature has exercised. The very words for different poetic forms: tragedy, comedy, lyric, epic—or for different verse meters: iamb, dactyl, hexameter—bear witness to the historical importance of their literature. The stories of Homer, the *Iliad* and the *Odyssey*, are cherished until this day and many children have dreamed of the mighty deeds of his heroes. What modern reader would not be awed by the breadth of Homer's vision of the human race, his insight into human emotions, the charm and meaningfulness of his parables? What poet or lover of poetry would not be captured by the infinite warmth and tenderness of the lyrics of Sappho, Pindar, or Anacreon? Their names may be less familiar than Homer's, but their influence has been felt, consciously and unconsciously. Their poetry has given direction to the form and content of songs and poems in all subsequent ages.

Equally potent has been the influence of the great Greek dramatists, Sophocles, Aeschylus, and Aristophanes. Their individual topics, whether mythological or political, have lost much pertinence, but the general significance of their work has remained undiminished. Antigone's appeal to unwritten laws that may be higher than any manmade rules; Oedipus's tragic involvement in predestined guilt; and Orestes's battle against the Furies, who are persecuting him for a crime even though it was necessary and preordained—never have these problems lost their hold upon our imagination. Our relationship to necessity, to a fate buried in our own nature as well as imposed by external forces, is a problem that not only persistently engaged the attention of Greek thinkers and dramatists, but has also captured, puzzled, shaken, and inspired the modern mind.

History

Greek civilization has often been described as unconcerned with history or as hostile to it, yet it produced some of the greatest historians. Among them were Herodotus, Xenophon, and, especially, Thucydides. The latter was perhaps even more conscious of the permanent significance of his work than were the poets (who, while giving expression to lasting thought, addressed themselves to contemporary audiences). As he himself states, he set out to write a history that was to be a treasure for all times. His method of presenting historical events has set no standards. A science of history was not evolved in Greece. But, with his artistic genius, the perfection of his treatment, the range of his presentation, the scope of his insight into the human drama, and his awareness of the limitations of human understanding, he left a work that has proved to be the very treasure he aspired to create.

Statecraft

The political problems of as small a country as Greece were in many ways very different from those that the modern, eventually industrialized, large nation-states have had to face. But what has made the political achievements of Athens, Sparta, Thebes, and others so imposing has been that they did not merely adjust themselves pragmatically to a given political form. Rather, the fundamental issues confronting any human community were thought through by the Greeks. They did not, like others, unthinkingly take over the despotic models or priest-dominated systems of their Oriental neighbors. Instead, they experimented with monarchy, aristocracy, oligarchy, democracy, and tyranny. Seeking independence, law, and order, and—at least in Athens—the free development of the citizen, they worked out constitutions of the most varied types.

Although they experienced, like others, the weaknesses of these respective forms of human government, the Greek philosophers and writers set themselves to the task of investigating various aspects of these forms, evaluating the relative merits and dangers. In poems, tragedies, and comedies, or in philosophical treatises, they set forth the conflicts between civic duties and personal aspirations, between society and individual. Thus, a body of political writings emerged that dealt not only with the realities of life in ancient Greece and with the problems of government and citizenship there, but also with the ideal of a utopian state where the conflicting forces might ultimately be reconciled.

Sports

The same sense of harmony that inspired Greek art and the Greek search for political order caused the Greeks to strive for the development of the individual, not only as a vehicle of spiritual aspirations, but with pride in the physical side of life as well. The beauty of the human body was a cherished ideal; valor was expected of all—and strength, fleetness, and grace. It was in order to further such ideals that the Greeks favored sports and instituted sporting competitions. Regularly, they held great festivals at Olympia, Corinth, and Delphi. True to the tradition of harmonious development of spirit, mind, and body, they generally started these events with religious rites, with a dedication to the gods. Then, during the next several days they held sports competitions, wherein racing, discus throwing, and wrestling played prominent roles. They concluded the celebrations with musical and literary performances in which composers, writers, and artists vied for laurels. Separate festivals with similar programs were held for women. So vital a part did these occasions play in Greek life that the very calendar of Greece was dated according to the Olympic games.

Surviving Greek Civilization

Enthusiasm for Greek life has induced many historians to idealize Greek institutions, Greek thought, and Greek habits to such an extent that they have neglected the darker aspects of conditions in Greece. Little has been said about some of the attitudes that lay behind the Greek artistic and philosophical achievements. Some have forgotten that the Greeks were vain and arrogant, and considered the entire world outside their borders "barbaric." They were hard dealing, inclined to cheat, prone to perjury and to treason. Of all peoples, they were the ones who unhesitatingly made one of their gods the protector of liars. They were quarrelsome, dishonest, greedy, brutal, and oppressive. Slavery was an integral part of their social institutions. They had little respect for laws; politicians and demagogues sacrificed the welfare of the state to personal ambitions. Homosexuality was a commonly accepted phenomenon, and prostitutes were praised in song while wives and daughters of the best households were little regarded and generally oppressed.

But the events occurring in the marketplace, the evil quarrels of daily living, and the abject, ugly condition of the Greek masses have disappeared as completely from our view as has the individual Greek citizen. What have survived are the immortal works of the few; the depth of thought of the greatest minds; the longing for freedom and free development of nation and individual, as expressed in deeds; the artistic creations that Grecian sensitivity to beauty made possible; the penetration of nature's secrets and the understanding of human life and ways—these have become a guide for all Western civilization.

THE ROMAN CONTRIBUTIONS

If the Greek heritage has been praised for its legacy of rationality, truth, and beauty, the Roman heritage has been extolled for its practical usefulness. Scant justice, however, has thus been done to Rome. For Rome, too, left in its innumerable monuments a large spiritual heritage to future generations; and one that can well challenge that of Greece.

Language

Like the Greek language, so has Latin made inestimable contributions to the civilization of the modern world. Just as with many Greek terms, numerous Latin terms found entrance into modern vocabularies, and with them the concepts and institutions for which they stand. Among Latin-English words are citizen, family, census, senate, monument, and arch. Other words, which originally were Greek, entered the Latin and were preserved by the Romans. The Western world thus owes to Rome a vast store of experience, embodied in language, which otherwise would have had to be painfully worked out anew and independently.

History

Most important among the legacies of Rome are those contributions that have taught the modern world a rational, reasonable approach to political conduct and nation-building. The political genius of Rome, its ability to rule itself and others, to adapt itself to changing conditions, to invent checks and balances in order to avoid excesses, to overcome the threats of social challenges, to regulate "the relationship of man to man," have altogether constituted an unequaled lesson for future Western civilization.

Preserved and evaluated by Livius, Tacitus, and others, the history of Rome furnishes insight into the evolution not only of Rome, but of any great people. It's history is embodied in the traditions of every Mediterranean nation, in monuments erected in the most varied countries, in their languages, law codes, and institutions. These Roman achievements, unlike those of Greece in its time of glory, were less the work of a few individuals with outstanding genius than (as the German historian Theodor Mommsen once wrote) the result of "extraordinary deeds" by "ordinary men."

Law

Underlying the structure of the mighty empire eventually built by the Romans was a concept of law which, though it had many roots in Greek philosophical thought and derived as well from the many examples provided by the political systems of other Mediterranean nations, was nonetheless unique in the ancient world. Roman law was a living procedure, adaptable to constantly changing situations. Only toward the very end of the empire, when decay of the state had progressed far, did the law become codified in its various aspects.

Roman law embraced the relationship between individuals. It progressively defined civic rights and the membership of the citizen within the common republic. Its vocabulary is still used and its procedures serve as models even today. Its stipulations in regard to property, the conduct of business, matters of inheritance, marriage, and divorce, and numerous other fields have sown the seeds for the codes of justice among all Western nations. Moreover, international rules worked out by Rome have constituted the beginning of endeavors on a long path toward a universal organization that would do justice to all members of the society of nations.

Architecture and Public Construction

In architecture, the Romans are known less for their originality than for their genius at adaptation. To a large extent, they adopted the artistic concepts that the Greeks had evolved. They built temples which, following the styles of Greece, inspire through harmony of form and elegance of structure.

But what they took over they also applied to different sorts of architectural projects, to types of construction that reflect an enterprising spirit and an inventive genius not shown by the Greeks. To these buildings, Rome lent much of that same kind of beauty that had flourished in Greece. Mighty waterworks were completed, aqueducts were installed, bridges with noble spans were thrown across rivers and canals, viaducts were laid across valleys and a *Cloaca Maxima* (sewer system) was built that has astounded modern engineers. The most distant parts of the empire were connected by a remarkable system of roads, many of them still in use. For hundreds of miles, walls and forts were erected along endangered borders.

Beyond such necessities—witnesses of the practical inclinations of an empire-building society—the Romans also created remarkable public monuments for the beautification and glory of their state. Such projects simultaneously helped solve social problems—they furnished work for the unemployed—and provided entertainment for the discontented classes. The Romans erected triumphal arches, constructed columns celebrating victories, and adorned these structures with inscriptions and representations of Rome's deeds of glory. They built public baths, a Colosseum and, in numerous cities, large arenas. The private houses of the rich, such as those found in long-buried Pompeii, were embellished with beautiful frescoes, reliefs, mosaics, and fountains.

Literature

As in architecture, neither did Rome in the field of literature initiate many new styles. The Romans did not think of many new literary approaches and thus did not show much originality. For its epics, Rome borrowed the hexameter from Greece. For its lyrics, Rome used and adapted the verse meters of Sappho, Alcaeus, and others. For its prose, it took Herodotus' and Thucydides' histories or Aesop's fables as models. In the form and content of its drama, Rome reflected that of the tragedies and comedies of Greece.

One of the most important Roman literary masterpieces, Vergil's *Aeneid,* a work of lasting grandeur, would have been impossible without the model of Homer's *Iliad* and *Odyssey.*

Nevertheless, at certain times (especially during the Renaissance) the literature of Rome has meant more to Western civilization than that of Greece. The writings of Cicero (which embody the author's eclectic philosophical views and possess little of the genius of Plato and Aristotle) and his orations (which hardly equal those of Demosthenes) have been praised again and again as the embodiment of worldly wisdom and have exercised a profound influence. Stoic philosophy has become known chiefly through the writings of Seneca and Marcus Aurelius. Epicureanism found a home and tradition in the wealthy Roman Empire rather than in Greece. Among the poets, Ovid and Horace are better known to the modern world than most of the Greeks (to be sure, the fact that a greater quantity of Latin poetry than Greek has survived may partially account for its popularity). For the stage, Rome produced the plays of Plautus, Terence, and Juvenal.

To these lasting contributions can be added the works of the great Roman historians—Livius, Caesar, Tacitus, and many others—who by transmitting the deeds of their compatriots have helped to shape Western civilization. It is through their eyes that Rome's history is viewed, that Rome's glory is appraised, and that Rome's mistakes and vices are recognized. Roman moral judgment has permanently affected the attitude of the West and has impressed upon it standards that have become an inseparable part of the civilization within which modern people act.

Surviving Rome

Like all great empires, Rome fell. Its people, too, exhibited human weakness in all their diversity. Like the Greeks, Romans were arrogant and brutal. Ruthless toward their enemies, they were also fickle friends. Corruption ran rampant within the bureaucracy. Greed animated those who should have dispensed justice and arbitrariness marked those who should have looked after the welfare of the state and its citizens.

The Romans extolled bravery. Wading in blood, they extended their empire. They exploited the lands and peoples that they conquered. At home, they kept the masses in servitude by brute force. They never achieved a stable societal structure: a constantly reviving revolutionary element, produced by war and misery, had to be kept in check by force, gifts, bribes, or costly amusements. Ethical principles were seldom heeded except insofar as they served the ruling classes of the empire. Disillusioned citizens, longing for a peaceful and pure life, turned away from public affairs and sought refuge in the stern, solitary atmosphere of Stoicism.

Yet, Rome, like Greece, left an unparalleled heritage. The stories of Lucretia, Fabius Cunctator, and Brutus have taught lessons of devotion and fulfillment of duty that have never been forgotten. Roman fortitude in adversity during the war against Hannibal, Roman uprightness as tragically exemplified by the two Catos, Roman statesmanship as shown by Augustus, and the Roman peace, as it prevailed under a Trajan, Hadrian, or Marcus Aurelius, have remained treasures of Western civilization and symbols of a conquest greater than armies could achieve.

Selected Reading

Kirchner, Walther. *Western Civilization to 1500* (1991)

2

The Medieval Heritage

The story of Greece and Rome is ended. The empires have disappeared; the societies they represented are dead. A cycle was completed. Most of the areas where they once flourished passed into the hands of different kinds of people. Western civilization found new centers in France, Germany, England, Spain, and other parts of the world. Not only in the Mediterranean area, but also in the center of Europe and along Europe's Atlantic borders, as well as in Italy, the story of Western civilization continued. Whether it was in the fourth, fifth, or as late as the seventh and eighth centuries that the ancient world made room for medieval civilization is a fascinating question. On our answer to this question may depend our whole attitude toward the problem of survival of civilizations, including our own.

In any case, sometime between A.D. 375 and 732, a new age began. This new age, the "Middle Ages," does not represent so much of a closed book, a finished story, as do ancient times. The centers of medieval civilization and many institutions of medieval society, unlike most of those of the ancient world, live on. No break has occurred during the fourteenth, fifteenth, and sixteenth centuries; the Middle Ages almost imperceptibly evolved into modern times. In eastern, western, and northern Europe, new areas were added to old established centers, and in these new areas, the traditions of the old were carried on.

MEDIEVAL CONTRIBUTIONS

Four factors especially demark the fundamental departure of Western medieval civilization from that of ancient times: (1) a geographic shift of the centers of power and civilization from the eastern Mediterranean basin northward to all Europe; (2) an influx of Germanic races into the Roman world and the emergence of a number of new political and social units carrying forward not only the Roman, but also the young, fresh, "barbarian" German heritage; (3) an economic transformation that followed the decline of the commercial markets in the wide Mediterranean Empire and the transition from a slave-owning, capitalistic society to an organization based on a feudal, local economy; and (4) the introduction and impact of Christianity.

Language

At the beginning of the medieval epoch, not a single modern Western language existed. At its end, almost every one of the Western national languages, all of which would evolve into the languages of today, had emerged. Latin was preserved throughout the Middle Ages as a means of international communication. But when modern times began, the linguistic tools we use today and that form our thinking had been shaped. Vocabularies and grammars of present-day languages had developed from Latin and Germanic roots and, in the East, from Slavic sources. They had been enriched, moreover, by numerous new words, either coined in order to express new thoughts and designate new instruments or taken over from other civilizations. By then, the tongues of the various nations, that is, the languages spoken by the various peoples or tribes, predominated both in daily life and popular literature. They also began to be used in religious literature and services and in scholarship. Thus, modern languages constitute one of the chief legacies of the Middle Ages.

Religion

In addition to the development of languages, one of the most outstanding contributions of the Middle Ages was the preservation and propagation of Christianity. The introduction of Christianity in the Western world as the Roman Empire's official religion, in such a way as to have enjoyed an almost monopolistic status, coincides with the beginnings of medieval times. By then, the creed of all major Christian churches had been formulated at Nicea and, ever since, it has prevailed. The Bible was translated into Latin, and it has become the property of all succeeding generations. Christian ethics were imposed upon pagan views and, even if at no time entirely triumphant, they have remained ideals toward which the Western world has been striving. The Church, Catholic or Orthodox, throughout the Middle Ages became the dominant social influence upon all the peoples of Europe. It permeated every facet of medieval life and thought. With its artistic and educational tenets, its calendar, its law, and its services as well as its political and economic power, it set the pattern for the secular and spiritual conditions that have given direction to all subsequent ages.

The Church imposed an order and a unity that even a later division into nations has never entirely obliterated. The Catholic Church created, with its papacy and hierarchy, an organization that has survived as a potent factor in modern times. Even so-called "heresies"—doctrines not approved by the official church—made their contributions. For through their challenge a constant process of purification has been forced upon the Christian church, and the Christian faith has been kept as the guiding code of the West for almost two thousand years. This has been enriched by rebellious and defending forces alike.

Philosophy

Naturally, Christian thought dominated all speculation about transcendental questions. Its influence has caused philosophers to engage in a search for ultimate goals and standards of logic and ethics different from those of the ancient world. Church fathers, such as Augustine, Ambrose, Jerome, John Chrysostom, and others, especially in the fourth century, started medieval philosophy on the new path.

But it was only in the twelfth and thirteenth centuries that a complete system of Christian philosophy emerged. Under the guidance of the universities and of so-called "schoolmen," among whom Peter Abelard, Albertus Magnus, and Thomas Aquinas stand out, an attempt was made to preserve or revive the Greek heritage, to follow the Greeks on the path of logic and rationality, yet not to sacrifice any part of the Christian and Church tradition, or any of its mysteries and transcendental teachings.

During the thirteenth century, the scholastic attempt was carried forward by two schools, the "Realists" and the "Nominalists." The former were closer in their thinking to Plato; the latter relied more on Aristotle. Though neither challenged the Christian foundations, the Realists insisted on the primacy of universal ideas and their exclusive "reality," whereas the Nominalists emphasized the role of the "particular" evidences of God's creation in nature and their significance. The Nominalists paved the way for a future naturalistic, scientific approach. The long struggle of the two sides forced them to make the greatest intellectual efforts, and these have again and again nurtured modern thinking and investigation.

Even apart from scholastic philosophy, the Middle Ages provided a mighty stimulus to modern philosophical pursuits. Scientific speculations about cosmos and nature by men such as Roger Bacon and, more important for philosophical developments, the mystical views and "experiences" expressed or witnessed by St. Francis and Meister Eckhart have stimulated again and again the speculations of later times. Indeed, the various forces of Scholasticism, of science, of mysticism, and of a revived classical philosophy constitute one of the most lasting contributions of the Middle Ages.

Learning

Religious thought and philosophical speculation gave direction to all forms of education in medieval times. After several centuries of stagnation during the early Middle Ages, secular knowledge resumed its path toward broader enlightenment. The Middle Ages gradually created an educational system, whose aspirations could, at least in part, form a basis and offer inspiration for developments in the modern world. Primary schooling in medieval times emphasized discipline, which was considered necessary for the formation of character, for the learning of reading and writing, and for Bible studies. This approach was, however, weakened as modern times progressed. The more advanced curriculum, which provided training in grammar, astronomy, music, and so on, also did not find permanent imitation.

But the university, a creation of the eleventh century, has been of unique importance. Professors and students began to meet in "universities." Within an atmosphere free from outside interference, they devoted themselves to the study of the universe and of mankind in its manifold aspects. Their studies embraced the four faculties of theology, law, philosophy, and medicine. Jews and, particularly, Arabs contributed to these studies by their accumulated wisdom in such fields as astronomy, agriculture, classics, science, and medicine. The four faculties of the universities as well as their rites and forms have proved to be of fundamental importance for the progress of Western civilization ever since. It was largely in the universities that the ever-striving spirit that has characterized Western civilization was fostered.

It was through universities that the training in logical thought was provided, which, in many instances, made possible the flowering of all secular activity outside their walls. Thus, receptivity was also created for many scientific considerations. Interest grew in the accomplishments of other civilizations. Paper, the compass, and glass were adopted from them. This heritage, in turn, stimulated original contributions, such as the invention of gunpowder and, toward the end of the medieval period, the printing press with movable type.

Art

Medieval art rivals all other medieval accomplishments in its importance for later times. It has exercised an influence at least equal to that of the art created by the ancient world. Just as there is hardly a community in the West in which imitations of Greek temples and columns cannot be found, so too there is hardly one in which the round Romanesque arch or, more frequently, the pointed arch of the Gothic cathedral and town hall, the stained-glass window, the imagery of Mary and the Christ child, and the paintings of the early Renaissance are not represented, copied, or imitated. The countless wonders of the Gothic style have, indeed, found duplication, often incongruously, in such a variety of modern buildings—churches, universities, private homes, stations, office buildings—that they have become an integral part of our lives. The unthinking modern individual is seldom aware of their origin. Cathedrals, which show Gothic style in its ultimate beauty, were, it has been said, "built before God, not before man."

The more humble artistic achievements of the Middle Ages, those shown by articles made for daily household use, have also left an indestructible heritage. The small arts, the handicrafts in all trades, have excited the imagination of Western civilization ever since.

Mosaics and paintings, successively in Byzantine, Romanesque, Gothic, and, finally, Renaissance style, are not only on display in museums, where they are the pride of town and nation. They are also to be seen in homes, often as transformed in the work of later generations of artists.

Each medieval creation bears witness to the individual genius and detailed, loving care of the individual master. Even if the creations of the early medieval periods with their special beauty and symbolism are not always meaningful to the uninitiated, those of the Renaissance, of Giotto, Fra Angelico, Botticelli, van Eyck, Memling, and hundreds of others have become part of the lives of millions who may not be conscious of the names of painting or artist.

Literature

Medieval literature has also made lasting contributions to Western civilization. Twofold were the merits of medieval scholars and writers. They preserved the literary and intellectual accomplishments of Greece and Rome, copying them down with infinite patience, commenting and interpreting. They then added to the ancient heritage their own creative works. Early during the medieval period, a minuscule (lowercase letters replacing the capital letters used by the Romans) was developed. This rendered easier the labor of writing by making writing more fluent, and helped to increase the treasury of great thought that could be preserved.

Many of the books written or reproduced during this time were prepared in beautiful lettering. Innumerable manuscripts with their splendid illuminations are witnesses to the medieval interest in literature; they are an inspiration to modern endeavors. We possess, in Latin and in later vernacular tongues, Church translations and commentaries; mighty hymns, such as "Ave Maria" and "Dies Irae"; great epics, like *Parzival, Tristan and Iseult,* the *Nibelungenlied,* and *La Chanson de Roland;* histories, chronicles, and scientific treatises; the love songs of troubadours and minnesängers; a vast heritage of folk songs; and a not yet sufficiently appreciated body of prose works. In the late Middle Ages, individual masterpieces stand out. Towering among them are the works of three Italians: Dante, Petrarch, and Boccaccio.

Music

Much of the writing and folklore was originally destined to be accompanied by music. The sound has long passed; the voices are dead. We know little more of it than parchment or paper can preserve with notations for music, or than instruments that have survived and been adapted to modern use can tell us. Yet, the oral tradition has not been entirely lost. Through it, the sonorous Gregorian chant has come down to us across the centuries; so too have thousands of lovely and mysterious folk songs and dances, which have never ceased to be repeated, generation after generation. Significantly, in many regions of the West, folklore did not become a conscious heritage until rediscovered during the past two centuries.

Statecraft

During the Middle Ages, all of the great modern European nations emerged as separate entities and within territorial limits that approximate those of today. France and Germany became the common heirs of Charlemagne's empire. England, conquered and settled by numerous invaders, was fused into the unit which it still represents. Russia emerged as a nation centering around Moscow. By the end of the Middle Ages, the Italians, though not yet attaining independent statehood, possessed a common language and common national aspirations. Spain had become a united country, Portugal a separate one. The Scandinavian countries were formed. A basis was laid for Switzerland, Hungary, and other nations. As a whole, medieval times put an end to the unity which the Western world under Roman rule had once possessed. Notwithstanding the attempts of the Catholic Church to preserve at least a spiritual unity, a multiplicity of states emerged with those separate and identifiable characteristics that are known to us in modern times.

Law and Legislation

Besides the evolution of nations, the Middle Ages made other important political contributions. While feudal ethics and economics found no acceptance in later times, certain aspects of medieval legal developments have been of great significance. The Middle Ages left to the field of law a threefold legacy: they preserved the heritage of ancient Rome, they evolved Church canons that have retained validity in the Catholic world and have influenced other areas, and they developed what became known as "common law."

Originating with chiefly Germanic concepts of justice, native in northern and eastern Europe and distinct from those of ancient Rome, this common law gradually expanded through oral tradition and through usage. It came to constitute, though uncodified, an integral part of the mores, ethics, and laws of the modern age. Courts and judges through their decisions, as well as lawyers and professors of law through their opinions, have established certain principles in conformity with an old spiritual heritage.

Closely interwoven with this growth of the medieval system of law was that of a number of political legal institutions. Most important among them were "diets" and "parliaments," which assumed rights of public legislation. These have left their mark upon all subsequent ages. They were composed of representatives of "estates" or classes. To a large extent, modern class stratification is based on medieval organization. Remnants of the medieval status of the aristocracy and of many ruling families have even survived into our own modern times. Titles and privileges go back to medieval patterns, but medieval times anticipated also the broader constitutional rights that were later claimed by the bourgeoisie.

Commerce and Discoveries

The heritage of medieval economic organization has been investigated, but, for lack of sources, is not yet sufficiently known. Yet, both in economic theory and in practical matters of commerce, the Middle Ages passed on a rich inheritance. Christian scholars as well as historians and chroniclers left treatises to posterity that reflect deep insight into questions of just price, interest-taking, monopoly, and profit. Economic theory forms part of as fundamental a work as St. Thomas Aquinas's *Summa Theologica*. He and others sought to direct natural human urges, such as ambition and greed, into channels where they would not conflict with the ethical demands of Christianity.

Likewise, practical aspects of medieval economic life and economic organization have been influential. Guilds, developed in the Middle Ages, have remained meaningful. Aware of certain principles of morality, they sought to limit competition, which was considered a vice; they promoted high standards of quality in workmanship. The Middle Ages also experimented with organization of communal labor, communal property, and planned production. During medieval times, many principles of banking, credit, exchange, and capital formation were taken over from the East or worked out independently. Numerous achievements of this kind gave direction to later entrepreneurial activity and exercised an influence on various political experiments—even in the Industrial Age.

Perhaps one of the chief reasons for the continued importance of some parts of the medieval economic system was that a vast expansion of European trade took place during the Middle Ages. Commerce had to adapt itself to worldwide markets. The enterprises of the Italian towns in the Mediterranean area, of the Hanseatic League in the Baltic, the Portuguese ventures to the Far East, and the Spanish explorations into the Atlantic regions were not merely precursors, leading to modern business activities. In many respects they represented undertakings of the same order as modern entrepreneurship and therefore were subject to very similar conditions. They thus could teach important lessons.

Cities

Lastly, the Middle Ages saw the founding (or, after Roman beginnings, the refounding) of almost all the great cities of Europe. By 1500, most of the great commercial centers of Italy, Germany, France, Spain, England, Scandinavia, and Russia that have played a role in modern times had been established. The development and rise of towns necessitated ways to organize them. People had to be attracted, shifts of population had to be managed, special laws and privileges had to be developed, and a division of labor had to be adopted. All of these would set patterns for later times.

THE "DARK AGES"

Like all other periods in history, the "Dark Ages," as the Middle Ages have sometimes been called, were full of misery. Pestilence, war, and starvation were rife. Intolerance, often in the name of religion, was greater than almost ever before. Those who did not share the beliefs of the powerful were declared heretics or were outlawed and persecuted; some were burned at the stake. The oppressed poor, tied to the soil and, as serfs, deprived of the right to move, had no recourse against the arbitrariness of their local masters. Though standards of honor were established and extolled in heroic poetry, treachery and falsehood prevailed.

Pride in clean and healthy bodies, as had once existed in Greece, was lost. Disease and suffering were rampant, owing to a wide disdain of nature and body and to an otherworldly orientation of the mind. Praise of womanhood was sung; the cult of Mary was initiated. Yet women were maltreated and held in contempt as the begetters of evil. Superstition was widespread, and the age, like most of the preceding ones, was marked by insecurity and fear.

Yet, the "Dark Ages" have also illuminated the modern world with their faith, scholarship, and the beauty they created. They brought forth ideas, and they established ideals that have remained meaningful. The faith and ethics of Christianity, the standards set in learning and philosophy, the works in art and literature, stand unique. They have enriched the modern world no less than did the highest achievements of Greece and Rome.

Selected Reading   Kirchner, Walther. *Western Civilization to 1500* (1991)

3

The Beginning of "The Modern Age" (1492–1517)

Not arbitrarily is the Modern Age dated from about 1500. The historical period from then until now possesses cohesion and a common outlook. Naturalism, individualism, and nationalism give it a special meaning.

Moreover, the global expansion of Western civilization constitutes a distinguishing characteristic. Whereas the Classical Period had embraced the evolution of civilizations around the Mediterranean Sea and in the Near East, and whereas the Medieval Period had enlarged the horizon by including all Europe as well as most of the Old World, the Modern Age takes in the entire globe.

The Modern Age had its beginnings in one of the most glorious epochs in Western civilization. Justly does Preserved Smith write in his Age of the Reformation, *p. 3 (1920): "Though in some sense every age is one of transition and every generation sees the world remodelled, there sometimes comes a change so startling and profound that it seems like the beginning of a new season in the world's great year. . . . Spring has come."*

That is what happened. Within "the span of a single life" (for convenience's sake, Smith takes the life of Luther, 1483–1546, as his measure) there appeared a great number of the most memorable personalities in history. And in all fields of human endeavor and human understanding—exploration and enterprise, science, art, music, literature, religion, and state-building— there were created some of the most momentous works known to history. This first generation of modern times was "great in what it achieved, sublime in what it dreamed; abounding in ripe wisdom and heroic deeds; full of light and of beauty and of life."

WESTERN SOCIETY AROUND 1500

The society that brought forth such accomplishments was a true child of the Renaissance. It was devoted to beauty; it was enterprising and skeptical. It rejected many of the past religious traditions and past authorities and yet was itself religious and reverent. It undertook to penetrate the secrets of nature with unaccustomed curiosity and confidence. Youth played a more important and leading role than it ever has since: men, and sometimes women, of thirty, twenty-five, twenty, and even sixteen years of age occupied many of the most influential posts and achieved feats of lasting significance. Truly could the young German poet and humanist Ulrich von Hutten sing: "It is a joy to live!"

Social Aspirations

Unlike the cultural atmosphere of medieval times, when the longings toward otherworldliness gave direction to many of the greatest achievements, the spirit of the Renaissance tended toward worldly things—toward a full development of people's natural gifts and a full gratification of the

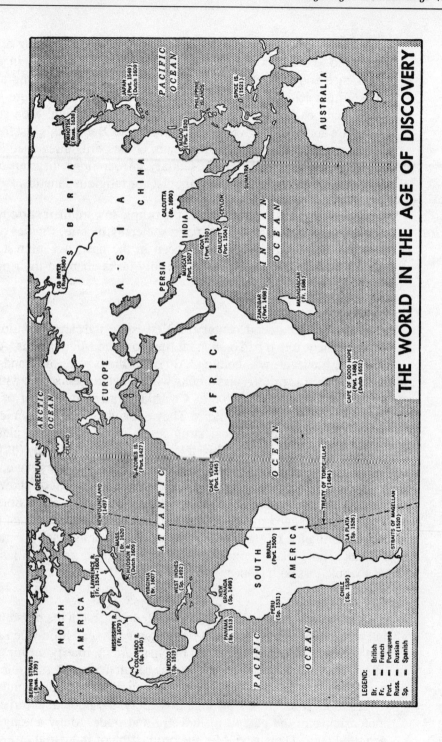

THE WORLD IN THE AGE OF DISCOVERY

LEGEND:
Br.   British
Fr.   French
Port. Portuguese
Russ. Russian
Sp.   Spanish

senses through the attractions offered by this world. Among all layers of society do we witness a thirst to enjoy life and all it could offer in meaningful experience and in transient pleasure. It was a time of great moral, cultural, and spiritual achievement. Albeit, it was also an age of pleasure-seeking, of intemperate eating, drinking, dressing, and lovemaking. Men and women risked life and limb in adventure and enterprise. Behind this lust for life stood the expectation of pain and early death. Great perils threatened in the form of wars, murders, pestilences, unsanitary surroundings, disasters on the seas, and persecutions by political antagonists or religious fanatics.

Social Stratification

The changes in the attitudes of the people toward their surroundings had a very slow, yet distinct, effect upon societal structure. Classes or "estates" remained essentially as they had been in the past; but interest in secular matters and, with it, attention to worldly tasks changed their outlook and occupations.

CLERGY

In the early sixteenth century the first estate, the clergy, continued to play the prominent role it had enjoyed throughout the Middle Ages. A change in this role, however, was coming. Although there were thousands of higher prelates, humble priests, and monks who devoted themselves with unabated zeal and piety to the service of Christianity, a vast number of them also indulged in worldly occupations. They expanded their economic activities; they participated in political struggles as well as secular pleasures and ambitions. A pope such as Alexander VI of the Borgia family (d. 1503), with his greed, politics, mistresses, children, and poisons, may have constituted an extreme of clerical depravity. But many others, too, showed greater interest in art, devotion to science, ability in languages, perfection in Renaissance manners, and participation in humanistic endeavors than they did in the performance of their duties. Soon, low morals, lack of training, and neglect of duty characterized even certain reforming groups. Thus, the clergy as a whole lost both respect and importance.

NOBILITY

The second estate, the nobility, rivaled the first in the pursuit of worldly interests. The medieval code of honor came to mean little when gunpowder and other inventions undermined the standards formerly set for the conduct of a nobleman; his military occupations began to play a lesser role. To a large extent, princes had to hire soldiers (mercenaries) to do the fighting.

In order to retain his prestige in society, the nobleman turned his mind increasingly to the pursuit of industry and trade. Many among the nobles acquired land. They used it for the production of industrial crops, exploited its mineral resources, and participated in business ventures. With the wealth thus acquired, they indulged in the entertainments of the age and the furtherance of secular interests in scholarship, art, literature, and science. A new ideal for the cultured noble was set up, originating in Italy: the ideal of *virtù*, i.e., of manly activity, intelligence, achievement, and conduct, devoted to all facets of Renaissance life.

Significantly, women shared in the interests and activities of the upper classes. Though they were in some respects, and in many instances, still held down, treated with cruelty, and abused as the "begetters of evil," some of them attained prominent positions. They exercised a greater influence upon political and cultural developments during this period than in most previous ones. Women ruled as queens, served as regents, diplomats, and administrators of estates, and engaged in professions as doctors, lawyers, and teachers. They excelled as scholars, poets, and arbiters of arts and manners. Chastity was as uncommon among them as among men. Power and luxury were as much craved by them.

THE BURGHER

In the age of discovery, the townspeople or burghers, who together with the free peasants formed the "third estate," necessarily acquired increased prestige. Everywhere, merchants and bankers rose to prominence. Owing to the wealth of the burghers, not only ports such as Cadiz, Lisbon, Antwerp, and London, but also trading cities and centers of crafts such as Augsburg and Nuremberg in southern Germany gained far-reaching influence. The Fugger family of Augsburg—whose interests extended to textile industries, silver and copper mining, wholesale trade, and banking—with its influence on the emperors and kings of Germany, England, Spain, and Portugal, was exceptionally powerful. Other businessmen with less wealth than the Fuggers could also influence the political fate of great commonwealths. Moreover, artisans gained in influence inasmuch as the demand for objects useful for the beautification of the surroundings or for new production methods increased.

Within the burgher class there developed a differentiation between the standards of the wealthy and those of the poor. The rich took the nobility as their model; they participated in Renaissance pleasures and aspirations. The poor were more limited in their search for pleasure. Among them, new standards of morality began to emerge emphasizing restraint, sobriety, frugality, and duty. This trend was accelerated during the course of the century by the influence of religious reform movements. It was also accelerated by the gradual worsening of the economic conditions of the lower classes brought about by unemployment, rising prices, and beginning capitalism, which in its early form deprived people of security and imposed new economic burdens. Crime increased. Beggars infested the towns; highwaymen made life unsafe for travelers and merchants.

THE PEASANT

Around 1500, the vast majority of the population in Europe was still composed of peasants. This was true even in a small country as active in trade as the Netherlands. However, considerable changes also occurred within this class. In the East, especially in Poland and Russia, a tendency toward greater enslavement of the peasantry was noticeable; but serfdom in central and western Europe continued to diminish.

With the growth of towns and trade, the need for free labor increased further. Simultaneously, changes in agricultural production methods reduced the usefulness of the institution of serfdom. As a result, many serfs were released and left the villages. Others who stayed gained at least partial freedom.

This emancipation movement benefited the peasants to a limited degree only. As the canvases of Pieter Brueghel the Elder, Hieronymus Bosch, and other painters show, many peasants indulged in dissipations (for which the upper classes set an example) and sought special enjoyment in feasting (something made possible because the food supply had become more ample than ever before). Social evolution, however, brought new hardships for them. Many who migrated to towns found life there even more difficult than at home. Deprived of security, peasants in various lands revolted. But they could not reverse the trends of the time.

ECONOMIC CONDITIONS

The most significant factor shaping Western society around 1500 was the expansion of its horizon. New technical means had become available. There were new types of ships, maps, nautical instruments, and superior weapons. Wealth was accumulated with which to equip expeditions. Political authority was established that could give protection to them. Scientific experience was gained that made success possible. A degree of economic organization had been achieved that not only could provide financial backing but also enable entrepreneurs of various specializations to combine in common undertakings.

Geographic Explorations

Possessing the material resources, men of genius, animated by the enterprising spirit of the age, could undertake to turn long-held dreams into reality. Their incentives were threefold, the three ever-present "G's": Gospel, Gold, and Glory—the desire to convert others, to enrich themselves, and to win fame.

Explorers set out in search of new shores. Columbus reached America in 1492. Vasco da Gama sailed to India via the Cape of Good Hope in 1498. Amerigo Vespucci landed on the continent (which has been named after him). Balboa crossed this continent and in 1513 sighted the Pacific Ocean. The Portuguese Magellan, with courage and perseverance, performed perhaps the most heroic feat of all; he undertook the first circumnavigation of the earth, and (though he himself perished on the trip) one of his five ships actually accomplished the round trip. John Cabot reached the North American continent near Labrador. In 1521, Cortes conquered the Aztec Empire in Mexico.

Somewhat later, Pizarro conquered for the Spanish the Inca Empire in Peru. The Portuguese built an empire of their own in the East Indies. Strife over the new possession was avoided by a Line of Demarcation established by the pope in 1493. It was amended one year later by the Treaty of Tordesillas, which assigned to Portugal most of the eastern, and to Spain most of the western, colonies.

ECONOMIC IMPACT

The discoveries had far-reaching influence upon European life. Economically, they provided enormous quantities of coveted gold and silver. They also secured vast new sources of food, especially fish. Soon, the value of the agricultural resources, game, and fish of many colonies overshadowed that of mining. Many new products, such as maize and potatoes, were introduced in Europe and changed prevailing food habits.

POLITICAL IMPACT

Politically, the discoveries strengthened the monarchs who enlarged their personal dominions and augmented their wealth. A shift of power from old trade centers to new ones in different countries occurred. Eventually, the Atlantic sea routes grew in importance compared with traditional Mediterranean and Baltic trade routes. The redistribution of power resulting from the acquisition of colonies led to new struggles for trade supremacy and to new wars.

SOCIAL IMPACT

Socially, the discoveries benefited merchants of the burgher class, who gained prestige through acquisition of new wealth. They affected the poorer layers of the population by providing them with food that could be imported and thus with new means of sustenance. Under the circumstances, populations grew. The newly discovered lands lured the adventurous to emigration. Moreover, as knowledge about the earth increased, old beliefs had to be given up and thinking habits changed. Lastly, discoveries led to the transformation not only of the Old World, but also of the new lands, which had to change their own ways of life in accordance with European desires and customs.

Economic Reorganization

Geographical discoveries, combined with the individualistic, enterprising spirit of Renaissance times, fundamentally influenced economic developments.

BUSINESS ORGANIZATION

The enormous expansion of markets and development of a money economy, strengthened by an ample supply of precious metals flowing from the New World as well as from Europe itself (for example, from Hungary), laid the basis for the rise of modern capitalism and private enterprise. Thus, the Fugger family of Augsburg represented entrepreneurial activity of a new magnitude and importance. A sharp competitive spirit aiming at personal monopolistic advantages in production and internal and external trade replaced former social attitudes and economic morals. A greater leniency of the Church toward people investing capital and receiving interest, which had formerly been forbidden, aided in a rapid formation of capital in the modern business sense. This, in turn, led to the organization of new business structures.

Best known among these were the so-called "joint-stock companies," which were corporations of merchant adventurers who pooled their resources—at first temporarily for one specific undertaking, later permanently for repeated ventures. They chose directors and sea captains to transact the actual business for them, while they restricted their own activities to accumulating gains from investments. They often secured charters from their governments granting them monopolies in certain areas or on certain commodities. The necessary capital was raised for extensive, though often very risky, enterprises.

One of the most famous joint-stock companies was the Muscovy Company in England. Toward the middle of the sixteenth century, it secured a monopoly over the Russian trade. Later, various companies from different countries were founded that carried on the trade with the Near East and the East and West Indies. Provisions for greater credit facilities (for bills of exchange and for paper certificates), new tools used in the mining and the textile industries, and more rational division of labor through specialization in production methods all further augmented Europe's economic potential.

EXPANSION OF MARKETS

With the help of the newly created facilities, European producers and traders could reach out for previously untouched markets. They exported horses, cattle, and agricultural products. They established new overseas production centers for Old World products, such as sugar. They introduced such hitherto unknown produce as potatoes, tomatoes, tobacco, maize, and quinine. They also increased the imports of familiar produce such as coffee, rice, silk, and cotton. From Newfoundland, they brought fish; from China, tea. Gold and silver provided not only for monetary funds, but also for a greatly expanded jewelry trade that made use of Indian pearls and rubies. New "needs" were artificially created. A commodity of special importance contributed to the wealth of the European countries: the slaves who, transported from Africa, were used as a labor supply for the New World. Spanish, Portuguese, and, later, English traders specialized in slave traffic.

PHILOSOPHY OF MERCANTILISM

Through the new economic practices, conditions evolved that underlie the system known to present-day economists as "mercantilism." While some aspects of mercantilism can be traced to ancient and medieval economies, others depended upon conditions evolving in the early modern period. The ideal of the mercantilist philosophers was to strengthen the position of their nations. Believing that the position of a nation depends upon the "bullion"— gold, silver, precious stones—amassed by it, they held that the nation should export more than it imported. This they sought to achieve through increased industrial production, establishment and exploitation of colonies, monopolization of crucial raw materials, and by building up both a merchant marine and a carrying trade that would be able to exclude competitors.

Such measures could, of course, be taken only with the help of a powerful government that backed the commercial enterprises. Mercantilism thus implied a measure of government interference in economic affairs. But, since the bourgeoisie already tended to favor firm central governmental control, government interference was tolerated. Those nations in which centralization under strong rulers had advanced most took the lead.

AGRICULTURAL CONDITIONS

Inasmuch as mercantilism favored trade and required increased productivity, agriculture had to adapt itself to changed conditions. Commercial farming of industrial products that yielded higher returns replaced subsistence farming insofar as tools and organization permitted. Once many peasants had begun to migrate to cities, their lands were sold for profit. Large farms were established and worked by an impoverished laboring class. Common lands were taken over by landlords. In countries such as Spain and England, many of the farms were enclosed and used for sheep-grazing and wool production.

THE ARTS AND SCIENCES

Some historians have been inclined to see in the economic developments of the Renaissance period the main reason for the artistic achievement of the early sixteenth century. According to them, the wealth and leisure enjoyed by the upper groups of the population made it possible for great artists to develop their talents and for their art to be duly appreciated by a cultivated society. However, such a view cannot be accepted. As always, the primary factor was the genius of individuals. Fortunately, people of outstanding genius lived at the time who—often in the face of grave obstacles—devoted themselves to achieving what their unique talents inspired and made possible. Other societies at other times, equally prosperous, have failed to show similar appreciation.

Painting and Sculpture

Encouraged by popes, princes, and wealthy burghers, Renaissance Italy especially continued to bring forth an astounding number of the greatest masters in the fine arts. It suffices to mention painter, architect, and thinker Leonardo da Vinci *(Mona Lisa, Last Supper)*; Raphael *(Sistine Madonna, Madonna of the Chair)*; Michelangelo *(Ceiling of the Sistine Chapel, Moses)*, equally great as sculptor and painter; Titian *(Charles V)*; and the sculptor and goldsmith Cellini.

But not less amazing are the great Germans Dürer *(Holzschuher; Trent; Knight, Devil, and Death)*, Cranach *(Luther)*, and Holbein *(Erasmus, Anne of Cleves)*. England had little to offer. But in France there were eminent artists, among them Jean Clouet *(Francis I)*. And there were in most countries many minor painters who, had they lived in times less overshadowed by the greatest, would have been considered unique.

What distinguished the paintings of the High Renaissance from that of Byzantine and medieval times was above all the natural, realistic forms the great masters gave to objects and persons in sculpture and painting. They paid careful attention to the anatomy of the human body. Perspective was introduced, and portrait painting, formerly not practiced, gained an important place. Abandoning the two-dimensional, stylized representations of earlier times and, in painting, the golden backgrounds, the artists filled the backgrounds with views of beautiful and grand landscapes and castles. Human beings engaged in their daily pursuits appeared increasingly in paintings. Yet, even when the masters depicted everyday occupations and pleasures, they did not forget the vanity of earthly aspirations. They produced some of the most beautiful religious paintings and also generally set those that represented worldly scenes within the frame-work of the spiritual preoccupations of their age.

Music

The early sixteenth century, outstanding in art, is known also for its music. As a "Golden Age of Song," it saw the flourishing of the motet and, after 1520, the madrigal—both compositions for voices, the former on sacred, the latter on secular, texts. In many countries, popular song festivals were held; the art of singing was promoted by guilds (Hans Sachs and the *Meistersinger*) The Catholic Church and religious reformers—especially Luther himself, who composed enduring hymns—competed in beautifying Church services by organ music and encouraged singing among the community. Netherland composers taught their art and style in many countries. With previously unknown perfection, their works for voice and for instruments were performed at the courts of princes and nobility as well as in the houses of wealthy burghers.

Literature

Owing to the mid-fifteenth-century invention of printing with movable type, popular education became more widespread. New educational ideals arose. Luther, in particular, favored widespread teaching of the fundamentals of reading and writing. He advocated kindness toward children and understanding of pupils in addition to discipline. With the increase in literacy, the demand for books accelerated. The great controversies of the age brought forth a stream of pamphlets, tracts, and brilliant works on classics, history, criticism, education, and politics.

HUMANISM

The intellectual trend known as *humanism,* with its interest in classical studies and in things human rather than otherworldly, penetrated from the southern into the northern countries. One of the greatest humanists of the age was Erasmus of Rotterdam (d. 1536), a scholar, a promoter of classical culture and learning, and editor of the Greek text of the Bible. He wrote *The Praise of Folly,* which ridiculed such human weaknesses as avarice, credulity, pedantry, and gluttony. As an advocate of peace and reason, Erasmus opposed the excesses, violence, and coarseness of the age. He admonished princes and churchmen to abandon evil traditions, to reform, be tolerant, and devote themselves to the true service of Christ. Other leading northern humanists were the statesman Thomas More, the pamphleteer and poet Ulrich von Hutten, and Johann Reuchlin, who compiled a Hebrew grammar for Bible studies and vigorously took part in the controversies of the age.

Numerous French and Scandinavian writers, as well as some Spanish writers, followed the Italian, German, and English example. They combined the pagan and Christian (the classical and medieval) heritage and published widely read works of lasting merit. Permanently important histories and biographies of many sorts appeared: Guicciardini's history of Italy,

Gomara's history of America, Vasari's lives of Italian artists, and Benvenuto Cellini's famous autobiography.

LUTHER

A special place in literary achievement belongs to Luther, who with his translation of the Bible into German created a work of beauty and majesty. The dialect that he used prepared the way for the modern High German tongue as generally spoken today. The English Bible translation by Tyndale was based on Luther's edition.

POETRY AND DRAMA

Compared with the great religious and humanistic literature, however, poetry and drama attained lesser heights. There were few who excelled in literary works of imagination. The perhaps best known, the Italian Ariosto (d. 1533), was by no means a great writer. In his own time, however, he was appreciated widely and subsequently served as a model for several generations. Popular drama, miracle plays, and poems in the classical style were generally imitative and no longer inspiring.

Natural Sciences

The broadening horizon of Western people, their inquisitiveness and secular interests, directed their attention to closer observation and investigation of natural phenomena. Moreover, the geographical discoveries stirred their minds and enlarged their scientific understanding. A great amount of new knowledge was gained in geography and anthropology. Discoveries brought new inventions and improvements in technique. But also in other areas, which had no direct connection with geographical discoveries, outstanding advances were made.

The greatest was perhaps reflected in the work of Copernicus (d. 1543), who showed that the earth circles about the sun. Rather unwillingly, people came to realize the relative insignificance of their own world within the larger scheme of nature. Of comparable importance was the growing understanding of human physiology. Vesalius (d. 1564) dissected and described the human body. Leonardo da Vinci (d. 1519) examined and charted many of its organs. Servetus (d. 1553) investigated the pulmonary circulation of the blood. Paracelsus (d. 1541) sought new therapeutic methods. Similar interests led Gesner (d. 1565) to compose a history of animals and Agricola (d. 1555) to study mineralogy.

The exact sciences, which were based on rational deduction and observation, were still intermingled with pseudosciences based on acceptance of authority or superstition. Standards set for scientific work by Leonardo da Vinci, who called for mathematical thinking and experimentation, were not generally accepted. Many scientists continued to attempt to solve the mysteries of life and nature with the help of astrology, alchemy, and plain magic. But since these unscientific methods did not stand the test of time, historians have been inclined to pass them over in their descriptions of the interests that captivated the minds of sixteenth-century people.

Political Science

A special place in the scientific endeavors of the age belongs to the numerous political writings. Despite widespread adherence to the theoretical propositions of medieval thinkers, these writings show a clear, realistic approach to political problems. Many works appeared discussing the duties of princes and of highborn ladies. Erasmus wrote such a book. More influential was the internationally used *Courtier* by Castiglioni, the standard work on courtly manners and on Christian behavior in public affairs. The English humanist and statesman Thomas More (d. 1535) wrote *Utopia*, which describes an "ideal commonwealth" based on Christian concepts. Through the nobility of its conception, *Utopia* exercised a strong influence on later political thought.

MACHIAVELLI

But none of these works compares in historical influence with that of Machiavelli (d. 1527), author of *The Prince*. In this book, Machiavelli, who as a humanist was well acquainted with classical literature, analyzes with penetrating insight into human psychology the sources of political power and its "demoniac" nature. Drawing upon experience and showing no concern with morality, he counsels the princes how best to gain, maintain, and use power. Self-interest alone, he holds, should dictate their actions. His work has remained unique in the field of rational statecraft.

Influenced by the great tradition of classical and medieval times, the High Renaissance introduced the Modern Age. The focus of attention was no longer upon sin and salvation, but upon the activities of human beings and the configurations of their natural surroundings. Worldly concerns now occupied the mind. Nobles and burghers engaged in commercial activities and sought wealth, which brought them new power—more than the sword had earlier provided. Industries were expanded, resulting in greater division of labor, and a new class stratification developed. Wealth served the princes in new types of warfare. They would hire mercenaries when formerly they had been relying on knights bound to them by concepts of honor. It was a time of often overwhelming change and upheaval. Great passions in all areas of human endeavor led to often cruel behavior in human relationships but also to astounding cultural achievements. The literature, art, and philosophy of the times attest to these achievements.

Selected Readings

Burckhardt, Jacob. *The Civilization of the Renaissance in Italy* (1937)
Cambridge Economic History of Europe. 7 vols. (1965)
Einstein, Alfred. *A Short History of Music* (1954)
Gardner, Helen. *Art through the Ages* (1970)

Hay, Denis, ed. *The Renaissance Debate* (1965)

Hutchinson, Jane C. *Albrecht Dürer* (1990)

Janson, Horst. *History of Art* (1969)

Magnus, Laurie. *A History of European Literature* (1934)

Nussbaum, Frederick L. *A History of Economic Institutions of Modern Europe* (1933)

Randall, John H. *The Making of the Modern Mind* (1940)

Ranke, Leopold von. *The History of the Popes* (1847–51)

Shepherd, W. R. *Historical Atlas* (1964)

Zinsser, Hans. *Rats, Lice, and History* (1935)

4

The New Monarchies

The atmosphere created by the new interests and directions of the active forces in society brought forth a new political organization in Europe. For several centuries, feudal traits had been on the wane, and tendencies toward greater cohesion within the territories of various national groups had appeared. These tendencies were supported by rulers who sought to extend their personal power. They were also promoted by economic necessities: the increase of productivity and the expansion of commerce. These changes necessitated the development of a strong central authority, such as absolutist monarchical forms provided. Thus came into being what is known as the "New Monarchies."

In a "New Monarchy," the ruling princes had to overcome the challenge of a feudal nobility. They succeeded in concentrating decisive power in their own hands; in reducing the influence of estates, parliaments, and diets; and in controlling the military forces, the jurisdiction, and the finances of their realms. In their endeavors, which put an end to much of the strife of the feudal age, they were usually supported by the burgher class, whose wealth and jealousy of the privileges of the nobility provided the princes with the means to strengthen their own monarchical rule.

WESTERN EUROPE

The development of the "New Monarchies" was much more rapid in western Europe than in other parts. Owing to the opportunities that the discovery of new lands offered, a shift of the center of authority and power from empire and papacy in Germany and Italy to the western monarchies took place. This shift was paralleled by a corresponding shift in initiative and leadership. The western regions of Europe bordering on the Atlantic and profiting from the new trade routes to the wealth of Asia and America adapted their political organization more speedily to the demands of modern times.

Portugal

A "New Monarchy" developed early in Portugal. It gained strength owing to the acquisition of colonies in the Indies and in Brazil. It benefited from the influx of Oriental products, spices and jewels, the income from the slave trade, the national strength gained through sea power, and support by the merchants and bankers interested in colonial expansion. Lisbon, the capital city of Portugal, soon surpassed the greatest older trading city, Venice, and the Portuguese king assumed a virtual trade monopoly. Concentrating in his hands the lucrative Indian spice trade, he firmly established his power and could dominate nobility and burghers alike. By allowing foreign participation in Portuguese trade ventures, he also avoided conflict with England.

Spain

The acquisition of colonies determined the new greatness of Spain under Ferdinand and Isabella, as it did that of Portugal. Gold and silver flowed into the treasury of the rulers, who since 1503 had held a monopoly on trade with America. They conferred this monopoly upon a Casa de Contratación. Ships sailed annually from the ports of Seville and Cadiz in convoys to bring colonial products safely home. However, unlike the ruler of Portugal, the Spanish royal house used its position less for accumulation of bullion than for its own political aggrandizement.

After Queen Isabella's death, the king secured—in addition to the large territories of the New World—domination of southern Italy and of trade routes in the western Mediterranean. He built the most powerful and effective army in the world, commanded by some of the greatest generals of the time. Piracy and highway robbery were checked. Firm order under strong monarchical supervision was maintained.

King Ferdinand carried forward the unification of the country, which had started with his marriage. Under central authority, a common, royally supervised, but essentially weak parliament *(Cortes)* was created. Religious dissidents were suppressed, the popes conferred the right to make Church appointments to the Spanish king, and the Inquisition became a tool in his hands. A generally valid law code based on Roman law was introduced, which even the nobility had to observe. Law studies flourished and arts were protected. Unfortunately for Spain, commercial interests had generally been the domain of existing brotherhoods of towns *(hermandades)*, and the king continued to give these conservative forces his protection, so that with high taxes rigorously levied, a vigorous, enterprising, independent middle class could not develop.

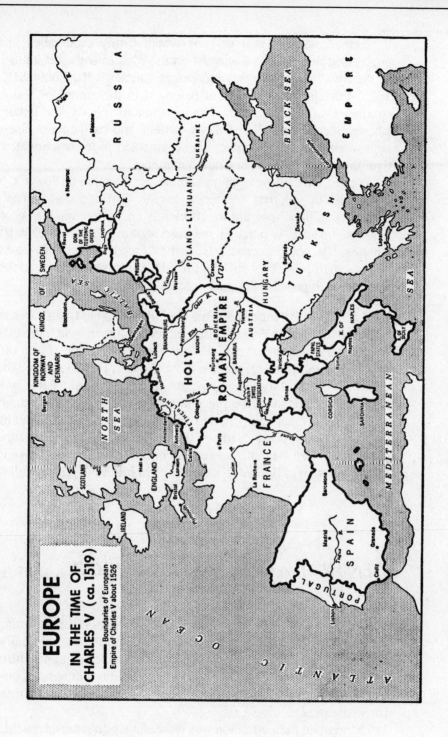

EUROPE
IN THE TIME OF
CHARLES V (ca. 1519)

——— Boundaries of European
Empire of Charles V about 1526

France

France, with its seat of government firmly established in Paris, had progressed under King Louis XI on the road toward the status of a "New Monarchy." Under Louis's successors Charles VIII, Louis XII, and (after 1515) Francis I—all of whom belonged to the House of Valois—France continued on the same path. The representative body, the Estates-General, whose functions paralleled those of diets and parliaments elsewhere, was kept weak while royal power was augmented in jurisdictional, administrative, financial, and also in Church matters.

Yet, France's development was slower than that of Spain's. Neither did it succeed in securing colonies—despite Cartier's discoveries in the St. Lawrence region—nor did it sufficiently encourage modern economic tendencies. Instead, it pursued the wars against the empire in Italy, which Charles VIII, out of expansionist desires, greed, and fear of Hapsburg power, had begun in 1494. Francis I continued the struggle and wasted the resources needed for improving France's internal conditions.

England

Like other Atlantic seaboard countries, England, with less than a third of the population of France, also entered a stage in which the establishment of a modern nation became possible. Henry VII of the House of Tudor had already reestablished respect for law and order. He had favored the merchant class, amassed a large treasury, and secured control of the judiciary. The nobility, decimated in the preceding times of trouble, was deprived of its military power and compelled to obey his wishes. But it maintained its hold on all important posts. Henry VII's successor, Henry VIII, adhered to the same policy. Parliament, however, continued to function, even though its effectiveness was limited, for the political initiative rested with the Crown.

CENTRAL AND EASTERN EUROPE

In the regions of Europe that did not border on the Atlantic Ocean, the traditions of the past remained strong. Because the politically dominant powers of Central Europe benefited little from the economic shifts occurring in the age of discoveries, they were forced into a defensive position. This caused them to seek the preservation of the existing social organization in their countries.

Moreover, their attention was increasingly directed eastward, where two new great powers, Turkey and Russia, had emerged. Neither Turkey nor Russia shared in the political evolution of the West. Thus, neither could set an example of political modernization. Yet, with the vigor of rising nations, both began to make their influence felt on the European political scene, and principally on the neighboring German Empire.

The German Empire

At the beginning of modern times, the empire was still an international organization, extending beyond Germany into areas inhabited by diverse national groups, such as the Dutch, Burgundians, Swiss, Italians, Czechs, and others. The empire was composed of seven electorates, many smaller states, numerous ecclesiastical territories, hundreds of towns, and other areas governed by independent knights. It was held together by imperial authority which, though the office of emperor was elective, remained in the hands of the House of Hapsburg. It had a few federal institutions, such as a diet (which decided questions of finance and common organization that affected all members) and a federal court. But these institutions did not offer a fertile soil for the evolution of a strong centralized state.

Nevertheless, "new" monarchical trends were not entirely absent. While they did not pervade the empire as a whole, they could be found within the larger member states, such as Saxony, Brandenburg, Bavaria, Austria, and others. It would therefore be incorrect to speak of the political development of Germany as differing radically from that of the Atlantic nations. It was, however, on a more restricted scale, local rather than national, that the trends toward "New Monarchies" appeared.

Despite its lack of modern political evolution, the German Empire was to achieve early in the sixteenth century a position of power in the world almost unequaled in any earlier or later period. This was achieved through the shrewd diplomacy of the House of Hapsburg, which concluded numerous advantageous marriage alliances. It was furthered by the enterprising spirit of some individuals, especially the merchants of southern Germany and of the Low Countries. It was also enhanced by the economic opportunities afforded by the proximity of Eastern European production centers and markets with their resources of grain in Poland-Lithuania, metals in Tyrol and Hungary, and export markets in Russia and the Balkans. Dominating the central areas connecting the east and west as well as the north and south, the Hapsburgs undertook to exploit these advantages.

The Emperor Maximilian I (1489–1519)—an intelligent, chivalrous, well-educated, but weak-spirited man—did not succeed in enforcing his will upon the empire, in improving its cumbersome, outdated judicial and ad-ministrative machinery, or in leading the whole country toward unification. But he strengthened its position enormously by securing as dowry the rich Burgundian and Netherland domains. He then married his son Philip to the Spanish princess Joanna, through whom his grandson Charles was enabled to claim the entire Spanish Empire. In 1517, upon the death of his grandfather Ferdinand, this Charles, born in Ghent in the Netherlands in 1500, actually became king of Spain and all her colonies. In 1519, upon the death of his other grandfather, Maximilian, the same Charles was elected German emperor. To win the election, however, it was necessary for him to engage in a bitter contest with Francis I of France. This contest forced him not only to distribute lavish bribes to the electors, but also to make sweeping promises (contrary to the trends of the time) to maintain "German liberties." As Charles V, he was to rule for almost forty years over an empire "on which the sun never set." He was a man of high moral standards, earnestly devoted to his task, slow and wise in decision, and shrewd in his judgment of people. But he faced a task that surpassed his strength, even as it would have surpassed that of any other ruler.

Italy

The only Western country in which the new forms of government made no progress, either on a national or a city-state level, was Italy. No central authority existed there. Individual attempts at making the inhabitants conscious of common links remained without practical effect. Emperor, pope, and French and Spanish kings shared with the Medici, Sforza, Este, Gonzaga, and other famous Renaissance princes the domination of the area that only centuries later was to form the Italian nation. Almost all sectors retained the accustomed forms of government.

Moreover, wars fought by the Valois and the Hapsburgs over the disunited country desolated the land. The rivalries of the great powers checked the growth of a modern state system. The commercial importance of the country (formerly based on Italian business connections with the Moslems in the Near East) was diminished by the advance of the Turks and the opening of the direct seaway from western Europe to India.

Russia and Turkey

Centralization and absolutism, toward which the European national states developed, had long existed in the two Eastern empires. But owing to Oriental concepts of despotism and the lack of customary ethical restraints such as those prevailing in the West, they differed fundamentally from their Western counterparts. The term, "New Monarchy" is hardly applicable to the two Eastern empires. Both the Russian tsar and the Turkish sultan enjoyed a degree of absolute power unparalleled in the West. Their power extended to politics, law, and economic activity. Despite differences in these respects between East and West, both countries began, whether through war or peace, to move toward closer relations with the West. Diplomatic contacts were established. There was a lively interchange of visitors, travelers, and merchants. Descriptions of Russia and Turkey were broadcast throughout Europe.

The sixteenth century saw a rapid development of the nation-state. Spain, France, and England led the way. Each nation developed its own type of institutions, but everywhere a centralized monarchical structure ("New Monarchy") gained ascendancy. The nobility, though retaining many privileges, had to adjust. The three great empires, the German, the Russian, and the Turkish, on the other hand, failed to achieve modern forms of government. Under Emperor Charles V, the German Empire was to reach a pinnacle of prestige and power. But the type of central institutions that existed could not prevail over disruptive forces, which increased. Nor did Germany benefit from the resources of the New World and the Far East, both of which opened great possibilities to the seafaring nations for an expansion of their wealth and power.

Selected Readings

Clark, Sir George. *English History* (1971)
Guérard, Albert. *France: A Modern History* (1969)
Holborn, Hajo. *A History of Modern Germany* (1958)
Kirchner, Walther. *History of Russia* (1991)
Mack Smith, Denis. *Italy: A Modern History* (1969)
McNeill, W. H. *The Rise of the West* (1963)
Merriman, Roger B. *The Rise of the Spanish Empire* (1918)

5

The Age of the Reformation (1517–1555)

1518	Zwingli begins work in Zürich
1519	Charles V becomes German emperor
	Cortez begins conquest of Mexico
	Magellan begins circumnavigation of the world
1520	Suleiman the Magnificent becomes sultan of Turkey
1521	Luther before Diet of Worms
1523	Sweden leaves Scandinavian Union: Gustavus Vasa becomes king
1524	Peasants' Revolt in Germany
1525	Battle of Pavia: Francis I of France made prisoner of Charles V
	Death of Jacob Fugger
1526	Dürer, *Four Apostles*
1527	Rome sacked by troops of Charles V
1529	Turks besiege Vienna
	Diet of Spires ("Protestants")
1530	Augsburg Confession drawn up
1532	Pizarro undertakes conquest of Peru
1533	Reformation begins in England (Henry VIII)
1534	Rabelais, *Gargantua*
1536	Erasmus of Rotterdam dies
	Calvin, *Institutes of the Christian Religion*
1540	Order of Jesuits founded
1541	Paracelsus dies

1543   Copernicus, *De Revolutionibus Orbium Coelestium (On the Revolutions of the Heavenly Spheres)*

Vesalius, *De Humani Corporis Fabrica (The Structure of the Human Body)*

Holbein dies

1545   Discovery of Potosi silver mines in Bolivia

1547   Protestants defeated by Charles V at Mühlberg

1552   Protestants resume war

1553   Servetus burned at stake in Geneva

1554   Marriage of Mary Tudor of England and Philip II of Spain

1555   Religious Peace of Augsburg

Persecution of Protestants in England

Muscovy Company founded in England

1556   Abdication of Charles V

By far the most momentous event of the early modern period was the Reformation. It started as a reform movement within the Catholic Church and its original objective was no more than a purification of the Christian church and a renewal of Christian morals in European life. Indeed, the leading men of the Reformation were, and remained, theologians, and considered all their proposals for reform from the theological point of view. But the effect of their work was soon felt in all areas of European life—in politics, social relationships, the sciences and arts, and in the economic arena as well. Historians have for this reason been tempted to speak of the Reformation as a broad, international revolution—a term that certainly misrepresents the work and aims of the reformers, but that may have a measure of justification on the basis of the movement's wide effects.

THE REFORMATION

The urgent need of a reform in existing religious institutions was generally recognized outside as well as within the Catholic Church. Over the course of the centuries, doctrinal views had arisen that seemed to many to be in need of revision. But, more important, numerous practical abuses had penetrated all parts and layers of the institutions of the Catholic Church and threatened its entire structure. Therefore, many of the most devoted Church members concerned primarily with advancing the Christian way of life joined forces with those who sought reform for selfish economic advantages.

Church Abuses

The sins of the Church and of churchmen were many. Anarchy reigned within the Church. Central authority had been weakened. Kings and nations had assumed rights and duties that belonged to the Church. Among popes and bishops, moral corruption existed. Many, greedy and venal, pursued worldly policies and allowed nepotism and simony, which implied the sale of Church offices. Among the clergy, a shocking lack of training existed; the rank and file found themselves in desperate economic circumstances, while the hierarchy lived in luxury. Immorality and sexual promiscuity prevailed among many of the churchmen. Church services and the care of Church buildings were neglected by the priests. A large portion of the clergy interested themselves in science, art, and economics, rather than in the salvation of souls.

To all this should be added constant rivalries and jealousies among the members of the hierarchy, among various monastic orders, and between monks and priests. Bishops tried to hold as many lucrative Church offices as possible without fulfilling the corresponding duties. Moreover, errors of faith had developed, which led to errors in conduct. Popes misused indulgences and abused their power to censure and excommunicate. The Church maintained economic views derived from a period with an entirely different economic system and needs; it insisted on exemption from taxation and refused to divest itself of "unproductive" lands.

As always, there were many forces at work within the Church to improve external conditions, purify the hearts of its members, and reconcile Christian tasks with the humanistic trends of the age. But these forces proved weak. Their effects came too late.

Early Reform Movements

The greatest figure of the Reformation was Luther. Today, hundreds of years later, the immediate and direct influence of his work is continuously felt. Luther was not, however, a great originator: he was a great accomplisher. Many before him had urged reform of the organization of the Church. Some had attacked the same dogmas which Luther challenged: Ockham, Marsilius, Bradwardine, Wycliffe, Wessel, Huss, and many a humanist were among them.

SAVONAROLA

The last of their number was Savonarola, a Florentine who, shocked by the corruption of the Roman Court under the Borgia pope and by the widespread secular interests of the clergy, preached purification and repentance. When he became involved in Florentine political quarrels, his enemies succeeded (in 1498) in having him hanged and burned as a heretic.

Luther

Martin Luther was, in a sense, Savonarola's immediate successor. He was born in 1483, the son of a miner. At first, he studied law, then turned to theology and became an Augustine monk. He took his duties most seriously, prayed, fasted, chastised himself, and made a pilgrimage to Rome. When a new university was founded in Wittenberg, Saxony, his superiors sent him there to teach. Terrified by the corruption he had seen in Rome, doubtful as to many teachings of the Church, and convinced that only faith and the grace of God can lead to salvation, he posted (in 1517) ninety-five theses on the church door in Wittenberg, attacking one of the worst abuses, the sale of indulgences.

Indulgences were to bring remittance of, or a pardon for, sins if the sinner showed a contrite heart, confessed, accepted due penalty, and performed good works. But they were granted and often sold without demanding repentance or good works. The profits of the resulting big business flowed into the pockets of bankers and bishops, or were used for the beautification of Rome.

NINETY-FIVE THESES (1517)

The publication of theses, of statements debating theological questions, was a rather customary procedure. Luther's act, however, had extreme repercussions because of the logic and vigor of his statements and his implied challenge to papal authority. Pious Christians everywhere saw in his act the long-desired beginning of reform. Numerous worldly interests saw in it a means to escape some of the guidance or financial impositions of the popes. Princes saw in his act a basis for stopping the flow of money to Rome and for channeling it, instead, into their own pockets. They used it as an appeal to German national consciousness, and sensed in it an opportunity to break entirely with a degraded papacy absorbed in politics, whose heirs they themselves wanted to become. Rome therefore reacted vigorously, and a number of disputations and debates were sponsored between Luther and some of the leading Catholic scholars. These, however, led only to a widening of the breach.

DOCTRINARY TRACTS AND LUTHER'S EXCOMMUNICATION

In 1520, Luther took a further decisive step by publishing three pamphlets. Again, he described Rome's abuses, demanded reforms in morals and in dogma, attacked some of the sacraments, transubstantiation, and worship of saints. He again insisted that the Bible alone, with no additional precepts of the Church, constituted the final authority for a Christian. He emphasized that, on the foundation of God's Word, everyone could be his own priest and master and need be nobody's servant.

The pope threatened excommunication against Luther. But, in the presence of applauding Wittenberg students, Luther publicly burned the pope's decree or "bull." He thereby protested in behalf of the individual's inalienable right, as a Christian, to be subject to God alone.

DIET OF WORMS (1521); TRANSLATION OF THE BIBLE

The rebellion against established Church authority, thus started by Luther, led to a quick reaction on the part of political authority, for emperor and kings began to fear for their own position. Charles V, a devout Catholic, invited Luther to attend a diet of the German estates, which was to be held in Worms in 1521. Under safe-conduct, Luther appeared. Before the assembled princes, he courageously restated his position, as "it is neither safe nor right to act against one's conscience."

Charles honored the safe-conduct, but Luther was put under the ban of the German Empire, which deprived him of all legal protection in the empire. His political friends had to give him asylum in one of their castles, the Wartburg. There, Luther composed hymns, studied educational methods, and, particularly, worked on his translation of the Bible. But within a year, grave disturbances called him back to Wittenberg.

Social Consequences

Luther's attack on authority and tradition had released many revolutionary forces. Numerous preachers and theologians felt that he had not gone far enough. Groups seeking salvation in independent ways, mystics, lay brotherhoods and sisterhoods, and others, had existed before. Now additional ones arose that demanded the abolition of, or substitutions for, all dogmas and sacraments, images, and traditional worships. Often they also rejected worldly authorities, princely powers, and existing economic and behavior patterns. Some wanted to introduce free love and a completely free, communistic society.

Luther, who himself had rejected celibacy and had married in 1525, fought such extreme trends. But the stream could not be stopped. Anabaptists, who were against infant baptism, and other religious radicals caused widespread disturbances. Rebellions of knights against their overlords occurred, and eventually—as in Wycliffe's and Huss's times—a great peasant revolt broke out. In "Twelve Articles," the peasants protested against serfdom, illegal and extravagant taxes, restriction of their rights to common lands, and the abolition of customary law in favor of Roman law with its property concepts. They demanded emancipation and the right to worship God in their own chosen ways.

Luther had exhorted the lords to deal fairly with their peasants and to yield to justified demands. Anticipating John Locke, he had advocated the peasants' rights to defend themselves against unjust government. But he was shocked by the violence that the resulting peasant uprising brought. He gradually became more conservative and turned, with a violence of language not uncommon to his time, against the pillaging peasants (a change that cost him the support of many). He insisted on the right of the God-ordained secular powers to reestablish order and worldly authority by fire and sword. Yet, the entire social fabric of past ages remained shattered.

Political Consequences

The political effect of Luther's work was no less significant than the social consequences. In the German Empire, the forces of disintegration were strengthened. Many princes, foreseeing an opportunity to confiscate the wealth of the churches and monasteries located in their realms, adhered to the new religion and rebelled against the emperor. In England, on the other hand, the king himself took advantage of religious controversies to strengthen his personal rule. In Scandinavia, the conflict caused the Swedes, under the leadership of Gustavus Vasa, to break the links with Denmark and establish an independent kingdom.

In most regions, strife and internecine war resulted. On the international stage, the French used the newly developing dissensions for territorial aggrandizement. The papacy was torn between political ambitions and the desire to see Catholicism everywhere restored.

Effects on Imperial Policies

Of special consequence was the effect of the reform movement on the position of the German Empire and on the role of empire and papacy in the Western world. Despite numerous struggles, the two powers had always been interdependent. But at this critical moment, when the survival of both was threatened and unity should have been the first necessity, Charles V was deserted by the pope, who feared imperial might more than heresy.

The emperor was forced to meet the problems alone. With fortitude, he sought to stem the tide. He turned, first, against the French, who had once more invaded his possessions in Italy. His Spanish armies decisively defeated them and took their king prisoner. Francis was not released until he had promised to keep the peace and to make restitution of conquered lands—a promise which, with the connivance of the pope, he soon broke.

Next, Charles had to use force against the pope himself, the ambitious and luxury-loving Medici, Clement VII. In 1527, Spanish, German, and Swiss mercenaries, commanded by a French duke, seized Rome, which they sacked, destroying untold works of art and stripping it of much of its riches. For the time being, papal opposition was eliminated. A measure of cooperation between empire and papacy could be established. Then, Charles had to deal with the Turks, the arch enemy of Christendom, with whom the king of France had entered into close relations and whom he had enticed to invade the empire from the rear. In 1529, the Turks reached the gates of Vienna, where they were repulsed. But they did gain domination over Hungary.

Lastly, the emperor had to contend with the German princes. Toward them he tried a policy of moderation. In 1529, a diet was held in Spires. However, it produced no concession by the Catholic princes, so that the Lutherans protested against the decision. (From this protest the name

"Protestants" is derived.) In the following year, the Protestants drew up a statement of their faith, the "Augsburg Confession," which reaffirmed their creed. But owing to the mediation of the emperor, a measure of cooperation between Catholics and Protestants was worked out.

THE SPREADING OF THE REFORMATION

Soon, Luther's religious reform movement turned from a principally German development into a European movement. In doing so, it lost some of the parochial character that it had possessed because it included a number of specifically German grievances. In spreading the knowledge of the work of the reformers, Gutenberg's invention of the printing press with movable type was a factor of immeasurable importance. An enormous outpouring of books and pamphlets, characteristic for the age, conveyed the religious demands as well as the thoughts from all other fields to all parts of Europe; an increasingly literate public could absorb them.

Expansion on the Continent

SWITZERLAND

In Switzerland, the first country affected by the Reformation in Germany, Luther's initial steps in 1518 had promptly induced the priest Ulrich Zwingli of Zurich to advocate similar reforms. Zwingli, like other humanists, was skeptical of traditional, accepted views and demanded that only what the original sources said should be recognized. He therefore followed Luther in turning to a theological interpretation of the Bible itself rather than to Church traditions.

But he went further in regard to the purification of dogma and did not hesitate to include even the sacraments of baptism and communion, whereby he created a breach between his own adherents and those of Luther. Theological disputations between the two men failed to resolve the dogmatic differences. Thus, an early split in the Protestant camp resulted. Zwingli himself was killed in 1531 while accompanying Zurich troops in battle, but his work was carried on by others.

SCANDINAVIA

In Sweden and Denmark, too, Lutheranism spread early. The Swedes, once they had freed themselves from Denmark, which was ruled by Christian II (brother-in-law of Charles V), introduced Lutheranism. Shortly thereafter, the Danes themselves revolted against their king, mainly because of his economic policies and arbitrary rule. Having driven Christian II out of the country, they, too, accepted the Lutheran faith. They introduced it into Norway as well. The new faith was likewise accepted by large segments of the population, especially townspeople, in Hungary, Lithuania, Livonia, and the Netherlands, and even by some converts in France, Spain, and Italy.

Expansion in the British Isles

Luther's movement created a special situation in the British Isles. The Reformation was at first of little interest to the average British subject. But, subsequently, it found adherents both in Scotland and in England. It was not, however, the religious question but, instead, the personal problems of King Henry VIII that caused England's reforms to assume worldwide importance during the 1530s. Henry was a despotic and utterly selfish, though not incompetent, ruler who achieved little in international relations but much of importance in internal affairs. He prevented a resurgence of the power of the nobility, preserved order, strengthened royal absolutism, and chose to cooperate with Parliament (and even enlarged its powers) rather than to subdue it. He incorporated Wales into England.

It was he who carried out the break with Rome. He had originally attacked Luther. But when the pope refused to give him a dispensation so that he could discard his wife (Catherine of Aragon, a relative of Charles V) and marry his mistress, Anne Boleyn, who he hoped would bear him a son, he decided to make use of the predicament in which the pope found himself owing to the Protestant movement.

Step by step, with the help of successive advisers (some of whom he executed after they had served his purpose)—Cardinal Wolsey, Sir Thomas More, Thomas Boleyn, John Fisher, Archbishop Cranmer, Thomas Cromwell—he separated England from Rome. He had himself recognized as head of the English Church, dissolved the monasteries (whose wealth he confiscated), and discontinued the payment of taxes to Rome. In 1539, he arranged for Parliament to confirm a statement of faith, the "Six Articles," which, while preserving essential Catholic doctrines, in essence refused to acknowledge papal authority. Thus, a true moral and doctrinal reformation was not consummated in Henry VIII's England. But the position of the papacy was undermined. After Henry's death in 1547 the real reform work began.

OUTBREAK OF RELIGIOUS WARS AND THE RISE OF CALVINISM

The changes under Henry VIII obscured the religious issues everywhere in Europe and emphasized the political aspects of the reform movement. In vain did Luther hope for a reestablishment of Christian unity upon the basis of a Church adhering to the doctrine of justification by faith, implying that by faith alone the believer can be saved, and using a simplified service. Until his death in 1546, he remained extremely active, interpreting the Bible, instituting schools and seminaries, installing superintendents, writing numerous works, and giving advice to secular authorities.

But the political and economic implications and their unavoidable practical effect were beyond his understanding. Two distinct leagues, a Catholic and a Protestant one (the latter under the name of "Schmalkaldic League"), had already been formed in Germany. Once Luther's authority was removed by death, war broke out between them.

Schmalkaldic War

This war was the first in a long series of internal struggles between Catholics and Protestants in many countries. It indicated that the situation had developed beyond the possibility of compromise. By 1546, this impasse was recognized not only by the Protestants but also by Charles V. He, too, had worked for a reunion of the faiths—trying to reach it through the convening of a general Church Council. But the popes had opposed a general Council. Even after the death of Clement VII, popes unwilling to effect moral reform in the Church consistently withheld their cooperation. In their refusals, they were supported by France, which engaged in one war after another against the Hapsburgs and which profited from the split within Germany.

Charles had no alternative but to seek to reestablish unity by force of arms. He declared war on the Protestants, and a first battle, fought at Mühlberg (1547), brought him startling success: his forces routed the Schmalkaldic League and captured its two chief leaders. But the emperor's triumph served only to further frighten the pope and various foreign princes. Although Charles, showing his customary moderation, had imposed only a truce, the so-called "Interim" (1548), and had redoubled his efforts to find a permanent solution through a general Council, no reconciliation was effected. Hence, a few years later, when his chief ally deserted him and his armies were defeated, he finally gave up all hope for the reestablishment of unity.

Peace of Augsburg (1555)

In 1555, a peace of fundamental importance was signed at Augsburg. It granted each German prince the right to establish for all his subjects the religion that he himself professed. Thereby, Lutheran princes, and with them Lutheran states, gained equal rights and status with Catholic ones—even though the peace forbade any future conversion of Catholic bishoprics into secular Protestant states.

Abdication of Charles V

Charles suffered two other disappointments. His troops failed to recover territories in Lorraine, which the Catholic French, cooperating with Protestant German princes, had annexed. Also, the marriage of his son, Philip, to the English queen, Mary, daughter of Henry VIII, did not bring the hoped-for union of Spain and England. The marriage did not produce a child who could inherit both thrones.

Exhausted after forty years of endeavoring to guide the fate of the world, Charles finally decided to divest himself of his various crowns. In a series of emotionally charged ceremonies—especially that of Brussels in 1556—he installed his son Philip as his successor in Spain, Italy, and the Netherlands, and his brother Ferdinand in the German Empire and in Hungary. The Hapsburg possessions were thus divided, and he himself retired to a monastery in Spain where he died three years later.

Rise of Calvinism

By the time the Peace of Augsburg had been concluded and Charles had abdicated, the split in the Christian Church had in any case become irreparable. The Protestant forces had been augmented by another reformatory group—the Calvinists.

John Calvin (1509–1564), a French law student, was influenced early by Luther's thought. He had turned to theology and had fled France as a result of one of Francis I's sporadic, politically inspired persecutions of heretics. In 1536, he published his fundamental work, the *Institutes of the Christian Religion*. He found asylum in Switzerland, and at Geneva he eventually established his political and religious leadership. Like Luther, Calvin based his teachings on the Bible, not on Church authority; like Luther, he preached justification by faith.

But he accepted Zwingli's interpretation of the sacraments. He insisted that no man can achieve the good except by the will of God, who has predestined our actions. Therefore, man should abandon himself entirely to God, who, to a certain extent, reveals his will to man and who allows man to lead a virtuous, and possibly prosperous, life on earth and to do good works.

In the sphere of public affairs Calvin provided the Church with a hierarchical Church structure and demanded that it be given a leading role in the community. Pastors, teachers, deacons, and elders, constituting a supervisory council, were to direct all action and watch over education, morals, and orthodoxy. Such a Church government was actually established in Geneva. It saw to the abolition of all remnants of Catholic worship, censored books, prohibited all luxuries and most amusements, and emphasized prayer and work. It went so far as to drag the famous scientist Servetus, who had already been accused of heresy by the Catholic Church, but who also opposed Calvinist ideas of the Trinity, before its tribunal and to have him burned at the stake (1553).

EFFECT OF CALVINISM

Calvinism spread even more rapidly than Lutheranism. It was more international in character, was based more on rationalism and less on mystic beliefs, and was more in line with the economic trends of the age. It more easily reconciled Christian ethics with business points of view. It described thrift as a virtue and prestige as a sign of moral strength. It also allowed reasonable interest-taking—a fundamental requirement for the development of modern capitalism. It spread rapidly to the Netherlands, France, England, Scotland, and Poland. In many countries it became a powerful political, as well as economic, tool. In Scotland, where French Catholic influence within the royal family was resented, the fervent preacher John Knox spread its tenets.

THE COUNTER REFORMATION

Pressed from many sides, the Catholic Church finally initiated reforms—though too late to save Western Christian unity. Again and again, the Church had hesitated, deliberately avoiding recourse to the customary means of settling disputes, namely, through the convening of a general Council. The popes feared not only the power of the emperor in a Council, but also a renewal of the struggle between pope and Council for supremacy within the Church and, in addition, the opposition of the clergy to the papacy. They were wary of the nationalist tendencies all over Europe and anxious to avoid possible losses of authority, funds, and prestige.

The Beginnings of the Catholic Reformation

Nevertheless, for some time the reform movement within the Church had shown considerable strength. A number of reforming orders, such as the Theatines and Capuchins, had been founded; several reform popes had been elected. Most prominent among them was Hadrian VI (teacher and friend of Charles V), a Netherlander and for hundreds of years the last pope who was not Italian. But his reign had been short and he had been succeeded by Clement VII, a luxury-loving Medici and typical Renaissance prelate.

Only after Clement's death did the reform movement find new official support. Yet, when in 1545, at the insistence of Charles V, a general Council had assembled in Trent, the popes had still obstructed its work. Only after Charles V had abdicated and Hapsburg power had been divided did the moment seem propitious to the popes for promoting the reform work of the Council.

The Founding of the Jesuit Order

By the time the Council convened again, the popes had received unquestioning obedience and aid from an unexpected source, the newly founded Society of Jesus—the Jesuits. A wounded soldier, the Spaniard Ignatius of Loyola (1491–1556), had turned from his former profession to become a soldier of Christ. He had written a book of *Exercises,* which taught the need for prayer, meditation, self-control, practical moderation, and training of the will to obtain salvation.

He gathered disciples and organized an order, for which he won recognition from the pope and which he placed like an army at the pope's absolute disposal. The purposes of the order were to combat heresy, spread Catholic education, and undertake missionary work. For the sake of effective results, the Jesuits underwent rigorous training. Many of them became the most learned members not only of the Church but of secular society as well. They did not hesitate to ally themselves in their work with the powerful of this earth, to make questionable political compromises, and to employ all practical means force as well as persuasion, Inquisition as well as prayer—to regain heretical lands. They devoted special attention to the colonies and carried their activities as far as Japan.

Conclusion of Council of Trent (1563)

Thus strengthened, the popes reconvened the Council, which had held only intermittent sessions, and in 1563 brought it to a conclusion. They achieved what they had set out to do. Since the Protestants did not recognize the authority of the popes, or the decisions of any council unless based entirely on the Scriptures, a compromise with them was excluded from the outset.

Instead, the Council reasserted the Catholic point of view. It centered its attention on doctrine and ritual; it affirmed that the Scriptures and traditions are equally binding for the faithful and that the supremacy of the pope is incontestable. The Council published an "Index" of books that Catholics were forbidden to read without special dispensation. It refuted heresies and reaffirmed old dogmas. It prescribed measures to improve Church discipline and the morals and training of the clergy; it prohibited malpractices in regard to indulgences and adoration of saints; it abolished certain administrative abuses.

The Council of Trent thus concluded a reform of the Church from within and rejuvenated the Catholic-Christian spirit. Subsequently, in 1582, Pope Gregory XIII even introduced a new calendar, which, named the "Gregorian," after him, replaced the Julian calendar used since the times of Caesar.

Reformation and Counter Reformation left a deep imprint upon the Western world in the field of religion and beyond. They affected intellectual trends, economics, and national developments. They stimulated education, changed social relationships, and led to new legal concepts and new laws. As two or more different faiths were subsequently to live side by side, a measure of tolerance became necessary, and the possibility emerged from the individual to make a choice in religious matters. Indeed, the cause of individualism, which the Renaissance, humanism, and capitalistic enterprise had fostered, was also advanced by the Reformation.

Selected Readings

Bainton, Roland H., ed. *The Age of the Reformation* (1956)
Grimm, Harold, J. *The Reformation Era, 1500–1650* (1966)
Janelle, Pierre. *The Catholic Reformation* (1949)
Reid, W. Stanford, ed. *The Reformation* (1968)
Rice, Eugene F. *The Foundations of Early Modern Europe, 1460–1559* (1970)
Spitz, Lewis W. *The Protestant Reformation* (1966)

6

The Aftermath of Renaissance and Reformation (1555–1603)

1558	England loses Calais, last foothold on Continent
	Ivan the Terrible invades Livonia
1559	Publication of Prayer Book in England (Elizabeth I)
1562	Beginnings of religious wars in France (Huguenots)
1563	"Thirty-nine Articles" of the Anglican Church
	Council of Trent concluded
1565	Beginning of risings against Spain in the Netherlands
1568	Mary, Queen of Scots, flees to England
	Duke of Alba in the Netherlands
1569	Union of Lublin between Poland and Lithuania
	Mercator publishes map of the world
1571	Battle of Lepanto: Turks defeated
1572	Beginnings of War of Independence of the Netherlands (William the Silent)
	Massacre of the Night of St. Bartholomew in Paris
	John Knox, Scottish reformer, dies
1576	Titian dies
1580	Montaigne, *Essais*
	Russian penetration into Siberia
1581	Northern Netherlands depose Philip II
1582	Gregorian calendar introduced

1584 William of Orange assassinated

1587 Mary, Queen of Scots, executed

1588 Spanish Armada destroyed

1592 Alexander of Parma dies

1594 Henry IV gains Paris: end of civil wars in France

Palestrina dies

1595 Dutch colonization of East Indies begins

1597 Francis Bacon, *Essays*

1598 Franco-Spanish peace of Vervins: death of Philip II

Edict of Nantes

1600 Founding of English East India Company

1602 Founding of Dutch East India Company

1603 Shakespeare, *Hamlet*

Death of Elizabeth I of England

Youthfulness, confidence, enthusiasm, thirst for beauty and manliness (virtù), had marked the early sixteenth century and made possible the achievements of the High Renaissance. They no longer characterized the second half of the century. In only two corners of Europe, Spain and England (both of which had previously made few contributions to the glory of the age), do we find a sudden flowering of culture. But in these countries the Renaissance took on a more mature, more intellectual, aspect and found its major expression in literature and science. Many of the great artists were by then either dead or, like Michelangelo and Titian, in their old age. The great humanists (Erasmus, Reuchlin, More), the religious leaders (Luther, Zwingli, Calvin, Loyola), the mighty Renaissance princes and patrons of culture (from the Medici, Sforza, Este, and other families), had passed from the scene, as had Copernicus and Machiavelli. However, on the political stage, in addition to literature and natural sciences, the second half of the sixteenth century did bring forth a considerable number of personalities and events inspired by the great age that was coming to a close.

THE POLITICAL SCENE

After the abdication of Charles V in 1556, the idea of European Christian unity, as it had been conceived during the Middle Ages—ever since the crowning of Charlemagne in 800 and Otto the Great in 962—was not revived. Spain, France, and Germany were to make successive attempts at establishing some form of unity by imposing their own supremacy and leadership on the rest of the Continent. In each case, though, it was national ambition rather than a general European concept that directed their efforts. Indeed, after Charles V's abdication, the history of Western civilization, more than before, becomes the story of individual countries.

Often it is the character of a ruler that leaves its sharp imprint upon the civilization of an age. Thus, William the Silent of the Netherlands, Ivan the Terrible of Russia, Philip II of Spain, Elizabeth I of England, and Eric XIV of Sweden lent color and distinction to the second half of the sixteenth century. Among the dramatic events they witnessed and to which they contributed were the War of Independence of the Netherlands, the struggle over the Baltic question, the Battle of Lepanto, the Night of St. Bartholomew, and the destruction of the Spanish Armada.

Italy

On the European stage during this period, Italy played the role as target of action for other nations. The country underwent the decline or disappearance of its vigorous city-states and the weakening of the political position of the papal territories. Almost entirely under Hapsburg domination, it served as a bridge between Spain and Germany. The commerce of the Italian cities steadily lost its world significance; the wealth of other countries overshadowed theirs.

Germany

Despite being located in the heart of Europe, Germany similarly declined in political importance. The Hapsburgs produced no new ruler of the stature of Charles V. Their resources were exhausted in wars to maintain the empire and the Catholic faith. Such common institutions as the diets no longer functioned satisfactorily. The independence of the states comprising the empire increased and borderlands were lost. Thus, the Netherlands was joined to Spain, and subsequently its northern parts achieved independence. Livonia fell prey, first, to Russian, then to Swedish and Polish invaders. Western borderlands in Lorraine were annexed by the French and the bishopric of Basel joined the free Swiss cantons.

The eastern frontiers of the empire continued to be exposed to inroads by the Turks, who remained in possession of Hungary with its silver mines. Most of the eastern trade routes via the sea to the rich grain resources of the Slavic and Baltic countries fell into the hands of enterprising Dutch traders.

However, individual German states (notably Brandenburg, Saxony, Austria, and Bavaria) grew in strength and gained international prestige. Such states, rather than the empire as a whole, increasingly became the centers of German might and German culture.

Spain

The role of leadership in Hapsburg affairs accordingly shifted to the Spanish branch of the house. Philip II (d. 1598) proved to be an outstanding ruler. Though lacking the balance and wisdom of his father, Charles V, personally cruel, and jealous of his own best generals, advisers, and servants, Philip was a man devoted to the fulfillment of his duties as king. He worked tirelessly, persistent in all his undertakings. In a sense, he was the first Western ruler to understand, and build, a modern bureaucracy.

INTERNAL POLICIES

Under Philip II, Spain's great military tradition was maintained. Arts and literature flourished. Numerous universities were established, Catholic scholars were attracted, and geographical studies were advanced. Spanish architecture found its grandest expression in the mighty, somber palace of the Escorial built by Philip. Manners, fashions, and court etiquette and ceremonials developed that served as models for all Europe.

Yet, the administration of the enormous empire set tasks for which Spain was not equipped. The wealth coming from the colonies, mainly in silver, was largely wasted. It did not stimulate industry, but rather pride, sloth, and luxury. Since the Spanish nobles considered business activities unworthy of their attention, and since the merchant class was small, foreigners were allowed to exploit the country's natural resources. Taxation remained high. Monopolies hindered fruitful economic activities and debasement of the currency became unavoidable. The government lost its credit standing through repeated bankruptcy of the treasury.

Simultaneously, agriculture declined, and large estates, given away by the Crown as rewards to nobles, were used mainly for pasture. The population, impoverished, gradually decreased. This process of economic decline was speeded by the expulsion of Jews and Moors who, through their trade and agriculture, had contributed much to the country's prosperity.

RELIGIOUS POLICIES

Philip maintained strict absolutism. Though a devout Catholic, he did not permit political influence by the Church. He kept the clergy dependent, using the Jesuits for the advancement of Spanish aims in Europe and America. On one occasion, he even made war on the pope and besieged Rome.

COLONIAL POLICIES

Just as Philip dominated in the affairs of the Spanish clergy, so he personally supervised, despite the obstacle of distance, the administration of government in the New World. He followed the established policy of appointing viceroys, but, in matters of policy, he kept them subservient to the "Council of the Indies." The *encomienda* system (landholding by the feudal nobility and forced labor by natives) was retained, and large estates were granted to Spanish nobles in the colonies. After the intervention of the friar Bartolomé de las Casas with Philip's father, Charles, the Indians were no longer subjected to slavery. Trade with the New World remained a royal monopoly. Large fleets were sent there annually, under the protection of convoys that fought off the English and French pirates and smugglers.

FOREIGN POLICIES

In foreign policy, Philip pursued the sole aim of defending the Spanish Empire. He was only partially successful. Closely cooperating with the German Hapsburgs, he fought and decisively defeated France. Allied with Venice and the pope, he engaged in war against the Turks. In 1571, he was victorious at Lepanto, one of the greatest naval battles of all times, upsetting Turkish domination in the western Mediterranean. He invaded Portugal in 1580, when the royal family there had died out, annexed the country, and thus gained its rich dependencies in Africa and Asia.

But in vain did he seek to retain control of the Spanish and Portuguese links with the colonial empires. Throughout his reign, he had to fight the English on the seas. After years of struggle, his ambitious plan to destroy the English navy and to end English competition with the help of a great fleet, the "Armada," miscarried. In 1588, the Armada, after being defeated by the English, was destroyed by storms. In all his costly foreign policies, Philip used and supported Catholicism, out of conviction as well as expediency, so that it ultimately appeared as if the defense of the old faith was the main objective of his policies.

The Netherlands

Despite Philip's high ability and industriousness, his reign ultimately turned out to be disastrous for Spain. His failure is attributable not so much to repeated bankruptcies or to loss of the Armada or to a revival of French power as to the crucial mistake that he made in the Spanish Netherlands.

OPPRESSION; DUKE OF ALBA

The Netherlands constituted the greatest asset within Philip's realms. He had inherited them from his father who, being a native, had understood how to retain their loyalty. Philip was dependent upon their wealth. But, instead of promoting Dutch and Flemish trade and winning good will, he tried to rectify a catastrophic financial situation in Spain by extending the crippling Spanish sales tax to the Low Countries. He thereby threatened the merchants with ruin. Moreover, through his arbitrariness and arrogance he exasperated the Netherlanders, who were accustomed to a large measure of freedom. Finally, through the protection of the Catholic faith, the enforcement of the decisions of the Council of Trent, and the Inquisition, he sharpened the antagonism of the largely Calvinist Dutch toward their Spanish overlords.

When the Netherlanders petitioned for reforms, Philip sent an army under the Duke of Alba. The Duke had shown his genius as a general in campaigns in Africa, in Italy, and at Mühlberg; he was later to show it also at the conquest of Portugal. When he sought to enforce Spanish rule and Philip's taxation system, the Netherlands rebelled. Alba crushed the revolt and executed two of the leaders, Egmont and Horn. But a third leader, William the Silent, of Orange, escaped to become the hero of liberty in the great struggle that ensued.

WAR OF INDEPENDENCE; WILLIAM OF ORANGE

The War of Independence of the Low Countries against Spain has remained an inspiration and model throughout the ages. William was a true Machiavellian; *The Prince* was his constant companion. He was called "the Silent" because he knew how to hide his thoughts behind a flow of diverting conversation. He was successively Catholic, Lutheran, and Calvinist. He married four times—for purposes of expediency. He was French (Orange), German (Nassau), and Dutch. An inefficient general, he was regularly defeated by Alba. He knew as little of economics as of military science.

But William had an inflexible will. He was a political genius who knew how to command the loyalty of others. He showed tolerance whenever his political strategy called for it. He was modern in his point of view and he was interested in realities rather than in appearances.

Under his leadership, the Dutch and the Flemish recovered from their defeats. They equipped a small navy of so-called "Sea Beggars" to harass Spanish shipping. After the recall of Alba in 1573, they forced the Spanish army to relinquish most of the country. In 1581, the independence of the Netherlands was declared. But the war was not yet won. When Philip II sent Prince Alessandro Farnese of Parma to Flanders, Farnese, a man fully the equal of William in political acumen, succeeded in regaining the southern areas of the Low Countries.

In the midst of the struggle, in 1584, William was murdered; but the Netherlanders fought on, stubbornly and courageously. They did not succeed in freeing the entire country. The country was divided: its southern portions remained Spanish and Catholic; the north established itself as an independent republic in which Protestantism was predominant. There, the Orange family provided political leadership. Soon, under merchant or "bourgeois" control, the economy became again the most flourishing of Europe.

France

The internal policy of France centered around the religious problem and the struggle for maintenance of royal authority. Its foreign policy was guided by opposition to the Hapsburgs and, particularly, to Spain. But France was in no position to establish good government at home or enforce its will abroad. Not only was it decisively defeated by Spain in 1559, but religious wars ravaged the country and undermined law and order.

RISE OF THE HUGUENOTS

The dominant issue in France during the second half of the sixteenth century was the issue of national unity. The Reformation had split the country. Two parties had been formed: the Catholic, directed by the Guise family; and the Protestant, or "Huguenot," led by the Calvinist princes of Condé and Navarre and by Admiral Coligny. Periods of persecution of the Huguenots alternated with periods of toleration.

France might have emulated Germany (where, ultimately, both religions were recognized and existed side by side) or Spain (where Catholicism existed exclusively). But it followed neither example. Indeed, the historical importance of the events in France lies in that it was not the religious question but a political one that became the chief problem. As so often happens, the conflict between the two groups turned into a triangular struggle. A third party, the "Politiques," was formed. This party, which was not greatly concerned about religion, put nationalistic aims and centralization of government above all other considerations.

Without delay, the queen mother, Catherine de Medici, who had an ambitious, intriguing character, embraced its tenets, for they coincided with her own absolutist aims. She played the other two parties against each other. Thus, the country was torn by internal strife. Disorders, unmatched elsewhere, occurred. The climax came when Catherine, faced by the possibility of a Protestant triumph, turned openly against the Protestants and instigated the outrage and horror of the Night of St. Bartholomew. Under the pretext of a reconciliation, she lured the Protestant leaders to Paris, whereupon these men and some twenty thousand of their adherents throughout France were massacred (1572).

CIVIL WARS AND RELIGIOUS SETTLEMENT

The events of the Night of St. Bartholomew led, after the shock of the stunning blow had passed, to a prolongation of the internal wars. The Politiques now sought to destroy the Catholic party. Politiques, Catholics, and Protestants—each party led by a Henry—continued to fight the other two in ever-shifting alliances (War of the Three Henrys). After utter exhaustion had been reached, the country impoverished, farms destroyed, international prestige lost, and two of the Henrys murdered, the survivor, Henry of Navarre, of the House of Bourbon and leader of the Protestants, succeeded in ending the struggle.

Putting the political issue before all others, he made terms with his opponents. He obtained recognition as king and converted to Catholicism. But he also pleased the Protestants by issuing the Edict of Nantes in 1598. This edict granted the Protestants freedom of conscience (the right to public worship) and the right to hold office. He guaranteed the latter right to the Protestant minority by permitting them to possess and to fortify, as a guarantee of their safety, a number of towns of their own in France.

England

The ambitions of individuals, disruption in domestic affairs, and foreign wars brought ruin to France. Meanwhile, a comparatively peaceful era and concentration on its national aims made it possible for England to enjoy a period of prosperity that coincided with the English Renaissance. The term "Renaissance" is possibly somewhat misleading: achievements in such areas as sculpture and painting were scant and mediocre. Nevertheless, we find typical Renaissance traits in music—with the development of the madrigal—and in literature—with the masterpieces of Tudor poets and dramatists, especially Shakespeare. In the splendor of its court life, the English also began to rival other Renaissance courts.

ECONOMIC EXPANSION

In England during the second half of the sixteenth century, the enterprising Renaissance spirit also asserted itself in commercial affairs and in geographical explorations. The shipbuilding industry expanded rapidly. Sea captains and pirates made England the foremost maritime power. Hawkins, Raleigh, and Drake sought trade routes westward. Chancellor established an eastward route to Russia via the northern tip of Europe. Jenkinson initiated English trade with the tsar and, indirectly, through the tsar's realms, with Persia.

Overseas expansion led to industrial expansion and the establishment of joint-stock companies after Italian models. Business enterprises formed by a group of merchants financed these undertakings and charged a captain to carry them out. They were precursors of the modern stock company. To further these enterprises, a regular credit system was built up. As in Spain, so, too, in England the results were a decline in independent farming and the wider introduction of enclosured farms. This shift led to increased sheep grazing and, in turn, stimulated the textile industry. The townspeople and the merchants improved their economic position. The national standard of living reached a higher level.

RELIGIOUS SETTLEMENT

Unlike many of the Continental powers, sixteenth-century England was spared religious wars. Under Edward VI (d. 1553), who succeeded Henry VIII, the political-religious changes made by Henry began to be extended to the realm of religious doctrine. Through two successive "Acts of Uniformity," a *Book of Common Prayer* was introduced. Protestant views regarding the authority of the Bible, justification by faith, and the nature of the sacraments were accepted.

Edward's successor, Mary Tudor (d. 1558), favored Catholicism. Her reign brought harsh persecutions of Protestants, hundreds of whom perished. Her own life was tragic and her rule short. Married to Philip II of Spain, she embraced not only the Catholic faith, but also the Spanish cause, which was contrary to English commercial interests. Moreover, in 1558 England lost its last stronghold on the Continent, the port of Calais.

In turn, Mary's successor, Elizabeth I (1558–1603), reverting to the policy of Edward VI, reintroduced a Protestant form of worship. Elizabeth accepted the innovations that had been introduced by the Acts of Uniformity, but she modified somewhat their anti-Catholic emphasis. The "Thirty-nine Articles" set forth the Anglican confession of faith. A party of so-called "Puritans" desired more far-reaching changes, but, in order to preserve an all-national Church that the ruler could control, they were suppressed. For the same reason, Roman Catholics were now persecuted, perhaps no less than the Protestants had been during Mary's regime.

EXTERNAL AFFAIRS

England's foreign policies under Elizabeth were dominated by rivalry for commercial expansion and by fear of the power of Spain, France, and Scotland. This fact drove the country into sharp opposition to Catholic nations. It led to a bitter, repressive policy in Ireland (which Spain tried at times to use as a stepping-stone for an invasion of England). It disturbed the relations with Scotland and its Catholic ruling house of Stuart. Indeed, it brought death to Mary Stuart (Mary, Queen of Scots), the queen, a fugitive from her own country and a refugee in England. Accused of participating in Jesuit conspiracies against the life of Elizabeth (who was her cousin), Mary was executed in 1587. The religious rivalry led to incessant, though undeclared, war with Spain and constant attacks on Spanish shipping. This situation reached its climax in 1588, when open war broke out and the Spanish Armada was defeated. On the other hand, opposition to Catholicism—and to Spain—brought cooperation with the rebelling Netherlands. As to France, no consistent policy could be pursued, inasmuch as English-French relations depended upon ever-changing French relations with Scotland and Spain.

ELIZABETHAN ACHIEVEMENTS

By the time Elizabeth died, the English treasury was exhausted. Parliament had become restive. Nevertheless, and despite the personal shortcomings of the queen, the Elizabethan Age stands out as a glorious era. Through the influence of literature, better education, and science, a gentler spirit had come to pervade England, a country which the Italians and French had long regarded as barbarian. Elizabeth's regime, supported by capable advisers of the queen, whom she chose well, had built the foundations of political power, economic prosperity, and a vigorous, self-reliant body of citizens. Parliament and the bourgeois class, which were to hold the key to the future, emerged strengthened. Nor did the nobility shun participation in commercial activities. Coal mining and shipbuilding flourished. Finally, a church grew up that combined traditionalism with Lutheran and Calvinist reforms and supported national unity under the monarch.

Scandinavia and Poland

The great issues of the day—the religious struggles, the capitalistic enterprises, and political centralization under a strong ruler—also continued to affect the small nations of northern and eastern Europe. These issues led to a further redistribution of power, which affected the entire Baltic area. Yet for more than a century after the discovery of America, Baltic trade still remained more important than the transatlantic traffic.

DENMARK-NORWAY AND SWEDEN

Denmark-Norway, having lost control over Sweden in 1523, sought to adapt itself to the changed conditions. It succeeded in reestablishing order at home and brought religious strife to an end, with consequences favorable to the Lutheran cause. It also built up its economy with the help of the huge income derived from tolls that Denmark levied upon ships passing from the North Sea into the Baltic Sea through the "Sound," the only navigable lane available and a narrow passageway controlled by Denmark. But the kings continued to squander their resources in futile wars against Sweden.

The Swede, on the contrary, made better progress. Having won their independence under the able, cautious, parsimonious Gustavus Vasa, they developed their rich copper and iron mines, increased their production, channeled traffic through their own ports, and built up a large treasury. This policy enabled them (under Gustavus's sons and successors) to survive bitter wars against Denmark, Poland, and Russia. With the conquest of Estonia in 1561, they became the foremost Baltic power. Yet, Sweden, too, lacked the economic resources, the population, and the modern commercial spirit that would have enabled it to compete successfully with the Western trading nations.

POLAND-LITHUANIA

Like the Swedes, the Poles cherished dreams of a large empire and of dominion over the Baltic sea lanes. In 1525, they had already established their overlordship of Prussia. In 1562, their Lithuanian partners incorporated southern Livonia. Poland compelled Lithuania to accept complete integration in 1569. Poland forced Danzig into submission and in 1582, after a series of wars against Russia, annexed large Russian territories.

Such diversified holdings demanded an efficient and tolerant central authority. But while arts, crafts, and literature flourished and the upper nobility enjoyed a life of luxury, the country as a whole did not develop the necessary progressive spirit and internal cohesion. The generally weak, elective monarchy was motivated since the end of the Council of Trent by the aim of proselytizing in behalf of Catholicism. It failed to control the unruly, chauvinistic nobility which, itself divided, dominated the law-giving institution, the diet or *sejm*. Little was done to promote trade and the development of a merchant class. Nowhere else was the social gulf among classes, nationalities, and religions so great as in Poland. Thus, conquests of territory contributed, not to the growth of the commonwealth, but to its destruction.

Russia

In the meantime, Russia was being governed by one of its most eminent rulers, Ivan IV (Ivan the Terrible). Ivan IV continued the work of consolidating the Russian realms begun by his grandfather, Ivan the Great. He succeeded in incorporating the vast territory along the entire course of the Volga. He attempted to conquer Livonia (Estonia, and Latvia) in order to gain ports giving Russia access to the sea. Failing in this, he established permanent connections with the West by welcoming English merchants who had opened the northern route around the North Cape.

Ivan IV brutally suppressed all potential opponents and kept princes (boyars) and the Church under his absolute rule. He personally monopolized many economic activities, and surrounded himself with a powerful bureaucracy that was at his complete command. He catered to English and Dutch traders, who increasingly replaced the Hanseatic merchants on the Baltic sea lanes. He strengthened the new links with the West by inviting craftsmen to visit his country, by introducing Western techniques, and by expanding diplomatic relations.

It was under Ivan the Terrible that Russia started its eastward march across the Urals. A band of intrepid Cossacks, led by Yermak, invaded Siberia in 1580 and began Russia's mighty eastward movement. As a whole, Ivan IV's reign meant rapid progress for Russia politically and economically, and expansion eastward. But it also led to territorial losses in the West, to moral debasement, and to all the vicious consequences of autocracy, which endangered internal stability.

THE SOCIAL AND CULTURAL SCENE

With the fading of the great age of the Renaissance in the second half of the sixteenth century, there began a period that in art history is known as "Mannerism." This era constituted the link between the High Renaissance and the coming baroque period. Despite the name, this age of transition was not devoid of sincerity and originality. Although works of genius, such as had been produced in the two preceding centuries, were rare, there was still left a love for the beautiful and for *virtù,* which made possible the creation of works of art that fulfilled the Renaissance ideal.

Society

During the course of the Reformation and the consolidation of national states, major changes in society occurred. On the one hand, royal courts and their bureaucracies gained additional power. On the other, wealthy burghers and professionals secured ever-greater influence. As much as twenty percent of the total population now lived in cities—about twice as many than used to live there. Those who benefited from the opportunities towns offered for commercial and banking activities sought equality in status with the nobility. Skilled craftsmen likewise gained from urbanization, but common laborers sank to lower levels. The gulf between upper and lower classes deepened.

The peasants likewise failed to improve their lot. Rebellions, to which they often resorted, gained them little. New economic conditions brought them somewhat more freedom, but did not relieve them from their poverty. Nor did the peasants benefit from the wealth that poured in from the colonies.

Life expectancy remained low for all classes. Hygienic conditions hardly improved. Medical knowledge and care made some progress, but epidemics such as cholera and syphilis still raged and attacked all layers of society, and nature's disasters took their toll everywhere. Ulrich von Hutten had sung that "it is a joy to live," but a gloomier mood seized the world toward the end of the century.

The Military

With the age of chivalry disappearing and national armies not yet formed, the military became somewhat of a class unto itself. Mercenaries made up most of the land forces. In the second half of the sixteenth century, infantry composed of these forces found employ on the many battlefields—from Scotland to Livonia, from the Netherlands to Hungary, from Sweden to Spain and southern Italy. Even on warships the infantry fought on decks after boarding the enemy's ships. Cavalry was no longer of the same use as in earlier times, and the knights lost the distinction which the possession of horse and servants had given them. The mercenaries were fickle. They freely offered their services to those leaders whose victorious records promised rich booty; they changed sides readily when profitable. Strategy and tactics had to be shaped to fit these conditions. Equipment with muskets rather than pikes or swords was needed and gave additional power to those who could afford the costs. Artillery became indispensable, especially for beleaguering fortresses. Scientific work was needed to help develop weapons (even great artists like Leonardo were commissioned to improve canons and fortifications). War, as usual, furthered science and technical occupations. Weapons necessitated the expansion of mining and industrial production.

Art

Among the great painters, those of the Venetian school, which had begun to flourish later than those in Florence and Rome, preserved longest the tradition of the earlier masters. Elsewhere, craftsmanship rather than genius marked the work of the leading artists. A younger generation of artists showed less youthful exuberance, less passion. Affected by the later, disintegrating trends of the Renaissance, they were inclined to follow traditional patterns and to exaggerate emotions. One towering figure stands out: El Greco (d. 1575), who lived in Spain *(View of Toledo; Great Inquisitor Guevara)*. His sense of the tragic is expressed in his beautiful, somber, deeply emotional canvases.

Music

In music, too, a different spirit became noticeable. The fresh and vigorous trends of the early century, which had popular appeal and were enjoyed by a broad audience, gave way to a more delicate style as demanded by a narrower, refined society that preferred classical features. The Catholic Church was worried because it sensed the worldly, sensual background of much of the art in the late stages of the Renaissance, and at the Council of Trent a special session was devoted to music. There, the participants warned against the imitation of classical models, condemned the influence of pagan morals, and demanded a purification of music along the lines of Christian tradition, accentuating severity and restraint.

Soon there emerged one of history's outstanding composers, the Italian Palestrina (d. 1594), who had studied under Renaissance Netherland masters. He fulfilled the demands of the Council, yet preserved and furthered the stylistic innovations of his predecessors, their polyphonic style and counterpoint. The earnestness, clarity, and tonal purity of his motets and masses were cherished by popes and art patrons alike. Palestrina, his contemporary Orlando di Lasso, and a school of their followers have ever since been regarded as preeminent forces in the development of early modern music.

Simultaneously, secular music was cultivated both in Protestant and in Catholic countries. The Netherlands and Germany, with their continued emphasis on harmony, lost the lead they had held previously. Italy, perfecting instrumental melody, came to the fore and inspired musicians in other countries. Even England, which had excelled in various forms of music (and which, with masters like William Byrd, continued to create independent works of remarkable beauty), was influenced increasingly by Italian music.

New or improved instruments, such as the harpsichord and the violin, appeared. Many compositions were written for instruments instead of for voice alone. Furthermore, music was written for theatrical performances. Toward the end of the sixteenth century, through a combination of music and drama, the modern opera was born.

Literature

Printed books increased in number and influence. Excellent histories were written, such as one centering on Philip II by Cabrera and a *Universal History* by De Thou. (Other histories—for example, the *Ecclesiastical History of the Magdeburg Centuries* and a history of the times of Charles V by Sleidanus—served propagandistic purposes in favor of religious causes.) In Spain, the novel made its appearance. Everywhere, descriptions of travel, such as the accounts collected by the Englishman Hakluyt, became popular.

With the increase in books, poetry and drama found an ever-growing audience. Authors such as the Italian Tasso (d. 1595) and the English Spenser (d. 1599) and Marlowe (d. 1593) gained fame in their own lifetimes.

France produced two writers of lasting significance. Rabelais (d. 1553), with the aim of entertaining, created in his *Gargantua* a mirror of human weaknesses, full of fantasy and humor. Montaigne (d. 1592), a sensitive, philosophical man of genius, was strongly affected by the skepticism of his age. He expressed doubt that human beings could ever acquire true knowledge, and in a spirit of unaccustomed detachment, wrote the *Essais,* in which he analyzed human nature so well that this work has served ever since as a guide to everyday living.

But the two most notable writers of this period were the Spaniard Cervantes (d. 1616), who wrote *Don Quixote,* and the English dramatist and poet Shakespeare (d. 1616). They probed the depths of human nature and aspirations, and with sympathy for human strength and human weakness they portrayed individual and national character with a mastery that has remained unsurpassed.

Science

In science, a basis for rapid advances had been laid by the Renaissance masters through their exact and imaginative approach, their sober observations, and their numerous careful descriptions of nature. No longer were they unquestioningly guided by the writings of classical authors who had dominated science so long. When classical views conflicted with observed facts, they were rejected.

In the latter part of the century, the Dane Tycho Brahe (d. 1601) was mapping the sky. The fundamental work of Copernicus was carried further by Galileo (d. 1642), who, after perfecting the telescope and making scrupulous observations that led to numerous discoveries, confirmed Copernicus's findings. Galileo realized the importance of insight and imagination, so long as they did not lead to "postulating in advance." He did not hesitate to propose hypotheses, but he based them on mathematical thought and then checked results experimentally. Galileo thus found and described the law of falling bodies and the motion of the pendulum. He enunciated the principle of inertia.

No less stimulating was the work of the English statesman Francis Bacon (d. 1626). Although, in his search for a scientific method, he overemphasized experimentation and observation, and although he lacked necessary mathematical knowledge, he prepared the way for future scientific endeavors by advocating an "inductive method of reasoning." Like Galileo, Bacon insisted on the necessity of doubting traditional concepts and values.

Advances paralleling those in astronomy and physics were made in other subjects. Gilbert of Colchester (d. 1603) made important discoveries in magnetism. In botany and zoology, new and advanced descriptions of plants and animals were published—even though much fanciful information still marked such scientific literature. Altogether, belief in pseudo-sciences, magic, alchemy, and astrology continued to dominate in many fields.

Geography

Progress in geography was aided particularly by the achievements of the preceding half-century. Maps drawn in the second half of the sixteenth century (for example, those of the German mapmaker Mercator) showed remarkable perfection after more than a thousand years of comparative stagnation in this craft. Mapmaking profited from the theoretical advances in science that made mathematical projection possible. It also profited from the practical experience gained through explorations and discoveries, replacing the numerous superstitions inherited from ancient and medieval times.

The new maps stimulated further explorations. Although no important new seaways were discovered, distant lands were explored. Large areas in America, Russia, and even Japan were made known to the Western world. Products such as coffee, which Venice began to import on a large scale, and the potato, which was first planted in 1584, became popular among Europeans.

Much of the work of discovery was undertaken by merchants. The traditionally conservative groups—the Hanseatic and Venetian traders—were pushed more and more into the background by enterprising Portuguese, Dutch, English, and Scotch merchants. The daring undertakings of these newer groups were backed by well-organized, powerful, and rich joint-stock companies. The travelers came home not only with profits, but also with intriguing accounts of the foreign lands they had visited.

Religion

As people turned their attention increasingly to exploration of the world around them, they lost some of their interest in questions of dogma. No theological works appeared in the second half of the sixteenth century that could compare in importance with those of the first half. Religious passions, however, remained strong, with bitter consequences upon the lives of nations. The

Inquisition lost much of its terror, especially after the outbreak of the War of Independence of the Netherlands, but the number of civil wars increased.

Catholicism recovered and regained strength in many lands. By 1600, the large Protestant minorities had been reduced in Poland, Austria, parts of southern and western Germany, the southern Netherlands, and France. In Spain, Portugal, and Italy, Protestant groups had been crushed. Catholicism had made inroads in Protestant northern Germany, England, and Scandinavia. Despite political changes in England, Ireland had remained faithful to Rome. Moreover, Catholic refugees from England and other Protestant countries founded colleges in other countries as rallying points for compatriots who were persecuted for their religious views. In many respects, the Catholics had adjusted more rapidly to the rational trends of the age than the Protestants who, cherishing a mystical faith, were inclined to adhere to the letter of the Scriptures.

In the latter part of the sixteenth century, differences in the evolution of Western European nations prepared the way for a political redistribution of power. This redistribution was not brought about without terrible convulsions. It was compounded by social and religious conditions. Internal wars shook France for more than forty years. Warfare ruined the German Empire. Spain lost its predominant place through a drawn-out, vain struggle in the Netherlands and, on the seas, against growing English power. England itself managed to live through a comparatively quiet time—with grave inner turmoil postponed until the next century.

War raged almost incessantly in the North between Sweden, Russia, and Poland, focusing around the Livonian harbors of Riga, Reval, and Narva, which served as intermediaries for the heavy East-West trade via Baltic sea-lanes. When Russia failed to gain access to the Baltic Sea, it turned its attention to the lower Volga region and Siberia, which small bands of adventurers had begun to open up to Russian penetration.

Yet it can be argued that political developments were overshadowed in importance by cultural advances. Science now began to lead the way into a different world.

Selected Readings

Butterfield, Herbert. *The Origins of Modern Science* (1949)

Chadwick, H.M. and N. K. *The Growth of Literature* (1969)

Davies, R. T. *The Golden Century of Spain, 1501–1621* (1954)

Hall, Alfred R. *The Scientific Revolution, 1500–1800* (1966)

Lovelock, William. *A Concise History of Music* (1962)

Mattingly, Garrett. *The Armada* (1959)

Pierson, Pieter. *Philip II of Spain* (1975)

Roll, Erich. *A History of Thought* (1974)

Trevor, Aston, ed. *Crisis in Europe, 1560–1660* (1965)

7

The Emergence of the Modern State System (1603–1648)

1604 Galileo: law of falling bodies

1605 Beginning of Times of Trouble in Russia

Cervantes, *Don Quixote*

1607 Jamestown settlement in Virginia founded

1610 Henry IV of France assassinated

1614 Dutch settlement on Hudson

Invention of logarithms

1616 Richelieu becomes minister in France

1618 Beginning of Thirty Years' War

1620 Settlement in New Plymouth founded *(Mayflower)*

Francis Bacon, *Novum Organum*

1621 Kepler's laws

1624 English settlements in East India and Dutch settlements in Indonesia

Decline of Portugal

1625 Grotius, *De Jure Belli et Pacis (Law of War and Peace)*

1628 Petition of Rights submitted to Charles I of England

Surrender of Huguenot-held La Rochelle to Richelieu

Harvey's treatise on circulation of blood published

1629 Edict of Restitution

Petition of Right

1630 Theory of mercantilism (Thomas Mun's treatises)

Swedish intervention in Thirty Years' War (Gustavus Adolphus)

1632 Battle of Lützen

Rembrandt, *Anatomy*

1634 Assassination of Wallenstein

1636 Corneille, *Le Cid (The Cid)*

Harvard College established

1637 Descartes, *Discours de la Méthode (Discourse on Method)*

1642 Civil War breaks out in England

Death of Richelieu

1648 Peace of Westphalia

The seventeenth century saw the development of trends that were to cul-minate during the eighteenth century in the so-called "Age of Reason." The passions and religious fervor of the preceding century were overshadowed by increasingly rational attitudes toward life. Even the seventeenth-century "religious" wars, which witnessed strange alliances between opposing creeds, reflect new political concepts rather than a concern about dogma and faith. New power relationships emerged. New aims, differing from those of the Renaissance and bearing witness to heightened national feelings, were pur-sued. A new type of diplomacy developed, one that was to endure until the twentieth century.

THE INTERNATIONAL SCENE

Two factors stand out in the political history of the seventeenth century: the rise of France in Europe, and the rise of England in overseas territories. The chief loser was the House of Hapsburg, both in Spain and in the empire. The position of superior power that Spain had held in the period following the discovery of America had actually rested on shaky foundations; the maintenance of that position had overtaxed the material and spiritual re-sources of the country. Similarly in the empire, the Hapsburgs lacked both the military and the economic bases for the preservation of imperial authority, and the bureaucracy needed for serving the central government. Meanwhile, France and England could build on structures adapted to the modern world that was emerging from the Renaissance. Furthermore, there

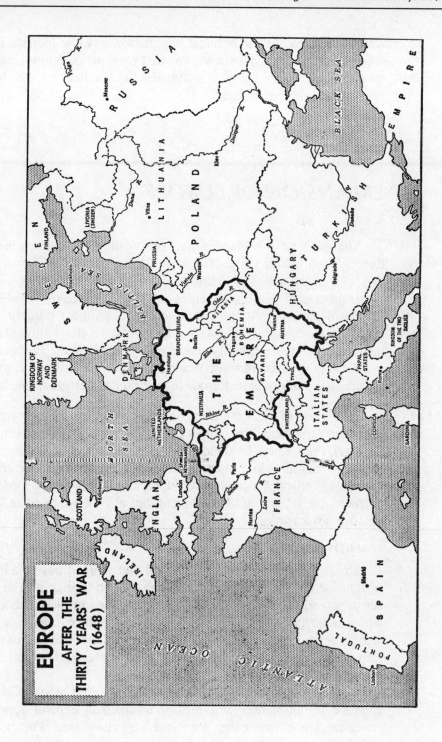

EUROPE
AFTER THE
THIRTY YEARS' WAR
(1648)

was a third area of wide political importance—its role indistinct during the seventeenth century, but already marked by signs of future greatness. This area comprised the colonial territories in America, to which European civilization was transplanted.

EXPANSION OF EUROPE

The drive of the Modern Age of Western civilization, expressed in Europe's worldwide undertakings, is without parallel in any other civilization. One of the most significant phenomena in the history of modern times is this process of "Europeanization" of the globe. The principal elements of European culture (religions, law concepts, political thought, languages, industrial techniques, customs and manners—the entire classical and medieval heritage) gradually spread everywhere. While European colonies and Eastern civilizations also made substantial contributions to the life of Europe, the contributions Europe made to them were very much greater.

Settlement of America

Settlement of the American continent was the most important phase of European expansion. The settlers came principally from four centers: Spain, Portugal, France, and England. During the seventeenth century, Spain tried both to consolidate and to extend its holdings, while France and England, joined by Holland, Sweden, and Denmark, not only established themselves in the northern parts of the continent, but also began to seize some of the Spanish possessions.

SPANISH AMERICA

Under Charles and Philip II, Spain had worked out an administrative system for its colonies; later rulers did little to change it. The policy was conservative. Government in America remained in the hands of viceroys, who were responsible to the home government. The *encomienda* system was also preserved. With the gradual exhaustion of the easily accessible mining resources, increasing attention was paid to the agricultural wealth and opportunities of the New World.

Spanish colonization was greatly aided by the Catholic Church, which enlarged its missionary activities and helped to expand Spanish rule to American lands. In Mexico, Peru, the La Plata region, Portuguese Brazil, Colombia, and Paraguay, the Dominicans, Franciscans, and, especially, Jesuits dominated in cultural and, sometimes, in political affairs. They adapted themselves to new surroundings, allied themselves with native ruling groups, and undertook programs of education, which gave them influence over the children. They thereby opened the gates to the influx of European institutions and customs.

The missionaries interested themselves in the economic welfare of the natives; they tried to protect the weak against exploitation. In Paraguay they went so far as to encourage communistic institutions. Of course, the civilization they introduced was indirectly beneficial to the home countries, which gained a large labor force and with its help could exploit the natural resources of the colonies.

FRENCH AMERICA

In American territory claimed by France, European culture was less pervasive than it was in the Spanish areas. French colonizing centered in Canada, where it began around 1611. Canada was a region sparsely populated and lacking readily available natural resources (except furs and timber). Consequently, compared with Spain, France showed much less interest in America. Emigration from France to the New World was negligible, nor did the French organize any nationally important trading companies for their colonies.

As a result, political and social conditions developed that differed markedly from those in Spanish America. The home government did not set up any elaborate administration, nor did it maintain close relations with the colonists and natives. Both groups were equally subject to the laws. In Canada, the precepts and influences of Catholic Orders were dominant.

ENGLISH AMERICA

England proved to be more active than either Spain or France. Its colonies in North America, which for a time had to compete with Swedish and Dutch settlements, were largely occupied by Protestants. At an early date, the English colonies set a pattern that differed sharply from the ones set by the French and the Spanish.

The English settled in Virginia, beginning with the Jamestown colony in 1607. Eventually, despite severe hardships and early political difficulties, they succeeded in establishing prosperous agricultural enterprises. Virginian wealth came to be based largely upon the production of tobacco, for which the English, following the Spanish example, found it advantageous to make use of black slaves. A trading company in England, the Virginia Company, was granted proprietary rights, but the actual administration of affairs was quickly taken over by a local representative assembly of the settlers.

In 1620, another colony, yet more independent of the home country (owing to dissenting religious beliefs), was founded in Massachusetts by Puritan emigrés. In accordance with the Mayflower Compact—an agreement entered into by passengers on the ship *Mayflower* during the journey to America—in this colony, too, a representative assembly of all freemen held the reins of government. In New England, during the early period of settlement, the problem of survival was even more difficult than it had been in Virginia. The settlers had to face similar disadvantages of climate and soil and, in addition, continuous internal dissension and the hostility of the native Indians. The success of the colonists must be attributed to their habits of hard work, their united defense (often brutal) against the natives, and their conviction as to the righteousness and eventual victory of their cause. During the 1630s, immigration to the New England colonies assumed substantial dimensions, and, in 1634, an English colony was founded in Maryland.

Expansion into Asia

The seventeenth-century establishment of European dominance in America was not at all matched by comparable expansion into Asia. The Europeans established themselves in numerous ports and some inland trading places; they entered into lucrative commercial relations. But no territories could be occupied as in America. No populations could be subjugated and their resources exploited.

Nor could the Europeans permanently introduce Western religious beliefs and social patterns. In the sixteenth century, Loyola's colleague, the Jesuit Francis Xavier, had spread the Catholic faith in southeast Asia. Early in the seventeenth century, Catholics in Japan may have numbered half a million, and even in China converts had been made. But, in the East, owing to the vigor of the old, indigenous civilizations and to the strength of their economic, social, and religious institutions, the process of Europeanization (already rendered difficult by strife among the Europeans themselves) was held back. The contributions of missionaries, traders, and soldiers were of little effect. Even this limited influence was restricted chiefly to southern Asia and failed to leave important traces in China and Japan.

EUROPE'S POLITICAL SCENE

It was during the seventeenth century that European expansion, especially in lands across the Atlantic, produced those changes in Europe's political power that had been foreshadowed in the Age of Discovery. Spain and Portugal, which had been the first to explore and settle the New World, were, however, not the ones to benefit permanently from their achievements. Whether for reasons of geographical location and climate or for reasons of individual ability and spirit of enterprise, it was not the Latin countries in the south of Europe but the seafaring nations in the Germanic North that reaped the fruits of colonization. Germany itself did not share in this development, nor did the Slavic East of Europe which, far removed from the Atlantic sea lanes, continued along its own independent cultural path.

Decline of Spain and Portugal

The death of Philip II in 1598 marked a decisive turn in Spain's role. Literature, music, and the arts continued to flourish, and the country entered what has become known as its "Golden Age." However, economic conditions deteriorated. Despite the work of the capable minister Olivares, the nobility, profiting from the weakness of Philip II's successors, regained their former influence.

The administration of the colonies became increasingly costly, while the wealth of the colonies was squandered for luxuries and for prestige. Ever more desperate efforts had to be made, especially in the struggle with England, to keep the sea lanes open. Prices continued to rise. Initiative was lacking. Emigration and wars checked population growth. The remnants of the Moorish and Jewish populations were eliminated in fearful persecutions. The army decayed and, under incapable kings, the bureaucracy failed to function satisfactorily. In 1639, the French took advantage of an uprising in Catalonia and invaded the country, thus further weakening Spain.

By then, Portugal, too, was engulfed in the general economic and political decline. When, by the middle of the century, the income from the East and the New World began to dwindle (partly because of the exhaustion of the great silver mines worked since 1545), power shifted from the Iberian domains of the Hapsburgs to the lands of rival dynasties in the north.

The German Empire

The possessions of the Austrian Hapsburgs, and with them the whole German Empire, underwent a similar decline, but for different reasons. Germany suffered from political fragmentation and lack of central authority. Trade decreased in the Mediterranean area, along with the commerce across the Alps that fed the great south German centers. Germany lacked the harbors needed in order to develop transatlantic trade. It was hurt, too, by conservatism, both of the south German bankers and of the north German merchants of the once powerful Hanse.

Leaders of genius became a rarity in the intellectual as well as the political, religious, and business spheres. Moreover, the Peace of Augsburg was often violated. The balance of strength continued to shift with the growth of Lutheranism in some regions, the strength of the Counter Reformation in others. Foreign powers—England, Spain, and France—saw opportunities to further their political objectives by interfering in German affairs and helping now one side and now the other.

THIRTY YEARS' WAR (1618–1648)

As a result, a terrible civil war broke out in 1618. It began as a religious war between Catholics and Protestants when, during negotiations, Emperor

Ferdinand II's ambassadors to Bohemia were hurled out of a window in Prague ("defenestration"). This war quickly involved foreign nations, for the Bohemians promptly deposed Ferdinand, who wanted to reintroduce Catholicism, as their king; they replaced him with a Protestant, the Elector Frederick of the Palatinate, who was a relative of the English king. Frederick suffered a major military defeat in 1620.

Shortly thereafter, although Protestant Denmark came to Frederick's aid, the imperial and Catholic forces again proved their superiority. Under the leadership of two great generals, Wallenstein and Tilly, the imperial armies forced the Danes and their Protestant allies to retreat. In 1629, the first two phases (Bohemian and Danish) of the war ended. Ferdinand regained the crown of Bohemia and in the same year promulgated an Edict of Restitution that cost the Protestants all the Church lands secularized and taken over by them since 1555.

In fact, it appeared that the war would end with the triumph of the Catholics. But, fearful of this eventuality, the foes of the Hapsburgs combined their efforts. They found a capable standard-bearer in Gustavus Adolphus, king of Sweden, devout Protestant, wise and generous statesman, and a leader shrewdly aware of Sweden's interests. Soon after his accession to the throne, he had entered the long struggle for Baltic hegemony; he had proved his generalship by conquering the Polish possessions in Livonia. He now saw a chance to help Lutheran brethren and simultaneously complete his domination of Baltic shipping by conquering Germany's Baltic coast.

As these aims implied war on the Hapsburgs, he obtained subsidies from Catholic France, whereupon a third phase (Swedish) of the war began. At the head of a splendid army, well equipped with artillery, he pushed deep into the heart of the empire. In his plight, the emperor had to recall Wallenstein, whom he had ungratefully dismissed, but who, with his enormous wealth in control of an army recruited by himself, was indispensable to the Catholic side.

In 1632, a decisive battle was fought at Lützen in Saxony. Wallenstein was defeated, and Protestantism was saved. But Gustavus Adolphus was killed. Without him, the Swedes were reluctant to continue the war; Wallenstein's star commenced to rise again. But when he began secret preparations for making himself ruler of a centralized German national state, he was murdered (in 1634), a turn of events that the emperor did not regret. In 1635, Ferdinand consented to a compromise peace, which was concluded in Prague. He revoked the Edict of Restitution, the main object of contention.

Since Hapsburg power was not yet broken, the French thereupon stirred up the Swedes anew. Moreover, they persuaded the Dutch to attack the Spanish Netherlands, induced the state of Savoy to seize the Hapsburg possessions in Italy, and put troops of their own into the field. Thus, the devastating war continued during a fourth period, which lasted another thirteen years.

PEACE OF WESTPHALIA (1648)

Peace was concluded in 1648 at Munster and Osnabrück, two towns in Westphalia. The empire survived and Hapsburg influence remained an important factor in European affairs; but imperial authority was greatly reduced. The central administration of the German Empire was further weakened and its more than three hundred component states were accorded almost complete independence.

Some of the individual states, such as Brandenburg and Saxony, gained territory and achieved status as European powers. The independence of Switzerland and of Holland was recognized. Calvinists gained equal rights with Catholics and Lutherans. The claim of France to the western territories of the empire in Lorraine, which it had annexed, was confirmed. So, too, was the claim of Sweden to the northern provinces along the Baltic Sea and the mouths of Germany's rivers.

The real winners of the war were France (which reached the peak of its power in Europe) and Sweden. Germany was devastated—even if not as much as has often been asserted. Still, in some regions the population had declined by a third or more. Towns and villages had to be rebuilt, agriculture had to be reestablished, and the intellectual centers had to be revived.

The Peace of Westphalia was supplemented by two additional treaties: one between France and Spain (the Peace of the Pyrenees, 1659), and another among Sweden, Poland, and Brandenburg (the Peace of Oliva, 1660).

Despite long negotiations and its numerous provisions, the Peace of Westphalia did not bring many changes. Yet, it marks one of the most significant moments in the history of Western civilization because it confirmed, and in a sense codified, the changes that had taken place in the political system of Europe. The aspirations toward international organization represented by the "Holy Roman Empire" were not revived. The "national state," exemplified by France, triumphed. Future interrelationships in Europe had to be based on the fact that in the diplomacy of the several countries religious considerations would be subordinated to those of national self-interest. Loyalty to the state replaced loyalty to religious institutions. During the Westphalian peace negotiations, new procedures and methods of diplomacy were worked out that were to persist for almost two centuries.

Russia

While Hapsburg power and the role of central Europe were on the decline, the countries on the flanks of the Continent were gaining strength and prestige. Russia emerged from a struggle with Poland to become the leading power in the East. Toward the turn of the century, Russia's ruling dynasty had become extinct. Boris Godunov, the last tsar's chief adviser, had himself elected as his successor. He proved himself to be a capable, far-sighted ruler, oriented toward the West. But as a "usurper," accused of having eliminated the rightful heir to the throne, he never gained the allegiance of the nobility and the trust of the people. A terrible drought in 1603–1604 added to his difficulties.

After Godunov's death in 1605, Russia went through a disastrous period of social revolution, political disintegration, dynastic rivalry, an invasion by the Poles who wanted to put a Pole on Russia's throne, and external war (the "Times of Trouble," 1605–1613). Out of this upheaval emerged a new autocratic regime and a new dynasty, the Romanovs. Only with their election in 1613 was internal peace restored.

The Romanovs ruled with the help of a new "service nobility." Through their holdings of land and serfs, the new nobility controlled the wealth of the country; simultaneously, it formed the backbone of the administration. The reorganization was achieved at the expense of the old, independent nobility, which was rendered powerless; of the peasantry, which was reduced to complete serfdom; and, eventually, of the Church, which was brought under tsarist control. A new law code was published in 1649. Of great importance was the fact that the Ukraine, largely inhabited by Cossacks, was conquered.

Thus Russia expanded westward. Closer contacts with Western nations were established. The balance of power between Russia and Poland was permanently changed in favor of Russia. Immigration, especially that of the Germans, English, and Dutch, was encouraged. European techniques, knowledge, artisanship, and luxury goods increasingly infiltrated the country.

The Netherlands

The increase of power of the large nation on the eastern flank of Europe was matched by the corresponding, if not greater, rise of western Europe. In the West, economic rather than military power formed the basis for growth and preeminence. Hence, a small country, such as Holland, was able to become a great power. When Antwerp had been ruined during the wars for independence, Amsterdam had become the financial center of the Western nations.

The advantages gained by the Dutch owing to this shift were augmented by a policy of tolerance. Refugees from various lands—including Jews, and especially those expelled from Spanish dominions—were readily accepted. They helped to establish wide trading connections. Owing to their industry and skills, the immigrants contributed to Holland's economic prosperity. The government was run by the wealthy burghers, who kept taxation low. Agriculture, fishing, the textile industries, shipbuilding, and transportation flourished. There was less class distinction than elsewhere and the level of cultural activity was high. Thus, Holland became a center of the expanding book trade. New universities were founded. Scholars and artists could do their work in an atmosphere of comparative freedom and tolerance.

England

In the Netherlands, the assumption of political power by the wealthy bourgeoisie and the subordination of military to economic objectives took place without grave internal crises, despite continued opposition of various groups to the landholding nobility. But the necessary adjustments in the other great maritime nation of the north, England, encountered much greater difficulties.

THE STUARTS

After the loss of its Continental possessions, England had become an insular power, restricted to its island, and this brought unexpected security. Nationalistic expansion was no longer directed toward European lands, but toward overseas colonies. However, internal tensions developed. Elizabeth, who had refused to marry, was succeeded in 1603 by James I of the House of Stuart. Under his rule and that of his successor, Charles I, the controversial issues about the condition and control of the Church and the immunities and rights of Parliament, all of which had been deferred during the reign of Elizabeth, were reopened. These issues were complicated by various factors: inflation, the increased costs of government, the heavy expenditures incurred by English diplomacy as carried on since the time of Elizabeth, and the wasteful factional strife at the Stuart court.

To meet this emergency, the king was compelled to increase taxes and customs duties and to sell administrative offices. In view of the accumulated debt, he had to pursue financial policies repugnant to a Parliament that desired, above all else, to maintain economic stability and prosperity. As parliamentary opposition grew, the king became more and more arbitrary, further increasing the general dissatisfaction.

Soon, every powerful group in the country was antagonized. Even a large part of the landholding nobility resented the king's rule, in spite of the fact that the Stuarts seemed to have special sympathy for them and that they held all major administrative offices and dominated in Parliament. Eventually, the opposition, though divided as to ultimate aims, was united in its desire to limit the power of the Crown and to participate in policymaking. The ensuing deadlock was reinforced by the friendly attitude of the Stuarts toward Catholicism and by their pro-Spanish point of view, which impeded the realization of English nationalistic and mercantile aims.

REVOLUTION

The widespread discontent was intensified by the unpopularity of the advisers appointed by Charles I and by his failure in foreign affairs. Finally, Parliament was induced to draw up a "Petition of Right" in 1628. This petition demanded an end to taxation without act of Parliament. It also opposed arbitrary imprisonment, billeting of soldiers in private houses, and martial law in time of peace. The king, though he insisted upon his "divine right," signed the petition. But in the following year, he dissolved Parliament and ruled without it for eleven years, during which the country prospered.

Opposition to royal absolutism again developed when the king, who was in dire need of new funds in order to combat piracy in the English Channel, tried to levy additional taxes. His right to do so was challenged by a burgher, John Hampden, but was sustained by subservient judges. Popular passions were further aroused by the king's conciliatory policies toward Catholics and by the harsh treatment which he and his archbishop, Laud, directed against nonconformist Puritans. This religious issue, added to the numerous other grievances, brought matters to a head. When Charles insisted on forcing the sects to accept the Anglican service, they took up arms in rebellion.

The king had to summon Parliament (in 1640) in order to recruit troops. Once reassembled, this "Long Parliament," which lasted until 1653, presented demands, namely, that the king must not be allowed to dissolve it at will, that meetings must be held regularly, and that all special jurisdiction claimed by the kings since Tudor times must be relinquished. Parliament insisted that it must control all income. Eventually it ordered the arrest and execution of some of the king's closest advisers, including Archbishop Laud.

CIVIL WAR

These demands and actions failed to solve the problem, for Parliament itself was divided. One party was sympathetic to royal absolutism; another favored the interests of the rich entrepreneurs; another supported the cause of the poorer parts of the population. There were still other groups, including the so-called "Levelers," who espoused communistic principles. In addition, Parliament was split by the religious issue. Anglicans, Calvinists, and Catholics disagreed about religious tolerance and state control over the Church.

The various economic and religious groups kept shifting their positions and loyalties in accordance with swiftly changing political circumstances. Thus, no clear alignment of sides had been established when, in 1641, a revolution broke out in Ireland over the question of settling Protestants in northern Ireland (Ulster). In 1642, the king himself, believing that the time to reestablish his own authority had arrived, took up arms against Parliament. Civil war began.

Twice beaten in battle, Charles I fled to Scotland, but was extradited and handed over to Parliament. Even at this point, taking advantage of the divisions within Parliament, he was able to defy the opposition until a determined Puritan minority under Oliver Cromwell organized a staunch and fanatical army that defeated the royal forces. The Puritans then reassembled the legislature as a "Rump" Parliament (purged of all members unsympathetic to their cause), which brought the king to trial. In 1649, having been adjudged guilty of treason, Charles was executed. Under Oliver Cromwell's leadership, the Rump Parliament set up a new government.

France

While civil war prevented the establishment of royal absolutism in England, in France absolutism reached its peak of development. Intelligent rulers, such as Henry IV (assassinated in 1610), and a long succession of unusually able ministers, who supported royal power, contributed to its success.

SULLY

The first of the great ministers was Sully (fl. 1600–1610), an intelligent, honest, and efficient Calvinist in the service of Henry IV. Under his guidance, a great deal was accomplished to repair the damage sustained from a half-century of civil war. Brigandage and highway robbery were suppressed and most of the dissolute army units were disbanded. Peace was maintained both within the country and in foreign affairs. The privileges of the nobility were severely restricted, and more officials from among the bourgeoisie were appointed.

The treasury was restored to a healthy condition by measures such as the farming out of tax collections, which meant that the right to collect certain taxes was sold to the highest bidder, who paid an agreed sum into the treasury and kept for himself what he was able to collect in taxes. The new system of tax collection, providing the treasury with a low but certain income, was used mainly to collect the *taille,* a property tax levied upon all landowners outside the ranks of the nobility. Sully put a stop to tax abuses, especially the imposition of illegal taxes; he made certain that the royal domain was managed on a profitable basis.

ABSOLUTISM AND MERCANTILISM

As there was widespread satisfaction with a system that had reestablished security and order, there was no need for action by the Estates-General, representing the people. The king and his first minister made all decisions. In economic affairs they adopted mercantilist policies with a principal aim of increasing production, accumulating bullion, i.e., precious metals, and strengthening exports. They facilitated trade by building roads, canals, and bridges, clearing land, and draining marshes. By means of subsidies and granting of monopolies, they aided long-established industries (e.g., paper and textiles) as well as new industries (e.g., silk manufacturing). And by selling offices, they secured a large income for the Crown. They sent explorers out to lay claim to new colonies, especially in Canada. They also enacted new navigation laws to prevent ships owned by foreigners from transporting goods to French possessions. In foreign affairs, they adhered to a traditional anti-Hapsburg policy, but avoided war.

RICHELIEU

The same policies which had been formulated by the stern and austere Calvinist Sully were pursued by the luxury-loving Catholic, Cardinal Richelieu, who in 1624 became chief minister under Louis XIII, the son of Henry IV. Richelieu was a learned man with wide cultural interests. He possessed an iron will, vast ambition, and a realistic understanding of politics. He put an end to the political irresponsibility and wasteful practices that had marked the period following the death of Henry IV and sought to strengthen the rights of the Crown.

Richelieu refused to convene the Estates-General, which had feebly attempted to regain its authority; they did not convene again for 150 years. He deprived the nobility of most of its remaining powers and ordered the royal forces both to seize its strongholds and to execute some of its leaders. By means of hard- fought military campaigns, he forced the Huguenots to surrender their fortified towns, which had been stipulated as inviolable by the Edict of Nantes.

The cardinal did not, however, destroy the Huguenots' religious freedom, for he was mainly interested in political matters. In fact, Protestant forces were Richelieu's chief allies against the Hapsburgs during the Thirty Years' War. Reforms were introduced in the army and the navy, enabling them to provide adequate protection for the colonies.

As in Sully's time, most of the government officials were recruited from the middle class. Provincial administrators (*intendants*), judges, and other high officials constituted a new social group, which consisted largely of commoners who derived their new nobility from office rather than from birth. It was called the *noblesse de la robe*. This bureaucracy remained the most politically influential segment of the population until the Revolution of 1789.

All of Richelieu's measures were designed to maintain French prestige abroad and Bourbon absolutism at home. When Richelieu died (1642), France was, indeed, on the road to supreme power in Europe. His very able successor, Cardinal Mazarin (d. 1661), who resembled Richelieu in being vain, greedy, ambitious, and shrewd, was just the man to preserve what Richelieu had built and to add to it. Mazarin's career ushered in the "Age of Louis XIV."

PHILOSOPHY AND ARTS

The Peace of Westphalia, terminating the intense religious and political conflicts engendered by the Reformation, laid the legal basis for the modern European state system. At about the same time, the works of the great thinkers on the Continent determined the future direction of Western intellectual endeavors. More and more, Europeans were devoting themselves to scientific investigations of nature, and this had a profound impact on their philosophy. Thus, both in the political and in the intellectual spheres, the mid-seventeenth century is correctly regarded as a dividing line between two major periods in the history of Western civilization.

Science and Philosophy

Among the scientists and philosophers representing the new spirit of inquiry that was to modify Western culture for centuries, three men stand out: Kepler, Galileo, and Descartes. Kepler (d. 1630) devoted much attention to problems of medieval scholarship and to astrology and other pseudo-sciences. However, he made one of the greatest contributions to an understanding of nature in formulating his famous three laws ("Kepler's laws"), which accurately described the motion of the planets. Galileo (d. 1642), notwithstanding persecution by the Catholic Church, continued the work in physics and astronomy that he had started in the previous century. Descartes (d. 1650) was a mathematician and philosopher who spent most of his mature life in Holland and became the foremost precursor of the "Age of Reason." He occupied himself with an investigation of our ability to "know"—and the limits of knowledge. He postulated the "self-evident" fact, *Cogito, ergo sum* (I think, therefore I am). From this fact, he proceeded rationally and logically to draw conclusions. He occupied himself with "truth" and ethics. To him, a steadfast son of the Catholic Church, God appeared as the "First Cause," but mechanistic laws ruled in nature. Cause-and-effect determined everything that occurred in the universe and a dualistic reality existed—a dualism of mind and matter. It is noteworthy that Descartes also developed the principles of analytic geometry and contributed to other sciences, such as optics.

OTHER CONTRIBUTIONS

The work of seventeenth-century cosmologists and philosophers was greatly aided by new developments in mathematics, anatomy, and physiology, and even social sciences such as law. Contributions to mathematics included the invention of logarithms by the Scotsman John Napier in 1614. In anatomy, a notable contributor was the Englishman William Harvey (d. 1657), who correctly described the system of blood circulation; he thus paved the way for the development of modern physiology. In law, the scientific trend inspired the Dutchman Hugo Grotius (d. 1645) to formulate proposals for a body of international law relating particularly to war and peace.

Education

Progress in science was closely connected with improved standards in education. New universities were founded in both Catholic and Protestant strongholds—e.g., in Catholic South America and in the Protestant Netherlands. A first college (Harvard, 1636) was established in North America. Among the leaders in the advancement of education during the sixteenth and seventeenth centuries were the Jesuit colleges. They had originally been designed to expound the decisions of the Council of Trent, to further the Counter Reformation, and to purge the schools of secular Renaissance influences and immoral authors.

Soon the influence of the Jesuit colleges spread widely. They helped to improve the training of the clergy so that the priests would not only deliver better sermons but also more conscientiously fulfill their other religious tasks. They promoted humanitarian activities within their own institutions and throughout the community. Francis de Sales and, especially, Vincent de Paul were among those who, influenced by their aims, earned lasting fame caring for the sick and the aged and building charitable institutions. The Jesuit colleges became important centers of all types of learning, successfully applying new pedagogical principles and particularly encouraging the accumulation of facts in many fields of knowledge.

Literature

In literature, the towering figure of Shakespeare still dominated in the first decade of the seventeenth century. He was followed by important, though less universally influential, poets such as John Donne (d. 1631) and Ben Jonson (d. 1637). Donne's lyrics show great originality and warmth of feeling. But Jonson's comedies are less full of the passions that marked the age of the High Renaissance; instead, they display the more moderate, rational, and reflective style of the baroque period. The latter is also true about the works of the famous writers in Spain's "Golden Age"—the dramatists Lope de Vega (d. 1635) and Calderon (d. 1681). While their works reflect a certain spiritual fervor such as the preceding century had shown, they, too, show rational tendencies, stylistic restraint, and a strong emphasis on form.

Art

In painting, sculpture, and architecture, the first half of the seventeenth century saw the baroque style come into full bloom. It flourished in all countries, though especially in Catholic regions. As in the case of other major movements in art history, the baroque style (1600–1750) passed through several stages of development. Many of the qualities associated with the term "baroque"—in particular, those of theatricality, overornamentation, sentimentality, and bombast—are derived from its later evolution. These characteristics, with their appeal to the senses, do not constitute the only, or even the most important, element of the baroque style. Like all art of the seventeenth century, the baroque was marked by dynamism, orderliness despite exuberance, an assertion of life and faith, and a mastery of form that has given it permanent value. A certain balance and harmony prevailed which, while providing a needed reaction to the individualism of the High Renaissance, emphasized intellectual strength and connected the art of the seventeenth century with the rational tendencies of the age.

Spain produced perhaps the greatest master of the baroque, the painter Velasquez (d. 1660). The baroque style was introduced in the north by the Flemish painter Rubens (d. 1640) and his school, who, even though they adhered to some traditional attitudes, opposed the Puritan trends of Calvinism and post-Trent Catholicism. Rubens was followed, though, by a new, more serene school of painting, including his pupil, the famous portrait painter, Van Dyke (d. 1641).

In sculpture and architecture, Giovanni Bernini (d. 1680) stood out as the foremost representative of the baroque style. It was he who designed the colonnades for the church of St. Peter in Rome.

Music

The baroque style developed in art became equally evident in the music of the seventeenth century. To some extent, the free inventiveness of the preceding period had to make room for compositions where inventiveness, no matter how intense the feelings, had to be reconciled with certain demands for a strict formal frame. The structure of music had to correspond to an elaborate system and possess a balance such as the taste of the time demanded. Even ornamentation became stylized. The polyphonic style was supplemented in what was termed "The New Music" (after an Italian composition published in 1602) by "monody"—compositions where only one voice carries the melody. Instrumental music, owing much of its inspiration to the songs of the sixteenth century, became popular and different types of string instruments came into use. The sonata form was created.

Italian opera made further progress and spread to the northern countries of Europe. In Germany, Protestant Church music flourished, with its beautiful choral preludes and other compositions, especially those written for the organ. The three outstanding masters of the period were Claudio Monteverdi (d. 1643) and Alessandro Scarlatti (d. 1725) in Italy, and Heinrich Schütz (d. 1672) in Germany. Thus, the period which saw the terrors of the Thirty Years' War and of the civil war in England, of the Times of Trouble in Russia, and of mass expulsions in Spain was by no means devoid of beautiful and inspiring achievements.

The first part of the seventeenth century presents as dismal a scene in the political arena as did the last part of the sixteenth. The climax came with the Thirty Years' War, beginning with religious strife and bringing in its wake death to millions, destruction of towns, and widespread misery. Soon the religious issues faded and, ultimately, neither ideological nor major national aims were involved, but only dynastic interests unrelated to the needs of the people. Ambitious "absolute" rulers were the ones who benefited.

On the other hand, with the basis for a new direction in Western civilization's cultural evolution laid in the preceding century, philosophy and science, regardless of what happened politically, became the focus of a world that searched for truth based on observation and knowledge based on logic. Questions of ethics and of metaphysics were by no means neglected. But doubt led to the application of reason and enhanced the need for experimentation. Great strides were made in mathematics, physics, cosmology, and biology.

Selected Readings

Anderson, Ingvar. *A History of Sweden* (1956)

Boorstin, Daniel. *The Americans: Colonial Experience* (1958)

Friedrich, Carl J. *The Age of the Baroque* (1952)

Kamen, Henry. *The Iron Century: Social Change in Europe, 1550–1660* (1971)

Livermore, Harold. *History of Spain* (1968)

Lossky, Andrew, ed. *The Seventeenth Century* (1967)

Maland, D. *Europe in the Seventeenth Century* (1966)

Marsak, Leonard M. *The Rise of Science in Relation to Society* (1964)

Pledge, H. T. *Science since 1500* (1947)

Rabb, Theodore. *Struggle for Stability in Early Modern Europe* (1975)

Tucker, Albert. *A History of English Civilization* (1972)

Weber, Eugen, ed. *The Western Tradition*, vol. 2 (1990)

Wedgwood, Cicely W. *The Thirty Years' War* (1939)

8

The Age of Louis XIV (1643–1715)

1649	English King Charles I executed
1651	First English Navigation Act
	Hobbes, *Leviathan*
1653	End of Fronde
	Cromwell becomes Lord Protector
1656	Russia incorporates Ukraine
1658	Death of Cromwell
1659	Peace of the Pyrenees
1660	Restoration of Charles II in England
	Peace of Oliva
	Death of Velasquez
1661	Death of Mazarin: Colbert named controller-general
1665–1666	Plague and Great Fire in London
1666	Death of Frans Hals
1667	Milton, *Paradise Lost*
	Beginning of War of Devolution
1669	Death of Rembrandt
1670	Pascal, *Pensées*
1672	Newton formulates laws of gravitation
	Jean de Witt assassinated
1673	Test Act in England
1677	Spinoza, *Ethics*
1678	Peace of Nijmwegen

Bunyan, *Pilgrim's Progress*

1681   Strasbourg annexed by France

1682   La Salle in Mississippi Valley

1683   Turks besiege Vienna

William Penn in Pennsylvania (Philadelphia)

Death of Colbert

1684   Leibnitz publishes method of differential calculus

1685   Revocation of Edict of Nantes

1687   Newton, *Philosophiae Naturalis Principia Mathematica*

1688   Glorious Revolution

Death of Frederick William, "Great Elector" of Brandenburg

1689   Act of Toleration; Bill of Rights

1690   Huyghens promulgates theory of light

Locke, *Essay concerning Human Understanding*

1697   Peace of Ryswick

1699   Peace of Karlowitz

1700   Charles XII of Sweden defeats Russians at Narva

1701   Beginning of War of Spanish Succession

1703   St. Petersburg founded

1704   Newton, *Optics*

Newcomen builds steam engine

1707   Union of England and Scotland established

1709   Peter the Great defeats Swedes at Poltava

1713   Peace of Utrecht

England gains *asiento*

1714   Peace of Rastatt and Baden

Leibnitz, *Monadology*

1715   Death of Louis XIV: regency of Duke d'Orléans

*T**he second half of the seventeenth century was not so much a period of new dynamic events as one of consolidation and gradual evolution. In political affairs, it witnessed the continuation of absolutism in France and of an opposite trend toward a parliamentary regime in England. It brought the rise of Brandenburg and continued progress in the Westernization of Russia. It also witnessed the growth of European civilization in the centers established earlier on other continents—especially in North America.*

But its truly great and lasting contributions were made in philosophy, science, and art. Not for Louis XIV's political exploits nor for the economic developments of his time is the age named after him so renowned; it is famous for the achievements of great philosophers, writers, and scientists. Their rational approach to life and to nature brought to maturity the ideological trends that had been growing in Europe ever since the views of the Nominalists had prevailed over those of the Realists during the late Middle Ages. The characteristics of the baroque, particularly its intellectuality and harmony, pervaded the cultural sphere. Since these characteristics developed most fully in France and spread from the example France set, they provided justification for naming the period the Age of Louis XIV.

THE POLITICAL SCENE

The Peace of Westphalia (1648) had signified open acknowledgment by European powers of what had long been a fact, namely, that the supreme position of emperor of the "Holy Roman Empire of the German Nation" no longer commanded wide respect; it had become essentially a shadowy honor devoid of practical significance. Even the etiquette of diplomacy was revised in accordance with the actual distribution of power. Special consideration was accorded not only to France but also to newly emergent nations such as Sweden and England.

France

When he came to the throne one year after Richelieu's death, Louis XIV was but five years old. He was ten at the conclusion of the Peace of Westphalia, twenty-three when he took the reins of government into his own hands, and almost seventy-seven when he died. Even if it had not been for the strength of his personality, such a long term as a ruler—the longest of any monarch in European history—could not have failed to leave a deep imprint, especially since he ruled during an age of "absolutism."

MAZARIN

During the first eighteen years of Louis XIV's reign, the direction of French affairs was entrusted to Cardinal Mazarin. It was Mazarin, a shrewd diplomat, who concluded the Peace of Westphalia, whereby France was raised to the first place in Europe. It was also he who sealed the fate of the French nobility. Seeking to profit from the financial straits in which the young king found himself, the nobility staged, in 1648, a rebellion, the so-called "Fronde." The rebellion aimed at reducing the powers of the bureaucracy appointed by the king. It was abetted by the highest law court, the Parlement of Paris, which was subservient to the nobility's interests. The Parlement demanded for itself the rights to control taxation, to appoint intendants (provincial governors), and to supervise legislation. This last right it could exercise by refusing to "register" any laws that it considered contrary to custom or infringing upon existing privileges. Had it succeeded, a development toward parliamentary government would have been unavoidable, although, owing to the composition and the policics of the Parlement, the traditional privileged classes would have gained more than the commercial interests.

But Mazarin energetically opposed the Parlement. He bloodily suppressed the Fronde and accompanying peasant uprisings. Simultaneously, he lent his hand, for the sake of unity, to the reduction of a puritanical movement within the Catholic Church, known as "Jansenism." This movement had had considerable influence on education. Though Catholic, it had tended in the direction of Calvinism; it was bitterly opposed by the Jesuits. When Mazarin died in 1661 and Louis XIV took personal control, the concentration of power in the hands of the king was such that a challenge had become impossible.

LOUIS XIV

Louis was a man of mediocre gifts, conceited and selfish, but industrious, persistent, noble in bearing, and inspiring. He never called a meeting of the Estates-General, nor did he permit the Parlement to obstruct his legislation. Whatever decision he personally made was final. He took counsel with advisers of his own choice only and continued to rely in his administration and for his law courts on the *noblesse de la robe*. Justice became somewhat more equable than under his predecessors, even though corruption persisted.

Arts and sciences found in Louis, in exchange for glorifying him, a liberal and understanding patron. Architectural projects, in particular, were greatly aided, although at excessive cost to the country. (One example is the enormous castle of Versailles with its famous gardens.) Court life set a model for all Europe: French etiquette supplanted the Spanish court ceremonial. French elegance was imitated everywhere and so were French manners. Yet court morality, with its mistresses and bastard children, was already out of tune with the standards the puritanical Calvinistic and the Counter-Reformatory trends had set and that the middle class, so important for all future developments, propagated.

COLBERT

Inasmuch as Louis XIV's glory was the chief political objective, all policies were keyed to its promotion. In the early part of his reign, Louis had the good fortune to find an unusually capable minister in Colbert (d. 1683). Colbert was a mercantilist who promoted industry through loans, bounties, tax exemptions, and scientific research. He sponsored the building of more canals, ports, and ships and simplified the customs system. In order to provide an ample labor force, he encouraged the French people through subsidies to have large families.

Colbert opposed idleness in the Church and in the lay populations. He abolished internal tolls. Through his support of commercial enterprises, such as the silk industry, and through the honest handling of funds, he greatly increased the tax receipts. He accomplished this despite the continued use of the inefficient farming-out system and despite all the shortcomings of an economy that placed the main burden upon the commercial and laboring classes, while exempting the rich nobility and the Church. Colbert also promoted colonizing activities. In his time, Marquette, Joliet, and La Salle explored the Mississippi region, with which a considerable fur trade developed. In India, the French colony of Pondichery was founded.

After Colbert's death, Louis XIV undid many of Colbert's achievements through wars, wasteful financing, and unproductive construction. Taxes became stifling to industry. Excessive government controls discouraged merchants and industrialists. Schools had to be closed. The population began to decrease; a terrible famine in 1709 added to the woes of the population. Worst of all, motivated by his desire to eliminate any dissenting and possibly rebellious groups (and thus guarantee stability and unity under the king) and also by his religious bigotry, Louis XIV revoked the Edict of Nantes in 1685. Persuasion had long been tried in efforts to convert Huguenots to the faith of the king and the majority. When its success turned out to be limited, a policy of persecution was instigated. Hundred of thousands of Huguenots were forced to emigrate—to the loss of France and the gain of the German states, Holland, England, and other countries that welcomed them.

FRENCH EXTERNAL POLICIES

Equally ruinous were Louis's foreign policies. Numerous wars were provoked merely for his personal "glory." The economic interests of the country were primary factors only in the first war (the purpose of which was to further the mercantilist policies of Colbert) and in the last war (the purpose of which was to establish overseas hegemony). All the other wars were contrary to the economic interests of France.

Enormous sums were expended to build an army superior to that of Spain—an undertaking achieved owing to the ability of men such as Louvois, Vauban, and Turenne. More money went into subsidizing allies, who were also lured with promises of territory that would be seized from the Hapsburgs. The myth that the natural borders of France were the Rhine, Alps, and Pyrenees served as an excuse for a policy of ruthless French expansion into Holland, Germany, Italy, and Spain. Finally, these wars of expansion proved to be exceedingly costly.

The first, the "War of Devolution," was fought for the possession of the Netherlands against a Triple Alliance of Holland, England, and Sweden. When peace was made at Aix-la-Chapelle (1668), it brought an extension of France's frontiers northward. A second war, undertaken against the Dutch, failed to bring further gains. Initial victories were followed by defeats, and the Peace of Nijmwegen (1678) constituted a draw. In the following years, subsequent to certain sham legal procedures by so-called "Chambres de Réunion," the German territory and city of Strassburg and several Italian towns were annexed.

These annexations became long-term gains. But, at the time, they merely served to arouse so much apprehension that in 1686 another defensive coalition against France, including nearly all the European powers, was formed. A third war, the highly destructive "War of the League of Augsburg," lasted until 1697. Then, in the Peace of Ryswick, Louis was forced to surrender some of his earlier conquests and to grant commercial advantages to the maritime nations.

Shortly thereafter, the Spanish line of the Hapsburgs died out. In an effort to prevent any further Austrian-Spanish family link and cooperation, Louis put forward the candidacy of his grandson to the throne. As a result, in 1701 a fourth war, that of the Spanish Succession, broke out. Again a "Grand Alliance" of most European powers was formed. Able generals such as the Austrian Prince Eugene of Savoy and Marlborough of England defeated the French armies. Only the death of the allied (Hapsburg) candidate for the Spanish throne and French diplomatic victories at the very end of the war saved Louis from utter ruin.

PEACE OF UTRECHT (1713)

Finally, in the years 1713 to 1715, peace treaties were concluded at Utrecht, Rastatt, and Baden. Austria thereby gained territories in the southern Netherlands and Italy. England secured vast colonial and commercial advantages, including rights to the lucrative slave trade (the *asiento*) in the Spanish colonies. Prussia increased its domain. The Dutch obtained land, fortified positions, and commercial rights in areas along their southern frontier.

As for France, it maintained its role as a great power. A French prince was allowed to keep the Spanish throne, though subject to restrictions. Thus, when Louis XIV died in 1715, cursed by the population, the glory of France, even in the political arena, was still not seriously impaired. Yet, Louis XIV's avowed love of war, his extravagance in building activities, the style of life at his court, and his exploitation of the population boded ill for the future of France.

England

French policies in the second half of the seventeenth century added to the nation's prestige and left a lasting impression throughout the Continent.

England's attention, on the other hand, was focused on its own insular affairs. By concentrating on immediate practical tasks, the English succeeded not only in overcoming the dangers of revolution and civil war, but also in laying a firm basis for their future as a world power.

CROMWELL

Four years after the execution of Charles I, Oliver Cromwell made himself "Lord Protector." During his administration, considerable political and economic progress was made, even though Parliament had since 1648 played a role subordinate to Cromwell and the army. New elections had not been held because Cromwell, whose backers were in the minority, could not risk them. Revolts were organized by royalists who were eager to put the decapitated king's son on the throne; others by the Scots, whom Cromwell sought to reconcile; still other by the Irish, who were brutally oppressed. No basis for a new, legal form of authority was developed.

Yet, Cromwell proved to be a capable ruler. Merchants benefited from the enforcement of navigation acts which aimed at excluding foreign ships from English ports. They profited from the fight against Dutch competition and from the stimulation of British shipping. Prosperous trade, in turn, encouraged industries, especially coal-mining and shipbuilding. Cromwell successfully defended the colonial possessions, organized new colonies, and defeated Holland and Spain—all of which helped to expand British trade. In the religious sphere, despite his strict Calvinist leanings, the Lord Protector tried to avoid trouble by means of a moderately tolerant policy.

RESTORATION

Notwithstanding its many successes, the Cromwell government was hated for its revolutionary origins, its absolutist trends, its Calvinistic moral standards, and its program of burdensome taxes favoring the military caste and the overseas merchants. Powerful conservative forces were especially resentful. Consequently, within two years of Cromwell's death in 1658, Stuart royalty was reestablished.

Charles II was recalled from exile. But before his "restoration," Charles had to agree to Parliamentary elections. The new Parliament restored the dominant position of the Anglican Church, proclaimed an amnesty for political opponents, and assumed supervision of the king's activities: his foreign policy, choice of advisers, purse, and military forces.

CHARLES II

The reign of Charles II was colorful. Despite disasters, such as the plague and a terrible fire that consumed large areas of London, it was marked by gaiety and artistic and literary achievements. It was an age of extravagance and immorality in which king and court, imitating France, set an example.

During this regime, wealthy individuals obtained more national influence. Some of the old-established feudal rights were abolished.

Political parties began to take shape: the Whig, which favored representative government and middle-class commercial interests, and the Tory, which supported royal rights, the Anglican Church, and the interests of the landed nobility. Yet, both parties, despite dissensions and corruption, followed policies designed to strengthen the country as a whole. Living conditions gradually improved.

THE GLORIOUS REVOLUTION (1688)

The division into parties gave the king, during his last years, an opportunity to increase his influence in the government and to secure the succession of his brother, James II. James, who was a Catholic, showed greater tolerance to Catholics; they had been barred from public office by the Test Act of 1673. Intolerance toward them remained undiminished in Parliament and in the community at large. James encouraged the return of absolutist trends. He also entered into close, economically undesirable cooperation and political alliances with Spain, France, and other Catholic nations.

The English consoled themselves with the hope that, since the old king had no sons, on his demise these trends would constitute no more than a brief setback. However, the king ultimately did beget a son, giving rise to new fears about Catholic influence. In 1688, a revolt, known as the "Glorious Revolution," began. Before blood was shed, James fled.

Mary, his Protestant daughter, and her husband, William of Orange, governor of the Netherlands, were invited by Parliament to take over the reins of government. Parliament reasoned that not only the Protestant cause, but also English international interests, would be served; Holland would be brought into a firm alliance and could provide a bulwark against France. Yet, Parliament was careful to impose certain conditions, specified in the "Bill of Rights," to which the new rulers and their successors would have to submit: Parliament was to decide all matters of taxation, to control the army, and to supervise legislation. Free elections were to be held regularly. A right of petition was to be guaranteed to all subjects. No excessive bail or excessive fines were to be imposed. No Catholic was to be king of England. Moreover, through an Act of Toleration passed in 1689, Protestant dissenters gained the right to free exercise of their religion, although, like Catholics, they were still deprived of political rights and were excluded from public service.

RESULTS OF THE REVOLUTION

Absolutism was thus defeated in England; Parliament emerged supreme. It was not a democracy that was created. Parliament suffered from traditional weaknesses, untrained representatives, and perpetual corruption. Furthermore, only men of wealth were eligible for membership; the government continued to be controlled by the landholding aristocracy. These men were wise enough to take the interests of the commercial classes into account so that business enterprises prospered.

Neither William (d. 1702) and Mary (d. 1694), nor their successor, Queen Anne (d. 1714), attempted to interfere with the functions of Parliament as set forth in the Bill of Rights. A union with Scotland, long desired by the English, was consummated in 1707. From then on, Scottish representatives sat in the same Parliament with Englishmen.

ENGLISH FOREIGN POLICY

The direction of England's external affairs during the entire period from Cromwell through Queen Anne's reign depended upon the maneuvers of Louis XIV. Accordingly, England was forced alternately into alliances with Holland, France, and Spain. The constant instability in foreign policy was intensified by divergent interests within England. On one occasion, Charles II (d. 1685) himself accepted bribes from Louis XIV.

But underlying all shifts of policy, there were three steadfast aims: eliminating competition in colonization; opposing Catholicism; and supporting the weaker powers on the Continent to counterbalance the predominant powers. These aims were largely achieved. With the help of a navy greatly strengthened in Cromwell's time, the English eliminated the Dutch as serious colonial rivals and annexed their American colonies. They displaced Spain in control of the seas and seized Spanish overseas territories.

England encouraged opposition to any Catholic rulers who tried to spread their religion abroad. It welcomed refugees from Catholic countries. Alliances with small nations made it possible for the English to join in the resistance to Louis XIV until France had been defeated and its bid for European hegemony thwarted.

Holland and Spain

The rise of England paralleled the decline of the two other great maritime powers: Holland and Spain. After three wars waged against them by England between 1652 and 1674, the Dutch lost their leading position in world affairs. Their merchant marine, formerly several times the size of England's, severely contracted. Perhaps the three factors contributing most to this decline were the continuous wars, the conservatism of Holland's wealthy ruling merchants, and the weakness of the central government owing to political strife.

In opposition to the party led by the House of Orange, which favored a unified and centralized country, there was another party led by men like De Witt, which favored provincial independence. Nevertheless, Holland remained among the leaders in finance, transportation, agriculture—especially vegetable gardening and floriculture—and fishing. It also maintained its prestige in scholarship, science, and the arts.

Spain, too, still excelled in literature and art, but its political and economic decline was more rapid. Poverty remained widespread. The population of the third estate increased very slowly. The masses had no influence in the royal absolutist regime, which was backed by a wasteful, ambitious landed aristocracy. Wars, both in the colonial areas and on the Continent, continued to drain the treasury; they resulted only in loss of territory in the New World (especially in the Caribbean area) as well as in Europe (along the Pyrenees).

Austria

The other Hapsburg power, Austria, understood better than Spain how to adjust to changing conditions. In fact, the Austrian Hapsburgs recovered rather quickly from the consequences of the Thirty Years' War. What they lost through the lack of German unity they made up for through an increase of their personal holdings, their *Hausmacht*. Despite the westward shift of economic and commercial centers, Austria recovered a key position in European international affairs. It resumed expansionist policies.

In 1683, their most dangerous enemy, the Turks, who had regained their strength under the able leadership of the vizier Ahmed Kuprili, once more penetrated to the gates of Vienna. The Austrians, with the help of the Polish king, John III Sobieski, won a decisive victory. Subsequently, the Austrian armies under the command of Prince Eugene pushed deep into the Balkans. In the Peace of Karlowitz (1699), Austria regained long-occupied Hungary from the Turks.

At home, the arts of the baroque flourished. Vienna became a foremost cultural center, excelling in music, architecture, philosophy, and court poetry. There was a great religious revival. The Austrian population increased substantially.

Brandenburg

Among the other German states, the most significant developments occurred in Brandenburg. This state, which had Berlin as its capital, was soon to become Austria's rival in a contest for leadership in Germany. Several factors contributed to its rise. Its territory was greatly expanded after the Treaty of Westphalia. It was centrally located and had an industrious population. In that age of absolutism, it was fortunate enough to be governed by a succession of able rulers.

The most famous was Frederick William of the House of Hohenzollern, the so-called "Great Elector" (d. 1688), whose measures during his long regime made it possible for the country to recover from the devastations of war.

Mercantilist policies were pursued. Subsidies, tariffs, and monopolies were arranged in order to promote industries, such as glass and textiles. Land was reclaimed and new agricultural products were sponsored. Even some attempts at colonization were made. A decline in population was counteracted by the welcoming of immigrants. In particular, exiled French Huguenots were encouraged to immigrate by the Edict of Potsdam (1685);

they were generously endowed with land, houses, schools, churches, and means to establish themselves successfully in agriculture and industry.

Simultaneously, a strong army was organized in which the nobility, deprived as elsewhere of its old feudal privileges and prestige, found a new, special field of activity within the framework of a centralized state. The bureaucracy was inspired with concepts of duty and honesty. Wars were avoided so far as possible. The unavoidable ones (waged sometimes with the help of French subsidies) against Swedes, Poles, and Austrians were essentially victorious. The success of the Great Elector's policies was made clear when, after his death, his successor (who inherited, in addition to Brandenburg, the Hohenzollern possessions on the Rhine and in Prussia) acquired the status of king.

Eastern and Northern Europe

Eastern European developments followed patterns different from those of both the West and the North, except for one aspect: constant warfare.

POLAND

Poland's bid for the subjugation of Russia, as attempted during the Times of Trouble in Russia, had failed. Thereafter, the country became increasingly disorganized. A luxury-loving upper nobility and a greedy, ill-educated lower nobility, the *slachta,* pursued private ambitions, nationalistic aims, and aggressive Catholic policies. Unwilling to subordinate their desires and aims to a strong monarchy, the nobility did not seek to create a functioning parliament or *sejm,* either.

As a result, the state, which appeared to be strong, was undermined from within. Life in the towns, which had flourished in the sixteenth century, stagnated. The changes needed to adapt to new conditions were neglected. This hindered the rise of a middle class as in Germany, France, or Italy. Consequently, the peasantry suffered; the position of the many Jews in the country deteriorated. Enjoying certain privileges in taxation and in the administration of their own communities, the Jews were both envied and disliked by their Polish neighbors and often maltreated.

Industrial production, which grew in neighboring countries, including Russia, hardly benefited. Agricultural activity was lively. Considerable income was derived from grain exports via Riga and especially Danzig. But the export trade remained mostly in the hands of German merchants and Dutch and English shippers.

Arrogance and ambition on the part of the upper classes, internal disorder, and lack of economic development brought external losses. The parts of Livonia which Poland-Lithuania had seized in the previous century were lost to the Swedes (1621); the eastern regions of the Ukraine fell to Russia in the Peace of Andrusovo (1667). The Cossacks—the freedom-loving, roaming inhabitants of the region who, although unreliable, had constituted a buffer against the Turks—were increasingly alienated. Through the "Union of

Brest" (1595), the Poles had tried to force the Cossacks into the Catholic Church and under the pope's authority which would have allowed them nothing more than to retain some of their rites from their traditional Orthodox Church. As a result, part of the Ukraine went over to Russia. Lastly, both Kiev and Smolensk were taken by Russia.

SWEDEN

In contrast to Poland, Sweden experienced its *stormaktstid* (great power stage). Capable rulers—Gustavus II Adolphus, later Charles X and Charles XI, and the great chancellor Axel Oxenstierna—understood how to assure collaboration between Crown, nobles, and a diet in which other sectors of the population also participated. With the help of the resources of Finland, which formed part of the Swedish Empire, a strong economy was maintained. Timber, iron, and copper furnished valuable export goods. Shipping flourished owing to Sweden's domination of Livonian ports and Baltic sea lanes. Despite Catholic Counter-Reformatory efforts, Lutheranism provided a strong bond between the peoples of the country. Schools were founded. Sweden's leading thinkers adopted the tenets of rationalism—notwithstanding the survival of myths and heathen beliefs among the peasant population. Descartes came to Sweden, sponsored by the daughter of Gustavus Adolphus, Queen Christina. He died there. The famous German jurist Pufendorf, became a professor at the University of Lund.

However, the wars that Sweden undertook against Denmark, Russia, Poland and in Germany exhausted the country, given its small population and limited resources. Successes could not be turned into permanent gains.

RUSSIA

Like most Continental nations, Sweden and Poland were heirs of the Renaissance. Russia traveled a different path. Neither many political nor cultural concepts of the West were introduced, even though a stream of English, Dutch, and German immigrants began to arrive. They brought, together with their skills, some of their ideas. The immigrants' main effect was felt in the field of industry. They founded some new industries, and they directed salt works, mines, glass factories, and more. A foreign, so-called German, suburb was founded in Moscow. This, and a steadily increasing trade by way of Archangel over the free northern seaways, increased contact with the West. So, too, did the acquisition of Western territories that the Poles had previously annexed. But it was mainly in the following century that such contacts and acquisitions would become significant for the development of Russian civilization.

The gap that existed between Russia and the West in regard to social, legal, and political institutions was demonstrated by two important events. One was the introduction of a new law code, adopted in 1649. At the very time when serfdom declined in the West, Russia introduced it. For more than a century, the Russian peasantry had steadily lost more and more of their right to free movement. Now, the law code of 1649 ensured their full attachment to the soil and confirmed the full rights of their landlords. Numerous revolts were the result, climaxed by a large-scale revolution led by a peasant, Stenka Razin. It failed. Power remained in the hands of the absolute "autocratic" tsar. While reducing the influence of the old nobility, he strengthened the role of his own appointees, largely petty nobles committed to service obligations who constituted the backbone of his bureaucracy. Their compensation consisted in landed estates or appointments to high administrative posts.

The other important event was the introduction of a church reform. It bore little similarity to the Reformation in Western Europe. It concerned mainly the elimination of errors that had in the course of centuries crept into the liturgical texts. Tsar Alexis I eventually backed the reformers, but thousands of adherents refused to accept the alterations to hallowed traditions. As schismatics ("Old Believers" or *Raskolniki*) who refused to recognize the creed of the official church, they were outlawed and persecuted. Thousands perished.

Thus, a split in the church occurred which was to last for centuries. The Old Believers held firm, even though the survivors of the persecutions were deprived of many of their civil rights. Not until the revolution in 1917 were they granted full citizenship rights. Unable to get administrative posts or land to work on, they turned, like other repressed minorities, to trading and other economic pursuits. They thereby contributed much to the growth of Russia as an economic power.

Still another development of major consequence marks Russian history during the seventeenth century: the extension of its territories. Borders now extended to China and the shores of the Pacific Ocean. Settlements were established in Siberia. Russia gained considerable wealth owing to Siberia's richness in fur-bearing animals, which provided the country's most valuable furs for export. Instead of taxes, the natives were required to provide the tax collectors with prescribed amounts of furs.

Colonies

During the second half of the seventeenth century, European overseas colonies underwent changes reflecting the shift of power among the parent countries. Spain found itself exposed to continued grave hardships, especially in the Caribbean area, owing to incessant attacks by English, Dutch, and French squadrons, pirates, and smugglers. In 1655, Jamaica, which because of its sugar production was regarded as one of the most valuable assets of the Spanish Empire, passed into the hands of England. Moreover, with all its wealth now added to the English economy, Jamaica, like other conquered areas, became another outpost for English commercial and cultural penetration.

Similarly, Portuguese domination in the East weakened as the Dutch and other antagonists seized one territory after another. Except for a few ports in Asia and Africa, it was only in Brazil that Portugal, albeit with difficulty, succeeded in maintaining an important position. The resources of Brazil helped to compensate Portugal for many of the losses suffered in the East. The newly discovered diamond mines, together with Brazilian gold and agricultural products, became sources of a steady income. The Dutch, in turn, though gaining colonies in Asia and Africa, lost their holdings in America (on the Hudson and on the Delaware). Lastly, in the Far East, all Europeans lost their rights and privileges in Japan. Foreign traders were expelled; Japan permitted only a small, narrowly confined, and closely supervised group of Dutch to retain a tenuous foothold.

Wherever changes in ownership occurred, corresponding changes in colonial life developed. These were especially pronounced in English North America. An ever-increasing stream of immigrants came to American shores. By 1700, all the original thirteen colonies of North America had been established. One of these was the prosperous Quaker colony of Pennsylvania, which devised a pattern of colonization based on their religious convictions, democratic concepts of sharing, mutual helpfulness, and hard work.

The French in America could not match the English development of colonies, although their mercantilistic-minded officials such as Colbert sought to promote exploration and settlement. Most of the French people were very reluctant to leave their beautiful and prosperous homeland. Despite the wealth in furs, timber, spices, fish, and sugar, their colonies had little attraction for them.

The three large colonizing powers developed three different systems of colonial organization. The French set up few institutions and left it to the traders to win the cooperation of the natives and secure profits for the homeland. The Spanish settlers remained under close supervision by their home country. The English colonists were given a large measure of self-government.

During the Cromwellian revolution, the English colonists took advantage of the troubles at home to strengthen their position. During the Restoration and the revolution of 1688 they further increased their liberties. Even though the home country regained much of its lost authority when the revolutionary period was over, the attitude of the English colonists remained strongly independent and self-reliant. Their primary attachment had become the one to the land on which they lived and they felt far removed from the scene of the wars against Louis XIV—into which they were drawn. The colonists referred to them as "King William's" or "Queen Anne's" wars, as if they were private undertakings of their rulers.

THE CULTURAL SCENE

The large space taken in histories of the time by the political events of the later seventeenth century bears witness to the growing influence that political institutions, political thinking, social relationships, and national aspirations were to exercise in the life of modern peoples. In the Age of Louis XIV, the modern European state system was completed and modern diplomacy was developed. Simultaneously, the tenets of the age found expression in many theoretical political writings.

Political Thought

The protagonists of absolutism included the Frenchman Bossuet (d. 1704) and the Englishman Hobbes (d. 1679). These thinkers defended the prevailing concepts of the divine right of kings, though they did not identify absolutism with arbitrary rule. Bossuet insisted that the royal will must be permeated with Christian doctrine. Hobbes, famous for this study of society and politics (*Leviathan,* 1651), thought that the royal will must be administered in accordance with the principles of a "natural" right to self-preservation. As Grotius had done, both demanded morality in international relations.

Their views were soon challenged by John Locke (d. 1704), who in his *Treatises on Government* and *Letter on Toleration* defended the idea that the relationship of ruler and subject is based, not upon divine right but upon a social order that binds both parties. In this view, all subjects have a right to liberty and property and may justly revolt if their rights are violated.

Philosophy

Locke, who was a man of affairs as well as a philosopher, derived his views from logic and observation, as his *Essay concerning Human Understanding* (1690) shows. Though he accepted the existence of God, he was an empiricist who relied on practical experience. Empiricist trends underlay the work of most other philosophers of the age—notwithstanding Hobbes's criticism of Descartes's "mechanistic" approach and Pascal's attempts to harmonize Christian thought with that of his own age.

Besides Locke, other leading philosophers were the Dutchman Spinoza and the German Leibnitz. Spinoza (d. 1677), like Locke, defended the individual's right to political liberty. He is most famous for his "pantheism," which implied that everything is a part, an evidence, of the divine and that "God" works as a mathematical law permeating the universe. Leibnitz (d. 1716) emphasized mathematically ascertainable laws of nature; he relegated God to the place of an initial cause. He saw the world filled with innumerable individual units of differing complexity, all independent of one another, following their own laws, yet in harmony with the world, the "best of all possible worlds," as made by God.

Science

An age so devoted to logical thinking, mathematics, and experimentation necessarily produced remarkable scientific results. Numerous instruments (e.g., the telescope, microscope, air pump, and pendulum clock) were invented or improved. Statistical systems were devised. Technical methods in industry and mining were improved.

The Frenchman Pascal (d. 1662), inventor of the barometer, developed a mathematical theory of probability. The Englishman Boyle (d. 1691) laid the foundations for modern chemistry by investigating the pressure properties of gases. Another Englishman, Halley (d. 1742), observed and described the comets. The Dutchman Huyghens (d. 1695) investigated theories of light and his countrymen Swammerdam (d. 1680) and Leeuwenhoek (d. 1723) studied microscopic organisms. Botanical works appeared in great numbers. In 1684, Leibnitz completed his system of the calculus, a monumental achievement.

NEWTON

But the greatest scientist of the age, and one of the greatest of all time, was the Englishman Isaac Newton (d. 1727). This many-sided genius, who was active in politics, independently devised a system of the calculus (1687). Yet, he carried on so many studies in physics, optics, and astronomy that he laid the basis for many areas of modern science. Occupying himself with the laws of mass and motion, he disclosed his greatest single discovery, the law of gravitation, in his great work *Principia,* published in 1687. In all his work, Newton rejected transcendental speculation or hypothetical reasoning. He insisted that the prime aim of the scientist should be to describe accurately natural occurrences and their ascertainable causes.

ACADEMIES OF SCIENCES

A special place in the history of this age belongs to the Academies of Sciences. The first was founded in London in 1662, to be followed (in 1666) by one in Paris and, later, by others in Prussia, Austria, Russia, and elsewhere on the Continent. Their activities included philosophical discussions about nature and its laws as well as the presentation of scientific papers on mathematical, biological, and physical problems. Many of the greatest minds of the age participated in their work and found in them the best forum for new ideas, testing them, and publicizing conclusions. Men such as Leibnitz considered them so vital to the development of the intellectual forces of a nation that he championed the founding of an academy of science to the Russian emperor as the tsar's foremost task.

Literature

From today's perspective, the advances of the sciences overshadow the late seventeenth-century accomplishments in literature and art. Yet, these achievements were by no means negligible. In France, creative writers included the celebrated dramatists Corneille *(Le Cid)* and Racine *(Britannicus, Athalie),* and the sharp, satirical critic of society, Molière

(Bourgeois Gentilhomme, Tartuffe). La Fontaine became famous for his *Fables*. At this time the trend toward classical literary tradition reached its height. The tradition demanded adherence to normalized rules and conventions, to precepts of "good taste," and respect for the rational patterns of the day.

But this trend also imparted a certain sterility to some literature of the Age of Louis XIV that not only deterred later generations, but as early as 1680 brought about a "Battle of the Ancients and the Moderns." Against the formal demands of the "Ancients," there arose a cry for freedom of expression by the "Moderns." Nevertheless, throughout Europe the classical French literature of the seventeenth century, as represented by the "Ancients," had a decisive influence. Everywhere, it was imitated and praised as the perfection of taste and the model for values. Only in England did writers of genius build or preserve a different tradition. There, Milton (d. 1674; *Paradise Lost*), Bunyan (d.1688; *Pilgrim's Progress*), and Dryden (d. 1700; poems, satires) stand out. Germany produced little; Grimmelshausen's *Simplicissimus* represents a lasting and potent literary contribution. But only the beginnings of a national literature emancipated from French models can be traced.

History

France made an important contribution in still another field. Mabillon (d. 1707), who undertook a methodological investigation of medieval documents, laid a foundation for systematic procedures and standards in history. The discipline of history thereby became an art and a science; it has since served as a source of basic information concerning social conditions and human behavior and as a record of human fate and aspirations.

Architecture

In the arts, the baroque style dominated. It was superbly expressed by means of numerous palaces for which Versailles, elegant and grandiose in concept and clear in line, served as model. The buildings, fountains, statues, and specially designed shrubberies and flower beds, all geometrically arranged to satisfy the taste of the age, were imitated everywhere. The graceful baroque style was well adapted to church construction. Some of its finest examples are found in southern Germany, Switzerland, and Austria.

In England, on the other hand, eminent architects continued resolutely in the classical, medieval, and Renaissance traditions. Christopher Wren designed St. Paul's Cathedral in London. The international influence of such architecture was slight. However, another side of the architectural arts in England came to constitute a real contribution to the stylistic concepts of all Western countries. This was the English garden. In contrast to the art of France, it emphasized naturalness. Lovely groups of trees or shrubbery, carefully and yet naturally arranged on wide lawns, appealed deeply to those who remained unsatisfied with the formal ornamental style of the Age of Louis XIV.

Painting

In painting, the French could pride themselves on the landscapes of Poussin (d. 1665) and Lorrain (d. 1682). A more lasting impression however, was left by other nations. Catholic Spain contributed one great painter, Murillo (d. 1682), but it was the Protestant, secularly oriented Dutch painters who excelled—masters such as Frans Hals (d. 1666), Vermeer (d. 1675), and the landscape painter Ruisdael (d. 1682). Yet, though their achievements may have been outstanding for any age, these artists were overshadowed by the genius of Rembrandt (d. 1669). His luminous portraits and moving biblical scenes have a power, depth, and human significance equaling the best ever created.

After the end of the Thirty Years' War, the persecution and expulsion of the Huguenots by the French, and the "Glorious Revolution" in England, religious issues ceased to dominate the political scene. Wealth, industry, banking, and shipping received ever-increasing attention. Peasant revolts and "cabinet wars" continued without bringing about major changes.

Spain and Portugal lost their prominent places; Sweden and, later, Brandenburg-Prussia emerged as major powers. The threat of Turkish invasions was put to an end. While in the East Poland lost in importance, Russia emerged as a factor on the European political stage.

The principle of absolute monarchy was perfected, except in England, where a parliamentary system took firm hold. In America, colonial rule persisted under Spanish and Portuguese viceroys and British governors. In steadily growing numbers, European immigrants entered the New World. A development took place that was to have grave consequences: black Africans were bought, sold, and sent as slaves into the British colonies.

In contrast to the misery that such trade brought, and to the wretched situation of the lower classes, was the luxury indulged in by the court of Louis XIV and its imitators all over Europe. Versailles set the example for style in building, dress, and manners. This age was also marked by works of fundamental importance, particularly in science, where logical, rational inquiry led to outstanding results.

Selected Readings

Beloff, Max. *The Age of Absolutism, 1660–1815* (1954)
Dukes, Paul. *The Making of Russian Absolutism 1613–1801* (1982)
Evans, R. J. *The Making of the Habsburg Monarchy* (1979)
_____ *The Cambridge Economic History of Europe* (1966)
Hatton, R. N. *Europe in the Age of Louis XIV* (1969)
Heckscher, Eli. *Mercantilism* (1934)
McKay, Derek, et al. *The Rise of the Great Powers, 1648–1815* (1983)
Slicher van Barth, B. H. *The Agrarian History of Western Europe* (1983)
Trevelyan, George M. *England Under the Stuarts* (1933)
Wolf, John B. *Louis XIV* (1968)

9

The Age of Enlightenment (1715–1774)

1719	Defoe, *Robinson Crusoe*
1720	"South Sea Bubble" in England
	John Law in Paris
1721	Peace of Nystad
	Montesquieu, *Lettres Persanes (Persian Letters)*
1729	Bach, *St. Matthew Passion*
1733	Beginning of War of the Polish Succession
1735	Linnaeus, *Genera Plantarium*
1738	Invention of flying shuttle by Kay
1739	Hume, *Treatise of Human Nature*
1740	Maria Theresa becomes empress (Pragmatic Sanction)
	Outbreak of First Silesian War (Frederick the Great)
1741	Dupleix French governor general in India
	Handel, *The Messiah*
1742	Thermometer of Celsius
1744	Second Silesian War
1745	Louisbourg conquered by British
1748	Peace of Aix-la-Chapelle
	Montesquieu, *L'Esprit des Lois (Spirit of Laws)*
1749	Bach, *Art of the Fugue*
1752	Franklin's experiments on lightning and electricity
1754	Beginning of French and Indian War
1755	Lisbon earthquake

1756   Outbreak of Seven Years' War

1758   Quesnay, *Tableau économique*

1759   Conquest of Quebec

Voltaire, *Candide*

1760   Battle of Wandiwash

1762   Rousseau, *Contrat Social (Social Contract)*

Gluck, *Orfeo*

1763   End of Seven Years' War; Peace of Paris

1765   Stamp Act for American colonies

1768   Watt's steam engine

1770   Cook returns from trip around world

1771   Arkwright's spinning mill in England

1772   First partition of Poland

1773   Reorganization of English administration in India

Beginning of Pugachev Revolt in Russia

1774   Turgot becomes controller-general

Goethe, *Sorrows of Werther*

The eighteenth century is known as the "Age of Enlightenment." To a degree, the Age of Enlightenment constituted a conscious reaction to the artificiality of the times of Louis XIV, but in essence it carried on the trends of that period. It spread the light of reason among wider groups; it called for action on the basis of rational thought. It emphasized science over religion, thought over faith, doubt over traditional authority.

The Age of Enlightenment believed that if scientific investigation were applied not only to inanimate nature, but to all aspects of human life, natural laws could then be discovered which, like Newton's law of gravitation, would explain human action. Then, human action could be so directed as to bring continuous progress to the nations. Thus, attention was focused upon investigations of phenomena in the natural sciences as well as upon investigations of social conditions, politics, and ethics.

POLITICAL ENLIGHTENMENT

The practical application of enlightened theories in the political and economic life of Europe was promoted by the appearance of "enlightened monarchs" or "enlightened despots." As the term "despot" indicates, the concept of the "divine right of kings" or of "absolute monarchy" was retained. Enlightened monarchs were, indeed, far from accepting ideas such as those of Locke concerning the natural rights of the governed in relation to their rulers. But they did show their affinity with the enlightened thought of their age. They did not claim that identity of themselves and their states which Louis XIV had expressed in the arrogant statement, *L'Etat, c'est moi,* which implied the sacrifice of the welfare of the individual to the glory of the king. Instead, they accepted ideals of tolerance, humanitarianism, equal justice, and other ideals that the Age of Reason proposed. Frederick the Great's enlightened dictum, "I am the first servant of the state," reflected the new views about the proper character and function of a ruler.

THE NATIONAL SCENE

With the exception of England (whose parliamentary system, despite its many weaknesses, did not necessitate paternalistic guidance by a monarch), of Poland (which was in the throes of anarchy), and of France (which remained too much under the spell of Louis XIV), almost all European countries had their "enlightened" rulers: Prussia, Frederick the Great; Austria, Joseph II; Spain, Charles III; Sweden, Gustavus III; and Russia, Catherine the Great. Denmark, Portugal, and Spain had ministers such as Struensee, Pombal, and Aranda, respectively. Frederick the Great of Prussia was the most representative example of enlightened despotism.

Prussia

Prussia had developed rapidly in the eighteenth century. In the time of Frederick's father, the efficiency of the government and of the army had been greatly improved. Under a deeply religious, despotic, and extremely parsimonious ruler, an honesty rare in eighteenth-century administrations had prevailed. Serfdom had been reduced. The judicial system was improved. Prussia's rank in Europe was firmly established.

EXTERNAL POLICIES

When Frederick II, "the Great" (d. 1786), came to the throne in 1740, he therefore inherited a most efficient governmental machinery. Making prompt use of his excellent army in three Silesian Wars, Frederick succeeded in doubling his realms and economic resources and in raising Prussia to the status of a first-class power.

INTERNAL POLICIES

His fame, however, rests not only on his generalship in war, but especially on his enlightened rule during thirty-six years of peace. Himself an irreligious man, he was a model of religious tolerance. Jesuits, Jews, and Protestants alike found refuge in his lands. Justice was dealt out speedily, humanely, and with great efforts at impartiality. Often, the poor were favored. Promotion for ability was common, even though Frederick reserved the top posts in the army for the nobility and retained many class distinctions. Agriculture was the king's chief concern. Immigrants were welcomed, wastelands recovered, and modern technical improvements introduced. Serfdom was practiced in its mildest form only. Housing for workers was provided. The raising of new crops, including the potato, was encouraged. The king supervised these matters personally. He resettled the veterans, to whom he distributed land, seed, and horses.

ECONOMIC POLICIES

In his policy toward industry, Frederick was essentially a mercantilist. He passed measures to stimulate production and trade and subsidized both the silk industry and the new porcelain industry. He founded a state bank and stabilized prices through state purchases in times of plenty or sales in times of distress. He developed mines in newly conquered Silesia. He prohibited the importation of luxury goods (e.g., tobacco and coffee) because payments for them would diminish his bullion.

Frederick's long and varied career encompassed a miserable childhood and youth under the strict hand of his despotic father, an industrious period in the service of the state, and an arduous old age. This pathetic, lonely person, who preferred to wear shabby clothes, had given up all his former love of luxury, comfort, the arts, music (he himself played the flute), and communion with philosophers (e.g., Voltaire, who had spent many years at his court). But when he died, his name was a legend everywhere in Europe.

Austria

In Austria, Joseph II (d. 1790) was Frederick's great admirer and imitator. Austria had started on a steep decline. Prussia was challenging Austria's leading position in Germany and Hapsburg princes proved incapable of modernizing their multinational state; they were bent mainly on the preservation of their *Hausmacht*. Austria could no longer maintain its standing. Joseph's mother, Empress Maria Theresa, though a kind, conscientious ruler, had pursued an overly conservative policy.

Joseph introduced new, enlightened policies. However, he pushed his reforms forward at such a pace that he caused as much disturbance, revolt, and setback as progress. Yet, Joseph did improve administration and education. He introduced civil marriage, abolished serfdom, and furthered toleration and equality for all, including Jews.

Russia

The remarkable improvements that enlightened despotism brought to numerous nations should not deceive us as to its inherent weakness. As its very nature required the continued use of arbitrary absolute rule, its advantages depended upon whether or not the government was in the hands of a conscientious and progressive monarch. It proved injurious if such a monarch was followed by a less progressive successor. This aspect of enlightened despotism was demonstrated by events in Russia.

PETER THE GREAT

Enlightenment came to Russia in the early eighteenth century largely owing to the personal influence of Peter I, "the Great" (d. 1725). Peter was a man of inexhaustible energy; he personally and conscientiously attended to innumerable duties and supervised an almost incredible amount of detail. He reformed the administration, removed clerical influences from state affairs, built a civil service based on ability, and reduced class discrimination in law courts. Following mercantilistic principles and the example of other enlightened despots he improved the economy of his state. In his time, the iron production of Russia surpassed that of England. He reformed the army and through successful wars expanded the national domain.

Peter accorded special attention to the Westernization of his country—a trend that had begun under his father, Alexis. He sought to improve educational standards and to introduce the teaching of foreign languages. He founded an academy of sciences. He obtained teachers from foreign lands, especially Germany, technicians from Holland, and traders from England. He sponsored explorations in Siberia and in the Pacific and Bering Sea regions.

Peter tried to transform the manners, appearance, and clothing of his countrymen in imitation of Western models; he founded St. Petersburg to provide a permanent link with the West (1703). But his impatience, arbitrariness, brutality, and vulgarity were gravely damaging to the nation. Weak, inconsistent, and generally luxury-loving successors, some of whom sought to eliminate the existing political and intellectual guidance of foreigners, almost ruined his work. Only when Catherine II, "the Great" (d. 1796), came to the throne were enlightened policies renewed.

CATHERINE THE GREAT

This German princess, though she led a dissipated life, excelled in intelligence, devotion to duty, administrative ability, and artistic and literary taste. Under Catherine's direction, French instead of German influences were strengthened. Plans for enlightened legislation were developed. Hospitals were improved, and she introduced inoculation.

However, the two fundamental weaknesses in the Russian system, autocracy and serfdom, prevented the development of a healthy peasant class, of progressive industry, and of a strong middle class. Many revolts of the peasants occurred (including the protracted and dangerous rebellion of Pugachev). Toward the end of the century, the nation, notwithstanding its territorial expansion, improved education, and increased production, faced greater social problems than at the beginning.

Poland

The rapid progress of Russia brought an end to the political prestige enjoyed by its smaller neighbors. In particular, it brought about the collapse of Poland. This collapse was hastened by the deplorable situation within the country—anarchical conditions, the arrogance and luxury of a small upper class, and the miserable status of the masses. Disunity among the upper and lower nobility made it impossible for any individual or group to run the government efficiently. This invited foreign interference and soon proved detrimental to Polish interests.

Moreover, an arbitrary policy in favor of Catholicism alienated Orthodox and Protestant sectors. The policy was doubly dangerous inasmuch as the majority of Poland's inhabitants were not Polish but Lithuanian, German, or Russian. In 1772, these conditions led to a division of the country among Russia, Prussia, and Austria, the so-called "first partition," which restored most of the non-Polish territories to the neighbors from whom they had been alienated.

Sweden

Sweden narrowly escaped the same fate. Its time of greatness under Gustavus Adolphus had been short. Not long after the death of Gustavus Adolphus, Brandenburg had begun to regain some of the annexed German lands. By 1721, Sweden's Livonian possessions had all been lost to Russia. The rest of its German territories had been relinquished to the German states.

With their territory reduced to its former dimension, the Swedes prudently took the necessary steps of adjustment. Absolutism was followed by enlightened despotism. Industry and trade prospered. The condition of the peasants (serfdom had never been widely practiced) improved substantially with the end of military adventures. A measure of popular representation by means of a national diet helped to stabilize the government on a sound basis.

Spain and Portugal

Enlightened despotism brought revival even to Spain and Portugal. Spain lost much territory in the Pyrenees region and in the colonies, as well as much of its population in numerous wars. Still, Spain gradually regained strength. Its recovery began in 1713, when the succession to the throne was settled. England had gained a stake in Spain's lucrative slave trade, but Spain adjusted itself to the new conditions. Trade restrictions were relaxed and new industries were established. The schools and the army were modernized. The downward trend of population was reversed.

Under Charles III (d. 1788) and his minister, Aranda, the government functioned honestly and efficiently. It reduced taxes to encourage private enterprise. In line with the trend toward a more centralized administration, it abolished internal customs barriers that had obstructed trade. In the colonies, the regime gave up the system of *encomienda*. It appointed able administrative officers and redivided the gradually expanding territory into appropriate administrative units. The pervasive influence of the Jesuits in state affairs was eliminated. Simultaneously, neighboring Portugal carried out similar reforms, both in Portugal and in Brazil.

France

Unlike other European countries, France, the home of enlightened philosophy, did not adopt progressive ideas in its own political system. Whether under the dissipated, but capable and intelligent regent, the Duke of Orléans (d. 1723), or under lazy, luxury-loving Louis XV (d. 1774), France retained the outmoded institutions of the previous century. Only in religious affairs was a more liberal policy instituted. The nobility retained its economic advantages. The administrative service and tax system were left unaltered. Colonization was but halfheartedly supported. The wasteful court continued to drain the treasury.

A crushing debt having accumulated owing to Louis XIV's ambitions and extravagance, the Scottish financier John Law attempted around 1720 to reestablish French credit. He organized a state bank, stabilized the currency, and took over tax collection. Law founded the Mississippi Company, a large colonial enterprise. But his fundamentally sound efforts to expand production and trade were misdirected, as a result of his personal ambitions. His efforts led to mad speculation and economic collapse. French credit fell to a new low. Under the circumstances, the peaceful policies of two able ministers, Dubois and Fleury, could not forestall the rapid political deterioration of the French administrative apparatus. Nor could the essential prosperity of individual merchants and peasants and the natural wealth of this (at the time) most populous and productive country in Europe prevent the decline of French power.

England

The evolution of the English government in the eighteenth century followed neither the pattern of French absolutism nor that of enlightened despotism. Nor did England's past political experiences, its social conditions, its technological and industrial advances, and its overseas commitments favor either such path. Instead, Parliament extended the scope of its political leadership. During the early eighteenth century, the Stuarts failed in attempts to regain the throne, which, after the death of Queen Anne, was handed over to Germans from Hanover.

The first two Hanoverian kings, being chiefly concerned with their Continental possessions, paid scant attention to English affairs. In consequence, Parliament was able to exercise its powers without hindrance. A financial storm arose from the speculations and collapse of the South Sea Company (an enterprise similar to that of John Law in France). But it was weathered without undermining the credit of the country. With commerce flourishing after the wars of the preceding century had eliminated Dutch competition, and with successes in international diplomacy, the authority of parliamentary government increased. A strong national bank, sound money, and an adequate and broadly based system of taxation—which, unlike the French system, did not exempt the nobility—supported a healthy treasury.

PARLIAMENT AND PARTIES

Under the cautious and efficient administration of Sir Robert Walpole (d. 1745), peace was maintained. Owing to Walpole's influence, enduring precedents for the conduct of government were established. As a "prime minister" (the first in English history) Walpole surrounded himself with advisers who could count upon the support of their parties—Whig or Tory—in Parliament. He thus secured the backing of Parliament (especially of the House of Commons), to which, in a sense, he thereby became responsible. The advisers themselves became the king's ministers. The group as a whole, the "cabinet," became the executive organ of the state. Bribery, dishonesty, and a policy of catering to interests of minorities and favored individuals may have continued to prevail under the developing system, and Parliament, which was composed of representatives of only a small fraction of the population—comprising mainly the privileged, wealthy landowning group—may not have represented the nation at large. Yet, the basic interests of the whole nation were safeguarded.

REIGN OF GEORGE III

The good functioning of the institutions as they developed was endangered when the third Hanoverian, George III (d. 1820), came to the throne in 1760. Opposed to the Whigs who had been in power for decades, George III chose his ministers not according to party affiliation, but according to his personal preference. He held them responsible to himself alone. However, his policies—often opposed by men like the elder Pitt (d. 1778)—were not crowned with success. During George's reign, England lost its thirteen colonies in North America.

Internal affairs took a course different from that which he envisioned. Notwithstanding his attempts to increase his royal prerogatives and notwithstanding widespread corruption, the parliamentary system developed further. In the economic sphere, mercantilist views were increasingly replaced by laissez-faire theories. With the progressive introduction of steam power, industrialism and modern capitalism set the pattern for future production methods and for relations between government and business.

THE INTERNATIONAL SCENE

The direction that the internal developments in the individual national states had taken in the second half of the seventeenth century and the path on which they proceeded during the following fifty years entailed new international relationships. By 1700, there had gradually and naturally developed a system of government that then became the conscious property of the European diplomats. It even provided a basis for a theory of international relations by appealing to the rational attitude of the age and to its sense of order. This theory is known as the "balance of power." On the Continent such a balance was not really new; it constituted a normal aim within the European community. It had existed within many an earlier state system, as in sixteenth-century Italy. But at the beginning of the eighteenth century, it gained importance because the danger of French hegemony under Louis XIV had again focused attention upon the problem. The "balance of power" meant that no single power or group of powers should be permitted to develop enough strength to dominate the others.

The policy of upholding it served Britain well. Since Britain stayed outside the system, it could use the policy to prevent the emergence of any overwhelmingly strong European competitor. Whenever the balance was upset, Britain would throw its weight on the weaker side. Assuming the role of protector of the weak, it would try to reestablish the balance.

The advantage of the system was that the independence of the various states (especially the smaller ones) could thereby be safeguarded. The disadvantage was that it hindered European cooperation and led to incessant wars because changes in the balance of power were unavoidable owing to the pressure of economic developments and to the emergence of strong-minded personalities in positions of authority.

International Objectives

Within the framework of the balance of power, of course, many of the old and long-standing trends in European policies persisted. France's objectives were to expand to the Rhine and to prevent a renewed collaboration of the German Empire and Spain such as had existed when both were under Hapsburg rule. England's policy was to keep European attention focused on European problems, rather than on overseas acquisitions, and to prevent the conquest of the entire Channel coast by any strong power. Hapsburg Austria's aspirations were to increase the *Hausmacht* and retain ascendancy over the Turks. Spain's ambitions were to preserve its Italian possessions and to keep its overseas trade routes open. Prussia's endeavors were to reduce Hapsburg influence in the German Empire and to secure the territories separating its outlying possessions on the Rhine and in East Prussia from its center, Brandenburg. Finally, Russia maintained expansionist zeal and its urge to gain access to the Baltic and Black seas.

Balance of Power and the European States

Such aims and aspirations led to numerous entanglements. Within the system of "balance of power," they could generally not be resolved except by resorting to war. Diplomacy, despite the assumed reasonableness of human beings, failed.

However, the wars were largely "cabinet wars," fought with small armies in restricted areas. They aroused little passion; they affected the general populations of the countries much less than either the religious wars earlier or the great national wars later. The destructive power of the weapons was limited. National and religious hatreds were absent. As if by convention, mutual respect and consideration among the warring yet interdependent princes prevented excesses in the conduct of war as well as the annihilation of states in the making of peace.

THE GREAT NORTHERN WAR (1700–1721)

Before Louis XIV's last war (the War of the Spanish Succession) had begun, another war had broken out: the Great Northern War between Russia and Sweden. After some brilliant initial victories, the Swedish king, Charles XII, considered one of history's great military geniuses, was decisively beaten at Poltava (1709). But it took the Russians another twelve years to evict the Swedes from all Livonia and to secure in the Peace of Nystad (1721) long-coveted harbors on the Baltic Sea. This achievement so increased the prestige of Russia that henceforth, in their diplomacy, all the European nations had to take Russia's views into consideration.

WAR OF THE POLISH SUCCESSION (1733–1735)

A new war broke out in 1733. Dubois and Fleury tried to keep France from being involved while it was trying to recover from the wars of Louis XIV. Nevertheless, the minor question of the succession to the Polish throne brought France into this new entanglement; Hapsburg and Bourbon vied with each other for control of the succession. The war ended with the failure of the Bourbons to secure the throne for their candidate.

WAR OF THE AUSTRIAN SUCCESSION (1740–1748)

The Hapsburg success was short-lived. Soon Austria found itself threatened from another side. Upon the accession to the imperial throne by Maria Theresa (for whose right of succession her father had sacrificed numerous Hapsburg interests), a series of other wars broke out. On the one hand, Prussia attacked Austria. Ignoring Prussia's promise to respect a "Pragmatic Sanction," by which most European powers had consented to Maria Theresa's succession, Frederick II of Prussia invaded and conquered Silesia (1741). On the other hand, France, which also sided against Austria, became involved in a new war with England.

This seemed to offer an opportunity for Maria Theresa to try to recover Silesia; but in 1745 her armies were again defeated by Frederick. France, her other enemy, was beaten by England, however; not until 1748 was peace restored (Peace of Aix-la-Chapelle). This prepared the ground for a revolution in the balance-of-power system. Both France and Austria, traditional rivals, were so weakened that neither had to fear the hegemony of the other. They therefore settled their age-old differences, came to an understanding, and allied themselves against the victors, Prussia and England.

SEVEN YEARS' WAR (1756–1763)

As a result, in 1756, a new war broke out, the Seven Years' War. This took on global dimensions. Russia joined the Franco-Austrian alliance against Prussia, while outside of Europe Spain became involved in the conflict against England. Thus wars were fought on three continents— Europe, Asia, and America.

In Europe, the war centered again around Prussia's struggle for the possession of Silesia. Despite a series of brilliant victories, Frederick soon found himself in grave difficulties. Only the death of Russia's empress, Elizabeth, solved his predicament. Elizabeth's successor, Peter III, was an admirer of Frederick; he withdrew the Russian armies. France and Austria were compelled to make peace on the basis of the status quo, and Frederick kept Silesia.

In Asia and in America (where the war became known as the French and Indian War) England, which contributed little but money to the European phase, gained the upper hand. The peace, concluded at Paris in 1763, cost France a large part of her overseas possessions.

RUSSO-TURKISH WAR (1772–1774)

Once the Seven Years' War was over, Russia turned its attention to the Black Sea region, which Peter the Great had tried to dominate. Russia started a war against Turkey, was victorious, and finally gained access to the Black

Sea (1774). Having once achieved this long-coveted aim, it began to push on relentlessly, seeking to secure all of the Black Sea coast. Russia's aim was to eliminate Turkish influence in Europe and Turkish domination of the straits (Bosporus and Dardanelles) as well as to gain direct and free access to the Mediterranean.

Balance of Power and Overseas Expansion

Despite alternating alignments of the European nations, the long series of wars that mark the eighteenth century brought shifts in the balance of power. The wars were fought in order to preserve existing power relationships rather than upset them. They increased the international prestige of Prussia and Russia without putting either of them in a position to attain continental hegemony.

Overseas, however, no balance of power was preserved. On the contrary, in all the wars that paralleled the European conflicts and that were fought in colonial areas—in particular the War of Jenkins's Ear (1739–1741), King George's War (1743–48), and the French and Indian War (1754–1763)—Britain expanded its power and empire at the cost of France and Spain. In both East and West, East India and America, Britain gained predominance.

EAST INDIA

At the time, East India seemed to be the most important colonial prize. It appeared for a while that France would be able to secure this prize; starting with its settlement at Pondichery, France had vigorously expanded its Indian possessions in mid-century. A competent agent, Dupleix, knew how to gain the good will of important local princes. In 1746, he annexed the large trading town of Madras. When, owing to French weakness at home, the town had to be ceded back to England (by the terms of the Peace of Aix-la-Chapelle in 1748), Dupleix concentrated on other areas and won domination over most of southern India.

But the English were determined to drive the French out. In Robert Clive, England found a leader equal to Dupleix in ability. Like the French, Clive sought the support of native princes. He impressed them as a man of action when he avenged the capture of Calcutta by a native prince. He wooed their services through generous gifts. Then he turned against the French.

Unfortunately for France, Dupleix, accused of dishonesty, had been recalled in 1754. His able successor, Lally Tollendal, obtained no help from the home government. Consequently, the British, who dominated the sea lanes and invested the necessary funds, defeated the French in the decisive Battle of Wandiwash (1760). Tollendal was recalled and put to death by an ungrateful government. Peace was concluded in Paris in 1763. Notwithstanding all the efforts and sacrifices of the French agents, and notwithstanding the economic importance of the colony, France had to surrender most of its holdings in India to the British.

Promptly, the British set about reorganizing the administration of their colony and exploiting its wealth. After recalling Clive without rewarding him for his services in the struggle against France, they deprived the East India Company of its control over the country. They subjected the government to strict supervision from London. Warren Hastings was sent to India as governor in 1773. With his regime a new chapter in Britain's—and India's—history began.

NORTH AMERICA

At the Peace of Paris in 1763, France lost not only India, but also most of its North American holdings. In the course of the eighteenth century, the French had tried to turn the colonial empire, which mercantilist theory and thirst for glory had driven them to acquire, into a possession that would yield practical returns. Their colonies in Canada, the Mississippi Valley, and the Caribbean islands showed considerable promise. Trading in commodities (sugar, timber, fish, and furs) and in slaves to and from the homeland and among the colonies increased.

However, not only competition with Britain but also the pressure of British colonists in North America upon the thinly settled French dominions hindered peaceful progress. As in India, the British home government backed the commercial interests, "the flag following the trade." In 1745, the colonists in America attacked and conquered the French fortress of Louisbourg. The terms of the Peace of Aix-la-Chapelle required the British to return the fort to France. But ill-feeling between the British colonists and their French neighbors led to continuous localized encounters, especially in Acadia (Nova Scotia) and in the Ohio Valley.

By 1754, these local conflicts had developed into a general war. Britain sent expeditionary forces to America, but they, as well as the American colonists themselves, were defeated. The resulting danger to the colonies brought more concentrated efforts, especially when the energetic and able William Pitt assumed the direction of affairs in England. Naval forces sent to America destroyed the French fleet. On land, British troops conquered Quebec and Montreal in 1759 and 1760.

Disaster now threatened the French. Belated Spanish intervention on the French side failed to reestablish a balance of power against England. Unable to continue the war, France and Spain had to submit to British demands. In the Peace of Paris, Spain gave up Florida. The French, choosing to retain the commercially profitable islands in the West Indies, ceded Canada and the Mississippi region.

The Thirteen Colonies

At the time of the Peace of Paris, the British people hardly foresaw that the most valuable part of their American possessions would be lost, at least politically, within scarcely more than a dozen years. During the Seven Years' War (the French and Indian War), the colonists had cooperated, if reluctantly, with the home country. Whether the colonists had originally come from England, Scotland, and Ireland or from Switzerland, Germany, and Holland, and whether they had emigrated for political, economic, or religious reasons, they were generally animated by a thirst for liberty.

They had moved to a new land not only for material gain, but also for independence and for freedom from compulsion. They objected to all exploitation of their land by the home country; they objected to British mercantilist tactics. Moreover, they pressed steadily westward from the seaboard and were angered at the interference of European issues and diplomacy with their own expansionist objectives. They had already secured a large measure of self-government, a prosperous economic status, and (as leaders like Benjamin Franklin demonstrated) a considerable amount of intellectual stature. In turn, they were unwilling to take upon themselves burdens which the British, having incurred large expenditures in the wars against France, tried to impose upon them without their consent.

They denounced a Stamp Act (1765), which Parliament devised as a source of revenue from the colonies. They forced its repeal in the following year. But Parliament, insisting upon its right to tax the colonies for revenue, imposed other burdens. The Declaratory Act, Townshend Act, Quebec Act, and so-called "Intolerable" Acts succeeded on another quickly, providing either for new taxes or for customs duties or fines. The situation was aggravated further because these impositions coincided with the absolutist tendencies of George III.

Violent propaganda started, supported by leaders brought up in the spirit of enlightenment: for example, Thomas Paine, who demanded a radical break with Britain. The dissatisfied colonists finally assembled a Continental Congress, which first prescribed a boycott of British goods. Later, in 1775, it raised an army. This was followed, in July 1776, by the assembling of representatives from the various colonies, who took the decisive step and declared the independence of the American colonies.

CULTURAL ENLIGHTENMENT

No matter how important the changes were which occurred in the political scene of England and the enlightened countries on the Continent, the social and intellectual pattern of the West was even more deeply affected by the economic evolution of the eighteenth century. Mercantilist practices had to be modified as the modern capitalistic system based on new production methods got under way. Agriculture and industry had to be adapted to the new technical knowledge and scientific spirit.

Industry, Trade, and Society

The changes were less noticeable in central and eastern Europe, which lacked colonial possessions and had only limited access to raw materials and markets. In the Western countries, however, the changes were evident. Private enterprises benefited from colonial supplies, technical advances and—especially in England—political conditions.

TRADE AND INDUSTRY

Everywhere, the coal and iron industries expanded. Serfdom, which had limited the industrial labor supply, steadily weakened or disappeared. Forced labor obligations were transformed into money obligations; this shift allowed greater mobility for the peasant and a broader labor market for the entrepreneur. An educated bourgeoisie aimed for higher material living standards and became ever more influential.

The Western countries steadily increased their trade relations with America, the Near East, and India. In order to maintain this prospering trade, they promoted domestic industries and were quick to introduce technical improvements. Spinning and weaving machines (invented by Hargreaves, Arkwright, and Whitney) were brought into use. Large organizations developed that introduced well-planned methods of production and distribution.

SOCIETY

The costs for the introduction of labor-saving industries had to be borne by the former free artisans and the workers who lost their jobs and independence and, as Hogarth's pictures from England show, lived in hopeless misery. The burden was also carried by the inhabitants of the Western countries' overseas possessions. Thus, England, besides exploiting the resources of India, sought to derive the greatest possible profit from the thirteen colonies in North America and from Caribbean possessions. Its exports included Eastern products, iron, and finished goods; its imports from the Caribbean—in a triangular trade (Liverpool-Boston-Havana)—sugar, molasses, and rum. Britain also monopolized the slave trade to the New World; it derived a large income from this source.

POPULATION

The industrial products created in Europe and the resources derived from the colonies contributed to the food supply, and thereby to population growth. Advances in medicine added to this trend. Microbes were discovered. The people benefited from a better understanding of physiology and from improvements in gynecology. The principles of hygiene were published and applied. Early in the century, families were very large, often with ten to twenty children, the majority of whom died in infancy. Families were smaller in the second half of the century, but more of the children survived.

On the Continent, women began to play a larger role in the world outside the household. Advanced education became available to greater numbers of them. In Germany and Italy, there were women professors in the best universities, such as those at Göttingen and Bologna. Women organized *salons* where the ideas of the day were discussed, and participated in important learned gatherings. But they did not yet excel in creating major works in art, philosophy, literature, or science.

Economic and Legal Thought: Humanitarianism

In line with these changing economic conditions and with the philosophical views emphasizing natural laws, the existing social organization was challenged. Economic thinking changed. Mercantilism, with its many regulations, appeared to interfere with the free play of "natural" forces. The freedom to be able to pursue those activities for which each citizen felt best suited was advocated as the basis of prosperity. Some economists, like the "physiocrats," headed by Quesnay (d. 1774) in France, held that it was not money or bullion that constituted wealth but rather a country's total national product. This in turn was said to result from exploiting the resources of soil and subsoil and the labor invested in producing goods. Others applied the theory of freedom to a broader area, focusing on trade and industry. They advocated the adoption of the doctrine of laissez-faire, believing that noninterference in the free and natural play of economic forces would work to the benefit of the nation. The most famous advocate of laissez-faire was Adam Smith (d. 1790; *Wealth of Nations*).

Underlying the thought of these economists was the twofold goal of finding natural laws and of contributing to progress, to the "happiness" of the human race. With this aim in view, the economists exercised a profound influence on law. Quesnay, for instance, advocated that governments confine themselves to restraining the evildoer and not interfere with the citizen's legitimate activities. In the view of Quesnay and his fellow economists, all have a right to work as they please as long as they do not hurt others. Adam Smith similarly favored the unimpeded right to work. Wealth, he argued, is the result of labor.

In the same spirit of promoting freedom and humanitarian aims, various reformers denounced restrictive laws. Beccaria, about 1764, objected to the use of torture. Prison for debtors was assailed as useless and inhumane. Serfdom was condemned. Superstitions, such as those responsible for the persecution of "witches," were ridiculed.

Science

The practical economic effect of rational thought and scientific orientation was clearly visible to the economists and scientists of the eighteenth century. They were, therefore, in favor of further efforts to expand scientific knowledge. Academies of science, like those of England, France, Prussia, and Russia, played a leading role in these efforts.

Expeditions for geographical discovery were sponsored; descriptions of foreign lands—of their fauna, flora, rivers, mountains, and populations—were published. Vitus Bering, a Danish explorer in Russian service, found the straits separating Asia and America. The Germans Gmelin, Steller, and Pallas, also in Russian service, explored Siberia, from the Urals to China and the Pacific. Other explorations were undertaken by the English and French in the New World. Automatically, European ideas were spread to many parts of the globe. Conversely, considerable influence was exerted by newly discovered areas upon the economics, politics, manners, and thoughts of the European nations.

The discoveries abroad contributed much to the imposing works of Buffon (d. 1788) and the Swede Linnaeus (d. 1778). Buffon described the animal world. Linnaeus undertook the fundamental task of not only describing plants but also classifying them on the basis of their reproductive organs. In physiology, Haller investigated respiration and the development of the embryo. Spallanzani (d. 1799) rejected the view that living matter can be generated by nonliving matter and proved that spontaneous generation does not occur in nature.

To the already flourishing fields of mathematics and astronomy, geniuses such as the Swiss mathematician Euler (d. 1783), and the philosopher Kant (d. 1804) made notable contributions.

In chemistry and physics, many discoveries were made. Boerhaave (d. 1739) and especially Priestley (whose work on oxygen, published in 1774, was fundamental) paved the way for scientific chemistry, which was soon developed by Lavoisier. Benjamin Franklin (d. 1790) occupied part of his time with scientific problems. His contemporaries owed him a broad understanding of electrical forces, of the significance of positive and negative electrical charges, and of the conservation of electrical energy. In medicine, immunization against smallpox was achieved.

Technology

Theoretical knowledge was soon applied to practical problems. Réaumur's work on the analysis of steel was published in 1722. Reliable measurements for longitude and latitude aided navigation. A steam engine was invented in 1705 by Newcomen and later modernized by Polzunov (1764) and Watt (1768). Even in the world of art, technology had an effect, as shown by the improvement of musical instruments.

Social Sciences

Developments in social science were as significant as those in the natural sciences. Three Frenchmen—Montesquieu (d. 1755), Voltaire (d. 1778), and Rousseau (d. 1778)—may have added little to the insights already gained by such English social thinkers as Locke and, later, his successor Hume

(d. 1776). But their practical influence as propagandists for the new social ideas far surpassed that of their English counterparts. In his *Persian Letters*, Montesquieu derided contemporary conditions in France; in his *Spirit of Laws* (1748), he emphasized the importance of the material basis of all social institutions and the influence of climate on the laws and character of a nation. He advocated a type of government limited by checks and balances. Voltaire, poet and historian, directed his wit against prejudice, unreasoning tradition, intolerance, and injustice. He firmly believed in the perfectibility of mankind.

Rousseau was the most sensitive of the three great Frenchmen and the only political radical. In his *Nouvelle Héloise* and his educational treatise *Émile*, he defended a new, utopian way of life that, he thought, could result from turning away from civilization and back to nature. Thereby, he hoped the people of the West would be led to virtue and happiness. In his *Social Contract*, Rousseau set forth his thoughts on the inalienable rights of all human beings and on popular government.

Rousseau's ideas were spread further by the so-called "Encyclopedists"—such men as Diderot (d. 1784) and d'Alembert (d. 1783), who, like Voltaire and Rousseau, faced censorship, exile, and imprisonment, yet pursued their work of propagating "enlightened" thought. They published a comprehensive alphabetical dictionary in which they used the entries for political, religious, and other terms to discuss enlightened ideas. It was such writings as these that composed the subject matter in the numerous salons, as well as in the pamphlets and newspapers. The increase in literacy increased their impact.

Religion

The entire movement of the Enlightenment appealed to the human conscience and humanitarian feelings. Yet, people's overconfidence in progress, their neglect of metaphysical urges, and their materialism were bound to lead to criticism and reaction.

ATHEISM AND DEISM

Only a few of the enlightened thinkers altogether rejected the thought of a God and religion. Hume, who saw religion as an outmoded state of human evolution, and d'Holbach (d. 1789), a determined atheist, were among them. But there was a strong trend in the direction of skepticism and atheism. This trend was attributable, on the one hand, to conventionalism and rigidity within traditional churches, and, on the other, to the failure to find a faith that would reconcile traditional religious beliefs with new scientific insights.

A vague middle position was provided by "deism." The deists rejected traditional revelation and with it the dogma of the existing Christian churches. While accepting a God as a first cause and as a source for the good, they built their views of the universe on the basis of rationalistic thought and mathematical laws.

PIETISM AND METHODISM

Deism lacked deep emotional appeal. It was soon surpassed in importance by a countermovement, antagonistic to rationalism, which had set in during the seventeenth century. This countermovement had originated with the German pastors Spener and Francke. Their initiative had developed the pietist trend. "Pietism" now brought to Christian communities a new devotion, spirituality, and charity, as well as a revived mysticism and missionary fervor. Emphasis was placed not on reason, but on the attributes of the heart. The movement satisfied the longings of many seeking a truly Christian life.

But with its individualistic tendencies, it also led to conflicts with state authority. Pietist groups, such as the Moravians under the leadership of Count Zinzendorf, were forced to emigrate. Many went to the New World, where they eventually exercised a certain distinct cultural influence. Likewise, many adherents of Wesley (d. 1791), who had sponsored a similar revolt in England against natural religion emptied of Christian content, came to America. Everywhere, the Age of Enlightenment thus saw two conflicting trends: the one toward rejection, the other toward reaffirmation, of the Christian doctrine.

Literature

The interests of the age and its preoccupations with societal structure and with laws of nature left a definite mark on literature. In France, the outstanding writers were Voltaire and Rousseau. But two works of special interest, the Abbé Prévost's *Manon Lescaut* and Bernardin de Saint-Pierre's *Paul et Virginie,* stirred even more deeply the hearts of eighteenth-century readers; they deserve mention as permanent treasures of world literature.

England contributed notable works such as *Robinson Crusoe* by Defoe (d. 1731), *Gulliver's Travels* by Swift (d. 1745), and satirical writings with their implied criticism of existing prejudices. A number of authors of wide renown appeared, including Pope (d. 1744, *Essays on Thais*), Fielding (d. 1754; *Tom Jones*), Samuel Richardson (*Pamela*), Sterne (d. 1768; *Tristam Shandy*), Oliver Goldsmith (d. 1774; *Vicar of Wakefield*), as well as Samuel Johnson and his biographer, Boswell (d. 1795).

Germany witnessed with Klopstock (d. 1803) and Lessing (d. 1781) the beginnings of one of its greatest periods in literature. Lessing in particular helped free eighteenth-century literature from the artistic structure of classical French tradition; he recalled the great and free heritage of Shakespeare to a public that had been inclined to forget or belittle the great English dramatist. Russia, too, began to produce significant literature; Lomonosov, and after him the future historian Karamsin, laid foundations for the literary as well as scientific evolution of their country.

A number of historians of lasting importance appeared in the mid-eighteenth century. Besides those who, in the tradition of Mabillon, investigated and edited sources, Voltaire and Gibbon *(Decline and Fall of the*

Roman Empire) combined artistic style with sound scholarship. Historical interest was thereafter steadily heightened. Classical studies increased rapidly. Excavations in Pompeii and in Greece by the German archaeologist Winckelmann revealed to the world the beauty and meaning of the classical heritage.

Art

With the growth of a reading public, the visual arts declined in significance. Few artists stand out. There were the three Italian baroque painters, Antonio Canaletto, Francesco Guardi, and Giovanni Tiepolo, the latter famous for his great wall and ceiling paintings. And there were three English painters Gainsborough (d. 1788), Joshua Reynolds (d. 1792), and the engraver Hogarth (d. 1764). All three were interested in social aspects. Gainsborough and Reynolds made portraits of the high nobility; Hogarth depicted the vices and misery of the poor. The baroque style turned into "rococo." Rococo possessed charm and intimacy. Its lovely buildings (palaces, theaters, churches), staircases, and furniture, with shell-like structures and curved windows letting in light, adorned the countryside of Italy, Spain, France, and southern Germany. But it increased the trend toward sentimentality, affectation, and overornamentation.

Music

Simultaneously, however, with the playfulness in the rococo arts, we witness in music some of the grandest, most meaningful works ever created. During the second half of the seventeenth century, the innovations of the preceding period had already borne many fruits. The violin and the violoncello had been brought to perfection. Composers of the stature of Corelli (d. 1713) and Alessandro Scarlatti (d. 1725) in Italy, and Purcell (d. 1695) in England had promoted the art of the contrapuntal style and created instrumental music of rare beauty. Reflecting both a rational trend and sincere emotion, they added purity, simplicity, and strictness of form to a content rich in thought and feeling.

They prepared the way for the great masters who were to dominate the first half of the eighteenth century. It was then that Johann Sebastian Bach (d. 1750) and George Frideric Handel (d. 1759) composed their works. Handel *(The Messiah),* besides writing numerous other works of the highest achievement, also excelled in the oratorio and opera. Bach did not publish any opera. It was in his compositions for orchestra, organ, and harpsichord; his church cantatas, chorales, and sonatas; his *St. John Passion* and *St. Matthew Passion;* and his *Art of the Fugue* that Bach embodied profound Christian inspiration and a human sense of beauty, grace, and compassion.

On the political stage, the ideas of the Enlightenment were spread widely through the writings of the prominent thinkers of the age, many of whom were French. They animated rulers, "enlightened despots" who in contrast to the style of Louis XIV considered service to their states and their subjects as their foremost duty. Under them, and also under England's parliamentary system, an outdated nobility found new tasks. It filled the middle and high ranks in administration, and in the army and navy. The commercial classes, bankers, and financiers benefited from the increasing trade and, owing to the numerous mechanical inventions, from rapid industrial expansion.

In the cultural field, the Enlightenment strengthened the scientific approach to the study of nature and human life. Plants, animals, and natural surroundings were described, illustrated, and classified. Biology and medicine profited from scientific methods. Studies of electrical forces led to major discoveries. The scientific trends caused many philosophers to question the value of religious beliefs and religious institutions. Some rejected all belief in an all-embracing God. But in reaction to such tendencies, there emerged also an opposite trend toward renewed faith and strict interpretation of the Bible, toward pietism and mysticism. Still others sought to reconcile conflicting ideas by accepting deist or pantheist views.

One field in the cultural life of the West reached a turning point in the period of the Enlightenment, and that was the field of music. A number of great German composers stood at the beginning of a full century of outstanding musical achievements.

Selected Readings

Cassirer, Ernst. *The Philosophy of the Enlightenment* (1952)

Gay, Peter. *The Enlightenment* (1966–69)

Gipson, Laurence H. *The British Empire before the American Revolution* (1936–56)

Gooch, George O. *Frederick the Great* (1947)

Hampshire, Stuart, ed. *The Age of Reason* (1956)

Hampson, Norman. *The Enlightenment* (1968)

Jones, J. R. *Britain and the World, 1649–1815* (1980)

Kluchevsky, Vasily O. *Peter the Great* (1958)

Krieger, Leonard. *Kings and Philosophers, 1689–1789* (1970)

Manuel, Frank E. *Age of Reason* (1951)

McKay, Derek, and Scott, H. M. *The Rise of the Great Powers, 1648–1815* (1983)

Raeff, Marc. *The Well-Ordered Police State . . . Germanies and Russia, 1600–1800* (1983)

Williams, Glyndwin. *The Expansion of Europe in the Eighteenth Century* (1966)

10

The Age of Revolution (1775–1795)

*T*he ferment created by the ideas of the Enlightenment spread rapidly among thinking people in all Western countries. Progress made possible by new methods of production added to the unrest. Impatience grew despite reforms introduced by enlightened governments. With a firm belief in the perfectibility of mankind, individuals belonging to the most diverse social strata demanded far-reaching changes in the organization of society.

In the face of this trend toward social evolution, many who held economic and political power stood firm. Instead of seeking ways to adapt themselves to the new situation, they rejected any idea of a retreat from their privileged positions. They hoped, in the spirit of Louis XV's "Après moi le déluge," to be able at least to postpone the day of judgment.

Nevertheless, the ideology of freedom and equality, and the fervor engendered by it, undermined irrevocably the faith in the old order, even that of those who had a material interest in it. Thus, without a serious economic crisis, the ground was prepared for a quick, violent transformation of social and political institutions.

REVOLUTIONARY MOVEMENTS IN THE COLONIES

The first great assault upon the traditional social system occurred in England's thirteen American colonies. They were comparatively free and prosperous and subject to rather generous, progressive government. The assault was led not by the oppressed, but by those who had little to gain except the fulfillment of certain ideals rooted in the spirit of the Enlightenment.

Birth of the United States

After the thirteen English colonies had declared their independence in 1776, they faced the task of making their program a reality. The struggle encompassed two phases: first, liberation from foreign domination, and second, establishment of a working government in line with the most progressive ideology of the age. Notwithstanding vigorous opposition by conservative forces, both tasks were successfully accomplished.

The American Declaration of Independence was worked out under Thomas Jefferson's guidance. Aside from enumerating the grievances against the British, it stated that man possesses "natural rights," that it is self-evident that "all men are created equal," that they have the right to "Life, Liberty, and the Pursuit of Happiness," and that government derives its power from the consent of the governed. It thus gave expression to the enlightened views of the century and sought to transform theory into practice. In this way, it set a model for the organization of democratic governments in many countries.

AMERICAN WAR OF LIBERATION

In order to achieve their goal of self-determination, the colonists undertook armed resistance against the most formidable power of the time. The war lasted seven years. But it was won, despite many setbacks and internal dissensions, by the American troops under the inspired leadership of George Washington (d. 1793). The English had the advantage of overwhelming naval superiority, but they conducted the war halfheartedly. Troops and generals sent to America were ill-equipped.

The Americans, on the other hand, had concluded alliances with France and Spain in 1778; they had received decisive support from them. American leaders, Washington in particular, performed their duties with great devotion and perseverance. In 1783, the English general Cornwallis, and his troops were forced to surrender at Yorktown, whereupon the British home government acknowledged American independence. The peace treaty concluded in the same year at Paris sealed Britain's loss of its thirteen colonies. Moreover, it forced Britain to hand back Florida and the Mediterranean island of Minorca to Spain. France gained nothing except acknowledgment of its claims to French settlements in America.

THE CONSTITUTION OF THE UNITED STATES

Even before the end of the war, the colonists had provided for postwar cooperation among themselves. They drew up the "Articles of Confederation." The articles vested most legislative and executive powers in the representative houses of the individual states; they limited the powers of the central government. This first attempt provided so weak a link among the various states that the formation of a healthy nation became a dubious prospect.

Moreover, economic conditions after the war were unsatisfactory. A number of revolts occurred and bitterness between factions persisted; efficient tax collection for the government was impossible for lack of a central enforcing agency. Issues such as westward expansion and the problem of slavery divided the states. During this period, the eastern seaboard states voluntarily surrendered their claims to western lands they could have acquired. This willingness also indicated some possibility of future cooperation. However, the leading figures in the colonies—Franklin, Washington, Adams, Jefferson, Hamilton—were concerned about the possibility of survival of the independent country in view of the dissensions within.

In 1787, several of them met with like-minded leaders in a new Constitutional Convention. With about seven states represented, the Convention under Washington's presidency agreed upon a constitution, whose drafting was largely the work of James Madison. It provided for a national government with three separate branches—legislative, executive, judicial–which were intended to provide checks and balances and thereby prevent the exercise of arbitrary power. Among other stipulations, it also provided for the separation of church and state. Although full of compromises, it constituted a workable frame of government. But by being much concerned with property rights, it lacked a statement about human rights. Amendments stating them explicitly had to be added subsequently.

With acceptance of the Constitution by the legislatures of all thirteen colonies (ratification by nine was required), the "United States" came into being. George Washington was elected the first president (in 1789), with his duties under the Constitution including those of enforcing the law, appointing judges, and acting as military commander-in-chief. The new nation began to function as a republic, and in a way very different from that of the European models. Through its progressive Constitution, the United States was to later exercise considerable influence on political and social thought and organization in Europe. Yet, the new nation was also a true child of Europe—of the French enlightenment and the Anglo-Saxon legal tradition.

Unrest in South America

The example set by the United States could not be followed in other colonial areas. In Spanish and Portuguese South America, training in self-government was lacking. A gulf existed between the Europeans, who included many wealthy and well-educated people, and the Indians, blacks, and mixed races who were in the majority. The European settlers feared that if they lost home support, then the lower classes would rise in revolt and overwhelm them.

Moreover, the economic situation did not favor independence. Despite the abolition of the *encomienda* system, agriculture was still backward, mining depended on the markets in the home countries, and business organization was weak. Uprisings against Spain and Portugal took place between 1780 and 1784. But, since allegiance was stronger than the spirit of revolt, the winning of independence was long deferred.

Activity in Asia and Africa

No revolutionary outbreaks occurred in other continents where independence movements would have had to originate with native (non-European) populations. The latter, notwithstanding their great numbers, never developed military power to equal that of the Europeans, who could therefore not only maintain their position but also extend their territorial holdings. Consequently, Europeans seized additional colonies in Africa and India. During Hastings's administration, India came almost completely under English rule. Furthermore, a whole new continent was opened for colonization when, in 1797, a penal settlement was established in Australia, which eventually developed into a prosperous commonwealth.

REVOLUTION IN EUROPE

Shortly after Europe witnessed the startling innovation of a republic in America, it was shocked by a terrible revolution against the "Old Regime" in France. This appeared to be another result of the philosophy of enlightenment. Revolts also occurred in other countries—in Belgium, Italy, and Poland. In still others, the threat of rebellion brought reforms. But none of these other revolutions compared with that of France in its dramatic and lasting impact upon all Western society.

Conditions before the Revolution

French institutions were not altogether backward. French rulers had not been entirely lacking in political enlightenment. After the death of Louis XV in 1774, attempts had been made under weak-spirited Louis XVI and his capable minister, Turgot (d. 1781), to improve agriculture. By abolishing the numerous internal customs barriers and improving the roads, Turgot provided greater freedom for trade. The privileges of the nobility were reduced, and the remnants of serfdom dissolved. Special efforts were made to end the abuses of an inequitable tax system and check the system of buying offices. Also, the highest law court, the Parlement de Paris, had been given increased authority. But the Parlement had been inclined to abuse its position in favor of the privileged classes; the reactionary forces everywhere were still strong.

Turgot was dismissed in 1776. The divisions among the French people in regard to law, customs barriers, and tax systems, all of which favored the traditional distribution of power, and the different weights and measures were essentially preserved. Class distinctions were upheld in favor of the first two estates (the clergy and the nobility). The third estate (the middle class and the peasantry—the latter alone accounting for four-fifths of the population) remained without political rights; they were discriminated against when seeking high positions and economic advancement. Overland traffic was unsafe, vagabondage commonplace. Moreover, each social stratum was divided within itself; each of the three estates had its wealthy and its poor constituents; often the wealthy individuals belonging to one estate cooperated with those in another rather than with members of their own estate.

Path to Revolution

Under such conditions, the incentives to revolt were many:

(1) There were the ideologies of the age, the philosophy of enlightenment, freedom, equality, and political rights for the bourgeoisie; the ideas of free enterprise, free development of trade, and free access to all positions in state and army according to ability instead of birth; the rejection of the corrupted morals of court and

nobility; and the opposition to existing types of censorship. Actually, many members of the nobility had themselves accepted these ideas. They gathered in fashionable *salons* frequented also by the intellectuals (the *philosophes*) of the time, and these *salons* became centers for the dissemination of the new concepts.

(2) There were political incentives, the example of the American colonies, and the dissatisfaction with foreign policies and with the military defeats of France at a time when a nationalistic spirit was spreading everywhere. Furthermore, there were the corrupt law courts and the still-existing, though seldom employed *lettres de cachet,* which meant arbitrary arrest at the king's pleasure. The entire system was out of tune with contemporary conditions under enlightened monarchies or parliamentary regimes.

(3) Many had personal grievances against the weakness of an otherwise well-meaning king, the haughtiness, interference, and extravagance of the queen, Marie Antoinette, and the influence of favorites, whose abilities contrasted sadly with those of the leaders of dissatisfied groups.

(4) Most important, however, were the economic motives for dissatisfaction. Although poverty was not exceptionally widespread in France and conditions in France among the lower classes compared rather favorably with those in England and other countries, confidence in the government's ability was lacking. The people had to contend with a steady rise in prices, intermittent food shortages—partly owing to bad harvests in 1788 and 1789—and recurrent periods of unemployment.

Moreover, many among the privileged were determined to preserve the inequalities of the tax system. The land tax, or *taille,* continued to be levied only upon the property of the third estate. The nobles, on the other hand, paid an amount that they themselves regarded as appropriate; the clergy confined itself to a voluntary "gift." The salt tax, or *gabelle,* was imposed upon everyone, but the tax on this indispensable commodity was burdensome primarily to the poor. The *corvée,* a tax in the form of compulsory work for the lords by those peasants who had not yet become free, was levied exclusively on the lower classes. In addition, the landed nobility enjoyed privileges, such as special-milling and hunting rights. Then, there were tithes, and extra tithes *(vingtième),* a wine tax *(trop bû),* and other levies. Nor could the peasants lighten their burdens through purchase of additional land, for this was prohibited.

Outbreak of the Revolution

The foregoing difficulties might have been overcome, had the public treasury not been depleted and had the Parlement not opposed legislation that would have made necessary funds available through taxation of the privileged groups. The credit of the government was soon exhausted. The king appointed as his chief minister Jacques Necker, who was popular but whom he dismissed again in 1789. Eventually, Louis was persuaded to call a meeting of the long-abandoned Estates-General. Elections were held. The people gave their representatives written instructions in so-called *cahiers* enumerating their grievances. In May 1789, the Estates-General assembled. It broke up in June over the question of voting, for the third estate composed of the middle classes and peasants feared that they would always be outvoted by the combined clergy and nobles. Their representatives, many of them young people and among these numerous lawyers, therefore convened on a nearby tennis court, where, under the inspired leadership of the noted orator Mirabeau, an oath was taken not to disband until voting by head was introduced and a constitution for all France was drafted.

The king capitulated. But this political victory by the lower classes did not solve their economic difficulties. Instead, it brought further unemployment and, finally, the first violent uprisings. On July 14, "the Bastille," where innocent political victims of absolutism were assumed to be confined, was stormed by a mob, and although the Bastille held only seven inmates, this event was a foreshadowing of the revolution to come. Unrest spread throughout France. Necker had to be recalled. Some of the nobility hastily fled the country. Ordinary citizens armed themselves and the people adopted a new, revolutionary flag.

The Constitution

In response, a memorable night session of the Estates-General was held on August 4, 1789. The privileged classes divested themselves of most of their prerogatives: serfdom was abolished; equality of taxation was introduced; eligibility for governmental jobs was extended to every qualified citizen irrespective of class or wealth; and all internal customs barriers were abolished. This was followed by a Declaration of the Rights of Man (August 26, 1789) proclaiming equality, liberty, and justice, and guaranteeing property rights to all.

In the face of these events, the king proved himself unequal to his task. He weakly submitted to a mob's demands and moved his court back from Versailles to Paris—"closer to his people." Revolutionaries formed "clubs" (Jacobins, Cordeliers, Feuillants, and others) and enthusiastic leaders (e.g., Marat, Danton, and Robespierre) took over their direction.

Thereupon, the Estates-General took another momentous step. In order to avoid imminent state bankruptcy, it decreed the confiscation of all Church lands. A new currency (the *assignat*), based on land, was issued. In the next year (1790), a constitution was drafted (the abbot Siéyès played a leading role as constitution-maker) establishing a limited monarchy. The country was redivided into eighty-three "departments," each administered by elective officers. Religious freedom was proclaimed. A jury system was introduced.

Voting rights were granted to the taxpaying segment of the population whether nobility or burghers. A representative assembly was given legislative powers and control of finances. It was largely composed of people influenced by the ideas of the enlightened philosophers. Furthermore, a "civil organization of the clergy" was introduced. Monasteries were abolished; clerical offices were to be filled by electoral vote of the communities; and papal power was confined to the right of consecration. The clergy, having lost their lands, were to have their salaries paid by the state and, in exchange, were to take an oath to uphold the constitution.

Repercussions Abroad

The new institutions meant a move toward radicalism. This, combined with the agitation of French *émigrés,* led to repercussions abroad. Foreign monarchs began to fear for their own safety and for the political system on which their authority rested. The situation worsened when Louis XVI was persuaded in 1791 to seek refuge abroad but, together with his entire family, was intercepted at the Belgian border. Strikes were called and bloody new riots occurred. Whereupon, the Austrian emperor decided to come to the aid of his French sister; and other monarchs joined him in organizing an army to invade France.

The Russian empress, Catherine—now old, conservative, and thoroughly afraid of any revolutionary movement—used the opportunity to act upon a scheme of her own. Fearing similar disturbances in anarchical Poland, she proposed and, together with the Prussian king, carried out a second partition of Poland. The Poles had begun to late to undertake overdue internal reforms. Patriots, such as Kosciusko, had begun too late to direct their efforts toward modernization of Polish institutions. Even a reformed Poland was no longer acceptable to its neighbors. The second partition was followed in 1795 by a third one, whereby Russia, Austria, and Prussia abolished the Polish state.

War

Meanwhile, in 1792, revolutionary France had answered the threats of the European powers with a declaration of war. A leftist party, the "Girondists," had taken over the government; it began to confiscate the property of the *émigrés* and to deport any priest who refused to take the prescribed oath in support of the constitution. When Louis opposed these measures, another move toward radicalism—typical of all revolutions in progress—occurred. His palace, the Tuileries, was invaded. The king and his family were subjected to numerous indignities.

Just then, an arrogant and ill-timed manifesto by the commander of the allies leading a victorious army into France contributed to the furor of the revolutionaries. Again, they invaded the palace, massacred the guards, and forced the royal family to seek refuge in the hall of the assembly. The assembly decided to jail the king and arrange for new elections on the basis of an equal, general franchise. Under the pressure of the Jacobins, who formed a more extreme left wing than the Girondists, the new assembly, the "Convention," proclaimed a republic. Meanwhile, at Valmy, the French troops gained their first decisive victory over the foreign invaders. This helped to strengthen the position of the Convention.

Terror

The Convention proceeded promptly to depose the king, introduce a new calendar—dating from the revolution instead of the birth of Christ—and abolish all remaining tax burdens on the peasants. It also brought the king to trial and (in January 1793) had him executed. Thereafter the guillotine worked constantly in a "Reign of Terror." This, in turn, led to a series of revolts in western and southern France against the revolutionary government and to an even more dangerous consequence—an all-European war. Spain, England, and Holland joined Austria and Prussia in an alliance against France.

Revolutionary France met the danger with resolute action. A general draft was ordered. A large army was promptly organized and a Committee of Public Safety was appointed. Composed largely of Jacobins, this Committee soon dominated both in the Convention and in the Girondist government; the latter was forced to resign. Centralizing all power, the Committee then pushed through legislation that actually abolished the very freedoms it advocated. When one of the most radical leaders, Marat, was murdered, Danton and Robespierre continued the revolutionary program. A new constitution was drafted. Laws were passed against speculators and against anyone suspected of disloyalty (Law of Suspects). Social legislation was broadened, though property rights were still respected. To supplant religion, a "Cult of Reason" was introduced, followed by a "Cult of the Supreme Being," which reflected vague deistic concepts.

In 1794, Robespierre seized complete control; he even had Danton arrested and guillotined. Robespierre was a fanatical devotee of Rousseau's utopian teachings, untiring and incorruptible. But, suspicious of everyone, he promoted the "Great Terror" whereby he intended to cleanse the nation and introduce the new age—that of universal brotherhood. He advocated equal rights for all, including women and Jews, and opposed the luxuries and manners of the former privileged classes; he insisted on simplicity in lifestyle.

Reaction

After five years of stirring events, insecurity, and disruption of traditional ties, a point was reached when the reestablishment of security and order seemed to many more desirable than liberty and utopia. A reactionary party emerged that succeeded, in July 1794 (9th of Thermidor), in overthrowing Robespierre's regime and sending him to the guillotine. The powers of the Committee of Public Safety were abolished, restrictive laws revoked, revolutionary clubs closed, and some priests allowed to return. In 1795—a year that brought an exceptionally bad harvest and a sharp depreciation of the paper money, the *assignat*—a new constitution was instituted that provided for a "Directory" of five men, and for two representative houses elected by people of property.

Thus ended the revolution. It had had no socialistic content; indeed, throughout the upheaval, property rights were regarded as inalienable. The small and weak working class, whose belated separate uprising under Babeuf was readily suppressed, gained nothing further for the peasantry. Nor did it bring political liberty, equality, or brotherhood, or solve France's financial problems. But it did end absolutism, feudal privileges, arbitrary arrest, the mercantilist economy, and Church predominance. It brought France glory by formulating the Rights of Man, fighting for them, and setting an example for other nations. It gained for the peasants full possession of their lands and freedom from feudal burdens, and it brought success to the middle class, which through its wealth became the dominating factor in the state.

The Age of Enlightenment ended, as far as Western civilization's political evolution was concerned, with revolutions in America and Europe. In some regions, they failed. In Britain's American colonies, a war of independence brought into being, however, a state with a government that, under a Constitution, attained many of the ideals with regard to freedom, government, and individual rights that the Enlightenment had cherished.

In Europe, revolution in France put an end to the numerous surviving remnants of feudalism. Recently, a French historian wrote: "The revolution is over." What he meant was that now, after two hundred years, the debate over its significance for Western civilization is exhausted. Perhaps the revolution was the most important specific event in European civilization since the Reformation. Its course from mild to radical reform, with accompanying internal and foreign war, and terror, all ending in reaction, has been considered a model for all revolutions.

Many of the hopes for "progress" voiced during the revolution were, as in its American counterpart, realized, even though some of the idealistic aims were lost. Neither the French nor the American revolution gave consideration to economic equality.

Selected Readings

Brinton, Crane. *Anatomy of Revolution* (1952)
Doyle, W. *Origins of the French Revolution* (1981)
Hampson, Norman. *The Life and Opinions of Maximilien Robespierre* (1974)
Hobshawn, E. J. *The Age of Revolution: Europe 1789–1848* (1970)
Lefebvre, Georges. *The French Revolution*, 2 vols. (1962)
Palmer, Robert R. *Age of the Democratic Revolution: A Political History of Europe and America, 1760–1800* (1959–60)
Rice, Arnold, and Krout, John A., et al. *United States History to 1877* (1991)
Robert, J. M. *The French Revolution* (1978)
Spaeth, Harold J., et al. *The Constitution of the United States* (1991)

11

The Napoleonic Era (1795–1815)

1796	Napoleon's Italian campaign
	Haydn, *Emperor Quartet*
1798	Napoleon's Egyptian campaign
	Wordsworth and Coleridge, *Lyrical Ballads*
	Malthus, *Essay on the Principle of Population*
1799	Napoleon becomes First Consul
1803	Purchase of Louisiana Territory by United States of America
1804	Schiller, *Wilhelm Tell*
	Napoleon becomes emperor
1805	Battle of Trafalgar
	Battle of Austerlitz
1806	End of Holy Roman Empire
1807	Reforms in Prussia (vom Stein)
	Fulton's steamship on the Hudson
	Introduction of Continental system
1808	Goethe, *Faust* (first part)
1812	Napoleon's Russian campaign
	War between England and U.S.A.
	Byron, *Childe Harold's Pilgrimage*
1813	Wars of Liberation against Napoleon
1814	Stephenson's steam locomotive built
1815	Battle of Waterloo: Napoleon exiled to St. Helena
	Congress of Vienna concluded; Holy Alliance founded

*A*s *often happens with revolutions, the French Revolution ended in dictatorship. A "gilded youth," which sought to "enjoy" life after the great issues demanding unselfish devotion had been settled, engaged in numerous follies in dress, manners, and behavior, and neglected the tasks that the newly gained liberty necessitated. But the man to direct France's destiny for the next two decades was already on hand: Napoleon Bonaparte (1769–1821). It was he who gave his name to the period from 1795 to 1815, from the end of the revolution until the end of the great international wars produced in its aftermath.*

The name reflects the predominantly political preoccupations of past historians but does not do justice to a period that belonged, culturally, among the greatest in Western civilization. And while it was France that excelled in the sciences, it was Germany (which played the least important and least successful political role) that contributed most to the greatness of the age in other cultural areas. Three names suffice to indicate achievements in that country: Kant, Goethe, and Beethoven.

POLITICAL STRUGGLES IN EUROPE

The counterrevolutionaries of 1795 were disappointed in their hopes, which the end of the revolution had aroused. Terror was ended, internal order was restored, and a measure of security was again provided for the average citizen. The fears of France's neighbors were alleviated. But the revolutionary and nationalistic elements in France were not satisfied with the results; they helped to pave the way for the rise of Napoleon. Obsessed with dictatorial ambitions, he gave Europe two decades of even more dangerous and destructive upheavals.

Rise of Napoleon

Napoleon, Corsican by birth, had studied military science in France and had been a member of Robespierre's party. He had excelled as a general of artillery in the war against the English. His exceptional ability, friendly relations with one of the members of the Directory, and advantageous marriage with an influential widow, Josephine Beauharnais, brought this capable young general the command of an army.

At his own suggestion, he was sent into Italy to terminate the war by attacking the Austrian possessions there. Although Prussia and Spain had signed a peace treaty at Basel in 1795, renouncing the entire left bank of the Rhine in favor of France, and although Holland had been defeated and had become a "Batavian Republic" under a French protectorate, Austria and

England had continued the war. The Italian campaign, conducted brilliantly by Napoleon, brought a string of victories and military glory to France. It made plunder available to fill France's empty treasury; it spread revolutionary ideas abroad. It ended not only with Austria's withdrawal from the war, but also with France's acquisition of extensive territory gained in the Peace of Campoformio (1797).

Having defeated Austria, Napoleon prepared to attack England. He contemplated an assault across the Channel, but instead chose to break England's "lifeline" to India through the conquest of Egypt. Napoleon conducted another brilliant campaign, winning a great victory at the Pyramids. But, after a British sea victory at Aboukir, he was unable to reach his objective because the French lost control of the Mediterranean supply lines. He was fortunate to escape with his life. He fled to Paris, leaving his army to perish in Egypt.

The Consulate (1799–1804)

Meanwhile, the Directory had squandered the spoils of the Italian campaign and had forfeited the confidence of the nation. Its foreign policy had by 1799 provoked a new anti-French coalition, this time joined by Russia. Russian and Austrian troops, under the command of Suvorov, had driven the French out of most of the Po Valley. At home, inflation raged, corruption made orderly government impossible, and new revolts staged chiefly by reactionary forces threatened. Napoleon regarded this as the opportune moment to carry out his own ambitious plans. In October 1799, he overthrew the government and dictated a new constitution, which provided for a consulate in which he himself took first place as the executive power. He saw to it that his action was confirmed by a plebiscite.

Napoleon's next step was to reconquer Austrian Italy. After another brilliant victory, at Marengo, and after defeating the Austrians again at Hohenlinden, he induced the latter to make peace at Lunéville (1801). He then turned his attention to England and successfully pressed the British to sign a peace treaty (at Amiens, 1802), which restored to France all colonies seized by England since the beginning of the war.

Napoleon then set to work on internal reforms, initiating a dictatorial but highly beneficial regime. The revolutionary era was declared at an end. The normal calendar was reinstated. A concordat was concluded with the pope. Although it did not return Church lands, it restored the prestige of Catholicism; dissatisfied priests, peasants, and burghers were pacified. Religious tolerance was extended to Jews. Government finances were systematized, a central bank was founded, and a new currency (the franc, backed by a sound tax system) was introduced.

Agriculture was promoted. The raising of new crops, such as sugar beets, was encouraged in order to make Europe independent of imports from British colonies. Roads, tunnels, harbors, and canals were built. The school system was expanded, higher education supported, and the French Academy reorganized. But censorship was strict and the propaganda apparatus worked to benefit Napoleon personally. By his appointments to local administrative posts and by dispensing honors, he secured supporters and faithful service to himself. Highly beneficial legal reforms were effected by means of the *Code Napoléon*. Based on Roman law, it embodied many of the liberal, equalitarian, and humanitarian concepts for which the revolution had been fought. It became a model for the Western world. It provided for equality before the law and confirmed the inviolability of property rights. But it deprived women of the gains secured by them during the revolution.

Napoleon's European Conquests

Personal ambitions and the very nature of his regime impelled Napoleon, however, to initiate dangerous foreign enterprises. Aspiring to become a "new Charlemagne," he had himself crowned emperor in 1804, and he then engaged in further wars. In 1805, he defeated Austria and Russia in his most famous victory, at Austerlitz, gained through tactics based on the great mobility of his forces. In 1806, he destroyed the Prussian army and conquered nearly all of Prussia. Numerous smaller German states were abolished; many were transferred to French jurisdiction. The Holy Roman Empire, which had endured nearly a millennium, declared itself dissolved and the Hapsburgs kept only the emperorship of Austria and their *Hausmacht*.

Another attack on England was contemplated, but invasion plans were abandoned after the French naval forces had been destroyed (in 1805) by Nelson's fleet at the Battle of Trafalgar. Nevertheless, Napoleon set up a barrier against England by prohibiting importation of British goods on the Continent, thus establishing the "Continental system." Moreover, his troops invaded and occupied most of Spain and Portugal, and even ventured to attack the papal states. Russia, defeated in East Prussia when coming to the aid of the Prussians, was forced to make peace and conclude an alliance with France (Tilsit, 1807). Napoleon then arranged a spectacular congress at Erfurt attended by kings, princes, and a host of famous people. It marked the apex of Napoleon's career.

Decline of Napoleon's Empire

Napoleon's conquests created a problem of overexpansion; he lacked the resources needed in order to protect and administer his acquisitions. The halfhearted, mutually distrustful alliance with Russia, providing for a division of European hegemony between the two partners, gave little assurance of safety.

Furthermore, Napoleon had to contend with serious new difficulties. His treatment of the papacy, culminating in the annexation of the papal states (1808) and the arrest of the pope, had alienated the Catholics and their sympathizers. Censorship and arbitrary restrictions had infuriated the liberals. The military campaigns had exhausted French manpower and had intensified the popular discontent within France. Most ominous was Napoleon's failure to subdue Spain which, with English help, resisted the invader. The revolutionary ideal of liberty seemed lost. A new nobility had supplanted the old. People were weary of war, but peace did not come.

Moreover, Napoleon was aging rapidly. His intellectual power and military genius seemed to be declining at the same time that his enemies were learning to overcome his strategy. His megalomania—reinforcing his habitual distrust of others and his steadfast loyalty to his family—had caused him to place his brothers and sisters on various European thrones. Their lack of capacity soon showed this move to have been ill-advised. Under their rule, the vast array of satellite states did not form a reliable foundation for the empire.

Nationalistic fervor now aided the cause of his opponents. In Spain, continued guerrilla warfare brought a constant drain on French strength. England gave no indications of wanting to make peace. Revolts occurred in Holland, Switzerland, Italy, and the Tyrol. Since the Continental system could not be enforced along all the coasts of Europe (enforcement would have been contrary to the interests of the various nations), it actually worked to the advantage of England rather than of France. Smuggling increased, bringing with it more discontent and greater disregard of law and order. In 1809, Austria risked a new war against France. Though defeated again and forced to allow the emperor's daughter to marry Napoleon after his divorce from Josephine, the Hapsburgs demonstrated the possibility of continued resistance. Finally, a rising anti-Bonapartist tide arose in Prussia, where, owing to statesmen such as vom Stein and Hardenberg, and General Scharnhorst, thoroughgoing reforms were undertaken. Planning a war of liberation, the Prussians adopted many practices from the French Revolution. They modernized and centralized the administrative system, abolished old-fashioned guilds, and eradicated serfdom. They extended the scope of religious freedom, and they founded new schools and universities. While the government adopted many of the liberal concepts of the Napoleonic law code, poets and educators stirred up a widespread feeling of national pride.

Russian Campaign (1812)

To meet the danger, Napoleon should have strengthened his alliance with Russia. Instead, he antagonized it by insisting on the enforcement of the Continental system. Finally, he decided to break up the alliance. Aware of his aggressive intentions, Russia brought an end to two wars in which it was engaged: one with Sweden over the possession of Finland, and another with Turkey over territory along the Black Sea coast.

In June 1812, Napoleon ordered a French invasion of Russia. The dramatic war (described in Tolstoy's *War and Peace*) began. The Russians were forced to retreat; after a terrible, but indecisive battle near Borodino,

Napoleon entered Moscow. But by then, Russia had collected its strength, whereas Napoleon had lost half his army. Beleaguered in the capital city, where shortly after his entry a terrible fire deprived his troops of supplies and shelter, and with winter approaching, Napoleon in vain tendered peace offers to the tsar. A Russian army under Kutuzov cut off his escape to southern Russia, where he had planned to spend the cold season, and the invaders were forced to retreat. This retreat became, owing to the severe weather, the disorganization of the French, and the Russian attacks, one of the worst military disasters in history.

Wars of Liberation

Under Prussian leadership, a widespread revolt against the French began almost as soon as the remnants of Napoleon's army reached German soil. Many of the conscripted foreign troops deserted. After numerous defeats and victories, an alliance of Prussian, Austrian, Russian, and Swedish troops defeated Napoleon decisively in the Battle of Leipzig (October 1813). The French troops were forced to flee back to France.

In the meantime, the combined forces of England, Holland, and Spain had attacked from north and south. In March 1814, an allied army marched triumphantly into Paris. Napoleon abdicated and upon the advice of the wily minister Talleyrand—a man who had already served the Catholic Church, then the revolutionary regime, then the Directorate, then Napoleon, and now his enemies—the victors reinstated the Bourbons. Louis XVI's brother, Louis XVIII, was called back from exile in England; he began to rule as a constitutional monarch under a "Charter." A "Peace of Paris" reestablished France's borders as they had existed in 1792.

Waterloo (1815)

A reorganization of the European political framework was undertaken in a congress, convened in Vienna. Prince Metternich, first minister of Austria, presided; Alexander I of Russia, the Duke of Wellington from England, and Hardenberg of Prussia were the chief figures. Almost all the nations of Europe participated in the splendid meetings. Eventually even Talleyrand, representing the new Bourbon France, was admitted.

Relations among the allies were tense. Austria and England wanted to reduce Russia's commanding power and prestige, whereas Prussia sought the backing of Russia for its numerous territorial wishes. France attempted to divide the victors by promoting the demands of various small nations.

Advised of these dissensions, Napoleon returned to France from exile on the island of Elba. But despite his enthusiastic reception in many places, his arrival was premature. Faced with this renewed threat, the allies composed their differences. At Waterloo (1815), Anglo-Prussian forces under Wellington and Blücher decisively defeated the hastily raised army of Napoleon. Again compelled to abdicate, he was now sent to the lonely, arid island of St. Helena, where he died in 1821.

Congress of Vienna (1815)

The Congress of Vienna concluded its proceedings in June 1815. With statesmanlike wisdom, the diplomats did not crush defeated France, but reestablished it within the borders it had possessed in 1790. Colonial issues had already been resolved by the two peace treaties in Paris (1814 and 1815). They had given England all it had demanded by way of colonies, including the island of Malta, and had made it heir to the profitable French slave trade. Germany was reconstituted as a loose federation of thirty-eight states with an Austrian as president. Austria itself regained and extended its Italian holdings. Prussia annexed large areas in central Germany. Russia seized most of Poland (which was made a kingdom under the tsar) and obtained recognition of its domination over Finland. Sweden, in exchange for Finland, took over Norway, which Denmark, Napoleon's longtime ally, had to relinquish. Holland and Belgium were united into one new state. In general, the congress aimed to restore their old domains to the legitimate rulers of the period before the wars or to give them due compensation. A belt of sufficiently powerful nations was drawn around France to deter it from future aggression.

National aspirations, which had been strengthened by the revolutionary spirit, were ignored in favor of an effective balance of power in Europe. At the insistence of Alexander I, the treaties were supplemented by a "Holy Alliance," an international organization intended to guarantee cooperation among the rulers and benevolent treatment of their subjects. This alliance was designed to safeguard both the international arrangements made at Vienna and the existing internal status of the various countries.

POLITICAL DEVELOPMENTS IN THE AMERICAS

Significantly, before the Napoleonic era had ended, America had begun to play an important part in Western affairs. Napoleon's wars did not involve the Western Hemisphere in the same way as the Seven Years' War had. Yet, the French revolutionary spirit and Napoleon's conquests had a radical effect on South and Central America. The conquest of Spain and Portugal by Napoleon removed the ruling dynasties, forcing the American colonies to search for a new governmental authority. The Napoleonic wars had an indirect effect in the United States, too, though less in terms of spreading the principles embodied in the Rights of Man, which were already adopted by the United States, than insofar as they forced the British to concentrate their attention upon Europe. They thus gave the United States an opportunity to build the nation without interference from England.

North America

At the time the French Revolution broke out, Washington had just become president of the United States. During his administrations, steps were undertaken to perfect the system devised by the Constitution. These steps were of considerable importance for all of Western civilization because they dealt with the issue of federalism versus a highly centralized union, state, or empire.

In the United States, a Bill of Rights was introduced into the Constitution by amendment, and a Supreme Court and a national bank were created; these developments involved intense controversies over the desirability of interpreting the Constitution broadly or of adhering to it strictly. The division of opinion divided the country, resulting in the formation of political parties. An amendment to the Constitution recognized the legal status of parties. Despite bitterness and strife under Washington's successors, Adams (elected 1796) and Jefferson (elected 1800), the struggle proved advantageous insofar as the issue of the interpretation of the Constitution was decided. Those who advocated the broader view prevailed, and a tradition of a legal opposition was established. Continued criticism led to progressive improvements.

In its external policy, the United States avoided European entanglements, but it could not escape them entirely. In 1803, the United States of America accepted Napoleon's offer to sell French Louisiana. It thereby not only protected itself against Spain, but also enlarged its territory enormously. It defended its right to unimpeded overseas trade. When forced to it by English blockades and embargo acts, the U.S.A. reasserted its position by even entering into a new war against Britain.

After victories and defeats (the English burned the newly built capital of Washington), a treaty was signed at Ghent in 1814. The peace treaty gave little to either side, but it reaffirmed America's independent statehood. Henceforth, the United States had an opportunity to develop its own resources further and turn its attention to expansion westward. It continued its march across the North American continent and attracted vast numbers of immigrants from European countries in search of economic advancement. It entered a period of "good feeling."

South America

In South America, the independence movement received new impetus when Napoleon's occupation of Spain and Portugal interrupted their exercise of legal authority over their American colonies. Revolts under inspiring leaders, such as Bolívar, Miranda, Morelos, and San Martín, occurred. By 1811, Venezuela and Paraguay had achieved independence. Mexico followed in 1814, the La Plata region in 1816, Chile in 1818, and Peru in 1821. Subsequent attempts by the Spanish and Portuguese kings to regain their authority failed, but so did all efforts of the South American nations to form a federation. The individual nations, however, were soon able to influence, first, the economic life and, later, the cultural and political life, of the Western world. Brazil, which also separated from its parent country, played a special role. Brazil alone did not become a republic, but in 1822 made Pedro, the son of the last Portuguese regent, an emperor.

CULTURAL TRENDS

While Napoleon's wars left hatred, destruction, and death in their wake, in other respects they had a permanent and beneficial influence on the progress of civilization. They engendered, especially among France's adversaries, enthusiasm, devotion, and idealism; they also disseminated many of the French *philosophes'* ideas and encouraged people abroad to build institutions promoting concepts of liberty and equality. The introduction of the Napoleonic Code in many parts of the Western world is but one example of this fact. The impact of the entire movement of revolution and war was so much deeper since it came at a time when the old political and social order was crumbling and the bourgeoisie, with its economic and progressive attitudes, gained predominance. People's minds were open to new and different ideas concerning politics, society, art, and science.

Advancements in Pure Science   During the forty years from 1775 to 1815, logical thought and the investigation of nature added many fundamental scientific insights to those gained earlier. These were embodied in a wealth of scholarly treatises of revolutionary character.

CHEMISTRY

In chemistry, the pioneer work of Priestley and Cavendish (d. 1810; studies of hydrogen, ca. 1766) was continued by these same men and by others—by Gay-Lussac, Avogadro, and most notably by Lavoisier (guillotined 1794). Lavoisier carried on the investigation of oxygen and hydrogen, established the fact that matter may alter its "state" but not its "quantity," studied the connection between oxidation and respiration, and placed chemical nomenclature on a scientific basis. He enunciated the principle of the conservation of mass.

OTHER SCIENCES

In biology, the works of the Swiss von Haller and the Frenchman Lamarck (d. 1829) were outstanding. In astronomy, Kant, Herschel (d. 1822), and Laplace (d. 1827) provided new insights into the structure of the cosmos. Laplace's conception of the origin of the planets opened new vistas for the study of the universe. In geology, Saussure (d. 1799) excelled, investigating rivers, mountains, and glaciers. In mathematics, besides Laplace—famous for his development of the calculus—Lagrange (d. 1813) was a leading figure. His special contribution lay in his investigation of geometrical problems.

MEDICINE AND ENGINEERING

In medicine, therapeutic studies were greatly advanced, tissue physiology was investigated, and vaccination was introduced by Jenner (1796). The danger of scurvy was reduced after experience with fresh fruits and vegetables had been gained during Captain Cook's trip around the world. In electricity, Galvani's discovery of animal electricity led to Volta's work (1799) on electrical currents and on the storing of electricity in batteries.

ARCHAEOLOGY AND HISTORY

In archaeology and history, a new stage was entered with Winckelmann's discoveries and Herder's philosophy of the history of mankind. As for philology, Napoleon's Egyptian campaign had brought the discovery of the so-called "Rosetta stone," which made possible the deciphering of hieroglyphs.

Advancements in Technology

Along with the advance of theoretical knowledge came progress in technology. In 1807, a successful steamship was operated in America. In 1814, Stephenson's locomotive was constructed in England. Balloons to carry human beings aloft were designed and used. Numerous improvements were introduced in two basic industries: mining and textiles. The use of interchangeable machine parts spread and made possible cheaper, more efficient production. Agricultural yields rose with growing understanding of nature and with the use of machinery. The production of iron and steel gained ever-increasing importance.

Britain took the lead in technological advancement. Its colonial empire, greatly expanded by new territories in South Africa and India, not only made industries possible, but also necessitated their expansion and modernization. This growth of industrial capacity enabled Britain to export goods to independent states as well as its possessions. Both European and American nations came to depend upon British machinery.

The English working population endured numerous adverse consequences of technical advances, suffering grievously through unemployment and low wages. The government was slow to extend protection to the workers. The "classical" economists of the age, in line with Adam Smith's laissez-faire policies, believed that, through free play of economic forces, adjustments would come by themselves; and they hoped with Jeremy Bentham (d. 1832) who adhered to "Utilitarianism," with its accent on practical aims, that the "greatest good for the greatest number" would eventually result.

Religious Liberalism and Mysticism

The utilitarian spirit, prevailing in economic thoughts and mechanistic trends, generated a reaction that was strengthened by the miseries accompanying revolution, war, and industrialization. This reaction expressed itself in a religious revival that took two different directions. On the one hand, it led to a liberal interpretation of Christian doctrine, with emphasis on love for all and on undogmatic tolerance. (Schleiermacher [d. 1834] in Berlin was to lead this movement toward religious liberalism.) On the other hand, a revival of mysticism took place, an inner rejection of the evils of the world and its self-assured knowledge. With this revival came a search for direct communion with God. Such feelings were expressed by numerous groups; typical was the Russian Baroness Krüdener, who sponsored a revivalist movement; her influence helped bring about the formation of the Holy Alliance by Alexander I. Simultaneously, there was a renaissance within traditional churches. In their search for guidance away from the materialistic path on which scientific knowledge seemed to lead, many people turned, especially, to Catholicism.

Philosophy

Philosophy was another field upon which the growing scientific and utilitarian spirit continued to leave a deep impression. Toward the end of the eighteenth century, belief in the unlimited possibilities of human understanding was badly shaken; so also was belief in the perfectibility of the human race. Philosophers came to acknowledge that there are limits to human knowledge, that scientific laws are inadequate to explain our ethical and spiritual nature.

KANT

It was the achievement of Kant (d. 1804; *Critique of Pure Reason*), to propose a philosophical system that embraced both an understanding of physical science and a recognition of the human moral instinct. Kant held that physical science gives a dependable knowledge of nature and its workings, but that moral law—an inner voice of duty—gives the human race a unique role in the material universe. This moral law, like that of nature, touches our rational nature, leads us to a sense of fellowship with all others. "Freedom," he insisted, is a condition necessary for the full development of human rationality and ethical behavior.

At least three great compatriots of Kant built on similar foundations: Fichte (d. 1814), Schelling (d. 1854), and Hegel (d. 1831). Like Kant, all three were heirs of the Enlightenment; all emphasized the need for freedom. Hegel postulated freedom as the ultimate aim of history, in the pursuit of which God's will expresses itself.

Music

The powerful forces of rational investigation did not dim the love of beauty and the spirit of imagination, fantasy, and vision that mark so many of the greatest achievements in art. Especially in music, some of the most beautiful works in world history were created. Germany continued, after the death of Bach, to be the center of European musical life. The great musicians of the time overcame the conventions, routine, artificiality, and constraints that the taste of the aristocrats who sponsored many of the composers imposed. For these patrons, music, to the extent to which it was not Church music, was often no more than an ornament at their social gatherings—and mere virtuosity was much applauded. But though abandoning to a certain extent the contrapuntal style of Bach, the good composers continued his work and gave expression to the deepest emotions and human feelings. Building on precedents that can be traced through the earlier, baroque period, as well, they devoted themselves to creating masterpieces for the piano (which thus gained new importance) and to producing symphonies and string quartets that stirred a new generation and yet would retain their appeal for all future ages. Haydn (d. 1809) was not only one of the most famous composers (*Creation, Te Deum*), but also a gifted teacher. He and his somewhat older contemporary, Gluck (d. 1787; *Alceste, Iphigénie en Tauride*), were in fact the most outstanding teachers since Bach and Handel. Gluck emphasized that "music is not just an art that pleases the ear, but one of the greatest means to touch the heart and arouse passion." The era's musical apex was reached with Mozart and Beethoven and their sonatas, symphonies, quartets and quintets and requiem masses—and their operas: Mozart's (d. 1791) *Don Giovanni, Magic Flute,* and *Marriage of Figaro,* and Beethoven's (d. 1827) *Fidelio.*

Thus, the musical world entered its own "Classical Age." Verbal descriptions cannot convey a sense of the inspired works of these great composers or even those of the many lesser ones. With the death of Beethoven, the last of the group, the Classical Age came to an end. In his later years, indeed, Beethoven himself introduced a new period—that of Romanticism.

Painting, Architecture, and Sculpture

Far less meaningful for future generations were the works in the fine arts created during the Revolutionary and Napoleonic periods. Perhaps there was an absence of artists of true genius, or perhaps painting, architecture, and sculpture were not so well suited to express the spirit of the age; in any case, little of great renown was brought forth in these areas. The Frenchman David (d. 1825) is practically the only painter worth mentioning—aside from the strange and very modern genius of the Spaniard Goya (d. 1828). Goya's scenes of the Spanish war against France endure as a realistic and gripping monument to the horrors of a time that prided itself on its idealism.

Nor was any high achievement shown in architecture and sculpture; these arts were rather influenced by neoclassicism, i.e., an imitation of classical models. With its simple, restrained lines and its clarity and dignity of style, neoclassicism was received as a welcome relief from baroque and rococo, even if its design lacked original, creative thought.

Literature

In contrast to the fine arts, literature provided an adequate and influential means of expression for the age. It came to a particularly high development in Germany. While Germany was politically and industrially backward, it produced in the late eighteenth and early nineteenth centuries some of the greatest writers of the modern age in literature—to complement its leaders in music and philosophy. The period from 1760 to 1800 is regarded as Germany's "Classical Age of Literature," which then was followed by Germany's "Romantic Age."

CLASSICISM

The two great figures in Germany's Classical Age, following Lessing, were Goethe (1749–1832) and Schiller (1759–1805). They expressed in classical form eternal human longings for freedom and self-expression. Their works (Goethe's lyrics, *Sorrows of Werther, Goetz, Wilhelm Meister,* and *Faust* and Schiller's ballads, *The Robbers, Wallenstein,* and *Wilhelm Tell*) have been translated into all civilized languages and have remained a source of inspiration ever since.

ROMANTICISM

Goethe and Schiller were followed by a long line of Romantic poets. "Romanticism" represents one aspect of the reaction against the artificiality and rationalism of earlier ages. The word is a much abused term for one of the most meaningful developments in Western culture. Although Romanticism's sentimentality, vagueness, and overenthusiasm were to antagonize later generations, its love of nature and of human beings in their noble aspirations, its search for inwardness, its sensitivity to beauty, and its youthful ardor and imagination were to remain ever-inspiring. It placed the accent of life on the worth of the individual.

The English Romantic movement was highlighted by the poems of Wordsworth, Coleridge, Byron, Shelley, and Keats. Of these English poets, Byron was probably the most widely read, even in Russia. His reputation was enhanced by his devotion to the cause of Greek liberty and by his early death.

German Romanticism inherited artistic restraint and clarity of expression from the preceding Classical Age. Among its most famous representatives were Kleist, Eichendorff, Mörike, who wrote beautiful lyrics and short stories, and E. T. A. Hoffmann, famous for his tales. Italy, France, and Russia, too, had their periods of Romanticism, the Frenchman Chateaubriand being regarded as one of the founders of the Romantic movement.

Everywhere, the ideal of freedom was extolled; imagination and sentiment, sometimes pervaded by mystic beliefs, fired poetic fantasy. The Romantic writers found a special source to draw upon, little considered in the past, in the stories and folk tales that had lived on in the oral traditions of the various nations and to which Herder, in particular, had drawn attention—calling to mind the long-buried treasures of the Slavic world. Folklore thus became one of the chief fountains of inspiration, not only for poets, but also for philologists, historians, social critics, and educators. Similarly, the Roman Catholic world of the Middle Ages captivated the emotions of many and in turn affected the religious trends of the age.

CULTURAL CROSSROADS: GOETHE'S FAUST

At this turning point in the history of modern times—a point when Western civilization appeared to stand on the threshold of change toward new horizons—stands Goethe's majestic two-part dramatic poem, *Faust*. Just as Dante's *Divina Commedia* came at the highest point of the Middle Ages and on the eve of the Renaissance, Goethe's *Faust* was written at a time of cultural transition. Goethe was a man of action as well as of thought, a scientist and philosopher, a statesman and prime minister, an artist and a poet. In *Faust*, he sums up the spirit of the Modern Age and expresses its aspirations. The protagonist, Faust does not adhere to formulated human or divine creed, but is an eternal seeker of truth. Disappointed by years of study, including the black art of magic, Faust makes a compact with Mephistopheles that stipulates that he must surrender his soul to the devil if ever he becomes satisfied—if ever he becomes ready to confess that he has achieved what he has been striving after. Mephistopheles tries Faust with pleasures, carnal love, wealth, classical perfection, and worldly power. But not until Faust is old and blind does he discern his goal: creative work, the winning of new life for a new and free people. This goal, of course, will never really be attained; it remains an ideal for which to strive. Thus in *Faust* is summarized the spirit of the modern world—eternally dissatisfied, eternally seeking, eternally striving, and through creative endeavor eternally aspiring toward new horizons.

*T*he Napoleonic Era was one of incessant warfare. Having risen through military exploits to a virtual dictatorship as emperor of the French, Napoleon made an attempt at dominating all of Europe. In the process, the European state system was altered and many of the ideas of the French Revolution gained wide acceptance. But Napoleon's attempt at domination failed when his invasion of Russia ended in disaster. He was ultimately banished to a small Atlantic island, where he died.

The American countries stayed out of the European wars, and ultimately benefited from them. In South America, the colonies seized the opportunity to begin wars of independence. In North America, the newly independent United States completed its liberation from Britain. It also began to build its own republican institutions, many of which were in harmony with the ideals of the French Revolution.

Some of the greatest accomplishments of the Napoleonic Era took place in cultural fields such as science, mathematics, archaeology, philosophy, music, and literature.

Selected Readings

Ashton, Thomas. *The Industrial Revolution, 1760–1830* (1952)

Bernal, J. D. *Science in History* (1954)

Dukes, Paul. *A History of Europe, 1648–1948* (1985)

Gershoy, Leo. *The French Revolution and Napoleon* (1964)

Grout, Donald J., et al. *A History of Western Music* (1988)

Herold, J. C. *The Age of Napoleon* (1963)

Lefebvre, Georges. *Napoleon.* 2 vols. (1935)

Rice, Arnold, Krout, John A., Harris, C.M. *United States History to 1877* (1991)

12

Nationalism, Liberalism, Industrialism (1815–1830)

1818	Chile and La Plata region declare independence from Spain
	Congress of Aachen
1819	Carlsbad decrees
	Bolívar founds Republic of Gran Coloumbia
	Scott, *Ivanhoe*
1820	Revolutions in Italy: Congress of Troppau
	Missouri Compromise
1821	Wcbcr, *Freischütz*
1822	Congress of Verona
	Independence of Brazil
1823	Monroe Doctrine
1824	Beethoven, *Ninth Symphony*
	Hegel, lectures on *Philosophy of History*
1825	Robert Owen's establishment of New Harmony, Indiana
	Dekabrist revolt in Russia
1827	Battle of Navarino
	Heine, *Book of Songs*
	Schubert, *Trout Quintet*
1829	Peace of Adrianople
	Catholic Emancipation Act in England
1830	Greek independence declared
	France seizes Algeria
	July Revolution in France

1830   Pushkin, *Eugene Onegin*

Victor Hugo, *Hernani*

*W*ars may not alter the course of events, but often tend to slow or accelerate changes already in progress. Despite the reactionary tenor of the Congress of Vienna, the Napoleonic Wars accelerated certain Western trends. For centuries, steady advances had been made toward the formation of national states. Now, the process was speeded up. The "Age of Nationalism" was at hand, and with it an age of "Liberalism" and "Industrialism."

Nationalism had been gradually developing within Western civilization since the end of the Middle Ages. An otherworldly orientation and the concept of an all-controlling Church had been giving way to wider, worldly interests. Gradually, the ideal of a united Christendom had become subordinated to the particular needs and ambitions of individual nations. Nationalism was based on the conviction that peoples with a common language, history, tradition, and attitude toward life should be united into single independent states. To such a state, all members should show their supreme loyalty.

Liberalism, which was usually coupled with nineteenth-century nationalism, was not only reflected in an attitude toward life but in a political and economic program as well. It aspired to guarantee the personal and political freedom of individuals and protect their human rights. It envisioned equal justice for all, a constitutional government, and the free development of all members of society according to their natural gifts and education, regardless of birth. Its main creed had been embodied in the "Rights of Man" of the French Revolution.

Industrialism was a correlative of liberal thought. The right to private property was one of liberalism's chief tenets. Therefore, liberalism favored the growth of capitalism. Capitalism, in turn, provided for the economic exploitation of the scientific discoveries of the past; it made possible the new production methods that eventually came to characterize all Western civilization. The machine replaced the work of the craftsman. An "Age of Industrialism" led to fundamental sociological changes, encompassing moral as well as material, and possibly even biological, aspects of Western civilization.

Nationalism, liberalism, and industrialism were viewed with disfavor by conservative groups of the populations: the royalty, many among the clergy, and the landed aristocracy. National aspirations, liberal views, and industrial production methods were, however, promoted by a young generation—heirs to the Enlightenment, who believed in "progress." They comprised idealists from many camps, especially professors and students, men and women, professionals and businessmen who had steadily gained in economic weight and intellectual leadership without gaining proportionately in political influence

PERIOD OF CONGRESSES (1818–1823)

The leading statesmen of 1815 were mainly conservatives. Having rearranged the political world at Vienna, they now sought the preservation of their product. Afraid of further change, they had devised at Vienna a system of international consultation that was to be used whenever a challenge arose.

Congress of Aachen (1818)

The first opportunity to apply this system arose when France asked to be relieved of various burdens put upon it after its defeat in the Napoleonic Wars. This issue was successfully resolved because some of the victorious nations desired an early restitution of French power to balance that of Russia. The statesmen met in a congress at Aachen (Aix-la-Chapelle) and agreed to end the occupation of France and to reduce its war indemnity. They refused, however, to settle other issues ardently advocated by the liberal bourgeoisie, such as the abolition of the slave trade and the widening of international cooperation. Incidentally, this congress was notable for the fact that it was under the influence of "bourgeois" international financiers among whom the Rothschild banking family was prominent. The assertion of their economic interests affected the political decisions of Austrian, English, and other representatives.

Congress of Carlsbad (1819)

The following year witnessed a second occasion for international consultation. Liberal agitation had increased, especially in Germany, where university students demanded constitutional government and longed for a united nation. In order to prevent the spread of such ideas, which would have undermined the domination of Austria, Metternich called a congress at Carlsbad. Suppressive measures were taken. Censorship of newspapers and books was established in Germany, and restrictions were imposed upon universities.

Congress of Troppau-Laibach (1820–1821)

Repression could not stop the growth of national and liberal sentiments. They showed themselves everywhere—in Italy, Spain, Portugal, Greece, and Latin America. Particularly threatening to the existing system were rebellious outbreaks in Austria's Italian provinces. A new congress was held in Troppau, Austria, and later continued in Laibach. Metternich succeeded in winning Tsar Alexander's support; under the banner of the "sacredness and inviolability of treaties," the two insisted on strict maintenance of the status quo.

But, in the meantime, divergencies of opinion and interests, both among nations and within each nation, had increased. Britain in particular saw its advantage in a relaxation of the Viennese system. It refused to cooperate in

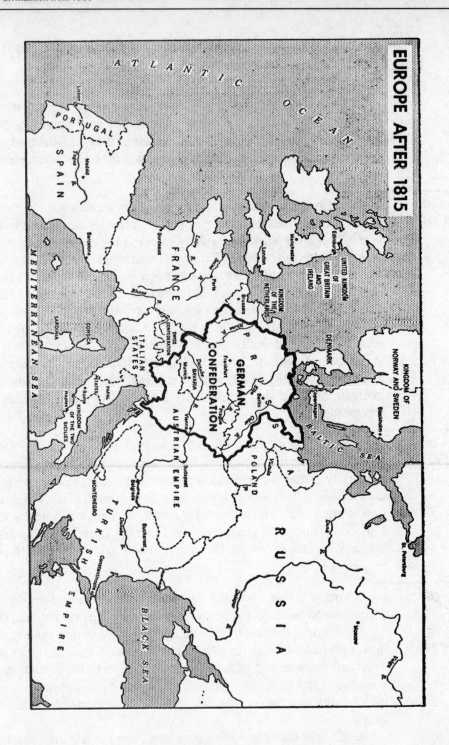

EUROPE AFTER 1815

the planned military action. In consequence, it had to be undertaken by Austria alone. A second issue jeopardizing the peace settlements, the Greek struggle for independence from the Moslem Turks did not lead to better cooperation. (Condemned in principle, Grecian independence nevertheless found support from both Russia and England, who were eager to reduce Turkish power.) Similarly, accord was not reached in matters regarding overseas revolts in Latin America.

Congress of Verona (1822)

The next and last congress was held at Verona; it concerned the national movements in Greece, Spain, and Latin America. The Greek issue led to the same dissensions as those of the previous year, and no international action was taken.

SPAIN

As to Spain, the old monarchy, which had been reestablished after the war, had been overthrown in a bitter rebellion; the liberal constitution of 1812 had been reintroduced. Fearful for its own political system, France, which had been readmitted to the council of nations, protested and demanded armed intervention. Again, England refused to participate in a military venture. France was left to act alone. It proceeded to subdue the Spanish forces and to restore the reactionary government of the king.

LATIN AMERICA

With regard to Latin America, Britain showed itself at still greater odds with the Continental powers. It saw an important prospective market in autonomous Latin American republics and wished to prevent the interference of other European powers. It therefore addressed itself to the United States. But the United States issued independently, in 1823, the "Monroe Doctrine." Thereby all attempts by the Congress of Verona to arrange matters in Spain's former colonies and to forestall the extension of the liberal-national revolt there were frustrated. European collaboration came to an end.

Results

The Holy Alliance and the congresses constituted an attempt at international organization and cooperation in line with objectives in large part generated by all-encompassing wars. The attempts of 1815 to 1823 came to naught; some of the victors used the new organization to prevent change. Perhaps it is correct to state that the congresses were "an offense to the moral conscience of Europe" (Robert Palmer). However, England's foreign minister, George Canning, had already rejected the concepts of morality as an unfit guide for national policies, even if, as he cynically added, "they justly immortalize the hero." National self-interest was extolled everywhere. A measure of international anarchy came to prevail that had been unknown to past centuries, during which it had been prevented by common dynastic principles, interests and connections.

REACTION VERSUS LIBERALISM (1815–1830)

Once the unrest of the postwar period had been calmed, reaction (or at least conservatism) triumphed in most parts of Europe. Not only in Russia, but also in Austria, Prussia, England, and Spain, the governments generally suppressed movements for an extension of civil rights and freedoms. France, for a time, followed a more moderate path, but eventually also reverted to reactionary views. The United States alone among the Western countries continued to build upon the foundation of liberal principles.

Yet, liberalism continued to gain ground among the educated classes in Europe. New disturbances affected the internal political conditions in the various European countries and upset the international order, which was now under the firm control of conservative statesmen. Within little more than a decade, liberal aspirations once again led to revolution.

France

In France, King Louis XVIII ruled from 1815 to 1824. While holding extremists in check, he followed a conservative path, in line with the Charter imposed on France. This Charter provided for monarchical rule, limited by certain legislative powers vested in an assembly. The assembly was elected by the landowners and upper-middle class, constituting about four percent of the population—the small well-to-do sector of the French people. The usefulness of such a system was extolled by writers like Joseph de Maistre in France and Edmund Burke in England. The very introduction of a Charter indicated a break with Bourbon absolutism and Napoleonic dictatorship. It permitted a beginning of popular participation in government. The Charter protected civil rights; the Napoleonic Code was retained along with other reforms.

The principles for which Charter and Code stood were, however, abandoned when Louis XVIII died and his brother, Charles X, succeeded him. Charles attempted to secure for his friends, the old émigrés of the revolution, an enormous sum to compensate them for the loss of lands. He sought to restore former Church privileges; he offended the spirit of the times by exacting the death penalty for thefts of sacred objects. He suppressed public opinion and imposed a stamp tax and other restrictive measures upon newspapers. In personal conduct, he displayed pre-Revolutionary royal splendor. Simultaneously, he tried to divert the attention of his people from his internal policies by catering to their frustrated thirst for glory; he engaged in a new military venture—an expedition for the conquest of Algiers. His ill-conceived policies brought about the breakdown of his own regime.

Central Europe

In Italy and the Germanies, Metternich's conservatism dominated. Except in three German states—one of them the small principality of Saxe-

Weimar where Goethe had been prime minister—no constitution was developed. The *Code Napoléon,* with its liberal spirit, was not retained. In essence, government was administered in accordance with principles of enlightened despotism. This conservative trend brought conflict with the liberals. In Italy, a number of secret societies were founded, like the *Carbonari,* which supported the liberal cause. In Germany, a comparable liberal movement led to unrest among students and to the formation of *Burschenschaften* (fraternities) and other liberal societies. The Italian movement attracted some outstanding leaders, among whom were the writers, Manzoni and Gioberti and the famous politician Mazzini. In Germany, idealistic thinkers joined the cause—the great scientist Humboldt, the philosopher Fichte, the statesman vom Stein, the poet Arndt, the Brothers Grimm, and many others.

However, liberal hopes in Italy came to naught when attempts at revolution failed in 1820 and 1821. Thereafter, justice favored the old privileged class again. Clericalism was supported anew, scientific education was hindered, and censorship controlled public opinion. Foreign domination remained.

In Germany, also, the liberal forces proved too weak. In 1817, students organized a festival on the Wartburg, where revolutionary speeches were made. In 1819, a liberal murdered a poet, von Kotzebue, who was accused of spying for reactionary Russia. This event spurred Metternich to call the Congress of Carlsbad; its decrees and repressive police measures put a stop to the agitation and initiated a period of calm and firm conservative rule.

England

Similar conservatism marked English policies, with the leaders convinced that a small upper crust should govern the ordinary people. The royal court was old-fashioned and dissolute. The office of prime minister from 1815 to 1830 was in the hands of the Tory party, which dominated in Parliament and passed little progressive legislation. The right to vote was even more restricted than in France. Modernization of agriculture was neglected, the common fields were almost entirely enclosed, and freeholders constantly diminished in number. Corn laws were passed that provided for protective tariffs on grain imports; they benefited the few rich landlords.

Little was done for the impoverished. A severe business crisis, following the war period, brought unemployment. When worker uprisings occurred, the government resorted to suspension of the *habeas corpus* in 1817 and, in one instance, in 1819, to bloody suppression. A stamp tax and censorship were introduced. Public mass meetings were forbidden. Little understanding was shown for the fact that while Britain grew rich—London inherited the position of financial center of the world formerly held by Amsterdam—and while the Midlands became "the workshop of the world," the workers and the lower bourgeoisie reaped meager benefits.

Only slowly, with improvement in business in the early 1820s, did a countermovement appear within the Tory party itself. So-called "liberal Tories," like Sir Robert Peel and George Canning, gained influence. Owing to their endeavors, penalties for political offenses were eased and the police system made more lenient. Tariffs were reduced, and trade policies were liberalized. The currency was stabilized through the introduction of the gold standard. Attempts to pass labor legislation were initiated. In 1828 and 1829, laws were passed that accorded long-withheld political emancipation to dissenters and Catholics in England. But more far-reaching liberal legislation had to await, in England as elsewhere, the impetus of the French "July Revolution" of 1830.

Russia

Despite the reputation for liberalism which the Russian tsar, Alexander I, had acquired in his youth, reaction proved to be the strongest political force in Russia. Liberal tendencies, which could threaten existing autocratic institutions, were crushed. Nationalistic aspirations, which caused unrest among subjugated nationalities like the Poles, were ruthlessly combated.

Early in Alexander's rule, his confidant, the minister Speransky, had proposed a reform program: consultative assemblies on the national level, a measure of local self-government, gradual reduction of serfdom, and lessening of class distinctions. After the Napoleonic Wars, plans were made for modernization of agriculture and industry. But the lack of qualified administrators and the resulting corruption, as well as the growing conservatism of Alexander, checked progress. Few improvements were undertaken in the educational system, the law courts, or the provincial administration. Serfs remained in bondage except on the estates of the German Balts, who were more progressive than the Russian landholders and foresaw the economic advantage of emancipation. The constitution and autonomy granted to the Poles were often violated. Universities were founded, but their work was subjected to police supervision. Obscurantism prevailed.

Additional bondage was introduced through the establishment of military colonies. The unhappy inhabitants of areas set aside for these colonies became permanent soldiers. Together with their families, they were subjected, even during peacetime agricultural work, to the absolute command of the military authorities. They received material care throughout their lives, but they lost all individual rights.

As a result, when Alexander died in December (Russian *Dekabr*), 1825, a revolt broke out. This "Dekabrist" revolt, initiated to bring freedom and constitutional government to Russian lands and led by idealistic, liberal young officers (most of them from the nobility), was put down with extreme brutality. From then on, the new tsar, Nicholas I, combated all liberal leanings. Again, Russia was insulated from Western influences. The old autocracy imposed its despotism anew.

The United States

While liberal political and economic ideas between 1815 and 1830 were largely rejected by the governments of Europe and all but disappearing in Russia, they were gaining ground in the United States.

Democratic institutions were strengthened. Voting privileges were consistently extended; educational opportunities were broadened. Upon becoming president in 1829, Andrew Jackson declared that, unlike his predecessors, he would emphasize fulfillment of the needs of ordinary citizens. With this aim, he attacked the existing banking system, which he reformed; an independent Treasury was created. He even opposed the courts. He surrounded himself with new men—political supporters who would replace political adversaries holding influential and lucrative offices. The resulting "spoils system" came into political practice.

Aside from these changes in political arrangements, a number of issues had to be dealt with which were unknown to other countries in the Western world. Some of them arose from the fact that, in the United States (as in Russia), farmers had the opportunity to cultivate wide areas of sparsely settled territory, an opportunity not available to those living in narrowly confined European nations, where the peasants from necessity, practiced intensive cultivation. Westward expansion at the expense of the American Indians became one of the most pressing issues. The Eastern tribes, already decimated in battles they had waged to defend their lands, were deprived of their possessions, expelled, and driven mercilessly beyond the Mississippi River. Their lands were then cleared of forests and given to pioneers, who prepared them for agriculture. Large areas were fenced in by cattlemen with barbed wire. Cities were built and irrigation projects started. Canals were dug. Settlers continued migration west, and resultant population shifts brought new political problems.

Just as agriculture and expansion multiplied problems, so did industrial growth. The United States government introduced protective tariffs—a measure that ran counter to liberal European economic theory. In addition, the government had to deal with the problem of immigration. This led to heated debates over preferential treatment and admittance of immigrants, from whom prompt assimilation and integration was expected.

Of still greater importance was the question of slavery. It brought bitter strife and was settled only temporarily, in 1820, by the Missouri Compromise, which delineated the areas in which it was legal to own slaves. Finally, there was the issue of the validity of federal legislation in states that objected to the laws and therefore assumed "nullification" rights upon federal acts. The struggle, involving preservation of the Union, at the time centered around the imposition of tariffs. It was, likewise, only precariously settled, in 1832.

The internal problems of the United States thus combined with factors peculiar to its geography and political origin, and led the country to follow a course in many respects radically different from that dominating the rest of Western civilization.

REVOLUTION

In 1830, whatever hopes conservatives may have entertained that they essentially could preserve the status quo in the face of concessions which, especially in England, had been forced upon them was shattered when a new revolution broke out in France. It was at first feared that this would lead to an upheaval comparable to that of 1789; perhaps this fear contributed to the quick surrender of the French king. But in its course the revolutionary movement did not again overturn society; instead, it was stopped in its early stages. Actually, the instigators had never envisioned more than the restitution of those liberal principles on which the post-Napoleonic settlement had been based. New social ideas were not at stake.

July Revolution (1830)

The July Revolution was brought about by the shortsightedness of Charles X, who violated the Charter and ignored petitions asking him to respect it. Finally, he issued "four ordinances," whereby the electoral law was arbitrarily changed to the exclusive advantage of the landowners. New elections were decreed, and the freedom of the press was further curtailed. On July 27, 1830, the printers went on strike and barricades were put up in the streets of Paris. King Charles X quickly fled. But the moderate royalist forces under the veteran leadership of Talleyrand and Lafayette succeeded in preventing bloodshed. They deposed Charles and accepted his cousin, Louis Philippe, prince of Orléans, as a suitable successor to the throne.

Louis Philippe had always boasted of his liberalism; he was proud of his "bourgeois" ways; and he could be expected to respect the Charter. The "four ordinances" were revoked; censorship was abolished. By the lowering of voting qualifications, the electorate was approximately doubled. The citizens' National Guard, formed to counterbalance the regular armed forces controlled by the king, was reorganized to ensure the gains of the revolution. The reforms satisfied the upper bourgeoisie; sporadic further revolts by the industrial proletariat (still poor and weak) were ruthlessly suppressed. By 1833, quiet reigned under the guidance of Louis Philippe's "July Monarchy."

Repercussions in Western Europe

The July outbreaks in Paris set off revolts in various parts of Europe. The neighboring Belgians, ever dissatisfied with the Vienna arrangement that had forced them into a union with Holland, rebelled. They clamored for constitutional government and national independence. Within a decade, Belgium was established as an independent state. Disturbances occurred in Switzerland and Italy, some of them successful in bringing about more liberal laws, as in Switzerland. In Germany, a number of princes hurried to grant their peoples long-promised constitutions. The German unification movement, advocated by liberal and national groups, made some progress, at least in the economic sphere. Under Prussian leadership, a *Zollverein* or customs union, created earlier, was broadened to include almost all the states of northern Germany. It facilitated the extension of the railway system and greatly served industrialization. In Britain, after fifty years of Tory rule, a Whig cabinet took over in 1830. Under Earl Grey, energetic work was started to reform the electoral law. In 1832, though not without meeting violent resistance, a first "Reform Bill" was passed. It abolished "rotten boroughs" (electoral districts which, though depopulated, had still enjoyed the traditional right of representation in Parliament) and created new electoral districts in urban areas. It thus broke the monopoly of the landowning nobility, with its medieval privileges, just as the Catholic Emancipation Act had broken that of the Anglican Church. It made room for broader representation of the bourgeoisie. While the industrial proletariat gained nothing and the composition of Parliament was not promptly changed, the First Reform Bill paved the way for future reforms.

Repercussions in Eastern Europe

The July Revolution indirectly helped the Greeks. Since 1819, they had struggled against the Turkish sultan. England and Russia had given them aid and in 1827 had destroyed the Turkish fleet at Navarino. Russia had continued the war until it could impose the Peace of Adrianople. With Turkey beaten and the liberal national movement invigorated by the July Revolution, Greece's claim to independent statehood was recognized. In 1832, the new nation was established.

Actually, it was only in isolated Russia that the July Revolution failed to have a tangible effect. There, the bourgeois class was too weak; the universities were too small and too firmly controlled. Ever since the Dekabrist rising, the autocratic government had been alert to any revolutionary action. The July Revolution did spread, however, to Poland. There, a terrible uprising ended with the brutal suppression of the rebels and the abolition of Poland's constitution. It accelerated the Russification of Poland and brought increasingly strict censorship to stifle all independent thought.

Revolutionary events dominating the late eighteenth and early nineteenth centuries gave way to reaction and a period of revived conservatism. A series of international conferences were held to preserve the Vienna system. In France, having regained the throne, the Bourbons pursued a strictly conservative policy. In Germany, Russia, Britain, and Spain, unrest was suppressed.

But a strong undercurrent for reform persisted; young people with liberal ideas caused sometimes bloody disturbances. The unrest came to a head when the Greeks rebelled against Turkish rule. They started a war for independence, which led, after ten years, to the creation of a modern Greek state.

Social conditions under the impact of industrialization likewise demanded change. A new French revolution broke out when increasingly reactionary policies of the king provoked the opposition. This revolution cost the Bourbons their throne for the second and final time. The forces released by the July Revolution spread to Belgium, Poland, and other regions. Belgium gained independence from the Netherlands, but elsewhere the results were not successful. Yet, while the young United States could continue to build its own institutions along lines envisioned by the founders of the republic or introduce such changes as practice necessitated, without revolutionary upheavals, wide reforms could not be postponed in Europe. Britain passed a bill which, by adjusting the electoral districts, broadened the electorate. In Germany, Spain, and Italy, the rulers took steps toward more liberal systems as well as economic changes and social betterment.

Selected Readings

De Ruggiero, Guido. *The History of European Liberalism* (1977)

Eldrige, C. C., ed. *British Imperialism in the Nineteenth Century* (1984)

Hayes, Carlton J. *Nationalism* (1966)

Jardin, A., and Tudesq, A. J. *Restoration and Reaction, 1815–1848* (1984)

Kohn, Hans. *Nationalism: Its Meaning and History* (1971)

Lincoln, W. Bruce. *Nicholas I* (1978)

Macartney, C. A. *The House of Austria, the Later Phase, 1790–1918* (1978)

May, Arthur J. *Age of Metternich* (1963)

13

Society, Arts, and Sciences (1815–1848)

The stirring events of the great French Revolution and the Napoleonic Age, despite the widespread suffering and sense of failure that ensued, did not destroy the idealism that had marked the preceding Age of Enlightenment. A strong element of unrest remained. Intellectual vigor was remarkable. Social questions and scientific problems were attacked with unequaled fervor. But, despite its efforts and enthusiasms, the generation that lived in the years following the Congress of Vienna experienced bitter disappointments.

SOCIETY: PRACTICE AND THEORY

In a sense, the Revolution of 1830 accomplished what the great Revolution of 1789 had failed to achieve. Professional men and those who controlled finance, trade, and the growing industrial apparatus gained almost everywhere a full share in the exercise of political power. "Bourgeois" views penetrated all facets of Western civilization.

New Social Stratification   In line with the trends of the times, social stratification was modified. The old nobility retained much of its landed wealth and its role at the royal courts and in the administrations of many countries. However, it no longer set the pattern in manners, taste, and social attitudes. The proportion of peasants in the population declined, even though they still comprised the overwhelming majority. Yet, they achieved no active political role. Industrial workers increased in numbers, but, owing to their economic weakness, were unable to influence either national or economic policies.

It was thus the middle class, the bourgeoisie, which most influenced the age. Within this group, it was the "captains of industry"—as the historian Carlyle called them—or successful self-made men who shaped the ways of modern society. Their specialized knowledge, ambition, and (in some cases) erudition and culture enabled them to challenge the old upper classes. They gained influence by means of hard work. They adopted or imitated many of the views and prejudices of the old society, but they were also receptive to modern ideologies.

As a whole, the middle class cherished liberal thought, to which it owed its rise. It generally advocated equality of opportunity, and favored the founding of schools and universities. It was interested in the progress of science. Although many of its members supported the religious institutions of the past, they now showed less religious fervor. They were tolerant in their treatment of minority groups, such as the Jews, who composed a significantly influential portion of their ranks. The latter were emancipated politically; many attained leading positions in science and trade. The middle class was devoted—though often more in theory than in practice—to "propriety," stability, and honesty; it served as a new patron of art and learning.

Women

In view of the political organization of the country, women in England could not participate in the conduct of public affairs, nor did they have political rights. In the building, mining, and textile industries, their labor was exploited as it had been throughout history everywhere. Long working hours at low wages and hard labor were demanded, not only in agriculture, but also in industry. Women of the well-to-do classes attended to their households, supported by maids; they occupied themselves with gardening, reading, writing (as did Jane Austen, d. 1817; *Pride and Prejudice*), and social gatherings. The political role of women in the United States was similar. But, as in other pioneering societies, the influence of women, especially in frontier regions, was considerable. Living conditions were largely determined by their activities and decisions.

In Continental Europe, conditions were different. Since industry was not as advanced as in Britain, there was less exploitation through industrial labor. Then, too, the women in Germany and France held a higher place in public affairs. Mme. de Staël, Mme. Roland and, later, George Sand in France and Bettina von Arnim, Rahel von Varnhagen, Caroline Schlegel, and Henrietta Herz in Germany exercised far-reaching influence. Their writings were of no less importance than their *salons*. In these salons, philosophers and generals, theologians and princes, historians and literary figures, gathered. Their discussions of existing views and problems led to action in various political arenas. Moreover, especially in Germany, women often took charge of businesses when their husbands had died early, and directed them, as did, for instance, Thérèse Krupp, the widow of the founder of the famous steelworks. To the numbers of active and influential women should also be added Baroness de Krüdener of Holy Alliance fame and others, such as the traveler Alexandra Gripenberg from Scandinavia.

Mechanization of Industry

The "rise of the bourgeoisie" owed most of its impetus to the mechanization of production methods. Mechanization brought changes so profound that later the expression "Industrial Revolution" was coined to describe the era—a misleading term, for no revolution took place, but rather a series of economic changes drawn out over a long period of time. These changes came first and proceeded most rapidly in Britain. Its insular position, fast-growing population, insufficiency of foodstuffs but control of raw materials at home and in its colonies, and —most of all—enterprising commercial spirit favored early adoption of new production methods. Mechanization of the textile industry started the spiral of general industrialization; it led to the growth of machine industry, which, in turn, stimulated coal and iron mining, shipbuilding, and, after 1825, railroad construction.

Railway construction—challenged in Russia as well as in the United States by canal building—thereafter became the chief motor force in the industrialization process. It demanded vast amounts of supply in coal and steel—for a century the standard measurement of a country's industrial progress. It gave jobs to large numbers of workers, stimulated the machine industry serving numerous branches of the economy, and opened the path for additional research and technical progress. Railways alone could provide the new needs for transportation and make it possible to reach the wider markets that developed with population growth and the demands of industrial workers who were not as self-sustaining as the peasants were . They opened up possibilities for passenger services that changed the living habits of millions of people. As large enterprises, they were in need of large amounts of financing, and this demand, in turn, contributed to the growth of banking.

Trade increased, prices rose, a boom resulted, and new industries came into being. European countries followed the British lead, albeit at a slower pace. In France, where coal and iron were scarce and agriculture was flourishing, and where cheap labor was neither as abundant nor concentrated in urban areas, industrialization was delayed. Spain, Italy, the Netherlands, and the Scandinavian countries lagged still further behind. But Germany's rise to prominence in industry, though later than Britain's and France's, was fast when it came in the 1830s.

Social Conditions

The mass poverty resulting from industrialization was most sharply felt in Britain, which became not only the industrial, but also the social, workshop of the world. It was there that theorists occupied themselves most intensely with the new economic and social problems.

SOCIAL THEORIES

Medieval thinkers had condemned covetousness, ambition, competition, and economic exploitation. Though not overly concerned with poverty, which was considered inevitable in human society, they had demanded Christian charity. They had insisted on a "just" price and had opposed interest-taking. They had approved regulation of trade and enforcement of quality standards through guilds and monopolies.

Most of these fundamental views had been reversed by the classical economic theory of eighteenth and early nineteenth-century Britain. Ambition was no longer considered a vice. Price determination by the laws of supply and demand, without reference to ethical principles, was regarded as natural and proper. Interest-taking was accepted as a normal function of the money market. Monopolies were condemned, and regulation of trade and production as to quality and quantity was left to "natural" forces.

In line with liberal trends, and inspired by Adam Smith's laissez-faire views, economists defended modern capitalism and private property. They extolled the division of labor and investigated the economics of money, rent, labor, and value. Most of them held to the liberal proposition that the free play of economic activities would bring the most favorable general conditions, that individuals are the best judges of their own interests, and that individuals serve society best when they promote their own interests.

But an increasingly pessimistic strain can be noticed even among these economists. David Ricardo felt that the various social interests could never be harmonized. Sismondi doubted that new production possibilities could improve the situation of the masses; he prophesied a succession of crises that would forever disturb social relationships. Malthus, following in this liberal path, insisted that population will always tend to outrun the means of subsistence; he therefore considered economic planning and artificial relief measures to be senseless.

SOCIAL REALITY

Evidence seemed to support such pessimistic views. Industrialization brought unforeseen results. The personal relationship between employer and employee was lost in the conduct of the new large-scale enterprises; individual workers became mere units in a chain of production. Their employment and wages came to depend less upon personal achievement than upon impersonal trends and business cycles. They no longer took pride in, or gained satisfaction and a comfortable living from, craftsmanship and skill. Low-paid, unskilled workers (often women and children) sufficed to attend to machinery; family incomes declined.

Many farm laborers were cruelly uprooted and separated from the soil from which they had drawn strength and a measure of security. They had to perform monotonous tasks as a result of the widespread division of labor. They were exhausted by excessive working hours and long trips to and from their work. Living in dismal slums, they no longer had the solace of the quiet and beauty of the countryside.

Scientific progress, however, did open up new vistas. It was now possible to prolong the average life span, to introduce new comforts of life, and to reduce manual labor through machinery that performed miracles of strength, speed, and precision. But, at first these benefits were only for the few and were paid for by both worker and peasant, whose lives were spent in toil. People's ruthless competitive instincts were stimulated; wealth was increasingly concentrated in the hands of entrepreneurs. The gulf between rich and poor continued to widen. Large fortunes were made, not only through the production of goods but also by finance. Even on the land, the newly gained freedom from serfdom was of little benefit to the peasant. The need for scientific farming methods, for fertilizer, for the planting of new mass crops such as potatoes and sugar beets, and, consequently, for financial means forced many to quit their homes. A smaller number of farmers could feed the increasing populations.

POPULATION

There was a change in the population ratio of town and country, as there was in the life span. Medicine and hygiene helped to prolong life and more people survived infancy. Around 1800, Spain and Britain counted about ten million inhabitants each, France and Germany almost three times as many, and Russia still more. The bourgeoisie (the "third estate") and the working class (the "proletariat") grew fastest.

Challenging Economic Thought

In view of such conditions, many leading thinkers in the second quarter of the nineteenth century began to occupy themselves with a revision of economic theories.

MODIFIED LAISSEZ-FAIRE

Jean Baptiste Say abandoned many of the positions of the classical economists; he taught that utility is the measure of value and that labor must be judged by utilitarian standards. Friedrich List advocated a certain amount of state direction and a protective tariff. John Stuart Mill, a foe of intolerance *(On Liberty, Essay on the Subjection of Women)*, somewhat later insisted, like List, that a measure of regulation and social reform directed by the state was necessary to guarantee the freedom of the individual. They all realized that the availability of industrial goods created "needs" that had not been felt before, and that consumption would rapidly increase.

UTOPIANISM AND ANARCHISM

A more radical departure from the laissez-faire theory can be traced to various idealistic groups of the first half of the nineteenth century. Of special importance were the "utopians" who, believing in the goodness of people if wisely led, expected a better future from the full development of their rational and moral qualities. Their views and aims were best represented by Robert Owen, an English textile worker who had become owner of a mill. Starting with social improvements in his own factory, where he limited the working hours of children, paid wages during periods of unemployment, and instituted schools for workers and looked after their health, he then turned his attention to British national problems. He moved temporarily to America and, in 1825, founded in New Harmony, Indiana, a colony for people who would renounce private property. Those who lived there adopted uniform housing, clothing, and education. They worked as a community and received credit for their labor in accordance with the extent of their participation in the activities of the community. The project collapsed, however, because the participants lacked the devotion and individual initiative Owen had expected.

A more scientific approach than Owen's can be ascribed to Saint-Simon. This noted Frenchman, a wealthy count and devoted Christian who sacrificed all his possessions for his ideals, taught that society must be scientifically planned, that true freedom consists in serving the community, and that spiritual values depend upon economic conditions. He held that property corrupts people. In this, his compatriots, Fourier and Proudhon, agreed with him. But not from society, church, or state—agents of law, protectors of property, and therefore vicious—did the latter two expect salvation. They expected salvation from the individual's rationality. Reason, they thought, would induce people to enter freely into contracts with fellows. On such a basis, a healthy, moral, and stateless (anarchical) society could be built.

In opposition, Louis Blanc extended Saint-Simon's views, insisting that, at least for the time being, the state alone could guarantee a fair distribution of wealth. He therefore demanded that governments attend to the task of organizing work. In many respects, Blanc represented the view of the modern socialist camp.

SOCIALISM

Socialism, which in its early stages was indistinguishable from communism, was not a nineteenth-century invention. It had antecedents in some of Plato's teachings, as well as in the Gospels, Thomas More's writings, and certain Egyptian and Aztec institutions. Nineteenth-century socialism differed, however, from earlier movements in that it addressed itself mainly to the new industrial worker and only indirectly to the peasant. It concerned itself largely with the relationship between entrepreneur and laborer and with questions of profit. Socialism embraced a great variety of views. Some socialists based their precepts on moral grounds, others on materialistic concepts. But all shared the fundamental principle that private property is evil and that the means of production, and possibly even those of distribution, should be in the hands of the community. They demanded an equal distribution of the national wealth, with remuneration for all according to their work or according to their needs. Traditional concepts, including inherited religious views, were rejected by most of them; socialists tried to be "scientific."

Social Legislation

Under the impact of utopianism, anarchism, and scientific socialism, both workers and governments acted to cope with the problems of the new industrial age. Workers and craftsmen who at the beginning of mechanization saw their livelihood threatened and had resorted to destruction of machinery gave up such desperate measures. Instead, they began to form associations and unions, which were to give strength to their cause. They organized the first trade-union, an illegal enterprise, in 1824. They also began to organize producers' and consumers' cooperatives in agriculture, industry, and trade. Thus they planned to bring a sector of the national economy under their own control and to share in the profits made possible by the new production methods.

Governments reacted by passing reformatory factory legislation, beginning with provisions for sanitation and the whitewashing of buildings, and continuing with regulations against the exploitation of children. In 1819, Britain forbade the employment of children under nine years of age for work in cotton mills. Factory codes (1833) and other laws for the protection of women and children followed, even though enforcement was slack. By 1847, a maximum working day of ten hours had been established for women and minors in certain trades. But all European governments held out against recognition of the workers' right to form associations or to resort to strikes. Nor did they propose unemployment-relief measures. They attributed poverty and hardships to the assumed laziness of the individual. In fact, especially in Britain, attempts were made to meet the problem of poverty by making governmental "poor relief" worse than poverty itself.

LITERATURE, SCIENCE, AND ARTS

Preoccupation of thinkers with societal changes did not hinder a vigorous literary and artistic life after the Napoleonic Wars were over.

Literature

Goethe died in 1832, one year after finishing *Faust*. Germany continued to create beautiful lyrical poetry (Heinrich Heine, d. 1856) and some of the most enchanting tales of fantasy (E. T. A. Hoffmann, d. 1822). Moreover, in a period when the drama was neglected and "became divorced from popular stage production," Germany contributed two eminent playwrights: Grillparzer and Hebbel. With penetrating psychological insight into the problems arising from the human situation, Hebbel paved the way for the modern drama. In France, the age of the novelist *(romancier)* dawned. Stendhal (d. 1842; *(The Red and the Black)*), Balzac (d. 1850; *The Human Comedy*), and Flaubert (d. 1880; *Madame Bovary*) wrote their great novels, and the elder Dumas composed his famous stories (d. 1870; *The Three Musketeers*). Perhaps the most important of these writers was Victor Hugo (*The Hunchback of Notre Dame*), who lived until 1885, and whose historical novels have continued to enjoy wide popularity.

In Britain, as in Germany, the Romantic movement continued. Keats (d. 1821; "Ode to a Nightingale"), Shelley (d. 1822; "Ode to the West Wind"), and Byron (d. 1824; *Childe Harold*) died too young to reach their full potential, but Wordsworth lived until 1850. He had won fame before 1800 with his poetry and essays, marked by rejection of classicist trends and by emphasis on a direct and warm relationship to nature. He continued to create similar works that served as models for many of his contemporaries. Romanticism lived on also in the historical novels of Walter Scott (*Ivanhoe),* in the writings of Thackeray (*The Vicar of Wakefield*), to a certain extent even in the social novels of Charles Dickens, who documented the underside of the Industrial Age, and in the writings of the Brontë sisters (Emily's *Wuthering Heights*). Literature in the English language was enriched by American writers, among whom Edgar Allan Poe (d. 1849; mysteries and poetry) and James Fenimore Cooper (d. 1851; *Leatherstocking Tales*) gained international renown.

Like the United States, Russia entered the world's literary stage as a newcomer. Its writers displayed unique artistic gifts. Pushkin (d. 1837; *Eugene Onegin,* "Queen of Spades") with his exquisite lyrics, powerful dramas, and enchanting stories stands at the beginning of a long list of Russian artists of outstanding genius. The novels of Gogol (*Dead Souls*) and Goncharov (*Oblomov*) depict the strange atmosphere of the Russian landscape, consciousness, and way of life; they have captured the imagination of readers everywhere. Writers of accomplishment also included Mickiewicz in Poland and Manzoni (*Promised Bride*) in Italy.

Philosophy and History

Except in Germany, the first half of the nineteenth century did not produce lasting philosophical works. In Britain, a shallow utilitarianism was expounded. Even Jeremy Bentham, with his sober studies of human nature and love of liberty and his desire for progress, showed in his search for the "greatest happiness for the greatest number" little insight into the human condition. But in Germany, Hegel, Fichte, and Schelling kept alive the traditions of the great thinkers: in the search for freedom, they saw the goal of history and the workings of Providence. Their idealism was opposed by a fourth eminent philosopher, Schopenhauer (d. 1860; *The World as Will and Idea*), who expressed deep pessimism. Not in moral attitudes, but in the will to live he saw the driving force of human action; ideas were but reflections of that will and of human selfishness.

Philosophical thought, which had been so closely connected with religion and then with the rational attitudes of the Enlightenment, came to be increasingly interwoven with historical studies. Out of combined progress in these fields came a new understanding of human attitudes and aspirations, and an account on environmental conditions. A great collection of historical sources was started in Germany, the *Monumenta Germaniae Historica*. B. G. Niebuhr wrote his fundamental work on Roman law; the famous modern historian Leopold von Ranke began his long and fruitful career.

Science

A major influence on nineteenth-century thinking was exercised by the physical sciences. The fundamental work of the eighteenth century was broadened and applied. Faraday discovered electromagnetic induction. Gauss, Helmholtz, Maxwell, and many others studied light, electricity, and heat and energy and laid a basis from which successors could carry on. They investigated electromagnetic waves and electrochemistry. Fraunhofer discovered the method of spectrum analysis. Thermodynamics was studied. New machinery, appliances, and lighting systems were invented. The most varied kinds of power-driven apparatus (for steamships, locomotives, and motors in factories) were created. Coal and steel became the most important industries. Likewise, the fields of geography and geology were scientifically developed (e.g., by Alexander von Humboldt and Sir Charles Lyell).

Art

While literature and science flourished, the fine arts produced less of lasting merit. Two painters of note appeared in Britain: Turner and Constable, the one famous for his paintings of Venice, the other for his landscapes. France took pride in Delacroix and Ingres. Among the best in other countries were the Swiss Böcklin, and the German Caspar David Friedrich, with their romantic landscapes. In architecture and sculpture, the neoclassical style of the early nineteenth century, represented by artists such as the Danish sculptor Thorwaldsen, gave way to another imitative art form, the neo-Gothic. Cities, which grew rapidly, showed an increasingly dismal picture: somber and pretentious dwellings and often graceless villas and public buildings began to mar town and countryside, especially in newly industrialized regions.

Music

Romanticism, which embraced many areas of human endeavor, became dominant in the field of music during the first half of the nineteenth century. The Romantic composers sought freedom of self-expression, delved into the mysteries of human life, and, above all, tried to depict emotion. Inspired by folk traditions as well as by patriotic movements, they created some of the most beautiful works ever written. One of the most famous Romantics was Franz Schubert (d. 1828). In addition to chamber music and symphonies, he composed *Lieder* (songs), which have become a permanent treasure of the musical world.

His tradition was carried on by composers like Schumann and Mendelssohn, and later Brahms. Outside of Germany, Berlioz (*Symphonie fantastique)* and the Polish exile Chopin in France excelled—Chopin equally great as pianist and as composer of nocturnes, dance tunes, and preludes. In German opera, the chief Romantic work was *Der Freischütz* by Weber, while in Italy Donizetti and Rossini *(Barber of Seville)* stand out. The Italian composers adhered rather firmly to traditional forms and lacked some of the depth of feeling evinced by the Romantics. They often catered to the demands of a public that wanted to be entertained and amused and was fascinated by such virtuosity as was displayed by the Italian violinist Paganini, who also composed *(Carneval of Venice),* and by the Hungarian composer and pianist Franz Liszt. Immensely admired by his contemporaries, Liszt's work enriched harmonic expression and greatly enhanced Church music. He became teacher to many excellent performers.

During the times of reaction and conservatism, industrialism advanced, and with it the role which the middle class could play. Wealth was accumulated by industrialists. Laissez-faire views supported such development, but it resulted in the deterioration of living standards among craftsmen, small businessmen, and workers. Voices calling for alleviation of suffering among the lower classes became stronger. New theories were developed, and some legislation, though inadequate, was passed to limit laissez-faire practices.

Music continued to flourish. Intellectual works in philosophy and history retained and even strengthened their place on the cultural stage of the European countries. In literature, new forms evolved and were accepted. The novel, in particular, emerged as a major force. Many works of considerable merit appeared in France, England, and Italy, and for the first time, significant literary contributions were made by Russian authors.

Selected Readings

Bruun, Geoffrey. *Nineteenth-Century European Civilization* (1959)

Cairns, John C., ed. *The Nineteenth Century* (1965)

Landes, David S. *The Unbound Prometheus: Technological Change and Industrial Development in Western Europe from 1750 to the Present* (1969)

_____ *The Cambridge Economic History of Europe.* 6 vols. (1966)

Trebilcock, C. *The Industrialization of the Continental Powers, 1780–1914* (1981)
Venturi, F. *Roots of Revolution* (1960)
Woodcock, G. *Anarchism* (1963)
Woodward, Ernest L. *The Age of Reform, 1815–1870* (1938)

14

The Bourgeois Era and Revolution (1830–1848)

1831   Faraday's experiments with electromagnetism

1832   First Reform Bill in England

       Goethe, *Faust* (second part)

       Beginnings of "Young Italy" movement (Mazzini)

1833   *Zollverein* founded in Germany

1835   David Friedrich Strauss, *Life of Jesus*

1836   Ranke, *History of the Popes*

1837   Invention of telegraph by Morse

       Dickens, *Oliver Twist*

1839   British-Chinese Opium War

       Belgium established as independent neutral state

1841   Straits Convention

       Carlyle, *Heroes and Hero-Worship*

1842   Chartist risings in England

       Comte, *Cours de philosophie positive*

1845   Texas annexed by U.S.A.

       Poe, *Tales*

       Dumas, *Count of Monte Cristo*

1846   Repeal of Corn Laws of England

1847   Helmholtz, *On the Conservation of Energy*

1848   February Revolution in France; revolutions in Italy and Germany

       California, New Mexico, etc., incorporated by U.S.A.

       First Pan-Slav Congress

Marx, *Communist Manifesto*
Balzac, *Comédie humaine* completed
Mill, *Principles of Political Economy*

In international affairs, the period from 1830 to 1848 was one of the quietest in European history. This fact proved the wisdom of Europe's most prominent statesman of the age, Prince Metternich. Despite his conservatism, he had succeeded in establishing a power balance that maintained a lasting peace for Europe. But internal affairs in the various European nations did not bear the same peaceful stamp. The conservatism of the statesmen acted as a brake on normal progress and as a stimulus to radicalism.

NEW CONSERVATISM VERSUS NEW LIBERALISM

As soon as the upper-middle classes had attained (through the revolutions of 1830) positions of leadership in most of western Europe, they themselves became a conservative force. The cause of liberalism was, however, not buried. It was carried on by individuals from many camps; they showed little evidence of "class" divisions and were motivated by idealism and conviction.

Britain

Owing to changes resulting from the growth of industries, Britain found itself in a precarious situation. Shifting social stratification, transformation of the British countryside, and new objectives in both economic and international affairs raised a variety of problems; satisfactory answers could be found only slowly.

GENERAL PROBLEMS

During the early thirties, the British continued to be plagued by tensions between the industrial workers, the new entrepreneurial groups, and the landowning nobility. Some social reform legislation, in addition to the political Reform Bill of 1832, was passed. Parliament published factory codes, improved health and sanitation systems, carried through church and municipal reforms, and made long-overdue arrangements for the abolition of slavery in the empire. But all this was insufficient. Numerous problems remained: urbanization, poor relief, the questions of free trade or protective legislation, of centralized or decentralized government, and numerous humanitarian issues. Riots occurred, and the threat of general revolution persisted.

POLITICAL PARTIES

Under the circumstances, the political leaders could no longer defer further steps toward modernization. In 1837, the accession to the throne of the young queen, Victoria, marked the turning point. Dissolute and extravagant court life was reformed, and the governing parties were reorganized. The old Tories split, and a "Conservative party" emerged. This party—opposed as it was to the increasingly important bourgeoisie, the rich industrialists in the Midlands, and the ambitious merchants—promoted mainly the interests of the large landowners. Occasionally it sought, under the influence of one of its members, Shaftesbury, an alliance with the working class. The Whigs also reformed. They came to be known as the "Liberal party." In line with the nature of liberalism, they found themselves divided into numerous factions. Some of the best-known members, like Grey, Palmerston, and Melbourne, were close to the more progressive Conservatives; others were radicals and insisted on speedy reforms; still others, like the Irish leader O'Connell, espoused special interests. Essentially, the Liberals stood for laissez-faire, trusting that the greatest progress would result if substantial freedom of action were allowed to the individual. Backed by a majority of the voting public, they formed a succession of cabinets.

But neither they nor the Conservatives represented the industrial workers. Consequently, other groups and movements arose, generally opposed to extreme liberalism as well as conservatism; some of them were anticapitalistic. Among them was the Anti-Corn Law League. It aimed at the abolition of the tariffs on grain that protected the landed gentry but adversely affected the industrial workers and the industrial entrepreneurs alike. Another was the Chartist group, which included factory workers, miners, and many intellectuals devoting themselves to the cause of humanitarianism and democracy. The Chartists demanded economic improvement for the workers, social equality for all, and radical changes (such as universal male suffrage) in the electoral system. But they did not agree as to the means— peaceful or revolutionary—by which to achieve their aims. They lacked sufficient funds to build an organization that would enable them to gain control of the government. Yet, they succeeded in keeping alive the issue of social reform. Millions of petitions were sent to the House of Commons to advocate their cause. Well-known public figures (including the reformer Edwin Chadwick) and leaders of the Anti-Corn Law League supported their program. But almost a century was to pass before their major proposals were to be carried out.

INTERNAL REFORMS

The internal realignments, the formation of new leagues and parties, and the vigorous political propaganda accompanying the changes could not help but increase general unrest, and this convinced the ruling forces by the middle of the 1840s of the necessity of making further concessions. Factory codes were improved and laws providing more adequately for the protection of workers were passed. Most importantly, in 1846, when Peel was prime minister, the Conservative Party, though split, had the Corn Laws repealed. A chief grievance of business and industrial workers was thus eliminated.

But repeal had many untoward consequences. It caused distress among the farmers, especially in nonindustrialized Ireland, where potato blight and subsequent famine had already hit hard. Repeal also eventually led Britain to adopt a more aggressive colonial policy in order to safeguard its imports of foodstuffs and its markets for industrial goods. It tempted the government to engage in wars that were both costly and damaging to its reputation. Once the repeal of the Corn Laws had been achieved, Chartists continued their demands for further reforms. But when another revolution broke out in France (the February Revolution of 1848) and danger of violence threatened England as well, the reform movement was interrupted. The government preferred to use repressive measures, a policy which caused widespread resentment; many left their country in order to seek a better life in the New World or in Australia.

FOREIGN AFFAIRS

The specifically British problems caused by the rapid growth of industry, finance, and trade led to a specifically British foreign policy. The country isolated itself even more from Continental affairs, satisfied that the existing balance of power was a guarantee of safety. It concentrated on overseas policies and the protection of the sea lanes to its various colonies. It expanded its Asiatic possessions by penetrating into Burma. In the 1840s, it launched an attack on China, prompted by a Chinese law prohibiting opium imports from India and by the destruction of English-owned opium stores in China. This attack, which was widely condemned because it implicitly coerced the Chinese to allow the sale of the dangerous drug (banned elsewhere), came to be known as the "Opium War." China, defeated, was forced to pay damages, to revoke the prohibition of opium, to open a number of ports to British traders, and to grant them numerous privileges on Chinese soil.

France

In France, a conservative course was followed during the reign of Louis Philippe. This king wisely turned his back on doubtful battlefield glory. His government, led in the 1830s by the historian Thiers, worked for internal prosperity. During Louis Philippe's reign, French population growth was resumed. Public works were sponsored, schools were founded, and relations with the Catholic Church were normalized. The arts flourished, and France once more took its place as an outstanding cultural center of the Western world.

However, dissatisfaction grew. Reactionary royalists who supported the claims of the deposed Bourbons, nationalists who dreamed of Napoleonic glory, liberals who demanded wider constitutional rights than the Charter provided, and socialists who wanted political power for the workers never reconciled themselves to Louis Philippe's rule. Within a few years, newspapers began to ridicule the king for his "bourgeois" ways and views, and Louis Philippe found no better means of dealing with the situation than the reenactment of repressive legislation.

This only increased resistance. Thiers resigned; another historian, Guizot, became prime minister. Through unpopular measures, his opposition to the Church, his refusal to enlarge the franchise, and his dishonesty in dealing with the parliament, Guizot contributed to a further decline of Louis Philippe's prestige. By the end of 1847, the opposition began to organize large public banquets that offered occasions for revolutionary speeches. When, on February 22, 1848, one such banquet was to be held, the government forbade it. This became the signal for open revolt. A third French revolution, the "February Revolution" of 1848, got under way.

Germany

As in France, so in Germany the period from 1830 to 1848 was one of external calm and internal seething. The influence of Metternich prevailed throughout, however, and notwithstanding minor modifications, his system remained in essence as he had planned it.

INTERNAL CONDITIONS

Most of the German states were governed efficiently, though in the tradition of enlightened despotism rather than according to liberal standards. Industrialization, with its initial social effects, had not yet been experienced in Germany to the same degree as in England and France. Economic conditions were comparatively favorable. German philosophers, poets, and musicians were admired everywhere; German universities, with their eminent men of science and scholars in the humanities, drew students from all parts of the world. But underneath, much dissatisfaction smoldered. Little account was taken of national aspirations or of liberal social demands. The cause of representative government made little progress; for example, newspapers and books remained subject to censorship. In most places, the nobility with its agrarian interests retained the highest administrative, military, and diplomatic positions, while the bourgeoisie played a subordinate role.

NATIONALITY PROBLEMS

Economic and social questions were complicated by problems of nationality. In the Hapsburg areas of the German federation, the numerous non-German nationality groups—Italians, Czechs, Hungarians, and others—began to clamor for self-government. But the Germans in all areas agitated for a closer union, for one great Germany. Fearful that the latter demand would endanger their multinational empire, the Hapsburgs opposed all unification moves. Vying for leadership within a German federation, Prussia, however, identified itself to a certain extent with the aspirations for one united nation.

This conflict in basic objectives, dividing the Hapsburgs and Prussians into hostile camps, was sharpened by their divergent attitudes in social and political matters. Austria appealed to the conservative forces and to the vanity of the small princes; Prussia aligned itself with the forces demanding change, established the *Zollverein* (customs union), and introduced trial by jury and freedom of the press. When general unrest mounted in 1847, the king of Prussia even called a diet or parliament composed of representatives of the people. But this measure was halfhearted, and no legislative powers were vested in the diet, nor was a constitution adopted. Thus, nowhere was real progress made toward the solution of critical problems. When the February Revolution broke out in France, unrest in Prussia was as great as it was in Austria; the call to revolution found a wide and enthusiastic echo everywhere in German lands.

Italy

Like Germany, Italy was disunited as a nation. In addition, most of its territory was subject to foreign rule: Sicily and Naples to the Spanish Bourbons; the Central Provinces (Parma, Modena, Tuscany) to various Austrian princes; and Lombardy and Venetia to the Hapsburg Empire. Only Piedmont and the Papal States had Italian rulers—the one the House of Savoy, the other the pope. All parts of the nation were badly administered. Progressive forces were suppressed economically as well as politically. The population was divided over political and religious questions. Neither industries and agriculture nor political institutions prospered; poverty was widespread. Intellectual activities were a major concern only among the small upper groups of the population. The anti-Catholicism of many people in this upper class prevented much contact between them and the masses.

Nor did unity exist among the leaders. Some were republicans, some royalists; some supported a unified Italy ruled by the pope, and still others were without any plan. A movement called "Young Italy" envisioned a *risorgimento,* a rebirth of the nation, but it remained weak. Rebellions, which occurred at regular intervals, achieved little. Thus, a revolt undertaken in Genoa in 1834 by a young enthusiast, Garibaldi, resulted in failure and the exile of its leader.

In 1846, new hopes for change were aroused by the election of a rather young pope, Pius IX, who was credited with liberal leanings and administrative ability. Metternich was not disturbed. He remarked cynically that "a liberal pope is inconceivable." The expectations of the patriots were not realized. They could look for leadership only from Piedmont, the one other independent Italian state. The House of Savoy, which ruled Piedmont, saw its opportunity and began, like the Prussian royal house in Germany, to move ahead on the road of liberal reform. It even granted a constitution. Although its sincerity about reforms remained as doubtful as that of Prussia, it could, because of the national issue, assume the desired role of leadership in Italy when the February Revolution occurred in France.

Russia

During the period from 1830 to 1848, while economic conditions and political trends were working slow changes in other parts of Europe and accumulating enough pressure to cause revolutionary outbreaks, conditions in Russia remained stagnant.

INTERNAL POLICIES

After suppression of the Dekabrist revolt, Russia had restored tsarist power, keeping intact the rule of the landlord class and the institution of serfdom. Adopting the slogan "autocracy, orthodoxy, nationality," the government made few progressive moves. It did adopt a new law code along lines proposed by the old statesman Speransky. It also improved public finance, modernized the administrative organization, extended some civil rights to the wealthier classes, and accepted more of the principles of private capitalism. But it suppressed all demands for constitutional government, social changes, and religious freedom. It did little to check corruption. Serfdom, the most critical problem, and a hindrance to Russia's modernization and economic growth, was left untouched. Constant local uprisings of peasants occurred. Equally ignored was the question of nationalities within the empire.

In vain did some of the greatest Russian writers raise their voices in criticism. They were silenced and exiled, their works suppressed. Circles concerned with political problems were banned. The movement of the Slavophils, which sought progress through reviving an imaginary Russian spirit manifesting cooperativeness and true Christianity, was looked at with disfavor, as was that of the Westernizers, who advocated social changes paralleling western European scientific and liberal trends. Universities were kept small, their students closely supervised; courses (for example, science courses) considered dangerous to traditional views were sharply restricted.

EXTERNAL POLICIES

Nationalistic external policies were vigorously, though not successfully, promoted. An expansionist drive was launched southeastward into the

Transcaspian regions and central Asia, but the expeditionary force perished in the steppes. Another advance was attempted in the direction of the Turkish Straits, stimulated by the fundamental aim of Russian policy to rule the coasts of the Black Sea and eventually gain domination of the Straits of Bosporus and Dardanelles.

Under Nicholas I, the Russians came close to their aim. In 1827, the Peace of Adrianople and, subsequently, the Treaty of Unkiar Skelessy (1833) gave them not only territorial concessions, but also special rights in the straits and a voice in internal Turkish affairs. In 1841, however, an end was put to this southward penetration. When new troubles in Turkey occurred, England, Prussia, and Austria insisted on joint international, instead of unilateral Russian, action. Thus, a turning point was reached in the development of Russia's foreign policies.

United States

Unencumbered by old-established aristocratic traditions, the United States, a republic in a world otherwise dominated by monarchs and vested landed interests, continued during the period 1830 to 1848 to escape most of the complex social problems confronting other Western nations.

INTERNAL CONDITIONS

The United States's population enjoyed civil rights. Hereditary privileged classes did not exist; the franchise, accorded in England or France to no more than a tenth or a twentieth of the population, was almost universal; the government and law courts were democratically organized. A new bank system was introduced, which provided for an independent Treasury department. Canals were built. The settlement of western lands continued to act as a powerful force for democratization. Although life (except for the upper-middle class of the eastern states and the plantation owners of the South) was comparatively hard and competition was sharp, America held out promise for all. Ever more immigrants came, even though a long depression hit the country in the late 1830s and discrimination was shown to many of them, particularly to Catholics.

Serious issues persisted, although they were of a different sort than those then raised in other parts of the Western world. Among them were the race problem and slavery, which involved also the question of unity between the agricultural South and the increasingly industrial North. The issue was sharpened through the introduction of the cotton gin, which altered labor conditions in the South. Those who wanted to maintain slavery were opposed by numerous anti-slavery groups in the North. Likewise, women's rights groups began to be formed. Nor was the issue of protective tariffs settled, or that of centralized government, or that of lagging enforcement of the law.

FOREIGN POLICY

Despite its safe geographical location, the United States had shown strong nationalistic tendencies. Fearful of European colonialism, it had proclaimed the Monroe Doctrine (in 1823), aimed at preventing foreign powers from gaining additional footholds in the New World. The successful development of the nation stimulated nationalistic feelings and a measure of imperialism. The westward movement was accompanied by the eviction or extermination of Indians. Economic imperialism was reflected in the tremendous growth of the lumber industry and in the swift development of mining for copper, silver, and gold. War was resorted to in order to annex territory: Texas in 1845 and other large Mexican areas in 1848. Treaties such as the compact with England regarding the Canadian border likewise served the purpose of expansion. Thus, while domestic unrest and international calm marked the European scene, in North America the situation was somewhat reversed. Internally, the country progressed without revolutionary outbreaks; but externally, expansion and wars marked the period from 1830 to 1848.

REVOLUTIONS OF 1848

The revolutions of 1848 were not as dramatic as the great Revolution of 1789. Their effect, however, was hardly less incisive. The French Revolution of 1789 came at the end of a period, the ancien régime with its feudal heritage; the revolutions of 1848 occurred at the beginning of a new age. They introduced the socialistic element into the political arena of the bourgeois world.

It was the year when Karl Marx published his *Communist Manifesto*. The same industries that gave the middle class its strength also had deplorable working conditions. Thus, there quickly arose a challenge to middle-class predominance. The benefits that the liberal creed held by the bourgeoisie were supposed to bring proved to be in many ways illusory. Instead of furthering "the greatest happiness of the greatest number," its unregulated functioning created unexpected misery and necessitated an early modification.

Revolution in France

When, in February 1848, the banquet forbidden by the government was held in defiance of the regime, cries of "Vive la république" were heard. In the night, street fighting began. Anxious to avoid any shedding of blood on his account, the king abdicated and fled to England—as Charles X had done eighteen years earlier. A republic was declared. Lamartine, a historian and Louis Blanc, a socialist, along with several other liberals, formed a provisional government.

PROVISIONAL GOVERNMENT

The new government was handicapped from the beginning. It had inherited an almost bankrupt treasury and could do nothing about the crop failures and business stagnation that had preceded its assumption of power. Dissensions became quickly evident. Socialists like Blanc and Ledru Rollin demanded immediate changes in the economic structure of the country. They insisted on the establishment of national workshops that would provide work—no matter how unproductive—for the unemployed. They demanded high taxes from the well-to-do, the nationalization of the means of production, and equal civil rights for all. They raised the red flag of revolution and formed radical clubs along patterns set in 1789.

The moderates agreed to the establishment of the national workshops, concentrated on political reform, civil rights, universal suffrage, and democratization of the National Guards. In April, elections were held in which they scored an overwhelming victory over the as yet small industrial working class. Now in control, they excluded the socialist representatives and rejected antiliberal and anticapitalistic proposals. This policy led to another rebellion. In May, a mob invaded the new assembly.

JUNE DAYS

The uprising was followed by further disturbances and a wave of arrests. The workshops were now closed, the jobless were sent to the provinces or drafted into the army. Agitation mounted, hunger riots broke out, and the leftist opposition joined forces with the reactionary right, both bent upon the overthrow of the provisional government. Toward the end of June, an organized rebellion occurred that the government proved unable to subdue, except by granting dictatorial powers to an army general, Cavaignac.

Under his regime, the revolutionaries were defeated, civil liberties were suppressed anew, and a constitution acceptable to the right and the center parties was drafted. Then, new elections were held to choose a president for the republic. The people in the provinces, eager to restore national unity and prestige, and the bourgeoisie in the cities, who wanted a government strong enough to deal with labor revolts, voted against the provisional government. On December 10, 1848, Louis Napoleon was elected head of the Second Republic.

Revolution in Germany

As soon as news of the February Revolution reached Germany, rebellions started. The long-suppressed opponents of the government believed the time for introducing liberal institutions had come at last.

END OF METTERNICHISM

In Vienna, liberals petitioned for constitutional government and civil rights. They were joined by members of the numerous nationalities forming the Hapsburg domains, who demanded autonomy. Barricades went up in the streets. In March, there was violence in Berlin and in the Rhineland. Outbreaks in Dresden, Munich, and other capitals followed. In Budapest, liberals and Magyar nationalists, under the leadership of Louis Kossuth, rebelled. The whole Metternich structure toppled, and the aged minister was forced to resign and flee. Everywhere, the German princes granted constitutions to their peoples. Even the emperor of Austria signed a constitution and acknowledged an autonomous status for Hungary and Bohemia. Such actions failed, however, to satisfy the liberals; they demanded, as a right of free citizens, constitutions of their own design. New revolts occurred in Vienna, Budapest, Prague, and Milan; the Slavs in Bohemia organized a first Pan-Slav Congress, and the Italians, under Piedmontese leadership, declared war on Austria. The emperor fled; in December 1848, he was forced to abdicate. But his Prussian colleague, Frederick William IV, proved more pliable. Unencumbered by nationality problems—except in some eastern parts where many Poles lived—he survived two days of violence and humiliation in March. He had promptly permitted a diet to meet and had watched it waste its time on a number of radical but unimportant acts, such as the abolition of titles and orders. By autumn, he had recovered control. He granted a constitution which, with its liberal stipulations, surpassed the expectations of even the more radical groups. Having taken the wind out of the sails of the liberal movement, he began to rebuild his own power. In a similar way, other German princes retained their thrones and regained authority.

FRANKFURT PARLIAMENT

Naturally, the revolutions in Germany were influenced not only by the liberal forces, but also by the problem of nationalism. In May 1848, the diet of the federation was replaced by a new, nationally elected parliament. Liberals, who predominated in the assembly, promptly attacked the problem of the unification of the country. They prepared a constitution that was to extend civil rights, suffrage, and personal liberties to all German peoples, and they discussed various plans for a united Germany: whether it should be a firm union or a loose federation, a monarchy or a republic, and whether Hapsburg Austrian territories and their numerous foreign dominions should be included to form a "Greater Germany" or excluded to leave a "Little Germany" under Prussian leadership.

But, since parliament lacked executive power, the dualism of Austria and Prussia proved to be an insurmountable obstacle. Too late did the advocates of the *klein-deutsche* (the "Little Germany") solution prevail; in April 1849, they offered the imperial crown to the king of Prussia, but he refused to take it from the hands of the representatives of the people instead of the princes. Nor did participation in a war against Denmark in support of the North German province of Schleswig further the cause of unification. Thus, the energies of the parliament were wasted, and soon it was reduced again to insignificance.

Revolution in Italy

Liberal and nationalistic aspirations succeeded in Italy no better than in Germany. Revolution in Vienna prompted uprisings of nationalists and liberals in Italy. In January 1848, revolts had occurred in Sicily; the ruling Bourbons had granted a constitution. In the beginning of March, many of the larger towns were ablaze: Naples, Rome, Florence, Venice, and Milan. Hard-pressed, Piedmont declared war on Austria. Simultaneously, patriots under the leadership of Mazzini and Garibaldi attacked the Papal States.

However, the poorly organized forces gained only temporary successes. In the north, the rebels were routed by Austrian Field Marshal Radetzky in two battles, at Custozza and Novara, and Piedmont had to sue for peace. Resistance collapsed in Venice, too. In the central region, Mazzini and Garibaldi had taken Rome, the pope had fled, and a Roman republic was established. But the two leaders proved incapable of organizing an effective government, and their republic came to an early end when French and Austrian troops came to the aid of the pope. In 1850, Pius IX returned. In the south and in Sicily, the revolt was suppressed by the former rulers. Everywhere, the old institutions were revived and nationalistic and liberal aspirations had to be deferred.

Revolution in the Smaller European Countries

Revolutionary fever spread to many of the smaller nations of Europe. In Switzerland, a new constitution was drafted which at last firmly established the unique multinational and multilingual republic, based on democratic principles and committed to a permanent neutrality, to which Switzerland still adheres. In the Scandinavian countries and in Holland and Belgium, too, institutions were brought into conformity with the demands of the age. A constitutional government was introduced in Hungary under Kossuth, but did not last. The Austrians invaded Hungary. When they were unable to deal with the Hungarian forces, they appealed to the Russians, whose tsar, Nicholas I, had assumed the role of "gendarme" of Europe. With the help of his troops, the rebellious forces were subdued; and Kossuth was forced to flee.

Repercussions of the February Revolution were felt among the Slavic nations subjected to Turkish rule, and in Spain and Portugal. Thus, with the exception of Russia, where autocracy and the police force cut through the roots of every liberal movement, and the United States, where citizens already possessed what European liberals were fighting for, the areas of revolution encompassed most of Western civilization.

Effects of the February Revolution

Historians have considered the revolutions of 1848 largely a failure, pointing out that the order existing since 1830 or earlier was not shattered. The upper bourgeoisie remained in control in western Europe, the middle class failed to win control of central Europe. Liberalism and nationalism continued as the dominant trends of the age; the political map of Europe was not altered.

Yet, a significant change had occurred. The working class had emerged as a claimant to power. Equalitarian trends increased. Liberal constitutions were adopted in most European countries. Serfdom disappeared in all areas except Russia and Turkey. A more pragmatic climate of opinion now prevailed, checking the overoptimism of the liberals. Nationalism, though still unsuccessful in both Germany and Italy, had shown its strength, it intensified among the peoples of these countries and among many additional national groups. Finally, the revolutions, ending in failure, drove thousands to the United States, where their enthusiasm, skills, and labor helped to build firm foundations for a society that conformed to their principles.

With the end of the revolution of 1830, a new period of comparative quiet began. Conservative governments held political changes in check, but technological advances forced social change upon them. England in particular was exposed to such pressures. A rapidly growing proletariat made reform necessary and the Whig party, replacing the Conservatives, carried out some reforms. Other European countries were under less pressure, but there, too, unrest increased.

In 1848, outbreaks resulted, far more violent than those in 1830. Once again, they erupted in France, but this time, with the exception of Russia, they engulfed all of Europe. The Metternich system collapsed. Karl Marx published his Communist Manifesto, *Socialist doctrines were added to the demands of leading liberal thinkers. Although the revolutions were ultimately suppressed, it was not before compromises were made. Many countries adopted constitutions and broadened welfare legislation. Social movements, largely purged of utopian aims and envisioning practical reforms instead, gained in strength and influence.*

Selected Readings

Albrecht-Carrié, René. *A Diplomatic History of Europe* (1973)
Cipolla, Carlo M., ed. *The Fontana Economic History of Europe*. 6 vols. (1973)
Craig, Gordon. *Europe Since 1815* (1971)
Dowd, David L. *The Age of Revolution* (1967)
Hobsbawn, E. J. *The Age of Revolution: Europe, 1789–1848* (1970)

Holborn, Hajo. *A History of Modern Germany*. 2 vols. (1965–69)
Macartney, C. A. *The Hapsburg Empire, 1790–1918* (1968)
Magraw, Roger. *France, 1815–1914* (1983)
Salvemini, G. *Mazzini* (1985)
Stearns, P. N. *The Revolutions of 1848* (1974)

15

Political Reorganization (1848–1870)

1849 Frankfurt Assembly dissolved
Macaulay, *History of England*

1852 Napoleon III becomes emperor
Cavour becomes prime minister of Piedmont
Harriet Beecher Stowe, *Uncle Tom's Cabin*

1854 Start of Crimean War
Opening of Japan to the West

1856 Peace of Paris
Bessemer process for steel manufacturing invented

1857 Indian Mutiny
Dred Scott Decision

1858 Treaty of Tientsin: opening of China to the West

1859 War between Austria and Piedmont
Mill, *Essay on Liberty*
Darwin, *Origin of Species*

1860 Garibaldi's expedition to Sicily
Chevalier-Cobden Treaty between France and England

1861 Kingdom of Italy founded; death of Cavour
Outbreak of Civil War in U.S.A.
Emancipation of serfs in Russia

1862 Bismarck becomes Prussian prime minister

1863 Emancipation Proclamation by Lincoln
Revolt in Poland

1864   Danish-German War for Schleswig-Holstein

French expedition in Mexico (Emperor Maximilian)

"First International" (workers' association)

Pius IX, "Syllabus of Errors"

The dynamic changes of the quarter century following 1848 contrast sharply with the relative lack of change prevailing during the preceding quarter century. In 1852, Louis Napoleon made himself emperor of France and Cavour became prime minister of Piedmont; the "tsar-liberator" Alexander II came to the throne of Russia in 1855; Abraham Lincoln was elected president of the United States in 1860; and, in 1862, Bismarck became prime minister of Prussia. Most of them worked not to preserve the existing institutions but to effect their transformation. In the pursuit of their aims, all—except the Russian emperor—resorted to force. Wars, though not of Continental or global scope, mark the period between 1848 and 1870.

By 1870, the balance of power established by Metternich had changed. The previously existing societal structures in East and West, in Russia and the United States, were altered in the wake of emancipation movements. A new aggressive spirit expressed itself in a renewed expansionist drive of Western civilization to other continents.

EUROPE BETWEEN 1848 AND 1870

The first few years after 1848 seemed to bring a renewal of reactionary political policies. However, this mood soon vanished. Progressive trends were increasingly felt in most European countries. Both liberal and socialist strength increased; concessions had to be made to the very forces that had been defeated in the revolutions of 1848. Constitutions were liberalized. The right to vote was everywhere extended to larger parts of the populations. Social legislation was broadened, and nationalistic ambitions were furthered.

France   The republican dream of the French enthusiasts of 1848 was short-lived. Within three years, the president of the Second Republic, Louis Napoleon, making free use of bribery and violating the constitution through arbitrary changes in the electoral law, had himself elected to another ten-year term as president. A year later, in December, 1852 he proclaimed himself emperor "Napoleon III."

NAPOLEON III (1852–1870)

Napoleon set to work shaping public opinion to suit his ambitions. He won over the well-to-do middle class by pledging the restoration of order; the working class by publicizing the socialistic leanings of his youth; monarchists, Napoleonists, and army officers by promising them glory; the bureaucracy by granting higher salaries; and the clergy by supporting the papacy against Italian nationalists and republicans. To all, he promised peace.

Once in power, this "sphinxlike" man muzzled the press, harassed the universities, exiled opponents, and permitted the schools to revert to Church supervision. He tried to control judicial decisions. He reintroduced universal suffrage, though allowing the representative assembly no more than a shadow existence. Yet, statesmen gave him the support withheld from his amiable predecessor, and thus enhanced his prestige. In some respects, he has been considered a model for later totalitarian rulers.

HEIGHT OF NAPOLEONIC SYSTEM

During his first ten years of rule, France prospered. Banks and credit institutes were organized and industries encouraged. The fashion industry was promoted by his wife, Eugénie. Railways and telegraph facilities were built and new methods in agriculture sponsored. An economic boom opened the possibilities for mitigating some of the hard conditions of laborers. Mutually advantageous low tariffs were negotiated with neighbors; the Chevalier-Cobden Treaty of 1860 provided for free trade with Britain. Broad new boulevards were constructed which beautified Paris and simultaneously served as a precaution against possible insurgents. A great international exposition and festivals to encourage trade made France the focus of world attention.

Ominous signs appeared, however, with Napoleon's ambitious foreign policies, which brought war after war. Within two years of his accession to the throne, France, in alliance with Britain invaded Russia. After victory was won, a pompous peace congress was held in Paris, from which the French gained little but vain prestige. Senegal in Africa was annexed. An extremely bloody war, waged in Italy against Austria in 1859, brought the acquisition of the Italian territories of Savoy and Nice.

DECLINE OF NAPOLEONIC SYSTEM

Owing to the experience of the Italian war, Napoleon III's ill-health, and fear of mounting discontent, the Napoleonic system was relaxed after 1860. Attempts were made to liberalize the government. Press and parliament were given greater freedom and influence. More attention was paid to the grievances of the working class, whose right to strike was formally recognized in 1864. But new foreign adventures wrecked the empire: wars were started in Morocco and Syria; Amman was invaded in 1862; large funds were invested in the construction of the Suez Canal; and when the United States became involved in civil war, an expedition was sent to conquer Mexico.

The disastrous expedition to Mexico began with the conquest of Mexico City and ended with defeat and the execution of Napoleon's puppet emperor, Maximilian. Another blow came in 1866, when Prussia defeated Austria and by means of generous peace terms put an end to the internal German rivalry that had always benefited France. Napoleon tried in vain to strengthen his position by offering further concessions within France and by attempting to obtain compensation from Prussia for French neutrality during the Prusso-Austrian war. In 1870, a new issue, the succession to the Spanish throne, led him to risk another war, this time against Germany. Within little more than a month, Napoleon was captured. While a prisoner in Germany, he was deposed. For the third time, France became a republic.

Germany

The Revolution of 1848 had meant a setback for German national as well as liberal aspirations. It had demonstrated the weakness of both middle class and proletariat—a weakness resulting from the initially slow development of industry and business, and the lack of great social leaders who might have inspired the middle class. Eighteen forty-nine had brought new uprisings in Vienna, new conflicts in Italy, and a resumption of the revolution in Hungary. All were in vain; reaction followed.

REACTION

In Austria, the new minister, Schwarzenberg, understood how to carry on the traditions of Metternich. He made minimal concessions to the new spirit. Rather, he helped reestablish the authority of the emperor and the prestige of the Hapsburgs within the German federation; he revived the conservative spirit of prerevolutionary days. Prussia likewise failed to promote either liberal or national institutions. Although the Prussian king perceived that the unification of the German states might make his state the leader of a new Germany, he was forced, after a conference with Austria at Olmütz in 1850, to give up such aspirations. Hopes disappeared both for a liberal Germany and for a united Germany under a constitutional monarchy. The southern German states followed the political example of Austria. Nothing more than the existing loose federation with its ineffectual Frankfurt parliament survived.

The next decade was conservative in political affairs despite the fact that, in 1850, the king of Prussia granted a constitution that provided for universal suffrage, though by classes. Progress was made in the economic sphere. Particularly in western Germany, industrialization grew apace; coal mining and steel production greatly increased. As in France, banks were founded, railways built, the postal service, once in private but now in public hands, improved and extended, and foreign trade expanded. The sciences flourished. The high standards of the German universities continued to make the country the West's center of scholarship. Not until a crisis occurred in Prussia over an army budget did grave political issues again stir the country. Then, however, a succession of rapid changes took place.

BISMARCK

In 1861, Prussia's parliament refused to appropriate funds demanded by the king for a new army program. The liberals tried to use this occasion to gain political concessions in exchange for support. The army, however, was of decisive importance to Prussia and as a last resort the king in 1862 appointed Otto von Bismarck as prime minister. He had been a representative at Frankfurt and more recently ambassador to Russia and then ambassador to France.

Bismarck was the son of a small landowner, a nobleman, and a conservative. He solved the budget problem by unconstitutional means, collecting the necessary taxes without parliamentary authorization. He strengthened Prussia's position by helping Russia to put down a Polish rebellion in 1863. Then, he induced Austria to join Prussia in settling another problem. The German provinces of Schleswig and Holstein had long been united dynastically with Denmark even after the German states had supported a Schleswig revolt in 1848. But, when in 1863 the Danish ruling family died out, the Danes decided to annex Schleswig altogether. Bismarck took advantage of this situation to whip up national enthusiasm against annexation. War was declared, and, despite a valiant defense by the Danes, the provinces were conquered. The administration of the territory was then divided between Austria and Prussia. But dissensions arose that gave Bismarck an opportunity to settle the issue of Prussian or Austrian leadership in Germany.

SOLUTION OF AUSTRO-PRUSSIAN DUALISM

War broke out in 1866. To the surprise of all Europe, Prussia beat the Austrians and their South German allies within seven weeks. The excellence of the Prussian army, its use of the newly invented needle gun, and the brilliant strategy of General Moltke were responsible for the victory in the one decisive battle at Sadowa. Peace followed promptly. Acting with prudence, Bismarck made no demands on Austria except that it not oppose a rearrangement of German affairs contemplated by Prussia. The only territorial loss incurred by Austria was the surrender of Venice to Italy, which had been induced to attack Austria from the south.

As a result, the Hapsburgs withdrew from involvements in internal German affairs; they devoted their attention to reconstituting their empire. A dual monarchy was established—that of Austria-Hungary. The two areas were governed by the same ruler and pursued a common policy in public finance and foreign relations, but each managed its internal affairs independently. The Hapsburgs failed, however, to extend similar local autonomy to the Slavs and thus carried out their reorganization only halfway.

In the meantime, Bismarck set to work on the reconstruction of Germany. North German states that had supported Austria were incorporated into Prussia; South German states were left independent, but concluded secret military alliances with Prussia and, in 1867, joined the Prussian Customs Union. The North German *Bund,* a new federation under Prussia's presidency, was formed; a common parliament was established.

FOUNDING OF THE GERMAN EMPIRE

It was then that, alarmed by the emergence of a greatly strengthened Prussia, Napoleon III asked for territorial compensations in Germany. His several suggestions were rejected. The position of France was further weakened when the possibility arose of a new dynastic combination, that of Prussia and Spain, which could menace France from two sides. Having had their own revolution, the Spaniards offered their vacant throne to a Hohenzollern prince distantly related to the Prussian king. The French protested. In July 1870, they ordered their envoy to ask the Prussian king, who was vacationing at Bad Ems, to withhold his consent. The king telegraphed his prime minister, and the telegram—the famous *Ems dépêche*—was edited and published by Bismarck in such a way as to inflame national feelings in both Berlin and Paris. Mass hysteria seized Paris.

In confusion, the French declared war and the Franco-Prussian War began. World opinion was mainly on Prussia's side. Prussian troops, joined by those of all other German states, overwhelmed the French forces. Two entire French army corps were taken prisoner—one, in which Napoleon III was captured, at Sedan, the other at Metz. When the German armies were at the gates of Paris, Bismarck arranged for the crowning achievement of his policies: in the French palace of Versailles, a united "German Empire" was proclaimed, and the Prussian king was designated as its emperor.

The nation was established as a constitutional monarchy—a union of some twenty states that embraced all German peoples except those living in the Hapsburg Empire. Shortly thereafter, Paris was taken. The Prussians exacted from defeated France a high indemnity and the return of Alsace and Lorraine to Germany. The latter provision was demanded less for national than for strategic considerations, as well as for the sake of the rich iron mines of the region.

Italy

Italy's path to unification was much more circuitous than that of Germany. Among the most serious obstacles were subjection to foreign rule, slow economic development, a lack of capable leaders, and the existence of the Papal States. The success of unification efforts hinged upon the role of Piedmont. Yet, in 1849, Piedmont itself was defeated in war and torn by inner struggles.

CAVOUR

Count Cavour changed the situation and prepared Piedmont for Italian leadership. Beginning his career as prime minister in 1852, he proved to be one of the most astute statesmen of his time. He realized that only liberal policies and economic strength could give Piedmont the necessary prestige and influence. Hence, he reduced tariffs, entered into favorable commercial treaties with neighboring countries, encouraged railway building, improved Franco-Italian relations by the tunneling of the Alps at Mont Cenis, and modernized the army. He made concessions to the liberals, such as legalizing civil marriage and suppressing mendicant orders (the Franciscans and Dominicans). But he protected Church life where it did not interfere with politics.

STEPS TO UNIFICATION

Cavour next applied his energies to external policies. His first objective was to "put Italy on the map." For this purpose, he joined England and France in the Crimean War, which demanded many sacrifices. However, it served Italian interests by enabling the king of Piedmont, after the victory, to show himself triumphantly in Paris and London and to have Piedmont participate in the Peace Congress of Paris in 1856. There, Cavour brought up the Italian problem, extolled Piedmont's future role, and laid the groundwork for an alliance with France, consummated two years later.

Once this was achieved, he provoked war with Austria. Supported by Napoleon III, the Italians defeated the Austrians in two extremely bloody battles at Magenta and Solferino. It was at Solferino that a young Swiss banker, Dunant, who happened to be present, conceived the idea of organizing a relief institution for the wounded and prisoners. Subsequently, Dunant founded the Red Cross.

Lest war be prolonged and new risks be incurred, the French emperor deserted the Italian cause shortly after Solferino. Fearing that Italy might become too powerful or that Prussia might intervene, he concluded a peace treaty with Austria at Villafranca. This treaty secured the province of Lombardy for Piedmont, but did not bring unity to the whole of Italy. Disheartened, Cavour resigned.

Yet, the process of unification had been set in motion. Within a year, Cavour returned to his premiership; the Central Provinces revolted against their various Austrian rulers and, by plebiscite, also joined Piedmont. In order to secure Napoleon's recognition of this second step in Italian unification, Italy had to cede Savoy and Nice to France.

Almost simultaneously, a third step was taken. With the connivance of Cavour, Garibaldi led a band of a "thousand" volunteers into Sicily and quickly succeeded in driving out the Spanish Bourbon rulers. Crossing back to the mainland, Garibaldi occupied Naples; simultaneously, Piedmontese troops coming from the north seized part of the Papal States. In 1861, the king of Piedmont was proclaimed king of Italy; Florence became the capital and a constitution was drafted. Only Venetia and Rome were still lacking to complete Italian unity. In the same year, Cavour died.

FULFILLMENT

In 1866, after Prussia's victory, Italy seized Venice. The capture of Napoleon III in 1870 enabled Italy to take Rome. As soon as the French emperor could no longer hold his protecting hand over the papacy, the Italians invaded the city and put an end to the temporal (or civil) power of the popes. A history of more than a thousand years was thus concluded. Denouncing the "evil" spirit of the time, Pius IX retreated into the Vatican. He refused ever to set foot again on the soil outside, thus making the popes voluntary prisoners for more than half a century. Rome became the capital of Italy. Many problems remained: Italy had achieved unity only with foreign help, its national strength remaining at a low level; it had not made peace with the papacy. Its economy, though improving, offered no firm foundation for a prosperous commonwealth. Jurisdiction did not include Italian populations in the southern part of South Tirol, in Dalmatia, Savoy, Nice, Corsica, and Malta. Yet, Italy had become an independent united country, with a constitutional monarchy. It had attained a certain amount of stability and could take its place among the modern nations of Europe.

Britain

If the period from 1848 to 1870 witnessed great innovations in France, Germany, and Italy, it brought few changes in Britain. Enjoying its "splendid isolation," its industrial wealth, and its "Victorian" way of life, Britain continued on the path of gradual democratization and of colonial expansion. With the backing of industrialists in the manufacturing cities of the Midlands, in Manchester, Birmingham, and Sheffield, the Liberal party stayed in power. Prime ministers of considerable ability—Russell, Derby, Palmerston, and, later, Gladstone—directed the government. Consistent support was given to business; various regulations helped to improve conditions for the working class. In 1867, when for a short time the Conservatives under Prime Minister Disraeli were in power, a second Reform Bill was passed which extended the franchise to large additional segments of the middle class. Emigration to all parts of the empire was encouraged so that ties with Britain would be strengthened and markets for British goods would be developed.

In foreign affairs, a vigorous colonial policy was pursued. British nationalistic sentiments were aroused and the various governments, especially in Palmerston's time, appealed to them. In Africa, British holdings were extended through missionaries and merchants, who were followed by occupation troops: "the flag following trade." New concessions were demanded from China. In India, an uprising of the natives in the British army, the so-called "Mutiny," was fiercely suppressed, whereupon the administration of India was put entirely under the direction of the British government.

In Canada, reforms were undertaken. In order to retain Canada's loyalty, Britain gave it control of its internal affairs in the 1850s. The British North American Act of 1867 recognized the change and Canada became a "Dominion." Special attention was paid to the safeguarding of communication lines between Britain and its colonies. Russia was prevented by the Crimean War from gaining free access to approaches to the Mediterranean. Subsequent wars and treaties with Persia and Afghanistan also prevented it from reaching the land route to India.

RUSSIA AND AMERICA

The years from 1848 to 1870 were also of decisive importance to Russia and the United States. Decisive events were the abolition of serfdom in Russia and of slavery in the United States.

Russia

For Russia, the decisive moment came with the Crimean War. It revealed the backwardness, inefficiency, and corruption of Russian institutions and forced the government to undertake long-overdue reforms.

CRIMEAN WAR AND RUSSIAN EXPANSION IN ASIA

Provoked by Napoleon III's meddling in Turkish affairs, but essentially reflecting British-Russian rivalry, the Crimean War (1854–1856) brought little glory to any participant. Russian soldiers fought valiantly; their defense of the fortress of Sebastopol has become famous. But their leaders and their equipment were lamentable. Motley French, British, Italian, and Turkish troops, though just as badly led, were able to defeat Russia and impose stifling peace conditions. Russia was deprived of all special rights enjoyed on Turkish soil; it was forbidden to maintain fortifications along its Black Sea border or to keep warships there. Various earlier conquests were restored to Turkey. With its drive southward stalled, Russia renounced further advances in Europe and turned its attention eastward. There, it met with better success. Penetrating central Asiatic regions, it occupied Tashkent, Bokhara, Samarkand, and Khiva; it also sent troops and settlers under Count Muraviev into the Amur region, forcing China to relinquish the territory. In 1860, Russia built the harbor of Vladivostok on the Sea of Japan. It penetrated Manchuria and occupied Sakhalin.

But these successes in the East, compensating somewhat for the failures in the West, did not make the government overlook the need for correction of the country's internal weaknesses. Nicholas I had died during the Crimean War. His son, Alexander II, faced the difficult task of converting Russian institutions to meet the demands of modern times.

EMANCIPATION

The defects of the Russian system were rooted in the institution of serfdom, which made it impossible to modernize and industrialize the country. Serfdom was universally condemned by economists, sociologists, and idealists. It was the chief target of the "intelligentsia," as an important group of the population was called. Composed largely of members of the free professions, students, and merchants, the intelligentsia had been driven more and more into opposition to all aspects of the existing political system. Many of them came from the ranks of the high nobility; they, too, preferred exile and disgrace to living under existing conditions, no matter how much, personally, they could have profited by them. The literary critic Belinsky, the politician Herzen, the social philosopher Samarin, the anarchist Bakunin—these intellectuals and innumerable others unceasingly protested against the evils of autocracy and its counterpart, serfdom.

Alexander may not have listened, but the lesson of the Crimean War could not be overlooked. In 1856, he appointed a commission to prepare the needed reform work. He insisted that any plan include provisions to give the peasants (1) freedom, (2) an economic basis for their lives (namely, land), and (3) due compensation to the former owners whose land was to be transferred to peasants. Owing to the steadfast cooperation of progressive landowners, the gigantic task of liberation was accomplished within five years. Neither fear of its possible revolutionary consequences nor opposition from reactionary quarters could stop the work. Nor could it be stopped by lack of financial means, bureaucratic impediments, or difficulties resulting from the diversity of conditions in the various parts of the empire.

On February 19, 1861, twenty-three million serfs and their families were declared free, and land allotments were made to them. A transitional period, however, was provided. During this period, the peasant did not gain actual ownership of the land but remained a member of a village community *(mir)*, in which ownership was vested, and which provided for communal cultivation of the fields. The *mir* received certain rights of jurisdiction over its members. It was responsible for the special "redemption tax," which, in the course of some forty years, was to reimburse the state for its compensation payments to the landowners.

FINANCIAL AND JUDICIAL REFORMS

Once the government had ended serfdom, it proceeded rapidly with additional reforms. It reorganized state finances and the tax system, created a state bank, and set up a regular budget. It abolished state monopolies and made numerous personnel changes. Educational reforms followed. Universities were given more freedom, women were admitted to secondary education, and public education was extended. Censorship regulations were modified.

In the political and judicial sphere, district assemblies *(zemstvos)* were established to decide local issues. Equality before the law was formally acknowledged; secret interrogation and flogging were prohibited. A jury system was introduced, and judges were freed of governmental control. Municipalities received charters for self-government. Finally, through universal conscription, the arbitrary levying of troops was ended. Reform measures were slowed down by a revolt of the Poles in 1863 and an attempt on the life of the tsar in 1866. But by 1870 Russia had, without civil war and revolution, achieved a reorganization that enabled it to enter the Modern Age.

United States

In the United States, foremost in the practice of liberal democracy, the same issue of involuntary human servitude and its economic consequences was the most inhibiting factor and burning problem of the period between 1848 and 1870. The issue concerned a smaller sector of the population than it did in Russia, but in the U.S. the practice of full "slavery," as opposed to "serfdom," was more revolting to modern people's conscience. It was also more complicated. It had an effect on the entire political scene, aroused regional jealousies, and involved racial antagonisms.

EMANCIPATION

During the 1850s, the United States experienced a rapid development of its productive forces; output in industry and mining increased, and railway construction proceeded rapidly, stimulating land grants as gifts to the railway builders. Additional areas of public land were sold at minimal prices, opening the way to ever more speculation and corruption, while providing pioneers with farmland. The discovery of gold in California released a stream of prospectors to the West, rapidly populating it with Americans, many newly arrived immigrants. National wealth grew and liberal political institutions continued to foster an enterprising, inventive spirit.

But grave problems remained unresolved. Ideology divided the northern and the southern states. Divergent economic interests between an industrialized North and an agricultural South could not be reconciled. The routing of railways across the continent, important for future development as well as personal gains of entrepreneurs, caused bitter disputes. Slavery as well as the status of fugitive slaves seeking shelter in the North created divisions. In 1854, the Missouri Compromise was repealed. Thus, at the very time when European nations were maintaining relatively stable governments, America was being subjected to widespread controversy and dissensions that threatened the peace of the land.

Into this atmosphere, Abraham Lincoln was elected to the presidency in 1860. Within a few months, the southern states seceded from the Union. Therewith, the issue of preserving the union came to overshadow the issue of slavery. The Civil War began. Both sides were poorly organized, but the North was better equipped, and richer. Owing to the ruthless use of updated weapons, the war caused extremely heavy casualties on both sides and fearful devastation in the South, where with hitherto unknown brutality little consideration was given even to unarmed civilian inhabitants. Victory for the industrially stronger North did not come until 1865. However, in 1863, about two years after Russia's freeing of the serfs, Lincoln had issued his Emancipation Proclamation. It freed the slaves. This measure failed to provide, in contrast to the laws passed in Russia, the freedmen with land as a basis for their economic future. It did not, in fact, even gain for them the equal rights set forth in subsequent amendments to the Constitution. More Americans were killed in the course of the Civil War than in the two later world wars added together. When Lincoln, soon after the end of the war, was assassinated, the South was treated as a conquered country. Confiscations, discrimination, carpetbagger plundering, and military occupation were heaped upon the vanquished. As to the slaves, their segregation was not ended. Yet, personal slavery was abolished, the country was reunited politically, and the balance of power shifted definitely in favor of the North. In the long run, the way was now open to further modernization and national prosperity.

EXPANSION

The vigorous United States pushed on to new tasks. In 1867, the government purchased Alaska from Russia, and in 1869 completed the first transcontinental railway. The government made available new territories for agriculture and encouraged business enterprise by passing more effective protective tariffs; a consequent boom helped even the defeated South to regain economic health and contributed immensely to the political strength of the nation.

THE WEST, ASIA, AND AFRICA

Events during the period from 1848 to 1870 changed the political and social structure of both the European continent and North America. They also transformed the relationships between Western civilization and the rest of the globe. A new era of expansion in Western countries began and their scientific methods and techniques spread to other lands. This process took place not only in regions completely or partially under Western domination, but even in independent nations that adopted Western ways on their own initiative.

Asia

The course of Westernization in Asia was different from that in Africa. Asiatic countries had developed a relatively unchanging culture on a high level, whereas numerous civilizations in Africa remained primitive. Of the Asiatic countries, one—Japan—succeeded in introducing many Western ways without becoming colonized. During the regime of Emperor Meiji, Japan, having been forced to open its ports to Western traders in 1854, averted the dangers of domestic revolution and foreign subjugation by adopting reforms along European models.

Other peoples of Asia had to accept Western ways involuntarily, through a combination of economic and military penetration. The Dutch occupied Sumatra and other parts of Indonesia, rich in sugar and coffee. They arbitrarily imposed Dutch customs and institutions. Weak, impoverished China, torn by internal disorders and rivalry between conservative and reform factions, had to establish diplomatic relations with the West. Forced to grant extraterritorial rights, China was also made to cede ports to Western governments. It even had to renounce many old ties with other Eastern nations. Only constant bickering among the Europeans themselves saved China from losing its independence; as it was, Britain, which had begun the Opium War, attacked the country once more. Together with French contingents, British troops looted Peking in 1860.

In India, after the Mutiny of 1857, the British imposed their jurisdiction and customs. Their policy of "salutary neglect," which meant indifference to the domestic needs of the country, was combined with a gradual enforcement of Western political and legal concepts; part of the upper class was slowly Anglicized. Many Indian students received an education in England. Indian markets and resources were integrated into the British economy. In Persia and Afghanistan, both England and Russia exerted a dominant economic and political influence.

Africa and the Americas

In Africa, the northern coast became the chief object of European penetration. Construction of the Suez Canal began in 1859; it was opened for traffic in 1869. French, English, and Spanish interests were built up among the Moslem peoples of North Africa—then largely under Turkish overlordship.

The Western nations also expanded their activities and influence in North and South America. Immigration, the settlement of vast areas, the building of railways, and the integration of the whole region into the Western economy acted as powerful forces, spreading in all parts of the Western Hemisphere the concepts, social customs, and industrial techniques of the West.

Imperialism

In the late nineteenth century, imperialism meant the building of European empires by embracing weaker, mainly underdeveloped, colonial nations; it constituted a violent form of nationalism. Like all colonizers, the imperialist nations often brought a modicum of order, law, and certain ethical and religious precepts. They also brought a measure of education to their colonial areas. But in their search for raw materials, industrial markets, fiscal revenues, and national prestige, the imperialists often ruthlessly exploited the inhabitants of these areas. For the sake of maintaining control over them, many wars were fought and many injustices committed; independence movements were suppressed.

After the revolutions of 1848, important changes occurred in the European political arena. Governments in most European countries took further steps, through action "from above," toward the introduction of constitutions which, though still limited in scope, included important steps toward representative government. France saw a brief period of social and economic progress followed by a decline, mainly owing to the ambitious foreign policies of Napoleon III. Germany, resolving leadership between Prussia and Austria in favor of Prussia, progressed toward unification. Italy likewise made great strides in the same direction.

The greatest changes occurred in Russia and the United States. Both countries, Russia peacefully, the United States in a devastating war, put an end to serfdom in Russia and slavery in America. Both enlarged their territories through wars, penetration, and settlement on their respective continents. Imperialism triumphed in England and France as it did in Russia and the United States. Western economy and diplomatic, military, political, and missionary institutions spread around the globe. Imperialism wove "a close net of common behavior and thought patterns" of Western origin around all parts of the five continents.

Selected Readings

Blum, Jerome. *Lord and Peasant in Russia* (1965)

Dehio, Ludwig. *The Precarious Balance: The Politics of Power in Europe, 1494–1945* (1963)

Hearder, H. *Italy in the Age of the Risorgimento, 1790–1870* (1983)

Hofstadter, Richard. *The American Political Tradition* (1973)

Kann, Robert A. *The Multinational Empire . . . Habsburg Monarchy, 1848–1918* (1950)

Kochan, M. and Abraham, R. *The Making of Modern Russia* (1983)

Kolchin, Peter. *Unfree Labor: American Slavery and Russian Serfdom* (1987)

Mack Smith, Denis. *Cavour* (1985)

Morison, Samuel E. *The Oxford History of the American People* (1965)
Pipes, Richard. *Russia under the Old Regime* (1974)
Plessis, A. *The Rise and Fall of the Second Empire, 1852–1871* (1985)
Waller, D. *Bismarck* (1985)
Webb, R. K. *Modern England, from the Eighteenth Century to the Present* (1980)

16

Revaluation of Values (1848–1870)

1865 End of American Civil War; Lincoln assassinated
Maxwell, *Treatise on Electricity*
Tolstoy, *War and Peace*

1866 Austro-Prussian ("Seven Weeks'") War
Italy annexes Venetia
Dostoevsky, *Crime and Punishment*

1867 Dual monarchy of Austria-Hungary established
Invention of dynamite (Nobel)
Second Reform Bill in England
Marx, *Das Kapital*
Ibsen, *Peer Gynt*
Purchase of Alaska by U.S.A.

1869 Opening of Suez Canal

1870 Jules Verne, *Twenty Thousand Leagues under the Sea*
Outbreak of Franco-Prussian War
Napoleon made prisoner by Germans, deposed by French
End of Papal States: Rome becomes Italian capital
Dogma of papal infallibility

1871 Founding of German Empire
Revolt of the *Commune* in Paris
Impressionist exhibition in Paris
Verdi, *Aïda*

*T*he rapid transformation of the political stage of the West by the thought, fervor, and endeavors of statesmen like Cavour, Bismarck, Napoleon III, and others, and by events like the emancipation of serfs and slaves in Russia and America, was duplicated in the contemporary cultural scene by equally rapid changes. In the sciences, Darwin's theory of evolution changed previously held concepts far beyond the field of biology for which it was conceived. In the arts, the traditionalism of a century was overturned by the impressionists. In literature, the novels of Dostoevsky and Tolstoy opened up new vistas into human nature, human passions, and the human subconscious. In the religious field, scholarly research and historical criticism of the Scriptures attacked inherited views, and a conflict took shape between a society trusting in science and progress and individuals vigorously reaffirming Christian tenets and creeds. Finally, the whole social pattern of Western civilization was called into question and repudiated by the work of Karl Marx.

DEVELOPING PATTERNS

History

A particularly important new role, in line with scientific views, was assumed in the middle of the nineteenth century by the study of history. A growing consciousness developed concerning the significance of the past to present conditions. Avoiding the often utopian, idealistic, and imaginative approach marking the Age of Enlightenment, historians now used sober, scientific methods; they engaged in conscientious source studies, on which they based their writings. They followed in general the principle stated by Ranke—to describe "what actually happened." Their method came to be applied in various fields outside that of history proper. But they combined their aim of pure scholarship with that of the *philosophes* of the eighteenth century, who had been ready to interpret, to educate, and to propagandize. Historical writings therefore became a force of national significance in preserving national traditions and promoting national consciousness. Especially influential were Carlyle and Macaulay in England and Bancroft and Parkman in the United States. On the Continent, Mommsen's masterful work on Roman history, written with detachment, was supplemented by historians like Sybel and Droysen, who acclaimed the Prussian state, and by Thiers and Michelet in France, who presented to their compatriots the glories of the French Revolution and Napoleon.

Literature

European literature mostly followed along paths established earlier in the century. Germany offered little that could compare with its past accomplishments. France continued to maintain a high level of prose fiction through the works of Zola, Maupassant, and others. Britain had a number of skilled essayists and critics, as well as several excellent novelists and poets—the latter including Tennyson and Browning. The United States contributed the poems of Whitman and Longfellow, the novels of Melville and Hawthorne, and the essays of Thoreau and Emerson.

A considerable number of significant works were created by women. In Britain, it was George Eliot and Elizabeth Browning, in Germany Droste-Hülshoff, in America Emily Dickinson and others who put their imprint on the literature of the age. A special place belongs to Harriet Beecher Stowe, who, with her moving *Uncle Tom's Cabin*, appealed to the conscience of the American people with regard to the abolishing of slavery. Her work evoked worldwide sympathy.

But in terms of the achievements of individual nations, it was Russia that produced the outstanding masterpieces of the time. In Russia, dissatisfaction with prevailing conditions led to a grave spiritual crisis. Out of the crisis emerged the searching, penetrating social and psychological novels of Turgenev *(Fathers and Sons)*, Dostoevsky *(Crime and Punishment, The Brothers Karamazov)*, and Tolstoy *(War and Peace, Anna Karenina)*. On the whole, it was the novel that appealed to the largest literate public, many of whom belonged to the upper-middle class.

Music

In the field of music, post-1848 Europe maintained remarkably high standards with brilliant performers such as Liszt, who through his new harmonic conceptions also contributed much to the art of composition. Still more significant were the achievements in opera. The nineteenth century found operatic creation at its apex. Towering over the excellent French composers, such as Gounod *(Faust)* and Bizet *(Carmen)*, were the two mighty figures of Wagner and Verdi *(Rigoletto, La Traviata, Aïda)*. While Verdi devoted himself to Italian opera, with its emphasis on voice and melody, and brought it to new heights through the greatness of his art, Wagner *(Tristan and Isolde, Nibelungen Ring, Parsifal, Meistersinger)* traveled an independent path, based on his view of opera as a musical drama that demanded serious texts of poetic worth. Wagner wrote his own librettos; he allocated to the orchestra a more essential role than previous composers had done. His work, based on sagas and folklore, may show many romantic traits, yet it constitutes one of the most beautiful and enduring expressions of the age. The symphonic and concert music of the mid-nineteenth century likewise attained excellence, with works by Brahms, the foremost symphonic composer of his time, and significant contributions by Berlioz and other composers, such as Bruckner and Johann Strauss.

Arts

Painting, too, received new impulses, which led to lasting achievements. Neoclassic as well as neo-Gothic, pre-Raphaelite, and other contemporaneous and often imitative art movements, as their names imply, were denounced by a younger generation. Some of the great painters of the middle nineteenth century staged a revolt against the traditional approach. Artists in Paris took the lead. Paris had grown steadily as an art center, where masters such as Corot, Millet, and the caricaturist and critic Daumier had produced and exhibited their works. Now, a new school of art, "impressionism," was developed by Manet, Monet, Degas, and other brilliant artists; they sought an artistic expression that departed sharply from the fashions, habits, and techniques of the past. Developing new concepts in the use of color and reproducing the luminous quality of the air, they depicted human life and nature in so fresh and inspiring a manner that they stimulated many disciples to carry forward the task of artistic reinterpretation.

By the mid-nineteenth century, the arts began to reach, through new channels, a still wider public than in the preceding two centuries. In the Middle Ages and early Modern Age, it had been the churches, foremost the Catholic and Orthodox Churches, which had in the West communicated philosophical thoughts and the great works in music, art, and architecture to the populations. They appealed to rich and poor alike. The same was true in Reformation times. But, thereafter, it was principally select audiences that could follow the philosophical developments and enjoy the arts in salons, academies, and social gatherings in the homes of the elite. Now, a wider public was once more reached. New outlets became available: concert halls, operas and theaters, and museums. Free lectures were given for the general public in special auditoriums, and newspapers reported and evaluated current political and cultural events.

Philosophy

In the field of philosophy, rationalist tendencies, which had steadily grown since the late Middle Ages, attained a final triumph. Despite the acceptance of numerous traditional concepts in metaphysics, rational analysis had in the seventeenth century characterized the works of Descartes, Spinoza, and Leibnitz. Eighteenth-century philosophers of the Enlightenment had similarly put their trust in reason rather than faith; following them—despite idealistic and ethical judgments—Kant, Hegel, and Fichte had also emphasized the function of reason.

This trend came to a climax in the mid-nineteenth century, with the philosophy of Comte, who rejected all views based upon metaphysical speculation. In his "positivist" system, he described metaphysics and religion as evidences of primitive stages of human development. To him, the future was to be shaped by science, based on logic and observable facts. Only by science would the human race reach its highest plane. A scientific approach also underlay the empiricism of John Stuart Mill, who directed his attention to social organization. Mill became an advocate of democratic and liberal concepts—even though he distrusted their effect on the human spirit.

The same confidence in reason as the best guide to truth inspired David Friedrich Strauss, who applied the scientific method to the Scriptures, which he subjected to a searching criticism. This investigation led him to challenge the historical accuracy of many parts of the Bible. Ernest Renan saw in the record of Christ's life the story of an extraordinary human being and the exposition of the highest ethical code. Together, Strauss and Renan added strength to a movement which rejected traditional, and especially transcendental, beliefs and which looked toward science, logic, and reason for guidance.

Science

Western civilization, having developed a steadfast confidence in reason and science, pressed forward in its investigations of nature. It searched for laws governing natural phenomena, and sought to apply scientific knowledge to practical problems.

PHYSICAL SCIENCES

In chemistry, Mendeleev, one of the first great Russian scientists, simultaneously with the German, Meyer, drafted the periodic table of the elements. There were many basic discoveries in both inorganic and organic chemistry. Liebig laid foundations for a broad application of chemical knowledge to agriculture. A petroleum industry was founded. In physics (especially thermodynamics and electricity), fundamental principles were discovered. Large industries applying the new knowledge evolved, including those developing new inventions (e.g., telegraphy and photography).

MEDICAL SCIENCES

Of the most immediate benefit for people were the scientific advances in medical sciences. Researchers studied physiology, especially the human cellular structure and nervous system. They also investigated problems of nutrition. Pasteur and Koch made fundamental contributions in bacteriology, and the germ theory of diseases was widely disseminated. Long-established theories of spontaneous generation were conclusively discarded.

As the causes of dread diseases were traced to bacteria, antitoxins and other means of preventive and curative treatment were developed. Epidemics such as cholera still occurred in numerous countries, but sanitation improved and, with it, public health. Antisepsis came into general use, and anesthesia prevented untold suffering. Similarly, in embryology, insights of lasting benefit were achieved.

BIOLOGICAL SCIENCES

The most notable advance, leading to new insights of basic significance, was made in biology. Many scientists, studying the life histories of plants, of lower animals, and of human beings, had concluded that an evolutionary process was taking place. Scientists like Erasmus Darwin and Lamarck, poets like Goethe, philosophers like Hegel, and social thinkers like Malthus had foreshadowed such views. The decisive step, however, was taken when Erasmus Darwin's grandson, Charles, explained life in terms of a struggle for existence, in which the weak members among plants, lower animals, and humans are constantly being eliminated and only the "fittest" survive. Thus, it was shown, a natural selection takes place and, through heredity, the natural qualities of those surviving are passed on from generation to generation until new species fit to survive are evolved. This theory of evolution was promoted with almost religious fervor by a number of Darwin's disciples. As it brought a deeper understanding of nature's evolutionary processes, it also led to a rethinking of traditional beliefs outside the field of natural sciences.

Religion

No area of human endeavor was more deeply affected by evolutionary views than was that of the Christian churches. The whole of science, scientific methodology, historical criticism, and the climate of opinion of the Age of Liberalism and Nationalism posed a challenge. To be sure, the Catholic Church had had experience in adapting itself to the demands and views of many successive ages. However, the Protestant churches, not open to authoritative reinterpretation, and many of them more rigid in their literal beliefs in the Scriptures, possessed less of such experience. Both were now forced to face a world where scientific explanations were accepted for the evolution of the universe, the creation of the human race, and the relationship of humans and nature. They had also to consider the various modern theories about the connections between the individual and human society, and between the psychology of people and their natural heritage.

CATHOLIC ATTITUDE

In the presence of such issues, the Roman Catholic Church, under the firm hand of Pope Pius IX, who had disappointed the expectations liberal and progressive thinkers had of him, took a resolute stand. Since the Age of Enlightenment, the Church had fought a new wave of irreligion and atheism. In the first half of the nineteenth century, it had succeeded, despite the progress of science, in making new conversions, including the case of the Protestant, Anglican churchman John Henry Newman in England, who had converted to Catholicism. It had the satisfaction of seeing in England the emancipation of the Catholics in 1829 and the reestablishment of the Catholic hierarchy in 1850. The Church had normalized its relations with France, and it had survived the onslaughts of the Italian nationalists and their occupation of Rome in 1848. Even among some of the foremost religious thinkers of Orthodox Russia it met with a friendlier spirit.

The Church therefore felt equal to dealing with evolutionary and other scientific views. Unconcerned with conflicting scientific interpretations, the pope put forth in 1854 the dogma of the "Immaculate Conception" of Mary. In 1864, he issued his "Syllabus of Errors." In eighty short statements he stated that science and reason are unable to explain all natural forces; that salvation cannot be gained outside the Roman Catholic Church; that the Church cannot dispense with temporal or worldly power; that marriage cannot be a Christian marriage without Church rites; and, in a last, most important paragraph, that progress, liberalism, and modern civilization are altogether at variance with the teachings of the Church. This strong statement, rejecting any thought of compromise, was followed in 1870 by the declaration of the "infallibility" of the pope in *ex-cathedra* pronouncements—pronouncements made from the altar of St. Peter's in Rome—on matters of faith and morals.

PROTESTANT ATTITUDE

Papal indictments of and warnings against the unrestricted belief in science, in human progress, and in contemporary civilization shocked many Catholics. They found even less approval among many Protestants. But divided as Protestants were into a multitude of groups—liberals with vague pantheistic ideas, fundamentalists with belief in the literal truth of the Scriptures, and a majority holding to various middle roads—they could take no united stand. As a whole, they found themselves less at odds than the Catholics with the climate of the time—capitalism, industrialism, liberalism, and nationalism. But science raised problems for Protestants, too. In particular, Strauss's historical criticism and Charles Darwin's evolutionary theories were difficult to reconcile with their traditional teachings. Indeed, scholarly investigation, unconcerned with Christian ethics, and Darwin's implication that organisms evolve in response to natural conditions led to a stronger reaction among many Protestants than among Catholics.

Social Theory

Science and evolution necessarily had an impact also upon social theory and were used by some of the radical thinkers to support their condemnation of existing social conditions. Socialists, in particular—who often found themselves in conflict with nationalism and liberalism, with religion, and with all traditions—gladly spread the scientific creed.

ANARCHISM

The most extreme socialist wing, the anarchists, rejected everything that in Western civilization was held in esteem, except modern science. Following Proudhon, the anarchists saw the "root of all evil" in the state. By coercion, the state corrupted people; its laws served only a small, propertied ruling group. Utopians at heart—including men like the Russian aristocrats Bakunin and Kropotkin—the anarchists expected progress and morality only from a scientific age when all peoples would enjoy complete political and economic freedom. By persuasion, or preferably by a cleansing revolution, they wished to create a new society in which law would be replaced by voluntary contracts. Only a fully free society, where neither state, family, marriage bonds, nor property and law would exist and where science and rationality would reign—only such a society, they thought, could be expected to bring perfection to humanity.

MARXISM

In contrast to the utopianism of the anarchists, another socialist trend was based on the scientifically conceived ideas of Karl Marx. A German by birth, Marx collaborated with his friend Friedrich Engels in writing a *Communist Manifesto* published in 1848. In 1867, while he was living in England, the first volume of his famous work, *Das Kapital,* appeared.

Marx's teachings are complex and open to various interpretations. With their emphasis on economic forces, they reflect the climate of his age and have become of fundamental importance in later times. Marx insisted that "history is the history of class conflicts," that the means of production and changing economic processes determine the law, politics, and morals of each succeeding society. He believed that with capitalism the world had entered a stage which would bring forth the last and greatest class conflict. He asserted that capitalism is interested in profits and not in the satisfaction of human needs; it deprives workers of an adequate share of the profits from their production by reserving for the capitalist all "surplus value" resulting from the laborer's toil.

Capitalism would lead increasingly to the concentration of wealth in a few hands and to greater misery for the masses. Labor had become a mere commodity available for the benefit of the capitalist. Dangerous business cycles would continue to haunt the world until the proletariat, the workers of all countries, had united, revolted, and brought about the collapse of the capitalistic system. Thus, through a dialectical process, according to which everything produces the seeds of its own destruction, capitalism would destroy itself. The state would wither away and all workers would be compensated for their labor according to their work and their needs.

Socialism in Action

If other socialist or communist theories had inspired many revolutionary outbreaks through the ages, Marxism, with its more scientific investigation of the relationship of economics and history, laid foundations for a far more relentless and thoroughgoing movement. Its practical effects were correspondingly far-reaching.

FORMATION OF SOCIALIST PARTIES

By the time the full impact of Marxism was felt, the situation of the working class had greatly changed compared with that during the early stages of industrial development. Socialists had gained strength through union. Toward the middle of the century, they had forced state authorities to recognize the right of collective bargaining. Then, realizing that political control was necessary for the emancipation of the workers, socialists began to form their first political parties. They sought representation in parliaments, where they opposed liberal as well as conservative aims. They rejected military appropriations and denounced the churches and nationalism. While thus repudiating the major creeds and loyalties of the age, they undertook to build a new loyalty—that to the international working class. For this purpose they founded, in 1864, the "First International" of labor unions.

LA COMMUNE

A new opportunity to strengthen the socialist cause, which by then had been profoundly influenced by Marx's teachings, came in 1870. Promptly upon the defeat of the French at Sedan and Metz and the collapse of the French Empire, revolutionary outbreaks occurred in Paris. Clubs on the order of the Jacobins were formed, and subsequent elections brought a great increase of socialist strength in the National Assembly. In March 1871, when many social and political ties were broken and a victorious foreign army stood at the gates of Paris, organized revolution began. The government was forced to flee to Versailles. A city council (the *Commune*), composed of radical and international socialists, was established as the executive agency. This revolution was of unique importance: whereas the revolutions of 1789 and 1830 had been sponsored by the bourgeoisie against the "old regime," and that of 1848 by an alliance of the bourgeoisie and the proletariat, the Revolution of 1871 was undertaken by the proletariat against the newly dominant bourgeoisie. Bakunin and many other socialists and anarchists took an active part in it, while Karl Marx, though considering it premature, applauded the aims of the revolutionaries.

The course of the uprising was, however, tragic. Both sides committed incredible atrocities. When the bourgeois government of France under the aged Thiers finally put down the *Commune*, a legacy of hatred remained that was to poison class relationships not only in France but throughout the Western world.

Russia gave the world some of the most outstanding works of fiction, presenting social, political, and religious topics with insights into the predicaments of the human condition in stories of unique artistry and depth. But high literary standards were maintained also in other Western countries as well, particularly in an ever-increasing number of published novels and dramas. Yet, in many ways, it was music, art, and science that marked the cultural world in the middle and late nineteenth century. Wagner and Verdi, Darwin and Marx, the impressionists, and a large number of scientists in physics, chemistry, and medicine all made a most significant impact.

Religion attracted new attention via its critics and defenders. On the one hand, there were Strauss and Renan or, in sharper form, Karl Marx, who challenged religious beliefs; on the other hand, there were those who held firmly to traditional values. Foremost among the latter was Pope Pius IX, who rejected the tendencies of modern times and tried to reassert the role of the Catholic Church as arbiter of faith, morals, and the values that the modern world should maintain.

Selected Readings

Berlin, Isaiah. *Karl Marx* (1963)
Brinton, Crane. *Ideas and Men* (1963)
Craig, Gordon. *German History, 1867–1945* (1981)
Hobsbawn, E. J. *The Age of Capital, 1848–1875* (1975)
Lindemann, Albert S. *A History of European Socialism* (1984)
Mason, Stephen F. *History of the Sciences* (1966)
Sinclair, Andrew. *A Concise History of the United States* (1984)
Stromberg, Roland M. *European Intellectual History Since 1789* (1975)

17

The Era of Bismarck (1870–1890)

1873	Three Emperors' League (Germany, Austria, Russia)
	Kulturkampf in Germany
1875	British purchase of Suez Canal shares
1876	Bell, telephone
1877	Outbreak of Russo-Turkish War
	Edison, phonograph
1878	Congress of Berlin
1879	Edison invents electric light bulb
	Ibsen, *The Doll's House*
1881	Assassination of Alexander II of Russia
	Tunisia under French protectorate
1882	Triple Alliance established (Germany, Austria, Italy)
	British occupy Egypt
	Beginning of Bismarck's social legislation in Germany
1884	Germany acquires colonies
	Nietzsche, *Thus Spake Zarathustra* completed
1887	German-Russian Reinsurance Treaty
	U.S.A. passes Interstate Commerce Act
1888	Van Gogh, *Sunflowers*
1890	Dismissal of Bismarck

A definite configuration in Western civilization is traceable during the period between 1870 and 1890. Politically, nationalism was strong everywhere. Democracy was stronger the farther west one looked; autocracy, the farther east. Economically, industrialism, based on scientific attitudes and technical inventions, was the chief manifestation of the age. It advanced quickly in the northern and Protestant countries, more slowly in the south and where Catholicism dominated. Culturally, the trend was toward wider participation of all groups of the population in national affairs, toward expansion of literacy, toward science, and away from traditional metaphysical beliefs. The arts flourished, but strong utilitarian tendencies were felt in many areas.

As a result, there developed numerous new tensions—internally between workers and entrepreneurs, externally between nations. But no major revolution occurred, nor did an all-embracing war break out. With the help of uncommonly able and responsible statesmen in the key countries, progressive legislation brought improvements for the less privileged classes. Capable diplomats aided in the settlement of international disputes.

THE EUROPEAN STATES AND THEIR ALLIANCES

The era after 1870 is frequently named for Bismarck, who in 1871 became Germany's first chancellor and who remained until 1890 the dominant figure on the international political stage. Having achieved the unification of Germany by means of three wars, he devoted himself for almost two decades to the preservation of a European peace that was to permit the consolidation of the newly founded German Empire. "Seldom," the liberal *Manchester Guardian* once wrote, "has power so vast been employed so well." The "Era of Bismarck" is marked by the growth and rooting of constitutional government in many countries, by worldwide industrialization and social progress, and by struggles between states and the Catholic Church as well as between capitalistic governments and socialist parties. Diplomatically, it witnessed a broad international system of alliances that replaced the old balance of power (an undependable ideal) that had been Metternich's aim.

Germany

The German Empire brought into being in 1871 consisted of some twenty states, most of them ruled by local princes. Owing to the enterprising spirit of its merchant class, the strength of its military establishment, and the efficiency and honesty of its administrative apparatus, it quickly attained a position as one of the great world powers.

INTERNAL AFFAIRS

In Germany the period from 1870 to 1890 was marked by economic growth and by the flourishing of intellectual, and especially scientific, studies in the universities. On the other hand, events of these two decades reflected exaggerated nationalistic trends. They demonstrated the weakness of the constitutional order, as conceived by Bismarck. They brought to the fore the specific problems of Catholicism and socialism.

Constitutional Arrangements. The German emperor, who was simultaneously king of Prussia, acted within the limits of a constitution that gave him authority to direct military and foreign affairs and to appoint ministers. Legislative power, however, was vested in the *Bundesrat* and the *Reichstag*. The former, having limited functions, was meant to constitute a conservative force. The great political struggles were fought out in the *Reichstag,* the popular representation of the German people. The *Reichstag* was made up of conservative, liberal, Catholic, and socialist parties; its members were elected by the entire male population.

Problem of National Unity. Bismarck's task of welding Germany into a powerful unit was not unlike that facing the United States with its sectional interests. The problems confronting the chancellor were rooted in differences of economic conditions between an agricultural east and an industrial west; in dissimilarities of religion, customs, and political traditions between southern and northern German states; in nationality issues involving Poles and Danes living in eastern and northern border regions and French inhabitants in Alsace-Lorraine. (Alsace-Lorraine did not become a separate state of the union; it was ruled from Berlin and, for some time, was administered poorly.) Yet, the population in all the states took pride in Germany's prestige, its economic progress, its army, and its educational system. A shared interest in German culture facilitated the task of unification.

Economic Conditions. Unification made possible the rapid expansion of Germany's industrial capacity. In steel production, Germany soon challenged and then surpassed Britain. Owing to its growing population and to excellent scientific research, Germany's chemical, electrical, and machine industries flourished. The organization of cartels and the modernization of techniques made production more economical and efficient. The merchant marine grew and a nationalized railway system proved successful. Trade connections with all parts of the world were established; and, during the 1880s, colonies were acquired. Despite a number of financial crises—including one crisis generated by the sudden influx of gold from payments of France's war indemnity—German banks and holding companies proved sound and gained worldwide importance.

Yet, agriculture suffered reverses, as in many other newly industrialized countries. Much concerned, Bismarck vacillated between a policy of protective-tariff legislation to further agriculture and a policy of low tariffs to further the new industries.

Confessional and Socialistic Issues. During Bismarck's administration, two great issues disturbed Germany's internal peace: One was the issue of the proper relationship between the state and the Catholic Church, the other the issue of socialism. The "infallibility doctrine" of the Church had raised grave misgivings throughout the Western world because it seemed to demand a double allegiance from Catholic citizens. Bismarck, in particular, was disturbed, inasmuch as separate Catholic interests in predominantly Protestant Germany could endanger the unity of the country; and his misgivings increased when a Catholic political party, the "Center," was founded and a struggle between Bismarck's government and the Catholics, a *Kulturkampf,* ensued.

The struggle centered around educational facilities. Bismarck wanted to see Catholic institutions under state supervision. He had stringent laws enacted against sectarian schools; he sought to bar or control Catholic religious orders. Everywhere, the liberties of the Catholics were infringed upon. But since Bismarck's repressive policy, though backed by liberals, did not succeed, he took advantage of the first opportunity (upon the death of Pius IX) to make a compromise. He revoked the restraining laws and sought the support of the Center party in order to fight a potentially more dangerous enemy: socialism.

After 1875, the various socialist groups had gained in power by merging into a "Social Democratic party." This party had won a number of seats in the *Reichstag,* where it opposed much of the imperial legislation and all military bills. The chancellor met this threat by means of two seemingly contradictory policies. On the one hand, he used force to impede freedom of speech and press and to exile or imprison socialist leaders. On the other hand, he wisely tried to deflate the program of the socialist party by satisfying as many of its demands as seemed justified. This latter policy led him to institute a bold program of social legislation that was to become a model for all nations. In 1883, he introduced compulsory health insurance for workers; in 1884, accident insurance; and in 1889, old-age insurance. Employers and employees had to share with the government the costs of such insurance. Similar social insurance systems were subsequently adopted by most Western nations and by Russia.

FOREIGN AFFAIRS

In foreign affairs, Bismarck hoped to achieve European peace and German security by isolating France and building German alliances with other nations. He sought friendly relations with England. He cooperated with the British in numerous practical issues and exercised restraint in regard to German demands for colonies. In 1873, he drew Austria-Hungary into a close alliance, for which he had prepared the ground by using moderation in the war settlement of 1866. He induced Russia to join this alliance, and thus formed a "Three Emperors' League"—despite Russo-Austrian rivalry and the agitation of Pan-Slavs, who advocated a commonwealth of all Slavic peoples and constituted the extreme nationalist wing among Russia's political forces. In 1882, he negotiated a second alliance system, which included Germany, Austria, and Italy, later known as the "Triple Alliance." He made treaties with Romania and other small nations. All in all, friendly ties connected Berlin with London, Vienna, St. Petersburg, Rome, Bucharest, and other capitals.

Yet, Bismarck did not succeed in maintaining all such ties intact. Relations with England cooled during the 1880s. Those with Russia likewise weakened. The Three Emperors' League was threatened in 1875 because of personal jealousies. It was suspended in 1878 when, following a victorious Russian war against Turkey, Bismarck failed to support Russia's demands for spoils. Furthermore, because of the incompatibility of Russian and Austrian aims, the league was allowed to expire in 1887. Although Bismarck considered Russia the "pivot" of German security, he succeeded in replacing the league only by a shaky and secret German-Russian "Reinsurance Treaty," which survived no more than three years. In 1890, the seventy-five-year-old chancellor was dismissed from office by the young emperor, William II, who had succeeded to the throne in 1888, and who refused to renew the Reinsurance Treaty. Thus ended Bismarck's international system.

France

Germany's vigorous economic and political growth from 1870 to 1890 was not paralleled in France. The required initiative was lacking. The population hardly increased. France continued to devote itself primarily to agricultural pursuits, whereas industries developed slowly. The war of 1870–1871 had left France without a legitimate government; the National Assembly was obliged to conclude the Peace of Frankfurt with Germany.

Not until 1875 was a regular government organized; and not until 1879, after many attempts by royalists to reintroduce a monarchy, was the "Third Republic" established. A parliamentary regime, with two legislative chambers, was set up, the members being elected by general male suffrage on an equalitarian basis. The legislature included many divergent forces—monarchists, liberals, republicans, and socialists. The president of the republic became a mere figurehead.

INTERNAL AFFAIRS

A number of years elapsed before the new government earned respect and confidence at home and abroad. Corruption marked its first two decades. Scandals occurred over the sale of Legion of Merit awards and over the building of the Panama Canal; and in 1887, General Boulanger, a new "man on the white horse" (reminiscent of Napoleon), aided by nationalists, threatened to set himself up as a dictator. Moreover, disunity was created by widespread materialism and religious skepticism among liberal bourgeoisie and the workers. Both clashed with the Catholic traditions of the conservatives and the peasantry, and led to much anticlerical agitation. Disunity was further increased by repressive acts against socialists.

Yet, beneath the surface, France did make progress in numerous respects. Its army was reorganized. Its economy recovered from the disasters of war and revolution. Living conditions for workers improved. Civil rights were no longer violated, as they had been in Napoleonic times. Artistic life continued to flourish and to attract foreign visitors. Advances in education were substantial.

EXTERNAL AFFAIRS

In external affairs, France was held down in Europe both by its own dreams of a *revanche* (revenge) for 1870 and by the strength of Germany on the Continent and of England on the seas. France failed to adjust to the new international situation. Moreover, by seizing Tunisia, which Italy coveted, and by establishing a French protectorate there, France incurred the hostility of the Italians. For two decades, France remained isolated. Yet, its Tunisian conquest compensated to a degree for the failure of some of its nationalistic plans. The Tunisian conquest was followed by an act incorporating Algiers into the empire. There, as in Tunisia, French law was introduced. Many settlers from France spread French customs, language, and culture.

England and the British Empire

The British Isles had remained untouched by the wars of France, Italy, Germany, Austria, and Denmark. In "splendid isolation," though carefully watching events on the Continent, Britain continued to devote itself to the affairs of its own empire.

INTERNAL AFFAIRS

After 1870, conservative and liberal governments alternated more rapidly than in preceding years. Both parties had outstanding leaders: the Conservatives Disraeli, the Liberals Gladstone. Though wholly opposed in their attitude toward life, both leaders worked capably and with success, each in his own way, for the aggrandizement of their country. They introduced urgently needed improvements in the educational system, which lagged behind those of the Continental powers. The economy made rapid progress. Measures for the protection of business interests and laissez-faire policies were now increasingly accepted by Conservatives; the unfair taxation system was revised. The workers gained by the legalization of labor unions, and relief came finally for the textile workers.

Progress was made also toward broader democracy through the introduction of the secret ballot. In 1884, a Third Reform Bill was passed; while it still did not make the right to vote general, it did confer the right on those who paid taxes. This meant that about three-quarters of the male population received that right. Anti-Jewish legislation, as it still existed in England, was removed, but nothing was done for women. Thereafter, radicalism became less extreme in its demands. Instead, a mild socialism was promoted by a "Fabian Society," founded in 1883. It was to usher in a socialist society by peaceful evolution rather than by violent revolution.

The problem of Irish self-government, which had long poisoned the relations between Irish and English, remained unsolved. Against much opposition, Gladstone sought to settle it by concessions. Land laws were passed in favor of Irish peasants. Religious peace was sought on the basis of an act, passed in 1869, that provided for the disestablishment of the Church of Ireland. But as an essentially agricultural land, with an almost medieval system of British landlords and Irish peasants, Ireland was bound to suffer from English policies, which were keyed to the trading and exporting of manufactured goods. Starvation conditions had existed ever since the potato famine of 1845. Irish hostility, derived from alien rule and kept alive by economic difficulties, smoldered.

EXTERNAL AFFAIRS

In external affairs, Britain pursued a vigorous imperialistic policy. It also became increasingly dependent upon its empire. The British consolidated their holdings in the Far East and built up their trade with China and Japan. They maintained their position in India by strengthening their communication lines and by acquiring, in 1875, controlling shares of stock in the Suez Canal Company. They purchased the shares from the Egyptian king, who had received them in exchange for his permission to allow the construction of the canal through his territory; however, his love of luxury depleted his finances, forcing him to sell the securities. Next, the British named Queen Victoria "Empress of India." They extended their sphere of influence into Afghanistan and Persia, thereby preventing a Russian approach to India, and they vigorously increased their colonizing activities in Africa. (Scientists and missionaries often formed an advance guard. For example, the famous Livingstone was led by his geographical interests and Christian zeal to explore central Africa. Commercial, and then political, entrepreneurs followed.) Britain also made an agreement with the Portuguese that made it possible for them to expand their acquisitions on Africa's west coast. Finally, when the ruthless exploitation and outrages of the Belgian king in the Congo became known, the British attended a congress, again convened by Bismarck in Berlin (1885), where an international agreement regarding more humane treatment of the natives of Africa was concluded. Principles for the colonization of Africa were laid down. Soon the map of Africa showed no unclaimed space.

Moreover, in 1882, at a time of riots in Egypt, the British navy, taking advantage of the situation, suddenly shelled Alexandria. This caused much loss of life among the population and inflicted great damage to property. Then Britain followed up this action by seizing the entire country.

English rule in Egypt was not oppressive. Law and justice were improved, and English purchases of tobacco and cotton benefited at least some sectors of the population. But Egyptian national sentiment was deeply hurt. A revolt led by the so-called "Mahdi," the leader of a Moslem sect, lasted a decade before it was suppressed.

Italy

Between 1870 and 1890, Italy experienced unique difficulties that affected adversely its political, as well as its economic and cultural, life.

INTERNAL AFFAIRS

Inexperienced in self-government, Italy struggled long for an efficient administration. Capable leaders and a sound bureaucracy were lacking. Funds were wasted, and corruption prevailed. Illiteracy was so widespread that it took a long time to build a working parliamentary system. National pride demanded the maintenance of a powerful army and navy, involving huge costs and excessive taxation; yet, the effort was hardly warranted.

More fundamental were other handicaps. The population increased rapidly. Because scarcity of raw materials prevented industrial development, poverty, too, increased. Many enterprising citizens chose to emigrate to America. Others joined radical parties that encouraged riots and peasant revolts; the anarchist movement grew. Finally, through a unilateral "Law of Guarantees," the Italian government accorded sovereignty in the Vatican to the papacy, paid an indemnity, and allowed religious institutions to function. Nevertheless, the popes remained unreconciled. In a predominantly Catholic country, this split inevitably created difficulties.

EXTERNAL AFFAIRS

An Italian foreign policy could be evolved only slowly; none had existed before Italy became a nation. Friendship with England and an alliance with Germany eventually formed the basis of Italian policy. The British had been favorable to Italian national ambitions. British good will continued to be important for Italy; since the British dominated the Mediterranean Sea and Malta, they could have become a threat along the extended Italian coastline. Germany had proved equally sympathetic. Despite Italian-Austrian rivalry over territories claimed by "irredentist" Italian nationalists, who sought the annexation of all territories where Italian people lived, the Triple Alliance was concluded between Italy, Austria, and Germany in 1882. A treaty of friendship was also negotiated between Italy and Russia.

Only with neighboring France did relations remain precarious. The attitude of the French had been vacillating during Italy's reunification struggle. France had seized Italian territories and had competed with Italy in colonial areas. In 1881, France took Tunisia.

Russia

The evolution of Russia from 1870 to 1890 continued to follow a path which differed from that of Western Europe. Intellectual movements asserted themselves, claiming for Russia a unique role in world history. Revolutionary and conservative groups shared these pretensions, though for divergent reasons. They expected their country to defeat the materialism of the West. Russia, they claimed, was animated by the spirit of true Christianity or by that of communistic, neighborly love and cooperation that could spread anti-materialistic, humane ideas. Significantly, such beliefs were held in the face of the deep national and social rifts that existed within the country, strong economic pressures toward greater Westernization, and Pan-Slav expansionist ambitions.

INTERNAL AFFAIRS

Few institutions existing in Russia in 1870 qualified the nation to take the role of leadership either among the Slavic countries or among the world powers. Although after emancipation and reform, the way was open for economic readjustment, autocracy was preserved and political modernization was slow.

Economic Conditions. Foreign capital, foreign entrepreneurs, and foreign technicians helped to develop Russia's natural resources. Numerous industries were founded. Coal, steel, and oil production rose and copper and gold mining increased. Soon after 1870, a vast railroad-building program was undertaken, serving, as elsewhere, both economic and military aims. The network was expanded southward in order to facilitate the export of grain and oil via the Black Sea and simultaneously to prevent a repetition of the military disasters experienced in the Crimean War.

Social Conditions. As a result, new social problems developed. Increasingly affected by Western trends, the growing and ambitious bourgeoisie found itself more and more in ideological conflict with the autocratic government. A like conflict existed between the government and the factory workers. The workers suffered as elsewhere from the hardships of early industrialization; they aspired to obtain political rights and economic improvement.

Still more dangerous to existing institutions was the dissatisfaction of the peasants. Legal restrictions and burdens weighed heavily upon them. Their individual holdings were generally too small for adequate subsistence. The redemption tax was high. Most peasants or village communes found it difficult to acquire sufficient additional land and to introduce modern techniques. The institution of the *mir,* with its collectivism, hindered initiative, reduced profits, led to much strife. Moreover, certain enterprising peasants (the *kulaks*) understood how to exploit the situation and to accumulate large acreage purchased from others who were unable to make an independent living. This *kulak* class became an important psychological factor in arousing resentment among the masses.

The government tried to meet the emergency by applying progressive, as well as repressive, measures. It continued the reform work, passed social legislation, reduced the redemption tax, gave more independence to the *mir*, and improved the *zemstvo* system. On the other hand, it maintained the autocracy of the tsar. It refused extension of civil rights and did nothing to eradicate the corruption permeating the entire bureaucracy. It intensified police methods, built up its espionage network in town and country, and continued the fearful system of exiling opponents to Siberia while leaving their families destitute at home.

Political Conditions. Under such circumstances, a threatening mood of resistance grew among all social classes. Idealists among the nobility, middle-class people desiring political rights, workers in need of further social legislation, peasants burdened by taxes and poverty, religious groups dissenting from the official orthodoxy, Jews agitating for equality, Poles and Finns and other aliens resenting both Russian domination and stepped-up Russification policies—all were united in assailing the existing institutions.

The intelligentsia became leaders of the discontented masses. Artists and writers, who played a more prominent role than ever before, often devoted their works to social criticism. To most of the reformers, a constitutional system in line with Western customs hardly seemed sufficient. Many felt that social rejuvenation would be possible only through revolution. In the 1870s, anarchists, whose primary desire was to destroy the state completely, gained an importance equaled nowhere else in Europe. Nihilists rejected all traditional values, and terrorists insisted that the times called for practical revolutionary deeds instead of mere theories. Together, nihilists, anarchists, and terrorists arranged for assassinations of leading officials, which culminated in 1881 with the murder of Tsar Alexander II. Marxists carried the teachings of Marx and Engels to the industrial workers.

"Populists" *(narodniki)* sought to gain salvation for Russia by winning over the peasants. The radicals instituted the *v narod* ("to the people") movement, which had two purposes: (1) young intellectuals were to live with peasants and become familiar with their ideas and needs; and (2) they were to propagate revolutionary ideas among the peasants. After the assassination of Alexander II, nihilism, terrorism, and populism abated somewhat. But despite stern measures of his successor, Alexander III, who fostered his grandfather Nicholas's aim of "autocracy, orthodoxy, nationality," Marxist socialism continued to grow. In 1883, an all-Russian socialist organization, forbidden at home, was founded abroad by Georgi Plekhanov. It devoted its efforts to spreading Marxist ideas among the Russian workers. Socialists agitated for shorter working hours and higher wages and sponsored strikes.

EXTERNAL AFFAIRS

In foreign affairs, Russia sought cooperation with Germany. It used the Franco-German War as a pretext to abrogate the Black Sea Clause imposed at the Peace of Paris. After Germany's victory, Russia formed the Three Emperors' League with Germany and Austria. By concluding this alliance and by, subsequently, making separate arrangements with Austria, Russia prepared to pursue its major aim: the resumption of its drive southward toward Constantinople.

The old aim of gaining control of Constantinople and the straits had become a major objective for the newly influential nationalistic forces in Russia, especially the Pan-Slavs. Ever since the first Pan-Slav Congress in Prague in 1848, they had looked forward to a mighty Slavic commonwealth under Russian leadership. When, during the 1870s, southern Slavic nations rebelled against Turkey and a "Young Turk" movement endeavored to modernize the country (which would have interfered with Russian intentions regarding Constantinople), the Pan-Slavs seized the opportunity and began to agitate for war. It soon materialized (Russo-Turkish War of 1877–1878). Backward technologically and weakened by the administration of corrupt and inefficient sultans, Turkey was quickly defeated. It was forced to sign a peace treaty at San Stefano whereby it had to surrender most of its European possessions, to grant independence or autonomy to its Slavic groups, and to agree to the formation of a Greater Bulgaria as a substantial power. It also had to give the Russians special rights in the straits, and to relinquish part of the Southern Caucasus. This treaty aroused fears in England and Austria, who wanted to preserve Turkey as a buffer, and the British insisted on the treaty's cancellation. They forced Turkey to cede Cyprus to them, and then undertook to defend the freedom of the straits. Thus threatened, Russia agreed to an international congress, which Bismarck was persuaded to convene in Berlin. The Peace of San Stefano was set aside, and the formation of Greater Bulgaria (which would have had an outlet to the Mediterranean Sea via the Aegean) was prevented. International, rather than Russian, control of the straits was arranged. Russia gained only some territory in the Caucasus and in Bessarabia as well as the recognition of the independence of Serbia and Romania. The outcome of the congress, which seemed to have rendered most of the war sacrifices futile, embittered Russia not only against England and Austria, but also against Germany because, in order to prevent a general European conflict, Germany had supported England. Not until 1881 was the Three Emperors' League renewed—and then only because of Russia's dependence upon German markets for its grain exports and on German supplies for its industrialization.

Frustrated in Europe, Russia resumed its Asiatic ventures. By 1884, Russian troops stood at Merv, not far from the Indian border. This advance led to further conflict with England and in turn brought another renewal of the Three Emperors' League. The league lasted until 1887 and was then replaced by the Reinsurance Treaty, which lasted until 1890.

THE UNITED STATES

In the period 1870 to 1890, developments in the United States became more and more like those in Europe. With the worldwide progress of democratization, including measures in behalf of civil rights, political differences diminished. In the economic sphere, the two decades witnessed in America, as in Europe, a rapid expansion of business and industry. Population growth was, however, more rapid in the United States, whose low death rate and high birth rate, combined with steadily rising immigration, resulted in an annual increase far above the rate in other Western countries. These demographic and economic factors enabled the United States to play an increasingly important role in world politics.

Internal Affairs

Notwithstanding cyclical difficulties, in addition to corruption and graft, material progress during the two decades after 1870 was enormous. Manufacturing and mining flourished. Large private fortunes were accumulated, while "equality of opportunity" became a watchword. Notwithstanding continued disagreements in the 1880s concerning the relative advantages of free trade and high tariffs, trade generally expanded. Farming did, as well, and it remained the chief occupational pursuit. Introduction of technical innovations—the telephone, phonograph, typewriter, gas lighting, sewing machines, and others—helped to establish the United States as a leading industrial nation. Urbanization accelerated.

This situation led to the emergence of numerous problems, some of which the United States shared with European countries. The United States, too, was beset by labor problems involving wages, working conditions, and spreading of slum areas and strikes. Numerous riots, some bloody, occurred. In the 1880s, an immigrant, Samuel Gompers, founded the American Federation of Labor.

Under such circumstances, the challenge of extreme liberalism had to be met, and a beginning was made with restrictive government legislation. To enforce it, a large bureaucracy was created. In 1883, the government enacted laws governing civil service. In 1887, the Interstate Commerce Act was passed to regulate the railroads; and in 1890, the Sherman Anti-Trust Act passed for the purpose of preventing business monopolies.

Moreover, a number of developments and problems peculiar to America emerged, primarily concerning (1) the aftermath of the Civil War, (2) the expansion of agriculture and the settlement of western areas, (3) the challenge of immigration, and (4) the promotion of financial stability. In contrast to European limitations, the agricultural area could be increased. Between the Mississippi River and the Rocky Mountains were vast regions that could be seized, where Indians lived with their buffalo herds. Gradually, these Indians were assaulted and largely exterminated. Their lands were fenced in with barbed wire. The buffalo herds were likewise nearly exterminated and the land was converted to cattle grazing and agriculture. As these regions became increasingly populated by American settlers, new states were formed and admitted to the Union.

The new problem of immigration now had to be addressed. The bulk of the newcomers no longer came from northern Europe, but from the southern and eastern European countries. They possessed a racial, social, and language background different from that of most earlier immigrants. More of them settled in urban centers than rural districts, and they were often exploited by irresponsible politicians who bought their votes and thereby vitiated the democratic process. Their integration into the mainstream life of the country was thus delayed.

Lastly, economic and financial developments gave rise to other serious problems. During the later part of the nineteenth century, the United States remained a debtor nation. This resulted in agitation to promote the use of silver as the basis for the currency, instead of strict adherence to the gold standard, which prevailed in most European countries.

External Affairs

In general, European problems in international relations held little interest for Americans. The United States entered into no alliances. It remained disinterested in the distribution of power overseas. For the most part, it stayed out of the race for territory. Nevertheless, it became involved in a number of foreign issues. Nationalism increased.

Population shifts to the West Coast and the acquisition of Alaska, as well as the occupation of the Midway Islands, west of Hawaii, which had taken place in 1867, forced upon the nation a more active role in the Pacific area, where American interests impinged upon those of Japan, England, Russia, and Germany, and necessitated both commitments and international conventions. A fear of "the Yellow Peril" resulted. Economic strength brought greater interest in Latin American countries and led to the First Pan-American Congress in 1889. The westward expansion within the United States and controversies with England dating back to the Civil War period made new agreements with England necessary; these were eventually achieved through arbitration by the German emperor and through the so-called "Halifax award," which settled the questions of the Oregon boundary and of the Newfoundland fisheries, respectively.

THE SMALLER NATIONS

The trends and problems of the great powers were duplicated among the smaller nations. However, few of these countries played any influential role on the international stage. Only among the Balkan nations did problems arise that led to wars. Only Portugal, Holland, and Belgium were active in colonial affairs. In all cases, a regulating influence was exercised by the great powers. Thus, in the Balkans, peace arrangements were dictated by the large nations. As a rule, the smaller countries devoted their attention to internal improvements. Switzerland and Denmark set an example with their advanced educational systems. They and other small countries succeeded in creating living conditions for their peoples often more satisfactory than those of larger countries. Democracy was strong in the small western and northern countries, while patriarchal and absolutist forms of government continued to prevail among Russia's and Turkey's neighbors in eastern Europe.

Unique roles were played by Switzerland, which had the most nearly perfect democracy in Western civilization; by Spain, which failed to rid itself of obsolete feudal institutions and which missed modernization in economic affairs as well; and by Latin American countries, where geographical disadvantages, underdeveloped economic resources, and political inexperience created favorable conditions for the rise of dictatorships. Even in Mexico, where a vigorous reform movement was led by Juárez, and after him by Díaz, progress in the direction of modern liberal institutions was slow.

Under the influence of Bismarck, peace was maintained in Europe. Only on the fringes did warfare erupt, between Russia and Turkey. Outside of Europe, force was employed by the various colonial imperialistic nations. Internally, considerable social advances were made. Most countries followed Bismarck's example and introduced old-age, health, and accident insurance, as in Germany. But rapid changes in industrial life brought ever new problems, which neither conservative nor liberal governments could satisfactorily solve. Socialism, seeking to meet the problems by introducing greatly altered social organization, was fought in Germany, France, Russia, Italy, and elsewhere.

But it gained in strength. Social democratic parties were founded and began to win seats and representation in constitutional assemblies.

In the meantime, the United States, where socialism did not become an issue, concentrated on perfecting its own internal organization and dealing with the numerous problems that came in the wake of the Civil War and the rapid industrialization of the country. A stream of immigrants came to the country.

Selected Readings

Cobban, A. *A History of Modern France*. 2 vols. (1962–65)
Craig, Gordon A. *German History, 1867–1945* (1981)
Croce, Benedetto. *A History of Italy, 1871–1915*
Eyck, Erich. *Bismarck and the German Empire* (1950)
Lukacs, John A. *The Great Powers and Eastern Europe* (1953)
Sheehan, J. J. *German Liberalism in the Nineteenth Century* (1982)
Taylor, A. J. P. *The Struggle for Mastery in Europe, 1848–1918* (1954)
Webb, E. K. *Modern England: From the Eighteenth Century to the Present* (1980)
Zeldin, T. *France, 1848–1945*. 2 vols. (1984)

18

Economic and Cultural Trends (1870–1914)

1891 Franco-Russian Alliance

1894 Dreyfus affair in France

1895 Jameson Raid

Discovery of X-rays by Roentgen

1898 European powers occupy Chinese ports

U.S.A. annexes Hawaii

Spanish-American War

Discovery of radium by the Curies

The period from 1870 to 1914 has been frequently criticized as an era of "bourgeois complacency." Actually, a measure of complacency did prevail among the middle class—and perhaps justifiably. Having gained dominating influence in the state, its well-to-do members were proud of their material wealth and comfort, the economic growth and prestige of their various nations, and their personal standards of "solidity and propriety." From education and literacy, they expected general progress in political and moral behavior. They celebrated important scientific discoveries, insights gained into the workings of nature, and the achievements of contemporary writers and painters.

But, far too often, they shut their eyes to many disturbing conditions underneath and to the currents that indicated growing dissatisfaction. These currents were felt not only by the less favored classes, but also by the privileged. Many leading thinkers questioned the possibility of continuous progress, whether it came, as many liberals believed, from the innate morality and good sense of people, or through science and education, or, as socialists believed, through revolution and emancipation, which they considered an inevitable result of an evolutionary process. Philosophers of the late nineteenth century reflected a deep pessimism. Many social thinkers were attracted by nihilistic views.

ECONOMIC CHANGES

In the five decades before 1914, sharp competition both among private enterprises and among nations led to enormous industrial expansion in most Western countries. This "second industrial revolution" is marked by the growth of the chemical and the electrical industries. Agriculture absorbed an ever-decreasing share of the available labor force and capital. Industrialization was beneficial materially, although the benefits did not reach the less favored classes until mass production became possible. Socially and politically, the effects seemed less promising. Class antagonisms increased. Socialist propaganda accused industrialists of exploiting the worker, gaining undue influence in political affairs, promoting colonialism, and instigating wars. Business affairs absorbed the energies of many outstanding figures: Carnegie, who built a steel empire; Nobel, who invented dynamite and built large munitions plants; Krupp, who presided over huge steel, armament, and machine industries; Rockefeller, who founded the Standard Oil Company; Alfred Mond, who organized vast chemical enterprises; and Werner von Siemens and Emil Rathenau in the electrical industry. Competition eliminated some while bringing others to the fore; unlike the former nobility, these captains of industry depended upon individual inventiveness and personal ability to maintain their positions, rather than class, birth, or even inherited wealth.

Population

The rapid increase of productivity was made possible by population growth. Despite emigration, the population in countries such as Germany, England, and Russia gained about sixty-five percent from 1870 to 1914. By then, about 425 million people lived in Europe, while another 135 million Europeans resided in overseas territory, making up a record third of the global population.

Many capitals with millions of inhabitants had arisen in the West: London, Paris, St. Petersburg, Berlin, Vienna, and Rome. City life offered excitement, opportunities, educational facilities, and independence, but also hurried, competitive, unhealthy, and insecure conditions. Still, migration from country to town continued unabated.

Industry

Urbanization not only facilitated industrialism and economic growth, but also made them inevitable. Innumerable technical inventions were devised. Heavy industries increased manifold. Chemical industries began the large-scale production of both medical preparations and many synthetic materials for manufacturing. Aspirin was discovered in Germany. The rubber and oil industries gained special importance, benefiting mainly the United States and England as well as enterprising small countries, such as Holland. To some extent steam power was replaced by electric power. In 1914, Germany produced one-third of the world output in electricity, with the United States a close second. Even small countries like Sweden and Switzerland, owing to natural resources, gained worldwide importance as producers of electricity and electrical machinery. Old industries found new markets—such as the textile industry after the invention of the sewing machine. New industries developed in the field of communication: the wireless and motion-picture industries. The transportation industry expanded. Trains and ships were improved in speed and comfort. The first electrical streetcars appeared in Berlin in 1879. Bicycles became a popular means of transportation and, after the German Nikolaus Otto had developed the first internal combustion motor, the first modern automobiles were built in the 1890s. Eventually, airplanes were constructed. In the United States, the Wright brothers undertook the first flight in 1903; within six years, the Frenchman Blériot crossed the Channel to England.

Progress in transportation supported numerous auxiliary industries, the construction of highways, the extension of railways, and the building of canals—such as the Panama Canal and the various inland waterways. The pace of life accelerated.

FINANCE

Industries grew rapidly, but business cycles increasingly caused uncertainties. Inventors and producers often did not have the funds to finance their business ventures. Through borrowing, they became dependent upon banks, trusts, and holding companies; power came to be concentrated in the hands of financiers and promoters. Financial institutions began to determine business policies. They put their representatives on boards of directors. They exerted pressure on their clients to conclude mergers and market-sharing agreements, or to form cartels. Small independent businesses diminished in number and influence. Large corporation, with limited liability, predominated. A comparatively small minority of stockholders exercised control despite a wide distribution of shares. Fluctuations of the market and business cycles speeded the process of consolidation into large units. London became the main financial market, but individual banks, such as the Crédit Lyonnais in France, gained power as well.

Agriculture

While industry was the most dynamic part of the Western economy, agriculture still comprised the largest sector. Only in England, where urbanization had progressed furthest and where half of the country's arable land was owned by less than one percent of the population, was the small landowner almost entirely eliminated. In Germany, a large percentage of the population still owned landed property or worked on the land. In France and the United States, more than half of the population derived their livelihood from agriculture; in Russia, almost three-quarters were peasants.

But, so far as increase in productivity is concerned, agriculture lagged behind industry. Age-old farming methods were widely retained in many regions. The system of agricultural holdings—whether those of large, almost feudal estates in eastern Europe or those of small individual peasant estates in western Europe—was not adequately modified to meet the new conditions. Although machines, particularly harvesting machines, came into widespread use, technical knowledge was not widely disseminated. Agricultural banks, credit institutes, and cooperatives, which sought to provide capital and efficient marketing organizations, achieved only limited success.

Economic Effects on the International Situation

The shifts in the national economies affected the international scene, destroying the existing power balance of the nations. Industrialization allowed "younger" nations to come to the fore; some older ones declined. Britain's position was particularly affected. It still had certain advantages: its colonial empire, London's financial prestige, and substantial profits from its carrying trade, foreign investments, and worldwide insurance. But as its share in world exports was reduced, its political influence diminished. The distribution of British manufactures (steel products, cutlery, machinery, and even textiles) encountered difficulties. Because of its dependence upon foreign markets and imports, England could not easily protect itself by means of protective tariffs. Britain's most successful competitors, Germany and the United States, had begun to industrialize late; they had benefited from British experience. They proved less conservative. They acquired more modern machinery; they more readily adopted new inventions and new techniques of production and distribution. They protected domestic manufactures with tariff walls. The United States, like Russia, had never accepted free trade; Germany, though vacillating, imposed higher duties than those in effect before 1870. Both countries used their newly gained economic dominance to further their political aims.

As for France, its wealthier classes proved overcautious. Instead of investing in speculative industries, they preferred safe investments which yielded high returns. They thereby prevented the country from gaining the position that brisk economic activity could have given it, even after the political debacle. During the period from 1870 to 1892, France, too, steadily increased tariffs.

Russia, too, increased its productive capacities. However, it gained little prestige in the world economy; the size and needs of its domestic market made it impossible for Russia to become a leading exporter of any products except grain and textiles. Its infrastructure remained weak.

Economic Effects on Social Conditions

Economic changes affected the power and prestige of nations; they also affected the life of the individual. More money was made available, and money could buy goods and services undreamed of in previous centuries. But the social distance between upper and lower classes steadily widened. People in the lower classes, on the other hand, could scarcely earn their subsistences. During depressions, such as those of the middle 1870s and the early 1890s, many of them lost their only capital—the opportunity to work gainfully. During the boom periods that prevailed in the years before the First World War, the same people suffered from swift inflation. Moreover, early in the twentieth century the use of assembly-line methods of production reduced the need for skilled labor, speeded up manufacturing operations, made work monotonous and exhausting, and created additional unemployment. Using a variety of means (propaganda, political parties, unions, and strikes), the workers, who were often led by idealistic members of the well-to-do classes, intensified their struggle for improvement.

EFFECTS ON SOCIAL LEGISLATION

The most important social consequence of the economic situation was the increasing introduction of social-security legislation. The German government had been first to realize both the value of satisfactory labor conditions to the state itself and the responsibility of the state toward its less fortunate members. In a series of persuasive speeches, Bismarck convinced the members of the *Reichstag* that fear of a "socialistic element" should not check laws promoting the welfare of all citizens. He therefore advocated, and Germany introduced, staggered income taxes that put the main tax burden on those who possessed capital; and, in the years from 1881 to 1889, the government passed laws for state-guaranteed accident, old-age, and health insurance, covering low-income industrial workers. This insurance plan was broadened and improved in subsequent years, and was imitated in most Western countries. In France, which had recognized labor unions since 1884, a series of factory codes was promulgated in 1892. In 1898, laws providing for workmen's compensation appeared. Old-age pensions were introduced between 1893 and 1910. In Russia, during the same period, government decrees brought the improvement of labor conditions and the adoption of various types of social insurance. Britain moved ahead more slowly. Yet, by 1911 it had not only passed social-welfare laws dealing with old-age pensions, workmen's compensation, and national insurance, but had also introduced staggered income taxes, land and inheritance taxes, and, the first country to do so, unemployment benefits.

Of the great powers, only the United States failed to follow the trend toward social legislation. The imposition of a federal income tax required a constitutional amendment which was not ratified until 1913. Federal inheritance taxes were not levied until after the First World War. Social insurance legislation was not enacted until the Great Depression of the 1930s.

EFFECTS ON ATTITUDE OF THE CHURCHES

The spirit behind social legislation was consistent with many demands of the principal religious denominations. Among Russian Orthodox and Protestant groups, it was mainly a few individuals and reform groups who associated themselves with political forces demanding social improvement and social security. As to the Catholic Church, Pope Pius IX had (in his *Syllabus of Errors*) denounced the uninhibited liberal view, and his successor, Leo XIII, had, in 1891, published an encyclical (*Rerum novarum*), in which he repeated Pius's condemnation of socialism, communism, and unchecked liberalism. Yet, simultaneously, Leo XIII pointed out the moral obligations of the wealthier classes. He also approved the determination that governments brought to their efforts to improve the living conditions of the masses and to restrict business practices harmful to the working class.

EFFECTS ON SOCIALIST PARTIES

Significantly, the endeavors of governments and churches to improve social conditions did not stop the growth of socialism. On the contrary, that movement accelerated. Workers used prosperous times to withhold their labor, a weapon which, however, misfired in times of depression. Still, socialism gained from the growing consciousness that industrialism had created problems that needed society's attention. Everywhere, socialist parties secured wide influence.

In Germany, the Social-Democratic party, founded by Lasalle in 1863, sent two representatives to the first imperial diet in 1871. When Bismarck's repressive laws were abolished in the 1890s, it sent more than forty representatives to the diet, and in 1914 their numbers grew to more than a hundred representatives, or almost thirty percent of the total. In France, despite equally vigorous suppression in the 1870s, the development was similar. Around 1900, a socialist was chosen as a cabinet minister. The same trends could be witnessed in the smaller countries of northern and western Europe. In Russia, moderate and radical socialists were elected to the Russian parliament, the *Duma,* where they had considerable influence.

In Britain and the United States, however, the socialists failed to secure representation. Socialist Labor parties were founded in both countries before the turn of the century, but, especially in America, Marxist ideology lacked appeal to the factory worker. In both countries, the tradition of a two-party system hindered the representation of smaller groups and prevented socialists from making much headway in elections. Yet, in Britain as well as in the United States, the socialists achieved some of their aims. The British Socialists contributed indirectly, in 1906, to the victory of the Liberal party, bringing Asquith and Lloyd George into power. The American Socialists supported Populists and other third parties in their efforts to accelerate reform legislation.

EFFECTS ON SOCIALIST PROGRAMS

All socialist parties steadfastly advocated the abolition of private property. They continued to oppose colonialism and militarism. They also worked for international cooperation of the laboring classes. In 1889, they organized a "Second International" of Labor, which identified itself with Karl Marx's teachings.

But, as time went on, it became increasingly difficult for them to preserve a united front. To many, Marx's theory that the class struggle is unavoidable and revolution inevitable seemed more and more doubtful. The skeptics organized a "revisionist" movement in Germany (with Karl Kautsky and Eduard Bernstein proposing modifications of Marxism), a Fabian Society in England, and a moderate "Menshevik" wing of the Socialist party in Russia. The anarchists lost whatever strength they had gained. In fact, not the radicals, but those socialist groups that advocated a transformation of society by legal and democratic means, gained the leadership of the labor movement.

CULTURAL CHANGES

In the period from 1870 to 1914, much fundamental theoretical work in science was accomplished. The investigation of radiation and atomic structure achieved important results. Einstein formulated his relativity theory. Attention was being given to applying the newly acquired theoretical knowledge to the solution of practical problems. Many technological inventions were made that affected every aspect of Western life.

But insight into the social and spiritual condition of the individual did not advance correspondingly. Nihilistic tendencies appeared in various humanistic fields. The generation maturing around 1900 (the generation of the *fin de siècle*) has often been described as wanting in spirit and enthusiasm and as showing decadence. This notion was not confirmed in the art world. Shortly before World War I, when the social world that had been created in the eighteenth and nineteenth centuries was crumbling, much meaningful original work was being created by impressionist and expressionist artists.

Science

The last quarter of the nineteenth century and the years before World War I brought a revolution in science comparable to that caused by Newton's discoveries in the seventeenth century. Scientific methods had been perfected. With the help of new instruments (themselves the result of scientific advances), observations were made, especially in atomic physics, which traditional Newtonian concepts could not explain. The work of Planck and Einstein offered solutions and new understanding. Similarly, in the biological sciences, the limitations of Darwinism were recognized; new hypotheses were formulated to explain facts obtained by means of new observations.

BIOLOGY AND MEDICINE

In biology, the theories of Darwin were spread by Huxley and other disciples. They influenced the various subdivisions of biology as well as anthropology, physiology, and sociology. The scientific data concerning plants or whole species of animals could not safely be applied to humans. Darwin's views needed to be supplemented. The mid-century discoveries of the Austrian monk Mendel, who formulated laws of heredity, contributed to a better understanding of evolutionary issues. The German Weismann disproved the inheritance of acquired characteristics. The Dutch botanist De Vries demonstrated that sudden variations (mutations) occur rather frequently in the evolutionary process. Biological investigations helped to redirect medical research. Diseases affecting human tissues were studied in the light of newly developed cell theory. Lister, Pasteur, Koch, and their numerous disciples made great strides in the field of bacteriology. There was notable progress in surgery; daring operations were undertaken by Virchow and other pioneers. Public health conditions were improved in response to a growing realization of the need for sanitation. The average life span increased further. Problems of nutrition were scientifically investigated and the importance of certain vitamins became recognized.

Most significant was the study of the nervous system, which in turn led to radical changes in the field of psychology. The Russian Pavlov described conditioned reflexes. The Austrian Sigmund Freud investigated the subconscious mind and began to develop the techniques of psychoanalysis.

Considerable thought was given to ethics in medicine. Views that disease was a divine punishment for sin had to make room for those emphasizing the obligation of doctors to cure disease, whether or not the patient was responsible for his or her disease, whether it was inherited, contracted during an epidemic, or "psychological." These considerations also involved modern government, which gradually came to shoulder responsibility for public health and for maintaining it in the interest of the entire population.

CHEMISTRY AND PHYSICS

Research in the field of chemistry brought extensive knowledge, which was found useful in practical application. Of no less importance was the fundamental work accomplished in physics. Photography was developed in France around 1840. In rapid succession, X-rays were discovered by Roentgen; electric waves were identified and analyzed by Hertz. The atomic structure of matter was investigated, and the functions of electrons were explored by Roentgen, Thomson, Millikan, and others. Becquerel discovered radioactivity.

In 1898, the Curies found radium; they showed that matter disintegrates spontaneously, releasing enormous amounts of energy. The work of the Curies stimulated further studies of matter (more specifically, the structure of the atom), of radiation, and of wave systems. In 1899, Planck published his fundamental work on quantum theory, which proposed that energy is emitted by atoms not in a constant flow but in an irregular pulsating movement. Planck called the amount of energy emitted a "quantum."

His theory was in turn followed in 1905 by Einstein's relativity theory. Einstein demonstrated that time and space are not absolutes, but that they are relative to the observer. He worked out a fundamental equation ($E = mc^2$), which stated the relationship between matter and energy. His findings, comparable in importance to Newton's discoveries more than two centuries earlier, were of fundamental significance not merely for pure physics but also for astronomy and new insights into the structure of the universe.

Philosophy

Scientific attitudes and methods impressed themselves so deeply on the thinking habits of Western society that the whole discipline of traditional philosophy had to be rethought. Metaphysical speculations were increasingly rejected. Empiricism—that is, the attempt to use experience alone as a basis for an explanation of "reality"—spread. The Austrian Mach taught that even our understanding of nature and its laws is limited by our imperfect sense perceptions. Only observation and logical thought can act as trustworthy guides to knowledge. Embracing this premise, utilitarian concepts seemed to constitute the most reliable teacher of the philosopher, and a form of pragmatism, as taught by William James—the major American contribution to philosophy—was widely accepted. There were also many adherents of a rigid determinism who believed that laws such as evolution governed events in history and nature; such laws allowed little scope for free will. This view led many to accept a relativistic philosophy in which ethics and morals, wisdom, truth, freedom, and goodness—objects of philosophical investigation throughout the ages—were no longer significant. Such an attitude negated religious doctrines and encouraged men such as Spencer and Haeckel to develop the new field of sociology.

Few voices rejected the mechanistic concepts underlying all these interpretations. One dissident, the Frenchman Henri Bergson, reemphasized metaphysical ideas, postulating an *élan vital,* which was passed on from generation to generation and constituted the main force in human evolution. More representative of the age was the German philosopher Friedrich Nietzsche. He attacked the Christian creed and both traditional and contemporary concepts of ethics. He called instead for a repudiation of conventional values, a "transvaluation" of values. He described the individual's will to power, especially the exceptional individual's will to power, as the source of great deeds and as the standard by which a person and his work should be judged ethically.

Education

The extension of knowledge and the acceptance of pragmatic and democratic attitudes created a need for changes in education. Elementary education became a necessity; compulsory schooling was introduced widely on the Continent. In 1911, England followed with the necessary legislation. Simultaneously, the United States, Russia, Brazil, and other countries of great size and multinational composition sought solutions befitting their special situations. But elementary education alone did not suffice; to disseminate new ideas and discoveries, revisions had to be made in the material taught in higher schools and universities. Knowledge was no longer, as in the Middle Ages, one body of data based on one set of premises. With the secularization of learning, a great variety of subjects and concepts had appeared; specialization increasingly marked the intellectual world. Disciplines such as chemistry, literature, and history had to be subdivided into numerous branches.

As a result, the universities began to organize specialized "institutes," while the secondary schools were divided into two groups: one stressing natural sciences, the other emphasizing humanistic studies. Instruction in religion was left largely to separate church schools. Art and music, once an integral part of higher education, were slighted or eliminated. Attempts of outstanding scholars to achieve a new unity were futile in the face of the necessities that the development of economic, scientific, and political endeavors had created.

Literature, Art, and Music

The *Zeitgeist* (or intellectual climate of the era) influencing science, philosophy, and education left its imprint on the world of literature and the arts. By 1870, the "Victorian style" (named after the English queen, Victoria) had become dominant. It was exemplified in architecture. Solid and pretentious, lacking in originality, architecture symbolized the way of life and the aspirations of the most successful members of the well-to-do bourgeoisie. Only slowly did a reaction develop against the ideology underlying the Victorian style, and only at the turn of the century did this critical attitude begin to show itself in works of an experimental nature—leading to "modernism," as it emerged in literature, painting, and music, as well as architecture.

LITERATURE

The literary developments between 1870 and 1914 clearly indicated this changing intellectual climate. During a first period, the Victorian style was represented by a poet such as Tennyson. The traditions of the great French romanciers in the age of Balzac and Stendhal were continued by Romantic novelists such as the younger Dumas. However, gifted younger writers turned increasingly to penetrating analysis of human nature, to naturalism and criticism of society. Most prominent were the French novelist Zola, the outstanding Norwegian playwright Ibsen, and his disciples, the Swede Strindberg, the Irishman Shaw, and the German Hauptmann. Their influential social descriptions and their interpretations are in contrast with the pessimism, and frequent cynicism, which characterize the works of others representative of the *fin de siècle*. To a certain extent, Strindberg and Ibsen, but perhaps more so the French novelist Maupassant—and also Anatole France—had represented this later trend. The Russian Chekov belonged also to the group which marked the "end of the century," and perhaps even Mark Twain, despite his earlier inclinations toward affirmation of life and humor. Other authors, such as Lagerlöf (Swedish), Kipling (English), and Conrad (Polish-English), who continued the great tradition of writing imaginative fiction, gave—sometimes within the Romantic mode—a sharp and sober picture of human character, longings, and weaknesses.

More experimental was a third group of authors, who began to win fame shortly before World War I. Partly under the influence of Dostoevsky and Tolstoy (who remained after 1870 the towering figures on the literary stage), they sought for entirely new forms to express their deep, psychological investigations of the human predicament, of human inner contradictions and the tragedy of life. Probing into the last recesses of the soul, into feelings of anxiety, fear, and guilt, writers such as Kafka *(Metamorphosis)* and Proust *(Remembrance of Things Past)* attempted a new approach in what came to be known as the "surrealist" manner. But it was hardly appreciated for at least a generation. Newspapers and journals came to exercise, through their art and literary criticism, a growing influence on public taste, in addition to that on political and social attitudes.

PAINTING, SCULPTURE, AND ARCHITECTURE

Comparable changes took place in the fine arts. After 1870, the work of the impressionist school with its emphasis on light and color continued. Then, toward the end of the century, there emerged the neo-impressionists and the "Fauvists" (van Gogh, Gauguin, Seurat, Cézanne, and Matisse) and, following them, the "expressionists," such as Kandinsky and Klee. It has been said that during the period 1870 to 1914, contrary to the democratic trend of the age, "a split occurred between artists and public" and that only an "élite" could grasp the meaning of many of the new paintings and their symbolism. But such splits and such limitations are, perhaps, in the nature of all works of art. In all times, many facets of artistic endeavor have been grasped first, if at all, by only a few people. No new situation was created when some of the greatest painters at the turn of the century found little appreciation among the public.

In fact, by turning away from classical as well as nineteenth-century traditions and by seeking to give expression to emotion and to reveal intrinsic meanings and to demonstrate their social consciousness rather than merely depicting the visible environment, the expressionists seem to have anticipated a world of which subsequent generations would become more fully aware. They left a more lasting impression and exerted a deeper influence than other fine artists, such as the Americans Whistler and Homer, who proceeded along more conventional paths.

In sculpture, France produced the extraordinary artist Rodin. In architecture, the Victorian style was challenged by numerous innovators who paved the way for modernism and to whom proportions and lines meant more than detail and ornamentation. The newly appearing skyscraper gave a special character to the environment.

MUSIC

Similarly, in symphonic and chamber music, the reaction against the Romantic spirit and against sentimentalism brought a sequence of masters, consisting of impressionist, then neo-impressionist, and eventually—in the last few years before the war—expressionist composers. Romanticism was still evident in the works of the Austrian Bruckner and later in those of the Bohemian Mahler and the Norwegian Grieg. Impressionism was represented by the Frenchmen Debussy and César Franck. Expressionism, with its new concept of atonality, came to the fore with the German Schönberg. At that time, there was also a long line of extraordinary Slavic (most of them Russian) composers, including Dvorák, Mussorgsky, Rimsky-Korsakov, and also Tchaikovsky, who tended to be, more than the others, in the Western tradition. The opera continued in the meantime along traditional lines, perhaps with the exception of Mussorgsky's *Boris Godunov*. In Italy, the best-known operas were composed by Puccini (*La Bohème, Tosca*), and in Germany the outstanding works were contributed by Richard Strauss (*Salome, Rosenkavalier*).

Religion

In the face of the secularization of Western culture, the churches found their hold on their members (especially the youth) increasingly difficult to maintain. The "conflict between science and religion" had begun to manifest itself in many directions. Some of the foremost contributors to the natural and social sciences sharpened the conflict by characterizing religion as a mere survival of old superstitions. Actually, the process of secularization did not require a denial of the ethical demands of Christianity or of the need for inspirational and charitable functions exercised by the churches. On the contrary, so deeply were the basic humanitarian sentiments and moral principles of Christianity embedded in the Western world, after almost two thousand years of its history, that they automatically became a function of the now all-powerful states. It became the task of secular authorities to provide social legislation (in lieu of Christian charity), to spread education, and to support the arts.

STATE AND CHURCH

During the transition from religious to secular sponsorship, many conflicts arose. Catholics, especially, proved less willing than the Protestants or the adherents of the Greek orthodox Church to subordinate themselves to national political institutions. Examples included the *Kulturkampf* in Germany, the struggle between Catholics and atheists in France, the controversies between the papacy and the new regime in Italy, and other conflicts between materialists and the Roman Catholic Church, such as those in Spain and Latin America. In some instances, the secular authorities consented to compromises favorable to a church, but even then the governments achieved their objectives on many points of disagreement. The materialistic trend generally assured them of victory in the battles against a church hierarchy.

In Germany, the *Kulturkampf* brought church property under lay control; all marriages performed by civil authorities became legal and the training of the clergy was placed under governmental control. In France, a comparable struggle led to the expulsion of the Jesuits in 1880, the elimination of religion from primary schools a few years later, as well as taxation of all ecclesiastical wealth, and finally, in 1905, separation of state and church. In Italy, despite the prevalence of strong nationalistic and atheistic tendencies, attempts to separate church and state failed. But the government retained possession of the city of Rome. It insisted on the legality of civil marriages and asserted its right to determine the relationship between state and church. Unilaterally, it decreed the neutrality of the Vatican and guaranteed the possessions of the Roman Catholic Church.

SPIRITUAL REVIVAL

These new relationships between state and church enabled religious institutions, particularly the Catholic Church, to rid themselves of political responsibilities and devote all their attention to spiritual matters. Consequently, a religious revival got under way. The Catholic hierarchy, while reaffirming traditional doctrines, concentrated on improving the education of the clergy and extending their missionary activities. In line with Leo XIII's *Rerum novarum* the Church continued to oppose merely utilitarian principles. The Protestant churches experienced a similar spiritual revival, which was reflected in the formation of numerous fundamentalist groups or organizations such as the Christian Science Church and the Salvation Army. There was also intensified religious activity within the Orthodox Church.

In Russia, the state-dominated church was opposed not only by the numerous atheist Marxists, but also by the "Old Believers." Some ten to twenty million strong, their fervor for a dedicated Christian life only increased with discrimination and persecution. The works of outstanding Russian philosophers bore a strong religious imprint. Tolstoy, Vladimir Soloviev, and Berdyaev infused Russian thought with the spirit of Christian love and Christian wisdom.

EXPANSION OF WESTERN CULTURE

Despite ideological conflicts and its many problems, Western culture was diffused so widely during the half-century from 1870 to 1914 that adoption of Western scientific thought, Western technology, and Western institutions became necessary for the survival and freedom of every civilization. Nevertheless, Westernization occurred voluntarily nowhere except in Japan. Everywhere else, as in China, Persia, Africa, the Arab countries, and the Latin American hinterland, Western ways were imposed upon the native populations. They became either completely or partially subservient to European nations.

Emigration to many parts of the globe contributed to Westernization. Half of the emigrants were absorbed by the U.S.A. Most of them came from Great Britain, Germany, Russia, Italy, and Spain. Sometimes adverse conditions at home, sometimes the attraction of the New World, and often individual, private reasons such as lust for adventure animated the people. Yet, up to a quarter of those who left eventually returned to their homeland.

Western Influences on Outside Cultures

Wherever it penetrated, Western civilization brought new patterns of culture through the preaching of Christianity, the introduction of humanitarian laws and European educational views, the teaching of European languages, and the dissemination of Western political ideologies. The contributions of Western civilization were numerous and varied—ranging from new inventions, techniques, and products (in transportation, manufacturing, agriculture, and mining) to improvements in health and medicine, and even to new modes of dress. Modern concepts of sanitation were widely introduced; the supply of trained doctors proved a blessing to millions. The Westerners eliminated many savage customs and superstitions; they checked tribal warfare. Slavery—though it survived for some time in Dutch and Belgian colonies and was used to obtain labor for building the Suez Canal—was abolished by law; it, too, eventually disappeared.

On the other hand, Westernization had its negative side for the native populations. Thus, some of their useful customs were often disrupted. While the Westerners helped to wipe out old diseases, they brought new ailments with them. Hasty changes in long-established habits of life and work wiped out some native populations. Neither were new methods in political affairs an unmixed blessing. The old forms of human exploitation by native rulers were often merely replaced by equally cruel alien ones.

Western Exposure to Outside Influences

While spreading to all parts of the world, Western civilization was itself subject to the influence of foreign cultures; it was compelled to solve new, challenging problems. Expansion had its disadvantages. Expenses for investments and for defense were often higher than the rewards. Most colonies failed to drain off the surplus populations of Europe. Instead they attracted limited numbers of often just the most independently minded, venturesome people. The colonizing nations also continued to engage among themselves in costly struggles for economic and military power. Often, they failed to achieve the autarchy, the economic independence, they had expected to derive from colonization. In fact, they became more dependent than ever before upon distant sources of raw materials and income.

Of course, colonization also had advantages for the West. The home countries were able to obtain needed commodities that contributed to their economic growth and profits, and to a higher standard of living. Financiers and other leaders in the community made fortunes from the exploitation of colonial resources. The possession of rich colonies made it possible for small European powers, such as Holland, to attain world prestige and influence.

Moreover, the expansionist drive aroused the imagination of many people who were dedicated to a cause, such as "the white man's burden," of bringing the assumed virtues of Western civilization to the "natives" and of converting the heathen to Christianity. A missionary spirit went hand-in-hand with the mercantile spirit. Native religions, customs, art, and even food habits had an invigorating influence on Western people. They fired curiosity. Without consideration of economic gain, adventurous people set out to explore the unknown.

New Western Horizons

Thus, after exploring various regions for material profits, Westerners turned to those that offered intellectual or emotional rewards. Scholars and adventurers sought satisfaction of their urge to know. Expeditions to unknown regions flattered their vanity, or catered to their national ambitions and desire to plant their nation's flag on untouched soil. For such reasons, Livingstone searched for the source of the Nile, while Stanley sailed to face terrible hardships in the Congo. Sven Hedin explored the arid inner regions of Asia and Tibet and visited Lhasa. English, German, and Austrian mountain climbers scaled the icy peaks of the Alps and Himalayas.

Extraordinary exploits were undertaken in the Arctic and Antarctic regions. Peary is said to have reached the North Pole in 1909. A whole group of intrepid Scandinavians achieved what for centuries had seemed impossible; the *Fram*, a ship equipped by Nansen, drifted from Norway to Labrador, almost by way of the North Pole; Nordenskjöld accomplished the first Northeast passage, Amundsen the first Northwest passage. In 1911 Amundsen, in a brilliant achievement, reached the South Pole.

In the forty-five year-period preceding the First World War, peace reigned in Europe. New industries developed and new industrial products supplemented old ones. Further fundamental advances in science and in analyzing nature's forces were made, as well as in important inventions that could find practical application. Financial institutions serving industries prospered. Agricultural production increased with the introduction of machinery and chemical fertilizers, reducing the need for hard labor. Transportation was modernized and speeded up. Migration from the land to the cities and emigration overseas accelerated. Living conditions for the masses improved.

The modern way of life was, however, criticized by the Catholic Church and, more effectually, by the strong socialist movement. Labor unions and political parties gained votes. The turn of the century brought a feeling of widespread "malaise," as expressed in philosophical and sociological treatments. The uneasiness filtered down to the masses who, by then, were more literate; they were influenced by the ever-widening stream of books, newspapers, and journals. Art, music, and literature reflected these feelings. The trend in art was toward nontraditional ways of representation, as shown by expressionists, by painters, and by architects, as well as in opera, polytonality and twelve-tone music, drama, and literature. Both normal and abnormal psychology were studied in new ways.

Government establishments seldom took an active part in furthering new intellectual trends. They concentrated their attention on their customary administrative tasks and their worldwide ambitions. They helped to spread the traditional principles of Western civilization and sought old ways of exploitation. Whether in America or Europe, governments paid little attention to Eastern or African lifestyles. But a desire for exploits in foreign lands continued to animate scientists and explorers. They made discoveries in the tropics, arctic climes, the deserts, and they penetrated to the most remote corners of the globe.

Selected Readings

Geary, D. *A Social History of Western Europe, 1848–1945* (1985)

Hayes, Carlton J. H. *A Generation of Materialism* (1963)

Milward, Alan S., et al. *The Development of the Economies of Continental Europe, 1850–1914* (1977)

Pollard, Sidney. *Peaceful Conquest: The Industrialization of Europe, 1760–1970* (1981)

Russell, Bertrand. *A History of Western Philosophy* (1945)

Shryock, Richard H. *Development of Modern Medicine* (1936)

Williams, Raymond. *Culture and Society, 1780–1950* (1961)

19

The Road to World War I (1890–1914)

1898	Germany builds large navy
	Fashoda crisis
1899	Outbreak of Boer War
1900	Boxer Rising in China
1901	Planck, quantum theory
1902	British-Japanese alliance
1903	Panama independence established
	Trans-Siberian Railway completed
	First airplane flown (Wright brothers)
	Shaw, *Man and Superman*
1904	Entente Cordiale of France and England
	Outbreak of Russo-Japanese War
1905	Peace of Portsmouth
	Revolution in St. Petersburg; a Duma introduced
	Independence of Norway established
	Einstein, relativity theory
1907	Anglo-Russian treaty over Persia; Triple Entente completed
1908	First Congress of Psychoanalysis (Freud)
	Young Turk revolt
1909	Expressionist school of painting started
1911	Italy annexes Turkish Tripoli
	Amundsen discovers South Pole

1912   Outbreak of First Balkan War

1913   Second Balkan War

Atomic structure described by Niels Bohr

1914   Panama Canal opened

Clayton (antitrust) Act in United States

Outbreak of First World War

*W*hen Bismarck retired from the political scene in 1890, the Western world entered a new stage in international relations. Prophets of supernationalism had long been at work. In Britain, the writer Carlyle, the journalist Bagehot, and the statesman Joseph Chamberlain had been fervent advocates of Britain's imperialistic role. The historian Lecky had gone so far as to proclaim that "real liberty is for supermen and opposed to democracy." France, stung by defeat in 1870, was inflamed to reassert national pride by men such as General Boulanger, Delcassé and Poincaré, and even Renan, author of the Life of Jesus.

In Germany, national passions and a longing for national glory were incited by historians such as Treitschke and Droysen, military men such as Bernhardi, and even Wagner, master of a new style in opera. In Russia, Pan-Slavists agitated for a great Slavic empire under Russian leadership; and many extolled a future messianic role for "Holy Russia." Italy nursed her irredentist dreams. Polish chauvinists demanded the restoration of their medieval multinational dominion. In the United States, too, repercussions of supernationalism were felt; the Spanish-American War and the policy of "walking softly and carrying a big stick" in foreign affairs, as expressed by President Theodore Roosevelt, were evidences of the all-encompassing trend.

Unfortunately for the peace of the world, the West possessed not only the spirit but, with its science and technology, also the means to make its nationalistic creeds an instrument of international policy and expansion. Competition among the nationalist Western powers led to new alliances and, eventually, to conflict.

INTERNATIONAL REALIGNMENTS

The first ominous step in the direction of war came at the expiration of the German-Russian Reinsurance Treaty. The lapse of the treaty in 1890 enabled France to end its isolation and to conclude a political, and subsequently a military, alliance with Russia. In this way, the large Bismarckian coalition system in Europe was gradually replaced by two competitive and opposed alliance systems: the "Triple Alliance" of Germany-Austria-Italy, and the "Triple Entente" of France-England-Russia.

Bismarck, who was dismissed in 1890, watched these developments with growing concern. He died eight years after his dismissal, embittered over the ingratitude of his emperor. Actually, the dismissal was not due to ingratitude, or even disagreements over certain external and internal policies. Rather, it reflected the gulf between old and new, and the changing temper and ambitions of succeeding generations.

New Course

The "New Course," which brought about the change, resulted in part from a shift in economic conditions and in part from personal influences. Bismarck's successors and Emperor William II believed that Germany's friendship with Austria was indispensable, but that it was incompatible with an alliance with Russia. They therefore risked giving up Russia; they hoped to compensate for the broken Russian alliance by establishing closer ties with Britain; William was the beloved grandson of Queen Victoria, and both Britain and Germany had already made overtures toward each other signaling the desire for closer cooperation. They had, however, overlooked numerous adverse factors: differences of political systems and ideologies, personal animosities, commercial rivalries, colonial disputes, and lack of popular support for common policies. They also overlooked the fact that the British parliamentary system did not lend itself easily to the making of a binding alliance. Moreover, the Germans trusted injudiciously in the idea that Britain would never reconcile its divergent interests—especially in colonial matters—with France and Russia. They therefore overestimated Britain's desire to ally herself with Germany. They risked offending Britain in a most sensitive spot: its domination of the seas. Ambitious to play a leading role on the sea, Germany started a large navy-building program during the 1890s under the able leadership of Admiral Tirpitz. This led to bitter competition that was costly to the taxpayer, a burden to strategists, and an impediment to friendship.

Dual Entente and Entente Cordiale

Its resulting coolness toward Germany encouraged Britain, at the turn of the century, to lend a favorable ear to French suggestions for renewed amity. By then, France was already strengthened through its new alliance with Russia. France and Britain had exchanged courtesy visits of statesmen and military units. They made a number of agreements, concluded an offensive and defensive alliance disclosed in 1895, and, most important, negotiated huge French loans to Russia.

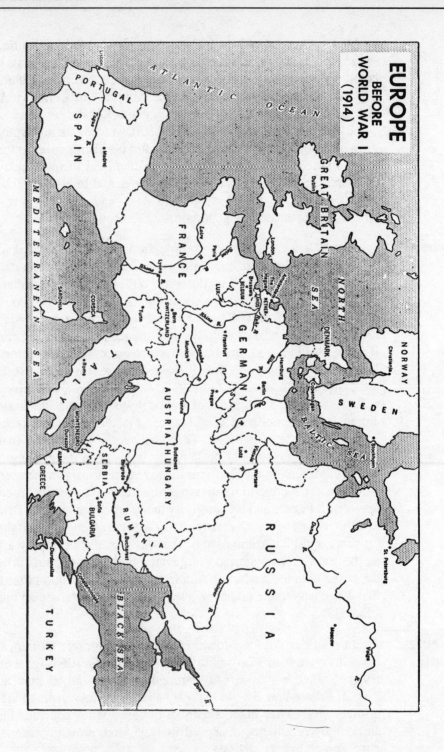

EUROPE
BEFORE
WORLD WAR I
(1914)

Now France, under the capable, single-minded foreign minister Delcassé, began to court Britain. In 1898, a clash between France and Britain occurred in the Sudan, which Britain coveted in order to build its African north-south connections from Cairo to the Cape. France wanted to occupy it for the purpose of building its west-east connections from the Atlantic to the Red Sea. Troops bent on their respective missions collided at Fashoda. Delcassé shrewdly used the occasion for a friendly settlement. He had the French troops called back. In exchange for renouncing plans in the Sudan, he settled for a free hand in Morocco.

This led to further rapprochement. When Edward, Prince of Wales, became king of England, he paid a visit to Paris; other state visits were exchanged. These events brought understanding and political agreements regarding North Africa, East Asia, and Newfoundland. Finally, an "Entente Cordiale" emerged. Without constituting a firm alliance, it laid the basis for frequent consultation and occasional exchanges of military plans.

Triple Entente

Franco-British relations remained insecure so long as France wanted to preserve an alliance with Russia in spite of British-Russian competition. (Such had previously been the dilemma of Germany in the face of Austrian-Russian rivalry.) Circumstances, however, favored France. In 1905, Russia was defeated by Japan and weakened by revolution at home. This paved the way for a settlement of Anglo-Russian misunderstandings. Russia's reverses forced it to give up its plans of expansion in the Far East and in the direction of the English lifelines through the Mediterranean. The reverses also changed the psychological climate. Revolution brought a parliamentary system to Russia, to the great satisfaction of British public opinion. No more than one area of possible conflict now remained—the Middle East. Conflict there was smoothed over by a peaceful agreement in 1907. The agreement allowed the British a free hand in Afghanistan; it divided Persia into spheres of influence, with the northern part reserved for Russia and the southern part for Britain.

With the Russo-English feud thus settled, France could proceed with its alliance system. Political and military missions were exchanged among all three countries. The Dual Entente grew gradually into the Triple Entente of France-England-Russia. Germany, limited to their Triple Alliance with weak Austria and unreliable Italy, no longer possessed the position of strength it had enjoyed in Bismarck's times.

NATIONAL READJUSTMENTS

In most countries, questions related to foreign affairs were given priority over domestic problems. All the Western nations experienced economic growth and, with it, an increase in social problems. All of them developed democratic and humanitarian institutions, albeit with the handicaps of burdensome bureaucracies and, frequently, powerful military groups that gained undue influence in the shaping of national policies. The extent and the speed of these changes varied in the different countries; subtle shifts in the strength of the nations were to have grave consequences for the individual citizen as well as for the peace of the world. Yet, this aspect of modern society, involving the relationships between domestic and foreign affairs, was seldom appreciated by people in positions of responsibility and authority.

The Continental Countries

Among the European nations, Germany was the first to adjust domestic economic and social policies to modern requirements. Within limits imposed by size and population, the Scandinavian countries, Holland, and Switzerland followed. The Southern European countries adapted themselves more slowly to the Industrial Age. In political matters, however, adjustment did not proceed from north to south, as in the case of economic and social change, but rather from west to east and southeast. The Atlantic nations were ahead of the central European powers on the path of democracy; in turn, the central Europeans were in advance of the Eastern and Balkan nations.

GERMANY

During the twenty-five years before the outbreak of World War I, few additional improvements were made in Germany's political institutions. Notwithstanding attempts by socialists to inaugurate radical changes and efforts by liberals to democratize government, widespread complacency persisted. Little was done to broaden constitutional rights, reduce military influences, extend secondary education, or improve the procedures of the efficient and honest, but sometimes harsh and overbearing, government officials.

Class stratification remained strong. The northern and eastern landholding nobility retained its hold on many offices. Simultaneously, it opposed land reforms that might have given agriculture the same basis for stability and progress that industry enjoyed. On the other hand, the country gained rapidly in strength as exporter, financier, and importer. Its role in international affairs steadily increased. Social insurance legislation was perfected.

FRANCE

A similar conservatism prevailed in large areas of France, especially in the provinces, where many people owned small landed properties, had adequate savings, and led a quiet and comparatively easy life. The leaders of industry were also conservative, lacking the progressive spirit dominating German economic affairs. Investments with safe returns were still preferred to the speculative financing of new enterprises that the times demanded. But among the inhabitants of the towns, radicalism and unrest were strong. Various issues and incidents kept political reform movements alive and prevented complacency.

First, there was the memory of military defeat, which stirred up nationalistic movements affecting political alignments. Second was the religious issue. Positivist groups following the ideas of Auguste Comte and atheists carried on a constant struggle against the Catholic majority. This conflict led to the suppression of monastic orders in 1903, and, after a quarrel with the Vatican over France's political relations with Italy, to the separation of Church and state in 1905. Third was the issue of socialism. Social legislation had followed the German model. But dissatisfaction persisted among the industrial workers, especially in the foundries of northern France and in the textile mills. Numerous strikes occurred. These were suppressed on several occasions with the help of the army. But the socialist movement grew. Even though radical syndicalism that favored direct action of labor unions through general strikes eventually receded, the socialist faction steadily gained influence in parliament and challenged the conservative forces.

Fourth was a revitalization of the progressive forces. This was sparked in 1894 by an anti-Semitic outbreak. Anti-Semitism was found, not only in France, but in most of the West. In France, it led to a crisis when a Jewish army captain, Dreyfus, was falsely accused of treason. After an unfair trial, he was condemned to exile on Devil's Island; it took twelve years and the fervent protests of such patriots as the famous writer Zola and the politician, Clemenceau to secure a reversal of the judgment and public amends to Dreyfus. The "Dreyfus Affair" deeply stirred French emotions and eventually brought a purge of a corrupt militaristic clique. It also led to improved legal procedures and, indirectly, to the strengthening of national security. Last was the issue of foreign policy, involving the alliance with Russia, the entente with England, the penetration into Morocco, the enlargement of the African empire in regions adjoining the Sahara, and the conquest of Madagascar. Liberals and socialists pointed out the inherent dangers of France's expansionist policy and the unfitness of France's agreements with autocratic, backward tsarist Russia; yet, the nation as a whole approved.

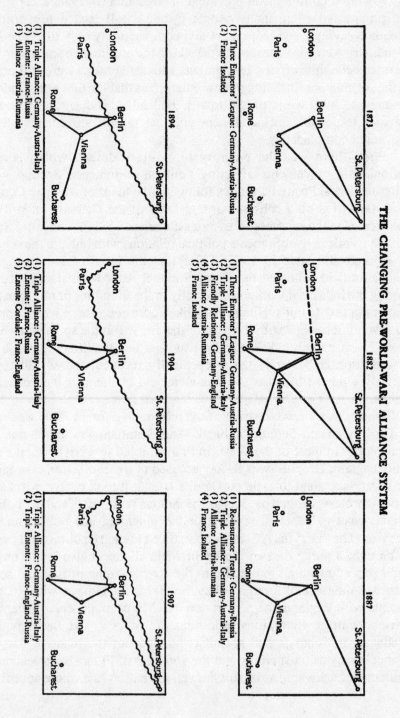

THE CHANGING PRE-WORLD-WAR I ALLIANCE SYSTEM

1873
(1) Three Emperors' League: Germany-Austria-Russia
(2) France Isolated

1882
(1) Three Emperors' League: Germany-Austria-Russia
(2) Triple Alliance: Germany-Austria-Italy
(3) Friendly Relations: Germany-England
(4) Alliance Austria-Rumania
(5) France Isolated

1887
(1) Re-insurance Treaty: Germany-Russia
(2) Triple Alliance: Germany-Austria-Italy
(3) Alliance Austria-Rumania
(4) France Isolated

1894
(1) Triple Alliance: Germany-Austria-Italy
(2) Entente: France-Russia
(3) Alliance Austria-Rumania

1904
(1) Triple Alliance: Germany-Austria-Italy
(2) Entente: France-Russia
(3) Entente Cordiale: France-England

1907
(1) Triple Alliance: Germany-Austria-Italy
(2) Triple Entente: France-England-Russia

ITALY

During the twenty-five years preceding World War I, Italy gained in stability and prestige. In the north of the country, important textile and machine industries were founded. Railway and shipbuilding programs progressed. Educational standards were improved. Legislation helped to mitigate at least some of the worst social inequities. Both the national government and the local political representatives gained in administrative experience. Notwithstanding a number of financial scandals involving members of the government, corruption diminished; slowly, an adequate bureaucracy was trained.

After 1900, the political situation improved. Anarchistic activities, which in that year led to the assassination of the king, Humbert I, abated. Dire poverty continued to prevail and class differences remained, not only in urban but also in rural areas and between the northern and southern parts of the country. Still, marxist and other socialistic movements gradually took on the same peaceful, constitutional forms as in other European countries. Moreover, Italy's foreign and colonial policies were conducted wisely. Ventures like the ill-fated expedition of 1896 for the conquest of Ethiopia were not repeated; instead, feasible aims were pursued. The conquest of Tripoli in 1911 helped to satisfy the nationalistic ambitions of the people.

THE SMALLER NORTHERN COUNTRIES

Similar political and social problems beset large and small powers alike. In Austria-Hungary, tensions were sharp between the various nationalities composing the empire. They often centered around Hungary, dominated by large landholders, and around Hungarian influence on the empire's policies. Much anti-Semitism existed, despite the integration of the Jewish upper class into their German surroundings. Moreover, worker dissatisfaction grew, although the country was less industrialized than the West.

Solutions varied with geographic factors, traditions, and available leaders. Democratic, political and social institutions developed in Scandinavian countries and in Holland, Belgium, and Switzerland. Military ambitions in all these nations continued to be negligible. International agreements guaranteed a neutral status to Switzerland and Belgium. A peaceful settlement solved one of the thorniest problems—the fight of the Norwegians for national independence. At the Congress of Vienna, control over Norway had been granted to the Swedish king, but Norway had never reconciled itself to this arrangement. In 1905, Sweden voluntarily recognized Norway's independence.

Intellectual activities flourished, especially in Scandinavia, where writers such as Ibsen, Strindberg, Hans Christian Andersen, and Lagerlöf, the literary critic, Brandes, and the composer Grieg gained fame, and where excellent school systems were built up. Progress was made in the development of industries wherever natural resources were available: iron and lumber in Sweden, electricity in Switzerland, coal in Belgium, colonial products in Holland. On the other hand, the major social debates of the age—socialistic movements and clericalism—brought strife to many small countries. As elsewhere, these problems were eventually settled. Cooperative institutions were created in Scandinavia and, making up for a large part of the national economy, contributed to economic peace and stability.

SOUTHERN AND EASTERN EUROPEAN COUNTRIES

Less promising was the development of the "second-rate powers"— Spain and Turkey and the new Balkan nations. They possessed few of the economic and social resources needed for modernization. They showed little initiative or progressive thought. Wealthy landlords, who often controlled political and economic affairs, were opposed to modern trends. Industrial development lagged. Colonial expansion, owing to geographical conditions, was not a solution available to any of these nations except Spain; trade was insignificant. Agriculture continued under antiquated methods and under feudal institutions. Yet, nationalistic ambitions were often manifest. Spain and Turkey had memories of past grandeur. The new Balkan states dreamed of future grandeur. But most of these states included national minorities within their borders and were plagued by disorders created by them. This also caused difficult frontier problems.

Spain, with a large part of the population living in abject poverty, was the victim of repeated revolutionary activity. Monarchical and republican forms alternated; parliamentary and democratic institutions proved futile. Governments ruled with the help of army and Church. In Turkey, not even the recognition of the independence of Serbia and Rumania, nor the subsequent establishment of Bulgaria, solved the nationality question. Revolts within the ruling cliques surrounding the throne contributed to a state of permanent political disorder. The aim of abolishing the despotic powers of the sultan and rejuvenating the state apparatus was not attained.

England and the British Empire

Under capable statesmen—the aged Gladstone and, after him, Salisbury, Balfour, Joseph Chamberlain, Asquith, and Lloyd George—Britain continued along its established lines. It lost its position as the leading industrial power to Germany and the United States; it also lost some of the markets in Latin America and elsewhere that it had dominated in previous decades. Still, economic conditions remained favorable and the population looked with satisfaction upon the material progress of the country.

Numerous political and social improvements were made. The judiciary was reorganized. Special, so-called "board" schools were formed to improve lagging educational standards and, by 1891, free elementary schooling was finally introduced. Social insurance was broadened to cover unemployment, which (as poverty once had been) was still often considered the result of laziness rather than of industrial conditions beyond the power of the individual workingman. A reform in the agricultural system, advocated by Gladstone, was eventually carried out.

The House of Lords demonstrated its lack of understanding of modern conditions by opposing such legislation and by advocating the use of force to break up strikes. In 1911, it was deprived of much of its power. Its right to veto legislation was sharply restricted. The working class gained steadily in influence. A Parliamentary Salary Act was passed to enable men without private means to become representatives in Parliament.

Yet, the laws providing voting rights for men still contained a number of special requirements that actually deprived some of the population of the possibility of exercising that right. Nor did women gain political rights. As a result, women (suffragettes) started a vigorous agitation for the extension of voting rights to women—an agitation that occasionally led to violence.

The British Empire itself was kept intact, even though Britain's relations to some of the larger and more important colonies had to be liberalized. In 1900, 1907, and 1910, the "dominion status" introduced earlier for Canada was granted successively to Australia, New Zealand, and South Africa. However, no timely solution was found for India. Despite vigorous protests, the Indians did not succeed in ending their colonial status. Nor was adequate progress made in the Irish question. Despite legislation providing for improvement in the status of the Irish peasants, Irish resistance under the gifted leadership of Charles S. Parnell was resolute. Even when violence broke out, the Parliament in Britain refused to permit the Irish the desired "home rule," and the issue remained unsolved.

Russia

While the Continental European nations and England saw between 1890 and 1914 progress in constitutional development, a combination of internal and external forces worked revolutionary changes in Russia. Pressure of radical groups from within, and of Western thought from without, undermined existing institutions.

INDUSTRIALIZATION AFTER 1870

For at least two decades prior to 1890, it had been clear that Russia, if it wanted to maintain its power and independence, would have to build modern industries. Around 1870 Russia initiated a large railroad-building program. After 1890, the process of industrial and technical modernization was speeded by the efforts of Count Witte; he had started his public career as minister of railways, then became minister of finance, and, finally, Russia's first prime minister. It was Witte who secured loans from abroad, especially from politically interested France. During the period 1891 to 1903, many new industrial enterprises were founded in western Russia, in St. Petersburg and Moscow, in the Don River region, and in the Urals; a Trans-Siberian railroad to Vladivostok was built and a Trans-Caspian and a Trans-Caucasian railroad were started. Witte also introduced protective tariffs, furthered social legislation, and established the gold standard.

REVOLUTIONARY ACTIVITY

Russia was thus well on the way to improved living conditions and industrial greatness. But, for lack of corresponding political changes, the total situation deteriorated; the gulf between rulers and subjects widened. Although, as elsewhere, anarchist violence diminished while the cooperative movement and moderate socialism gained strength, the revolutionary temper grew and was intensified by the continued lack of representative and constitutional government. The revolutionary spirit was shown not only by workers and peasants, but also by the increasingly important bourgeoisie and by the intellectuals—scientists, professors, writers, and artists, all of whom were highly responsive to Western influence.

The situation became more critical still when, after 1900, an unfavorable business cycle in Europe affected Russia. Disturbances once more spread in the industrial centers and among the peasantry. A new move toward radicalism occurred. The extremists among the socialists rejected the slow path of peaceful evolution by means of education, propaganda, and constitutional procedures. Insisting on revolutionary means, they gained new adherents and won a majority at a congress of Russian socialists and their émigré comrades held in 1903 in London. Hence they called themselves "Bolsheviks" (the "larger," the "majority") as opposed to "Mensheviks" (the "lesser," the "minority").

RUSSO-JAPANESE WAR (1904–1905)

At this crucial moment, the government became involved in a dangerous foreign enterprise. Stimulated by the imperialistic policies of other European nations, the Russians had already entered the race for colonies; they were especially eager to obtain concessions in China. Following the repression of a Chinese independence movement, the so-called "Boxer Rebellion," Russia had demanded a lease on the Chinese harbor of Port Arthur and had occupied Manchuria. Britain and Japan, themselves coveting economic and military predominance in China, had reacted to this advance by concluding an alliance in 1902. Thus backed, Japan attacked Russia in 1904. Unprepared industrially, Russia suffered severe defeats on land near Mukden and on the sea near Tsushima. In 1905, it sued for peace. A treaty was concluded that year at Portsmouth, New Hampshire. Russia ceded Port Arthur and half of Sakhalin to Japan and recognized Korea as a Japanese sphere of interest.

REVOLUTION OF 1905

In the meantime, revolution had broken out at home. For years, the Russian government had played a dangerous double game. Through its police and spies, it had often cooperated with the rebellious labor class. It hoped that, by supporting economic demands and even strikes against capitalists, it might deflect attention from the political shortcomings of the regime. But it had succeeded only in forfeiting the support of the bourgeoisie without gaining that of the workers. And when—led by one of the dupes of this system, the priest Gapon—workers of a large munitions factory in St. Petersburg used the wartime opportunity to press their demands for political rights, their illusion about the government came to an end. Singing hymns and marching upon the imperial palace to submit a petition, the workers were violently attacked. "Bloody Sunday" of January 1905 ended with thousands of victims dead or wounded.

This incident welded the antigovernmental forces into one. In vain did the tsar attempt to calm the opposition by halfhearted promises. Peasant uprisings spread. Strikes occurred in all industries. The various subjected nationalities prepared for a final blow. Patriots, outraged by the military loss to Japan, failed to rally around the throne. In October, a general strike was called, and violence in the countryside forced the government to make radical concessions. A "manifesto" was published, by which the tsar issued a constitution and granted autonomy to the Finns. Thus, autocracy in Russia finally ended; it was to be replaced by constitutional government.

THE BEGINNINGS OF CONSTITUTIONAL GOVERNMENT

The manifesto instituted a nationwide representative body, or Duma, with legislative powers, and to be elected by the various classes of the population. Financial and military decisions remained in the hands of the tsar. Political parties became legal: Conservatives; Cadets, or Constitutional Democrats; Social Revolutionaries, or right-wing evolutionary socialists; Mensheviks; and Bolsheviks.

By its concessions, the tsarist government split the revolutionary opposition, as had been done in France in 1848. The liberal bourgeoisie, relying on the Duma to press for further reforms, abandoned their alliance with the working class and the socialists. These struck once more in December 1905. The uprising was bloodily suppressed, and the tsarist government proceeded with its reform plans. Actually, it twice went back on its promises to the liberals, twice dissolved the Duma, and arbitrarily changed the constitution.

Without consulting the Duma, it also wrote, on its own initiative, the final chapter of peasant emancipation. At the suggestion of Prime Minister Stolypin, it annulled all remaining restrictions on the peasants and abolished the *mir*. Peasants from then on were no longer bound to village communities, but gained personal property rights to their lands, which they could now sell and leave at will. But once all this had been accomplished, a Third Duma was convened. With it began a real measure of constitutional government.

The United States

The year 1890 did not mark any drastic break in American history, such as occurred in European history. Social progress was steadily but slowly achieved. However, the administrations of Theodore Roosevelt and Woodrow Wilson seemed to many to represent the dawn of a new era for the Western Hemisphere as well.

INDUSTRIALISM AND SOCIAL LEGISLATION

Economically, the United States continued to benefit from the work in fundamental sciences carried on in Europe. Thousands of its citizens went there to study philosophy, mathematics, natural sciences, and medicine. But technological application of scientific discoveries, owing to the inventive genius of men like Thomas Edison, was more rapid than in Europe. Industries, deriving the necessary supply of laborers from the flow of immigrants, grew at an astounding pace. Early standardization of tools and parts made mass production possible. The small business owners were often unable to compete with entrepreneurs such as Morgan, Rockefeller, and Ford, who built huge industrial empires. Not even antitrust legislation could check their power. Nevertheless, socialism did not gain as in Europe. Threatened by depressions and unemployment, workers fought for better conditions and wages, organized strikes, and formed unions; but they did not adopt the concept of the "class struggle." A socialist party under Eugene Debs did not attract enough voters to gain representation. In agriculture, the recurrence of major depressions did not lead to political radicalism among the farmers. Unlike Europe, there was still enough land available for extensive, rather than merely intensive, cultivation of the soil. The farmers benefited, moreover, from the rapid growth of the national economy.

Democratic institutions made the government and the two main political parties sensitive to popular needs; and the challenge of third (reform) parties, such as the Greenback and the Populist parties, contributed to the timely passage of progressive social legislation. During the administrations of Theodore Roosevelt and Woodrow Wilson, many such laws were passed. Effective programs for the conservation of natural resources were instituted. The women's rights movement made some gains; in various states, women were granted voting rights.

IMPERIALISM

If socialist doctrine and various other economic and political problems of Europe were of less significance for the United States, the issue of imperialism did not remain alien to America. British interference in Venezuelan affairs released violent emotions and forced the British to submit the question to arbitration in 1899. The United States went to war against Spain, later annexing Puerto Rico and the Philippines and sponsoring Cuba as an independent state subject to American economic imperialism and political protection. The United States annexed Hawaii in 1898 and established naval stations in that area. Colombia was forced to renounce part of her territories. An American Zone was established where the Panama Canal was dug across the Isthmus. It was finished in 1914. The United States participated in the international action against China during the Boxer Rebellion and insisted on a subsequent economic "open-door" policy in the Far East. The Monroe Doctrine was reinterpreted to allow for possible United States interference in Latin American affairs. "Dollar diplomacy" supplemented military measures in the pursuit of U.S. imperialism.

PEACE AND WAR

Social institutions and aspirations, which had prevailed ever since Napoleonic times and had been accepted as typifying the entire nineteenth century, came to an end in 1914 when World War I broke out. With our knowledge, gained in retrospect, that war did come in 1914, we are inclined to see in the nationalistic developments before 1914 a path inexorably leading to this conflict and to violence. But the forces against war were also strong. The view cannot be maintained that war was the only means of solving the existing international problems.

International Movements to Prevent War

One of the major aspects of the nineteenth-century liberal creed was its humanitarianism—a heritage from the Age of Enlightenment. And one of the most important humanitarian aims was the abolition of war. As technology created ever more deadly weapons and as the spirit of the peoples was steadily poisoned by nationalistic propaganda and rivalry, the forces seeking to preserve permanent peace became increasingly active, and numerous steps were proposed, and some taken, to avoid a catastrophe.

PRIVATE INITIATIVES FOR THE ORGANIZATION OF PEACE

Most of the peace movements were initiated and promoted by private individuals, not by governments. Some of these individuals advocated Christian precepts rejecting violence. Others adhered to Marxist views rejecting nationalism. Some were pacifists, others in search of an international legal order. Some wished for peace in order to conserve existing conditions, others wanted it in order to reform society. The means by which the workers for peace proposed to maintain peace were also diverse: political alliances, international law, arbitration, congresses, disarmament, and education. They founded organizations to investigate the causes of war and explore the possibilities of avoiding it. Some of them tried to influence political leaders and electorates in the direction of peace by emphasizing the dangers and all-embracing character of modern warfare. Prizes were offered to men who contributed to the promotion of peace: Benefactors established funds, such as the Nobel Peace Prize and the Carnegie Peace Endowment.

In numerous countries, vigorous propaganda against military service was carried on. Socialists held their own "Internationals"—congresses at which nationalistic competition was denounced. At home, they voted in parliaments against military appropriations. Businessmen and bankers set up trusts and cartels whose profits depended upon peace, for they ignored national boundaries, divided up markets, and made foreign loans and investments.

OFFICIAL INTERNATIONAL AND PEACE ORGANIZATIONS

Governments could not afford to disregard the demands for peace put forward by so many segments of the populations. One of the first official organizations created before 1914 for the promotion of international cooperation, understanding, and peace was the International Postal Union. A Red Cross convention was signed that led to the creation of national Red Cross organizations subject to international rules. A number of disputes regarding borders and the interpretation of treaties were arbitrated, often involving major powers such as the United States, Britain, Germany, and Spain. International congresses were held.

In 1899, a Peace Conference was convoked at The Hague in the Netherlands. While it failed in many respects, it did succeed in founding a Permanent Court of Arbitration. In the Western Hemisphere, the Pan-American Union was established. An international sports organization was formed to provide opportunities for friendly competition among the youth of the several nations; and, in 1896, the first modern Olympic Games were held in Athens.

International Crisis Leading to War

Notwithstanding these peacemaking efforts, war came. It was ushered in by a long series of crises.

THE FAR EAST

Although the situation in the Far East appeared to be dangerous, it was not there that the real threat lay. In fact, the Western colonizing nations had, without resorting to war, divided the various Pacific islands among themselves, and international rivalry in China had abated. Before the end of the century, Germany had seized Tsingtao; Russia, Port Arthur; Britain, Weihaiwei; and France, Kwangchowan. The United States had secured economic advantages through its open-door policy. Even Japan had gained concessions. In 1895, after a successful war, Japan had deprived China of the Korean peninsula and the island of Formosa; it had also received economic privileges in China itself. A few years later, Japan had concluded an anti-Russian alliance with Britain and had then secured from Russia some Chinese spoils. Yet, international rivalry stopped it from extending too far. Thus, the tensions in the Far East were relieved. After 1910, a reform party emerged in China, the old dynasty was deposed, and, under the leadership of Sun Yat-sen, first steps were taken toward the building of a modern state that prevented a further spoliation of the country.

AFRICA

More threatening were the developments in Africa. Toward the end of the century, Italy invaded Ethiopia, where it was defeated; France and Britain clashed in the Sudan at Fashoda. The Egyptians and Sudanese under the Mahdi staged a desperate revolt against the British. The revolt cost the brutal Governor Gordon his life and subjected the British to a damaging defeat at Khartoum. Not until 1898 was the Mahdi defeated at Omdurman and native resistance ended. Finally, the French began to penetrate into Morocco. Each of these events had serious repercussions among the Western nations and caused conflict. Then, a critical situation arose in South Africa. Subsequent to the discovery of gold in the Dutch territories of Transvaal, an unofficial English expedition, backed by the imperialistic British prime minister of the Cape Colony, Cecil Rhodes, tried to gain control over the area. This "Jameson Raid" failed, but it led to war between Britain and the Dutch settlers, the Boers. The outbreak of the Boer War shocked not only Holland but all other European nations. Yet, it was vigorously pursued and quickly demonstrated the inherent dangers of all colonial issues for the peace of the West. Ill-will between Britain and Germany was provoked when the German emperor congratulated Kruger, leader of the Boers, for his valiant defense. The war itself continued until Boer resistance was crushed. A moderate peace was made and in 1910 the creation of the Dominion of South Africa gave, indirectly, a measure of autonomy to the Boers. However, animosity persisted, not only between Britain and the Boers, but also among the European powers.

BERLIN-BAGHDAD RAILWAY

Another crisis arose, in connection with a German railroad project. Everywhere, railroads served both economic and strategic purposes. The Russians built their famous Trans-Siberian Railway, the British planned a railroad from the Cape through the length of Africa to Cairo, and the Germans proposed one connecting Berlin with Baghdad via Constantinople. Lacking the capital needed for this enterprise, Germany suggested international participation, but Britain and, subsequently, France refused cooperation. The British feared for their Middle Eastern connections and did not wish to see Germany penetrate into areas at all near to India; the French sided with their newly won British allies.

The German proposal also antagonized the Russians. They had envisioned their own domination over Turkey and, ever since Bismarck's dismissal, had watched German policies with distrust. A rapprochement, attempted in 1905 in a conference at Björkö between Emperor William II and Tsar Nicholas II, was not brought about. Because of existing alliances, the agreement concluded by them was not ratified by either party. Eventually, the Germans appeased Russian apprehensions, but they never reconciled Britain to the Baghdad railroad plan. Nor were Russian and British fears lessened when closer German-Turkish collaboration was established by the appointment of a German general to be the sultan's military adviser—a position parallel to that of his British naval adviser.

MOROCCO

The Fashoda crisis had brought an agreement between France and Britain that favored French expansion in Morocco. But it had disregarded possible interests of other nations. As a result, Morocco faced considerable difficulty. Morocco was rich in lands well suited to agriculture and grazing; it was also a valuable strategic asset. In 1905, the Germans demanded concessions in Morocco and began to support Mohammedan nationalists opposed to French rule. William II paid a provocative visit to the Moroccan ruler at Tangier. This Moroccan development led to a serious crisis that was only with difficulty settled by an international conference at Algeciras (1906). There, France's Entente Cordiale with England brought its fruits; France was almost unanimously supported. Germany, which had undiplomatically provoked the issue, had to be satisfied with insignificant gains. Five years later, Germany reopened the issue through an equally undiplomatic act, sending a naval unit to the port of Agadir. This time a settlement was reached only with still greater difficulty. The international atmosphere was further poisoned.

BOSNIA

Despite the gravity of all these colonial disputes and the dangers of war which they involved, it was ultimately the situation in the Balkans which led to an irreparable crisis. Next to the issue of Alsace-Lorraine, Bismarck had always most feared the dangers of Balkan nationalism because of its implications for all Europe. All great powers collided there. Russia wanted to win the straits and dominate its Slavic sister nations; Germany and Austria wanted to expand southeastward. France wanted to preserve long-standing economic and cultural investments; Britain wanted to keep the other great powers away from the eastern Mediterranean, its chief link to India. In addition, Turkey sought to retain the rest of its European possessions. The various Balkan nations (Serbia, Romania, and Bulgaria—excited by their recently won independence—as well as Montenegro and Greece) were pitted against Turkey, against Austria, and against one another. No arrangement since the Congress of Berlin had achieved more than a temporary respite.

Early in the twentieth century, a national revival occurred in Turkey. The Young Turks introduced a constitutional monarchy under Sultan Abdul-Hamid. Had their reform succeeded, the great European powers would have lost the influence they were accustomed to exercise in the Balkans. In view of such a prospect, the two nations most affected decided to act: in 1908, the foreign ministers of Russia and Austria met at Buchlau. Following a program that had been outlined in the 1870s, the Russians agreed not to interfere with an Austrian occupation of Bosnia, and the Austrians not to interfere with Russian plans regarding the straits. The Austrians promptly helped themselves to their share of the bargain. But Russia, faced by other nations with vital interests in the region assigned to it, found itself stalled. There developed an extremely bitter resentment at what Russia considered Austrian duplicity. Serbia, with claims of its own on Bosnia, was not less incensed. The flames of Pan-Slavism were fanned, and what had been intended as a compromise turned into an additional controversy that brought Europe to the brink of war.

BALKAN WARS

A major disaster was temporarily avoided, but the crisis hastened a local upheaval in the Balkans. In 1912, Italy's annexation of Turkish Tripolitana had demonstrated the continued military weakness of the Turkish Empire. The Balkan nations deemed the moment ripe for rebellion against the sultan. The war was fought in two sections. First, Bulgarians, Serbs, Montenegrins, and Greeks invaded Turkey; they forced Turkey to make a peace depriving it of all European possessions except Constantinople. Second, these victorious rebels, plus Romania, went to war with one another. As one result, Bulgaria lost most of its spoils.

The Balkan wars foreshadowed future patterns of warfare. International law was violated by every belligerent; terrible devastations and massacres occurred. Peace brought only additional sources of misery: it forced migration of peoples and population exchanges, subjection of people to alien rule, economic disruption, and general impoverishment. Nothing was settled. Indeed, yet another splinter nation—Albania—was created. Dissatisfaction was general; a festering wound was to poison areas far beyond the Balkans.

SARAJEVO AND THE OUTBREAK OF WORLD WAR I

In June 1914, the final crisis occurred. In Sarajevo, Bosnia, a Serbian nationalist assassinated the successor to the Austrian throne, Archduke Francis Ferdinand. Enraged at the connivance of some members of the Serbian government and at the encouragement given by Russian Pan-Slavists to Serbian nationalism, the Austrians sent an ultimatum to Serbia that would have put a virtual end to Serbian independence. Assured that Russia could not and would not desert it as before, Serbia refused full compliance. Austria, counting on German support, lacked the wisdom to modify the conditions of its ultimatum. In vain some of the great powers set their diplomatic machinery in motion at the last moment to stop an outbreak which, because of treaty obligations, was bound to bring France into the war as an ally of Russia, and which was likely as well to engulf Britain, Italy, and, once more, most of the Balkan nations. On August 1, 1914, World War I broke out.

Internal Factors

It is often forgotten that internal political and party considerations in major countries sharpen international crises. The internal difficulties at this time were not insurmountable. But in order to maintain themselves in power, governments had to make concessions to right-wing forces everywhere: Britain to the anti-Irish, imperialists, and capitalists; Germany to agrarian reactionaries and industrialists; France to chauvinist politicians and army officers; Austria-Hungary to the nobility and the enemies of Slavic national aspirations; Russia to those bent on maintaining the dated social structure. In the United States as well, party considerations eventually contributed to war policies.

Following Bismarck's dismissal, the European international system that he had maintained to guarantee peace gradually dissolved. A steadily growing nationalism and colonialism increased tensions, and two opposing alliance systems were formed by the major European powers. Economic rivalry between the nations and internal social struggles contributed to the difficulties. Social-democratic and labor parties—in Russia partly of a revolutionary nature—gained in strength despite legislation passed in all countries to improve social conditions. In the United States, unrestricted capitalism reached an apex. Both the wealth and influence of leading entrepreneurs and enterprises increased.

Numerous conflicts between great and small nations raised the specter of war. Russia's war against Japan led to revolution at home. Clashes between European nations in Africa as well as among the Balkan peoples added to the danger. Pacifist organizations failed in their efforts to prevent war. The period of peace came to an end and World War I broke out.

Selected Readings

Fieldhouse, D. K. *Colonialism, 1870–1945* (1983)
Gollwitzer, Heinz. *Europe in the Age of Imperialism, 1880–1914* (1960)
Gulick, Edward V. *Europe's Classical Balance of Power* (1955)
Langer, William L. *European Alliances and Alignments* (1931)
Rice, Arnold, and Krout, John A. *United States History from 1865* (1991)
Wolff, Robert L. *The Balkans in Our Time* (1974)

20

War, Peace, and Revolution (1914–1919)

1914 First Battle of the Marne

1916 Battle of Verdun

1917 Abdication of Russian tsar: February Revolution

October Revolution in Russia: Bolsheviks (Lenin) establish communism

1918 German-Russian Peace of Brest-Litovsk

Armistice concludes First World War

Revolution in Germany, Austria, Turkey: republics declared

1919 Allied intervention in Russia; civil war in Russia

Treaty of Versailles; League of Nations

The years 1914 to 1919 brought such deep and clear changes that someday the period surrounding World War I may well be considered a no less decisive turning point in history than that of the Reformation years 1517 to 1521. During the first quarter of the twentieth century, new points of view concerning nature and society transformed science, religion, and the arts, and led to the evolution of new social and political structures.

Three fundamental changes are discernible: (1) The European state system, completed with the Peace of Westphalia in 1648 and modified in 1815 and 1870, broke down without being replaced by a new tenable system. Instead, the nationalistic objectives of every nation were acknowledged, with the consequence that instability prevailed throughout the world. (2) The European balance of power, established around 1713 (when the wars of Louis XIV ended), was destroyed. A regrouping took place, requiring the participation of an additional power—the United States of America—to assume the function of balancing the divergent groups. (3) The dominant influence of liberalism, which had been the aim of the most progressive forces of society since the Enlightenment, came to an end. Collectivism gained everywhere, and in one area—Russia—it achieved complete victory in its extreme socialistic form.

WORLD WAR I

The conflict that broke out on August 1, 1914, brought "total" warfare such as previous ages had not known. Other wars had affected all aspects of life, had engulfed military and civilian populations, and had inflicted "total" destruction. Such were the War of Liberation of the Netherlands, the Thirty Years' War, and the American Civil War. But "total" destruction applied only to those localities in which armies actually operated.

By the time of the First World War, division of labor and use of modern communications had increased the interdependence of large areas so much that the effects of war touched ever-widening areas. War embraced nations in their entirety. Mobilization meant the mustering of all productive forces at home, as well as of armies. The destruction of the enemy's industries, manpower, and morale became essential objectives. Thus, the blockade of Germany brought untold suffering to its civilian population. Only fundamental discoveries (such as Haber's discovery of the process of synthesizing ammonia and producing fertilizer artificially) enabled the country to continue the war. German submarine warfare had a comparable effect upon the English people. The war stimulated the inventive powers of nations. Many new weapons and techniques were devised or perfected, such as combat planes, armored tanks, poison gases, and air bombing.

Origins of World War I

Historical events and processes are too complex to allow an enumeration of "causes." At the most, a few tentative conclusions can be drawn. In the case of World War I, a number of basic contributing factors merit consideration. (1) The force of nationalism led to numerous crises involving overseas lands as well as European territories. (2) The existing system of competing alliances, less the result of aggressive intentions than of fear, pitted nations against one another. (3) The secrecy of diplomatic intercourse made the various nations suspect that sinister agreements were being made against their interests. Secrecy brought universal distrust and was therefore a threat to peace. (4) The absence of a "balance of power" proved as much a danger to peace as formerly the existence of such a balance had proved to be. The old system was not replaced by international cooperation, but rather by an anarchical state of international affairs rooted in nineteenth-century liberalism. (5) The feeling of the "unavoidability" of war prevailed, partly brought about by irresponsible sensationalistic journalism. (6) The instability of the economic system caused business cycles of booms and depressions and made large segments of the population lose their sense of security. Thus dissatisfaction with the existing economic order was heightened. (7) The scientific spirit and scientific inventions upset sociological patterns and mores. In addition, they changed the economic balance between nations and led to new jealousies. (8) The lack of foresighted leadership contributed to instability. Some statesmen, politicians, military men, and educators prepared for an armed conflict; others, with equal determination, devoted their lives to avoiding one. But the majority of leaders, though well-meaning, were weak and vacillating. The foremost statesmen lacked originality as well as independent judgment. They allowed themselves to be swayed by irresponsible advisers, political parties, the mob, or simply the general course of events. Thus, as Lloyd George once said, the nations "backed into war."

War Preparations

The world situation and historical trends pointed in the direction of war. Yet, the actual outbreak of World War I was made possible only by the maintenance of large military establishments on land and on sea and by the development of careful strategic plans.

ARMAMENTS

Compulsory military service was in effect in most Continental countries. Everywhere military budgets were extremely burdensome. France was most heavily armed, with almost two percent of its population in its land forces. Germany had proportionately a smaller, but more efficient army. England had a small army, a large navy. Russia had the greatest number of battalions, the poorest equipment. Austria had enough troops, but the diversity of their national origins detracted from their dependability.

STRATEGY

Germany's position in the center of Europe was the most precarious, in view of the possibility of attack from two sides—a constant threat that developed after the destruction of Bismarck's carefully built system of alliances. Consequently, its strategic preparations were the most elaborate. For allies, Germany could count only on the Austrians. Italy, although temporarily committed to Germany, eventually joined the other side.

SCHLIEFFEN PLAN

The Germans had therefore worked out the Schlieffen plan (named after a chief of staff) according to which, in case of attack from two sides, a holding action in the east against Russia was to be undertaken while efforts were to be made to reach a quick decision in the west against France. Troops were to march through neutral Belgium in order to attack the French from the north, occupy the coastline, cut off possible help from England, and force Paris to surrender.

ENTENTE PLANS

This plan was not unknown to the Triple Entente of France, Russia, and Britain. The British had not yet promised unconditional adherence to the Entente, but they participated in military preparations that included strategic talks with "neutral" Belgium. Entente plans called for a Russian thrust, first into Austria, then into East Prussia, and a French attack along the Rhine.

War Guilt

Analysis of the events that led to World War I shows that it would be unjust to conclude that the conflict was instigated by any one of the belligerents. The victorious nations later required Germany to acknowledge responsibility. Such one-sided accusation was made in order to gain practical advantages, although these ultimately did not materialize. An objective appraisal indicated that all the participants shared in the responsibility. Austria-Hungary and France were guilty because they followed policies of expansion and of revenge, respectively. Russia fostered a war atmosphere, nurtured Pan-Slavism, and allowed too much latitude to ambitious statesmen. England and Germany were animated by the generally prevailing imperialistic spirit. They could have refused to participate in such a war and thereby made it impossible, but they failed to do so. Among the German (as among the French) military and political circles were many who were not averse to the idea of a war. Germany's extensive navy-building program had contributed much to the tension and to ultimate disaster.

The Course of the War

The first two years of the war witnessed startling victories by Germany. As a result, almost the entire war was fought on the soil of Belgium, France, northern Italy, and Polish Russia. (Minor action took place in the German colonies.) The war was fought mostly on land by armies consisting of millions of conscripts on each side. Naval and air engagements were of comparatively little significance. Germany won many important battles, but failed to turn these into a decisive victory.

As the struggle continued, Japan, Italy, Romania, and various small nations joined the Allies, while the Central Powers gained the support of Turkey and Bulgaria. Participation by the United States ultimately decided the issue. Then not even the collapse of Russia (which relieved Germany of the necessity to fight on two fronts) could prevent the defeat of the Central Powers. In November 1918, they asked for an armistice.

CAMPAIGNS OF 1914 TO 1916

In a sense, the first three months of the war were the most critical. According to plan, Germany invaded Belgium, whereupon England promptly declared war on Germany. Nevertheless, the Germans conquered Belgium and pushed deep into France. But the Schlieffen plan was not consummated, for they did not gain control of the English Channel coast, and therefore could not prevent British aid from reaching France.

At the end of August, apprehensive of Russian penetration into Germany, the Germans reduced their forces on the Western front and sent them to the East. They succeeded in decisively defeating and repelling the Russian forces in the great battle of Tannenberg. But a consequence was that early in September their advance in the West was stopped short at the Marne River (First Battle of the Marne). What was planned as a short, lightning war turned into an interminably grim one. Throughout the year 1915, millions of soldiers faced one another in trenches, unable to strike a decisive blow. In 1916, the Germans attempted to break the deadlock. Two terrible battles were fought, one at Verdun, the other on the Somme River, bringing unprecedented losses to both sides. An important naval engagement took place off the shores of Jutland. But the situation was not changed. Only in the East, where the fronts were mobile, was a decision reached. The Russian armies were pushed out of German territory. Soon Austria, too, was liberated. By 1916, the Germans had penetrated deep into Russian territory.

CAMPAIGN OF 1917

The year 1917 began with no change in sight. Yet, that year proved to be decisive, for two major events completely altered the situation. The first event was the Russian Revolution, which overthrew the tsarist government and established a liberal democratic regime (the "Provisional Government") in February 1917. Although Russia remained in the war for a time, and even staged a mighty summer offensive, the failure of this effort merely hastened the disintegration of the Russian army.

The second event was the entry of the United States into the war. Strong pro-English leanings, democratic idealism, American investments in Allied countries, effective English propaganda (coupled with the interruption of news reports from German sources), and, finally, Germany's unrestricted submarine warfare, which cost the United States heavily in lives and goods— all these factors contributed to abandonment of American neutrality. Active participation by United States armed forces (comparatively few of whom saw action in battle) did help the Allies and gave them renewed hope. However, American reserves in manpower and weapons, economic resources, and food supplies were far more decisive in swinging the tide of war against the Central Powers. American aid did not actually make itself fully felt before a second phase of the Russian Revolution occurred. In October

1917 (November according to the Western calendar), the Provisional Government was overthrown by the Bolsheviks, who promptly concluded an armistice with Germany.

END OF WORLD WAR I (1918)

Early in 1918, the armistice between Russia and Germany was supplemented by a peace treaty, which was concluded at Brest-Litovsk. Germany insisted on the separation of Livonia, Poland, the Ukraine, and other territories from Russia; it posed as an advocate of self-determination for all peoples but actually hoped to impose its own control upon these areas. But Germany's victory in the East could not make up for the increased danger threatening her from the West. In the course of the spring and summer of 1918, the German armies were forced to retreat, and by September, it had become evident that, despite Brest-Litovsk, the war was lost for Germany. Her military position had become untenable, and internal unrest was brewing. To avert trouble at home, various steps were undertaken to democratize the country, such as granting universal, equal suffrage in Prussia. But this failed to placate Germany's enemies (bent on a complete overhauling of the German government) and Germany's own liberals and socialists. Desperately, in the fall of 1918, the imperial government offered to negotiate peace along lines laid down in "Fourteen Points" proposed by President Woodrow Wilson. Germany's allies (Bulgaria, Turkey, and Austria-Hungary) also sued for peace, and their rulers abdicated. Although Britain and France held numerous reservations regarding Wilson's war aims, the German government could hold out no longer, and an armistice was concluded in November.

THE HOME FRONT

Contributing to Germany's defeat were the difficult circumstances behind the front. Just as with sieges of towns during the Middle Ages, now whole countries were besieged and faced starvation. In all countries, therefore, much depended upon the organization of the home front and its resources. Industries had to be reoriented, raw materials provided, and food supplies secured. The courage of the population had to be maintained and their support guaranteed.

Russia and Germany suffered most. In Germany, the emergency had led to a mighty effort to organize a war economy. It was efficient, but with outlets to the world largely cut off (which made it also impossible to counter the enemy's propaganda or, in turn, to reach the enemy's populations), no effort was adequate. Nor was the attempt to put England in a similar predicament by means of unrestricted submarine warfare a successful one. The conviction in Germany that the war could be won diminished. Together with the military defeats of the army, collapse could, after four years, no longer be avoided.

ABDICATION OF GERMAN EMPEROR

By this time, revolution had broken out in Germany. The emperor had fled to Holland and, like other kings and princes of the individual German states, had given up his throne. A republic was instituted. There was street fighting in Berlin and elsewhere, soldiers and sailors deserted, and communists attempted to seize power. But the socialists, supported by the liberal democratic parties, took over the government. Thus, simultaneously with the end of the war, Bismarck's imperial structure fell to pieces. Democrats and socialists had to assume the heritage under difficult circumstances.

PEACE OF VERSAILLES (1919)

About one hundred years intervened between the Congress of Vienna and the Treaty of Versailles. During this period, the temper of the times had changed fundamentally. At Vienna, the defeated nation had taken part in the settlement, but at Versailles the voice of the vanquished was rarely heard. The prompt return of the defeated to the family of nations had been the aim of the victors in 1815, but the postponement of such a result was the objective of the victors in 1919. A balance of power was sought after Napoleon's downfall, whereas a permanent weakening of the Central Powers was desired by the Allies at Versailles. Statesmen at Vienna drew frontiers in conformity to historic dynastic rights and interests, whereas the spirit of nationalism and revenge dictated boundary arrangements in 1919. Moreover, for the first time, a non-European power, the United States, played a leading part in a European peace settlement, while Russia, which had been so prominent in the negotiations of 1815, did not even participate.

Terms of the Treaties

The decisions made at Versailles (spelled out in the treaty with Germany and, subsequently, in separate treaties with Austria, Bulgaria, and Turkey) were the result of numerous compromises. Early on, it became clear that the victors were pursuing divergent aims. Although President Wilson was a leading figure in the negotiations, his Fourteen Points were brushed aside whenever they seemed favorable to the interests of the defeated nations. Wilson's principles called for freedom of the seas, removal of economic barriers, disarmament, impartial distribution of colonies, evacuation by Germany of all territories occupied during the war, self-determination of subjected peoples, and the establishment of a League of Nations. Instead, the ideas of Premier Clemenceau of France, who presided at sessions of the peace

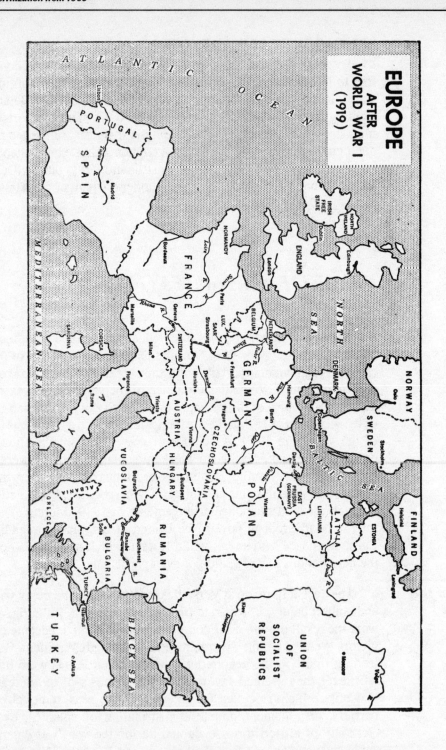

congress, prevailed. He advocated such harsh terms that, as he intended and openly avowed, they could not be fulfilled and Germany would be kept in permanent submission. Generally, he was supported by Prime Minister Lloyd George of Britain.

TERMS FOR GERMANY

The final treaty stipulated that Germany surrender all its colonies and special rights overseas, cede Alsace-Lorraine to France, and give France the right to control and exploit for a period of fifteen years the rich industrial area of the Saar. Germany was forced to give up its fleet—some units of which were scuttled by the crews—and a large part of its merchant marine. It had to cede territories in the west to Belgium, in the east to newly formed Poland, and, after a plebiscite, some lands in the north to Denmark. Danzig was made a free state, and a Polish corridor, separating German East Prussia from the main territory of the German republic, was created.

Germany's army was reduced to one hundred thousand men; conscription was prohibited. The production of many types of armament was either forbidden or limited. Germany had to accede to occupation of its western lands and agree not to maintain military forces in the Rhineland. In addition, it was ordered to pay, as reparations, a war indemnity the amount of which was left open; yet, payments were to begin immediately. Finally, it was forced to sign a clause acknowledging that it had caused the war.

TERMS FOR OTHER DEFEATED COUNTRIES

Separate treaties were concluded with Bulgaria, Turkey, and Austria-Hungary. Bulgaria lost Thrace, had to limit its armaments, and, like Germany, was ordered to pay reparations. Turkey lost practically all its non-Turkish empire in Asia and Africa. Most of this area either was taken over by France and England or, wherever separate states were created, was brought within the orbit of French or British influence. Turkey also agreed to the freedom and demilitarization of the straits.

Austria-Hungary was split into pieces, a decision that disrupted the economic unity that had been slowly forming in the middle Danube area. The territory was allocated to five nations as follows: to Austria, the German-speaking areas (except some which were handed over to Italy, Hungary, or Czechoslovakia); to Yugoslavia (newly formed out of Serbia), Bosnia and other provinces; to Poland, Cracow and parts of Austrian Galicia; to Czechoslovakia (formerly Bohemia), Moravia and parts of Galicia; and to Hungary, the Magyar areas, except Transylvania, which was ceded to Romania.

FOUNDING OF THE LEAGUE OF NATIONS

In a world torn by hatreds generated during the war and radically changed by its outcome, a just and durable peace settlement could hardly be expected.

Bitterness remained everywhere. Aware of this difficulty, President Wilson had fastened his hopes for necessary peaceful adjustments upon a League of Nations, which he had advocated in his Fourteen Points. France and England did not favor such a league, but agreed to it (just as Metternich had once agreed to the Holy Alliance), in the expectation that it might serve as a conservative influence.

The league was endowed with neither executive nor legislative power. It was to serve essentially as an open forum for international discussions. An International Court of Justice was connected with it, as well as various agencies concerned with humanitarian questions, health problems, labor conditions, the slave trade, and educational matters. The league was charged with administering the former German colonies, but all of them were surrendered either outright or as "mandates" to the victors. From the beginning, the organization was handicapped by the fact that three of the five great powers were not members: the United States because of domestic opposition, party politics, and demands for reservations with regard to some obligations under the league's authority; Germany because of its defeat; and Russia because of its communistic form of government.

Political and Economic Effects

The Peace of Versailles was signed in June 1919. It reflected the profound changes that nationalism, liberalism, and socialism had already initiated.

THE INTERNATIONAL SCENE

There were fifteen states in the Europe of 1815; now there were twenty-seven fully independent nations. These included the Balkan countries and Hungary, Czechoslovakia, Poland, Finland, and the three Baltic states—Lithuania, Latvia, and Estonia. The last great multinational empires of Europe—Austria, Russia, Turkey—were shrunken or destroyed. Self-determination by the nations, though promised, was put into practice only where it affected adversely the defeated Central Powers. It was not accorded to the peoples of colonial nations, such as India. Nor was it granted to Austrians who had voted to join Germany, to Germans who were transferred to Italy, to Yugoslavs who were likewise incorporated into Italy, or to Alsatians, the Irish, Macedonians, Slovaks, and other minorities. It was totally disregarded in eastern Europe.

With the help of France, and notwithstanding a decision by an international group fixing Poland's eastern boundary along a so-called "Curzon Line," the Poles invaded Russia and annexed western lands of Russia—White Russia. They invaded Lithuania and incorporated the capital, Vilna. They also seized most of Germany's industrial Upper Silesia, after the people, in a plebiscite, had decided 14 to 9 against them. Because the principle of self-determination was disregarded, minority problems also persisted in Turkey, Greece, Czechoslovakia, and elsewhere. They poisoned international relations even in cases where population exchanges were undertaken.

POLITICAL TRENDS WITHIN NATIONS

The war experience and the outcome of the war had the effect of swinging public opinion and political institutions sharply to the left. Few of the European monarchies survived. Nearly all the new states were established as republics; the defeated countries were so reestablished. The republics had either democratic or socialist governments. Socialists were the dominant minority in various central European countries. They also gained many votes and constituted strong opposition parties in many Western and Eastern nations. Communists ruled Russia.

THE WORLD ECONOMIC PICTURE

As in politics, so in economics, World War I upset the status quo. Capitalism had to adapt itself to new conditions. War had imposed many restrictions on capitalism; nowhere in Europe did it regain its former strength. One of the Fourteen Points had called for removal of economic barriers. It was ignored. Except for Germany, which was forced to open its borders to imports, European countries put up higher barriers against the free exchange of goods than those existing before the war. Russia almost entirely shut itself off economically from the Western world.

Everywhere, trends toward independence from foreign supplies increased. There was a shift in financial strength. London lost its leading financial position to New York, and the United States changed from a debtor to a creditor nation. European currencies depreciated. War reparations upset the international balance of payments and necessitated redoubled export efforts on the part of Germany; this hurt other exporting nations. Russia repudiated the debts contracted by tsarist governments, thus rejecting all repayments. Having granted Russia huge loans, France was the chief victim of repudiation, but Britain, Belgium, and the United States also lost substantial investments. Moreover, a sharp line of demarcation was drawn between the capitalistic and the communistic worlds. Some of the new nations in eastern Europe were built up by the Western nations as a guard, a *cordon sanitaire*, against Bolshevism because of its anticapitalistic organization. On the whole, the first steps in building a "world safe for democracy" seemed none too promising.

THE RUSSIAN REVOLUTION

While the Western nations were busy rearranging the political map of Europe, the attention of the Russians was directed toward constructing an entirely new social order. The significance of the Russian Revolution far surpasses the effect it had on the outcome of World War I. It was the first revolution in Western history to give the industrial workers political power and leadership in a major nation, and to introduce a socialistic system. It constituted a substantial defeat of the bourgeoisie and of the liberal-democratic system for which the middle classes generally stood. It generated forces that became worldwide in scope.

February Revolution (1917)

Ever since the Revolution of 1905 and Stolypin's agrarian reform, radicalism in Russia had decreased. Terrorist activities had ceased. Within its narrow limits, the Duma had come to gain influence and had started to build a constitutional system. The chief leaders of the radicals, notably Lenin, lived in exile; the times appeared unfavorable to them. But after 1910, and especially after the outbreak of war, the situation changed.

Inasmuch as social progress had been slow, the strain of war proved disastrous. Moreover, the war governments were managed by reactionaries, the court was filled with intriguers, and the tsar, Nicholas II, was personally incapable as a ruler. He and his wife, Alexandra, fell under the spell of Rasputin, a monk who with apparent success had administered to their ill son. The very fact of the influence of this greedy and dissipated man, even if he possessed rare common sense, indicated the corruption of the whole tsaristic system. Military defeats, manpower losses, widespread famine, and political graft hastened its disintegration.

Revolutionary activities were resumed. In the winter of 1916, Rasputin was murdered. In January 1917, strikes broke out, and mutinies occurred in the army and navy. The moderate parties in the Duma thereupon asked the tsar to yield wider powers to the parliament and to dismiss his government. Instead, the tsar dissolved the Duma. Thereupon, the liberal parties joined the socialists in the demand for his abdication. More strikes broke out. Soldiers deserted. Threatened from all sides, Nicholas II abdicated. The monarchy fell with him, and in February (March, according to the Western calendar) 1917, a Provisional Government was instituted by the Duma.

Provisional Government (1917)

The new government was administered mainly by representatives of the liberal parties. It established freedom of religion, women's rights, and the legal equality of all citizens. It attacked the disturbing nationality problem by starting the Poles on the road to independence and by helping other national groups make a beginning in self-government. It passed laws to provide for social welfare, and it promised the peasants redistribution of the land along lines to be decided by a popular assembly after the end of the war.

But in all its actions, the government was hindered by "soviets" (or councils) of workers and soldiers, which the socialists had set up and in which the communists dominated. The Soviet of Petrograd (as St. Petersburg had been renamed in nationalistic fervor) actually, if not legally, came to constitute a second governmental agency in the country; it interfered with the decisions of the regular government by supervising, countersigning, or rejecting its acts.

In April 1917, Lenin returned from exile, followed soon thereafter by Trotsky. Under their leadership, the strength of the socialist opposition grew rapidly. Lenin's simple, easily understood slogan of "Peace, Land, and Bread" appealed to the war-tired, hungry population—especially to the peasantry. Radicalism spread. Ever-widening circles demanded the establishment of the dictatorship of the proletariat. Soon, the more moderate members of the government, who had tried and failed to break the stranglehold of the soviets, resigned. A new offensive against the Germans collapsed. Then, in July, a Bolshevik uprising occurred; it was crushed, but only with difficulty. The liberal government was replaced by one under the Social-Revolutionary leaders Kerensky. He, too, was unwilling to accept the primary demand of the soviets—to end the war.

The situation thereupon deteriorated further. It led to a coup by one of the generals, who hoped to replace Kerensky's government with a military dictatorship. Kerensky was obliged to turn for help to the soviets, to free their leaders who had been arrested after the July revolts, and to call a "pre-Parliament."

October Revolution (1917) and Introduction of Communism

But it was too late. In October, Lenin, who had fled to Finland in July, returned and called for another armed uprising. The soldiers followed his lead. At the end of October (November in the West), the Provisional Government was driven out. Kerensky fled and most of his colleagues were arrested. Thus began the rule of the communists.

BOLSHEVIK LEADERS

The new government was formed by Lenin. Lenin was the son of a superintendent of schools who belonged to the lower nobility. Out of idealism, Lenin had engaged early in revolutionary activities. Single-mindedly, he had devoted his great intellectual and organizing abilities solely to the preparation and implementation of the revolution. He had spent most of his life in exile, had edited various communist newspapers, had published books and pamphlets, and had welded the nucleus of the Russian Bolshevik party into a centralized, efficient, and devoted group. His most important collaborator after the overturn of the tsarist government was Leon Trotsky, of a fairly well-to-do Jewish family. Trotsky was a man as fervent in his idealism and as willing to sacrifice as Lenin himself. But he was more erratic, more individualistic, and less able in matters of organization. Trotsky had been one of the leaders of the 1905 revolution. He had suffered years in prison and banishment. Not until May 1917 had he been able to return to Russia from exile in America. He became Lenin's commissar for foreign affairs.

Notable among other members of the new Bolshevik government was Stalin, a revolutionary from Georgia, whose parents were a shoemaker and a washerwoman. He studied at an Orthodox seminary, from which he ran away to devote himself to the Bolshevik cause. Less intellectual than either Lenin or Trotsky, he proved himself an efficient, ruthless, and practical revolutionary. By 1912, he had become editor of *Pravda,* the Bolshevik newspaper in St. Petersburg. Stalin was subsequently exiled to Siberia and did not return until 1917. Lenin made him commissar for nationality questions.

INITIAL BOLSHEVIK RECONSTRUCTION OF RUSSIA

Lenin's government did not hesitate to carry out the Bolshevik program. Without regard for international consequences, Lenin fulfilled his promise of peace. Russia's allies refused to recognize the necessity for Russia to leave its allies and end the war; they rejected the Bolshevik proposal of a peace without annexation and reparations, and sought to force Russia to continue the war. However, Lenin began negotiations with the Germans. Within a month, he concluded an armistice; in March, 1918, the Peace of Brest-Litovsk was negotiated.

With equal determination, Lenin initiated the work of socialist reconstruction. Private property and Church property were confiscated. Banks and bank accounts were nationalized. Factories were handed over to the workers (and later nationalized). The lands of the nobility and the rich were seized by the peasants.

All trading activities, except those of small businesses owned and operated by individuals, were taken over by the state. The employment of one person by another was forbidden. A new police force of ardent Bolsheviks was organized. Control over the army was assumed by party commissars. Every citizen was instructed to go to work for the new government. The peasants were ordered to deliver fixed quotas of their crops. As to Russia's international role, Lenin paid little attention to traditional values. He based his policies on the expectation of world revolution, which he envisioned as the inevitable result of the war. In the meantime, he concentrated on one task only: the maintenance of communist rule in Russia.

The war which began in August 1914 had its origin in an atmosphere of nationalism and economic rivalry. The leaders in the various countries failed to seek diplomatic means for settling the differences peacefully. All prepared for war.

Germany scored initial victories, but they were not decisive. Hopes for a short war faded: long, drawn-out trench warfare followed. Gradually, the geographic location of the Central Powers made itself disastrously felt. Lack of food and resources, added to heavy losses in manpower, undermined their strength. In 1917, the United States, with all its vast reserves, openly entered the conflict on the side of the Allies. A year later, Germany was forced to sue for peace. Thus, the end came in November 1918.

The Treaty of Versailles deprived Germany of territories in all border regions, regardless of the promised principles of self-determination for all peoples. The treaty also imposed degrading stipulations and demanded unlimited reparation payments. The Austrian-Hungarian Empire was divided up. A League of Nations, advocated by the United States, was founded but not endowed with power to act decisively on the international scene. It failed to become an efficient agent for peace.

In the meantime, a two-stage revolution occurred in Russia. It put an end to tsardom and autocracy, and ushered in, first a liberal-democratic, then a socialist (communist), regime.

Selected Readings

Beard, Charles A. and Mary R. *The Beards' New Basic History of the United States* (1968)

Carr, Edward H. *The Bolshevik Revolution, 1917–1923.* 3 vols. (1985)

Fay, Sidney B. *The Origins of the World War* (1928)

Joll, James. *The Origins of the First World War* (1984)

Mayer, Arno J. *Politics and Diplomacy of Peacemaking: Containment and Counterrevolution at Versailles, 1918–1919* (1967)

Nef, John H. *War and Human Progress* (1950)

Robbins, Keith. *The First World War* (1984)

Ropp, Theodore. *War in the Modern World* (1966)

Trotsky, Leon. *History of the Russian Revolution* (1958)

Ulam, Adam B. *Lenin and the Bolsheviks* (1969)

Williams, Jones. *The Home Fronts: Britain, France, and Germany, 1914–1918* (1972)

21

The Twilight of Liberalism

1920	Polish-Russian war
1921	Disarmament conference held in Washington
	The NEP established in Russia
1922	German–Russian treaty of Rapallo
	Mussolini establishes fascist regime in Italy
	Sinclair Lewis, *Babbitt*
	James Joyce, *Ulysses*
1923	French invade the Ruhr
	USSR established
	Stabilization of German currency
1924	Dawes plan for German reparations adopted
	Death of Lenin
1925	Locarno Treaty
1926	Nationalization of oil industry in Mexico
1928	Briand-Kellogg Peace Pact
	First Five-Year Plan initiated in USSR
1929	Stalin's dictatorship established; Trotsky banished
	Italy-Papacy concordat: Vatican City becomes sovereign Papal State
	Crash of New York Stock Exchange

With war and devastation any widespread feelings of security and complacency faded; but this very fading made possible the blossoming of vigorous new intellectual activity in Western culture. During the 1920s, scientific and technological endeavors broadened in scope and significance. Literature, painting, and architecture flourished, bringing to maturity the revolutionary art concepts that had been in their pioneer stages before the war. Political experiments in democracy, socialism, and communism generated much idealism. The New World, having come of age, now contributed in the same manner as had the European nations to the cultural accomplishments of the West.

CULTURAL TRENDS

Interest in the Western countries became more and more concentrated upon technology and the social sciences. Scientific advances continued, and scientific methods of research and experimentation were applied to the new disciplines of psychology and sociology. Science affected the work of philosophers, historians, and economists. It stimulated education, in which a new approach to the study of the process of learning was sought and experiments in new types of schools were undertaken. It influenced literature, which became less concerned with the character, ideas, and behavior of the exceptional individual and more concerned with the average person and with the collective behavior of the masses. Its effects can be traced in painting, architecture, and music, all of which gave expression to modern psychological and sociological trends. Even religious thought came to be increasingly reconciled to modern science.

Science and Technology

War had accelerated scientific work and the search for new technologies. The work of twentieth-century scientists increased people's realization of the complexities of the cosmos. In all scientific fields, further specialization became necessary.

PHYSICAL SCIENCES

The most spectacular advances were made in the physical sciences, particularly in research concerned with the world of the atom. Physicists such as Ernest Rutherford, Niels Bohr, and Erwin Schrödinger achieved fundamental progress in understanding the structure and the processes operating within the atom. Werner Heisenberg proposed an uncertainty principle, which postulated final limits on human possibilities of observation; it thus restricted, on the atomic level, the area in which scientific verification is possible and led to further advances in quantum mechanics. Astronomers developed the idea of a constantly expanding universe to explain many puzzling phenomena in this field. Albert Einstein elaborated his theory of relativity and began work on a formula that would be as all-inclusive in explaining the relationship of natural forces as Newton's gravitational laws had once seemed to be.

TECHNOLOGY

Numerous inventions made in preceding decades found practical application and altered the average person's lifestyle. The automobile, now more affordable, especially through the work of Henry Ford in the United States, became increasingly important for commercial uses and in private family life. It also affected national policies by creating a need for highway construction and a demand for oil, which influenced international policies. The airplane, whose development had been rapidly furthered during the war, came into commercial use. Priority was given to speed, not only for transportation but in almost all areas of modern life. In 1927 Charles Lindbergh accomplished the first nonstop transatlantic flight from New York to Paris. Radio was developed, bringing music and other programs to the average household, of which it became a part, like the telephone. Television had its first practical tryouts, and the moving-picture industry changed with the introduction of sound and color. Manufacturing processes were modernized. Stopwatch in hand, the American, F. W. Taylor had worked out in the late nineteenth century, every movement a worker was required to make at a given job, and the worker was thus strictly bound to a schedule. After the First World War the conveyor belt and the moving-assembly line, children of Taylorism, dominated the actions of the factory worker, who was reduced to functioning like a machine component. Although wages were generally higher because of wartime labor shortages, resentment grew, work-related ailments increased, and bitter opposition in the form of trade unionism resulted.

CHEMISTRY

New information about the molecular structure of matter enabled chemists to broaden their efforts to produce synthetic materials, with the result that rare or expensive natural products, such as rubber and silk, could be increasingly replaced by artificial materials. This development of synthetics also went beyond the realm of science by affecting economic, social, and political life. New products changed the habits and work of the average person and simultaneously redirected the policies of whole nations. They reduced the dependence of great powers upon their colonies for raw materials and led to the creation of new industries. This, in turn, eased some international tensions, generated others, encouraged nationalism, affected independence movements among colonial peoples, and eventually contributed to recurring shifts in the balance of power.

BIOLOGY AND MEDICINE

Aside from physics and chemistry, notable advances were also made in most other areas of science. Biologists made fundamental achievements in their study of heredity (including the phenomenon of mutations) and cell physiology. New therapies for a wide variety of diseases were developed. Vitamins were identified by Frederick Hopkins and penicillin was discovered by Alexander Fleming in 1928. Hormones and antibiotics were added to the physician's arsenal.

Progress in public health brought new methods for combating epidemics caused by mosquitoes, lice, rats, and other carriers of bacteria. Improved sanitary practices also contributed to better health and a longer life for millions of people. This led to increases in population, which resulted in crowded urban and rapidly growing suburban areas. Nevertheless, material standards of living could improve, since science—and particularly advances in chemistry, plant pathology, veterinary medicine, and agronomy—made possible a vast increase in agricultural production, so that the food supply was more ample than ever before.

PSYCHOLOGY AND SOCIOLOGY

Finally, the two new fields of scientific psychology and sociology made rapid progress. Psychologists applied the theories expounded by Freud and his disciples; they evolved new ideas in normal and abnormal psychology. Sociologists applied the research techniques of psychologists and arrived at interesting, though necessarily tentative, conclusions regarding collective behavior—conclusions that had considerable influence in the fields of philosophy, political science, and history.

Philosophy and Economic Theory

In a world dominated by scientific endeavors, philosophy continued to occupy itself largely with rational, materialistic, and social questions, rather than with transcendental or metaphysical problems. Such outstanding thinkers as Bertrand Russell, Alfred North Whitehead, John Dewey, and Ludwig Wittgenstein interested themselves in science and its methods, as well as in the effects of science on human society. Pragmatic tendencies were strong, and the theories of symbolic logic and logical positivism were developed. Logical positivism followed the example of nineteenth-century positivists like Auguste Comte in excluding metaphysical and transcendental concerns from the domain of philosophy. But they went further by devoting themselves to the technical analysis of language and to the belief that the meaning of any statement lies in its method of verification; the unification of all the sciences through a common logical language was the ultimate goal. The question and meaning of "progress" was reexamined. In line with evolutionary theories, the facts of history and experience, rather than abstract concepts, were adopted as the basis for most interpretations of the evolution of human society. Some philosophers, such as Oswald Spengler in his *Decline of the West* (1918–1922), came to view human history altogether as a biological process subject to natural laws. They insisted that every culture passes through a cycle of youth, maturity, and old age, with its resulting deterioration. In this philosophy we may measure the disillusionment that resulted from the First World War and the tremendous blow inflicted by the conflict upon the idealism and boundless confidence with which the generation entered the twentieth century.

Scientific and historical approaches also marked the work of economists. In the nineteenth century, Karl Marx had turned to history in order to understand economic developments; many twentieth-century economists, among them John Maynard Keynes and Joseph Schumpeter, adopted the same method. After studying the evolutionary social process in history, they reviewed and criticized the propositions of the classical economic theorists. In general, they came to reject all idealistic and utopian views; like many philosophers, they accepted "utility" as their standard. Some economists concluded that utility governed "value" and thereby, within the changing historical setting, the major phases of the economic process. They developed extensive statistical methods and, with the help of statistics, investigated business cycles, price movements, and all other characteristics of capitalism.

A special place of importance belongs to the German Max Weber (1864–1920), an influential sociologist who helped create the constitution of the postwar Weimar Republic. His studies concerning the relationship between society and the individual were embodied in his most famous work, *The Protestant Ethic and the Spirit of Capitalism* (1904), which, as its name implies, explored the effects of the Protestant Reformation—in particular, the new perception of wealth and its accumulation—on the growth of capitalism and, by extension, modern Western society. Weber's ideas helped to counter the influence exercised at the time by certain Marxist thinkers.

Education

Growing attention was paid to mass education in order to prepare Western schoolchildren, as well as adults, for the increasingly complex tasks facing them in the modern world: how to handle machinery and how to live alongside it; how to exercise newly won civil rights; how to use a constantly expanding leisure time. In the decade after World War I, therefore, while literacy was becoming nearly universal (spreading to the most remote regions of the United States and Russia), educational goals underwent a radical transformation. Study of the classics—a foundation of modern civilization—was curtailed in order to allow more time for study of the natural sciences. Instruction emphasized experience and practice rather than memorization, which had long been regarded as an indispensable tool of knowledge. Discipline was relaxed, and students were given greater freedom to achieve "self-expression."

With mass education, a leveling process began whereby uniformity in thinking habits was promoted. Numerous experimental schools were founded. Social adjustment to the mechanized modern world was considered a major task for "democratic" education. To be sure, opposition arose against the new trends in education; critics of the idea of "progressive education" held that lack of rigid intellectual training and discipline would lead to a return to barbarism. Even in communist Russia, a foremost advocate of progressive education, a reaction occurred during the 1930s.

Literature and the Fine Arts

The 1920s stand out as a time particularly rich in writers and artists of ability and significant accomplishment. It was during this period that the trends that had been developed under the leadership of the expressionists during the last decade and a half before World War I came into full flowering. With the upheavals of war, revolution, and postwar adjustment, many of the former restraints broke down. Writers and artists of genius could follow more freely their inclinations and proceed with important experimental work. Today there is little doubt about the broad historical and social significance of their works.

LITERATURE

The novel continued to offer artistic frame that seemed most appropriate to the temper of the time. It lent itself to realistic description and to criticism of the social scene. Among the leading writers of fiction were the Frenchmen Romain Rolland, André Gide, and André Malraux, the Englishmen Thomas Hardy (famous also for his poetry), John Galsworthy, and D. H. Lawrence, and the Russians Maxim Gorky, Alexei Tolstoy, and Vladimir Mayakovsky (all of whom were actually products of the prerevolutionary days). *Remembrance of Things Past* (1913–1927), by Marcel Proust, and *Ulysses* (1922), by the Irishman James Joyce, became foremost examples of that type of psychological study and penetrating observation of human instincts and behavior that have since become known as stream-of-consciousness writing. Unusually vigorous and important literary talents emerged in the United States with Sinclair, Lewis, F. Scott Fitzgerald, Theodore Dreiser, John Dos Passos, Upton Sinclair, and Ernest Hemingway; and in Germany with Heinrich and Thomas Mann, Franz Werfel, and Hermann Hesse.

Compared to prose, creative work in drama and poetry was of lesser importance. The American Eugene O'Neill, who rejected nineteenth-century farce for symbolic expressionism, and the Englishman George Bernard Shaw, who despite advancing age still remained one of the most productive authors and critics, excelled in drama. In lyric poetry, the most prominent writers were the Irishman William Butler Yeats, the American T. S. Eliot, the Frenchman Paul Valéry, and the Germans Stefan George and Rainer Maria Rilke. Of course, the largest audiences were not reached by the great writers but by newspapers, journals, magazines, and sensational novels.

Just as literacy was rapidly advancing everywhere in the West, means of communication were being invented that could dispense with the written word. Radio, cinema, photographs, cartoons, and illustrated advertisements (i.e., audiovisual media) were used to disseminate information, entertainment, and propaganda on an unprecedented scale. Though they often contributed to the corruption of people's tastes, they also contributed to their education and elevation. The film in particular, with a number of outstanding productions and excellent actors, such as Charles Chaplin and Greta Garbo, gained a major place in the cultural scene.

PAINTING AND SCULPTURE

In the fine arts, expressionism reached its climax and brought forth a movement known as surrealism. Many outstanding painters and sculptors concentrated on human psychology rather than on visual imagery. They sought to express an inner reality: a view of twentieth-century men and women as being torn by the multiplicity of modern problems that they had to face, without the confidence that a feeling of harmony with either nature or a world spirit had given them in other times. Artists revealed their concern with the social patterns of their age, which they sought to explain or criticize.

Outstanding contributors were the painters Pablo Picasso, who began a new phase of creativity in his life, and Diego Rivera, who was influenced by communist ideology, as well as the Swiss Paul Klee; and the sculptors Sir Jacob Epstein, Ivan Mestrovic, Aristide Maillol, and Henry Moore. Since these painters and sculptors often preferred an abstract type of expression, it was difficult for the average person to understand their works. Most people were drawn to other, more conservative artists who favored a simpler, more direct language. Especially in countries ruled by communist and fascist regimes, intellectualized, abstract trends were ridiculed and rejected, whereas artistic creations rooted in national folklore and serving, if possible, the ideologies of the regimes were promoted.

ARCHITECTURE

Vigorous and artistically meaningful developments also occurred in the field of architecture. Functionalism, which had begun to dominate building styles during the period before World War I, now spread rapidly. It emphasized simplicity, the utmost restraint in ornamentation, and clear, geometric lines. It sought to bring aesthetic values into harmony with the practical demands of life in an industrial age. City planning and apartment, factory, and office building projects engaged the attention of architects; social needs gave direction to their creative endeavors. The Bauhaus in Dessau, Germany, a school of painters and architects, became a center for modern concepts in building. Similarly, in the Netherlands, France, and the United States, the functional style with its characteristic aesthetic values made rapid progress. Owing to masters such as Walter Gropius, Ludwig Mies van der Rohe, Frank Lloyd Wright, and Le Corbusier, town landscapes in Europe and America began to change. Uncluttered lines and a variety of color began to give many of them an impression of beauty that most nineteenth-century towns, in their grayness and with their imitative styles, overornamentation, and slums, had sadly lacked.

MUSIC

In music, traditional harmonic concepts survived in most of the popular compositions; folklore continued to inspire their creators. But composers such as Arnold Schönberg, Igor Stravinsky, Paul Hindemith, Béla Bartók, and the by now older Finnish composer, Jean Sibelius went on with experimental works, some of them with the creation of atonal music. Like expressionist painting, atonal music failed to have an immediate appeal for the uninitiated; nevertheless, it attracted a growing audience of intellectuals. The Soviet Union produced Sergei Prokofiev and Dmitri Shostakovich. America's chief contribution consisted of popular and often "intellectualized" jazz. It had originated among black musicians, inspired broad audiences, and influenced many leading composers. While in the United States a special type of musical theater, the so-called musical, originated, few operas of importance were written. Classical and modern concert music came to be enjoyed by ever-widening audiences. Numerous excellent orchestras were founded, especially in America. Improved radio reception and better phonographs contributed to an unprecedented awareness of the great musical heritage.

Considerable attention was paid to the Czech composers Smetana and Dvořák, who had worked in the nineteenth century, and to the younger Janáček. However, unlike the German masters whom they admired and whose appeal was universal, they emphasized—a sign of the pervasiveness of nationalistic feelings—special national values. Janáček expressly admonished his students "to compose in the national style."

Religion

It is significant that the rapid progress of science, technology, and secular education did not intensify the conflict between science and religion, which dated back to the preceding century. Scientists began to appreciate the limitations and relativity of their knowledge, while most churches allowed a broader place for science in the mind of rational people. Atheism no longer claimed converts, as in preceding decades, except in Russia, where Marxist aims called for a condemnation of all religion as a form of superstition. The challenge of science caused the churches to reassess their teachings and ultimately to strengthen their spiritual forces. Even in Russia, the church gained rather than lost by this challenge and by the withdrawal of many who had adhered to it only out of convention.

Relations between church and state became more peaceful. With the spread of separation between church and state, governments exercised less control over religious institutions. Especially among Protestants, a spiritual revival led to a Neo-Orthodoxy, which had its roots in ideas expounded by the nineteenth-century Danish theologian Søren Kierkegaard. Neo-Orthodoxy asked for a reaffirmation of the Christian doctrine and a resolute acceptance of the fundamental tenets of Christianity, which demanded of the individual a "painful abandonment" to faith. The Catholic Jacques Maritain and the Protestant Karl Barth were the two outstanding theologians who adhered to this position; both insisted with equal fervor on the obligation of the faithful not to neglect their duty to promote human concerns in daily life and politics.

INTERNATIONAL TRENDS

Like most wars, World War I settled fewer problems than it created. The international arrangements made at Versailles were quickly shattered. The League of Nations proved ineffective. The gulf widened between the views of capitalist countries and those of Russia and between the interests of colonial powers and those of their dependencies. The fact that mechanized civilization, with its numerous pressures, required new attitudes was comprehended by few politicians.

Major International Problems

The two problems most disturbing to international relationships after World War I were communism and reparations. At first, the victorious Western powers sought to solve these problems by force, trying to suppress communism with armed might and to collect reparations under threats. When this method failed, they slowly settled down to the task of making compromises. Unfortunately for the peace of the West, they delayed too long.

COMMUNISM

At the end of the war, communism seemed to be only weakly established in Russia. Hoping, therefore, to be able to restore a capitalistic, liberal-democratic regime, four powers—America, Britain, France, and Japan—decided to crush the Bolsheviks. They invaded Russia in 1918 in order to force her back into the war against Germany. When the world war ended, they continued to support the old tsarist forces in order to oust the Bolshevik government. This "intervention" led to catastrophe. After two bitter years, foreign troops were forced to quit Russian soil. Simultaneously, Russian monarchists and anticommunists, led by Anton Denikin, Pyotr Wrangel, Aleksandr Kolchak, and other tsarist officers, either surrendered or fled the country. By 1922, the Bolsheviks were in full control of most of Russia. Regions that had attempted to establish independent regimes, such as Siberia, parts of the Caucasus, and parts of the Ukraine, were reunited with Russia proper and became components of the Soviet Union.

Thus within four years, communist power had firmly established itself. From then on, it became an ever-greater force in the world. Even when absent from international conferences, the Soviet Union had to be considered in all political settlements. It secured recognition from most European nations and gradually expanded its influence abroad through the *Comintern, the Third* (Communistic) *International*, which Lenin had sponsored in 1919.

REPARATIONS

Some of the French leaders at Versailles had insisted upon the imposition of extremely burdensome reparations; they hoped that reparations payments would not only help in the reconstruction of war-damaged France but would also make possible the permanent subjugation of Germany. These expectations were not realized. It quickly became clear that reparations were a two-edged weapon. By forcing Germany to increase its industrial capacity and to bend its efforts toward exports in order to earn the means for making reparations payments, the insistence on reparations caused a major disturbance for the Western economy. German currency became inflated to a degree never before experienced—at one point the paper mark was quoted in Berlin at two and a half trillion to the American dollar (the prewar exchange rate had been 4.2 marks to the dollar); the victors thus made it possible for the German government to pay its internal debt in inflated currency and thereby gain strength, while other countries experienced unemployment and a limited inflation. Moreover, unemployment and inflation led to a new radicalism everywhere. Mortgage holders, bondholders, and other creditors suffered, retired people were impoverished, and millions of people lost interest in the preservation of the capitalistic system. Finally a wedge was driven between the Allies themselves, especially between France and England (who desired economic stability) and between the United States and its European partners (who refused to pay war debts to the United States so long as they could not collect from Germany). In 1927, an economic conference called to find a solution to the problem failed to achieve its purpose. Thus reparations served neither the Allied interests nor the cause of world peace and reconstruction.

International Solutions

As time went on, the task of finding a basis, different from the Versailles Treaty, for rebuilding the Western community of nations became more urgent; but a solution was delayed as long as the aims of the Western states remained at variance. France desired domination on the European continent and therefore insisted on strict fulfillment of the stipulations of Versailles. Simultaneously, by entering into bilateral arrangements with Poland,

Czechoslovakia, and Yugoslavia, it sought to build up in eastern-central Europe an alliance system that would serve the double purpose of erecting a *cordon sanitaire* against communist Russia and a counterweight against German might. England, however, wanted the reestablishment of a balance of power: Not only should France be prevented from becoming a menace to England but communism should also be held in check. The United States, which refused to become a party to the Versailles Treaty, followed a policy of isolationism wherever possible. Germany sought a revision of the treaty and the reestablishment of its prewar position. Russia, which ranked fifth among the great powers and, like the United States, was not a signatory to the Versailles Treaty, detached itself completely from the West; Russia saw as its aims the consolidation of a socialist society at home and the spread of communism abroad.

RAPALLO (1922)

The divergent aims of the great powers foreshadowed a long period of negotiation. Since the League of Nations failed to fulfill the role intended for it, conference after conference had to be called. Various meetings took place in 1920. In 1921, a naval conference was held in Washington for the purpose of promoting disarmament. The only thing achieved, however, was a redistribution of naval strength. The arrangement was significant inasmuch as England, formerly the greatest power on the seas, had to accept a place of equality with the United States; Japan ranked third; while Italy and France shared fourth and fifth places.

A year later, a more important conference was held at Genoa, to which both Germany and the Soviet Union were invited. It led (owing to the failure of the victors to make concessions to the two outcasts) to a German-Russian treaty. This treaty, made at nearby Rapallo, changed the existing distribution of power as much as had the Franco-Russian alliance in 1890. Germany and Soviet Russia, both isolated and weak since the war, agreed upon formal political recognition and economic cooperation and thereby became powerful factors on the international stage. France reacted bitterly. In the following year, 1923, it used Germany's inability to pay reparations as an excuse for occupying the great German industrial region of the Ruhr. Both the United States and England refused to associate themselves with such a punitive measure and even withdrew occupation troops. As a result, the French invasion of the Ruhr gained little and further complicated the international situation.

LOCARNO (1925)

Under the circumstances, the need for a realistic attack upon Western economic and political problems became more urgent. Steps were finally taken at the initiative of the United States. In 1924, with the realization of the close relationship between political and economic problems, a reparations plan (the Dawes plan) was worked out. It fixed German reparations at a sum apparently commensurate with Germany's ability to pay; American loans were put at Germany's disposal so that Germany might provide for its new obligations.

Once adopted, the Dawes plan opened the way for a settlement of political disputes. This was achieved by a conference held in Locarno in 1925. Owing to the efforts of the French and German foreign ministers, Aristide Briand and Gustav Stresemann, respectively, an agreement concerning the disputed Franco-German border was consummated. The agreement guaranteed the maintenance of Germany's western boundaries as established by the Versailles Treaty. In the following year Germany joined the League of Nations. Simultaneously, the military supervision of Germany was ended.

BRIAND-KELLOGG PACT (1928)

Further steps toward the preservation of peace were taken in the next year. Inequalities in military strength continued to endanger world peace; regional meetings and disarmament conferences among the victors had accomplished little. Thereupon, the American secretary of state, Frank Kellogg, proposed a pact that provided for compulsory arbitration of future political differences. The pact was signed by the United States and the leading European powers in 1928.

Solutions to Colonial Problems.

World War I marked the end of an era of Western civilization, not only in Europe but also in the colonies. Under the pressure of world opinion, humanitarian views, and socialist propaganda, European political domination began to recede. Meanwhile, national movements led by native upper classes gained in strength. Germany and Russia dropped out of the colonial picture altogether. Germany, by virtue of the Versailles Treaty, had lost its colonies everywhere. Russia, in line with communist ideology, voluntarily renounced treaty advantages secured by tsarist governments in China, Afghanistan, Persia, and Turkey.

Other nations also had to modify their relations with colonial areas. The United States eased its controls in Central America and reformed the government of the Philippines. France, Japan, and Britain (though attempting to preserve their empires and even to enlarge them) also had to make concessions. France was obliged to give up some of its control in the Near East and to liberalize its policies in North Africa. Japanese troops were forced to leave Siberia, where they had made territorial acquisitions during the anti-Bolshevik intervention of 1918–1920.

Britain, the largest colonial power, had to make the broadest concessions. In 1923 it gave its dominions the right to make independent treaties with foreign powers. Between 1926 and 1931, it created the British Commonwealth, which provided for the equal status of dominions and parent country within the empire and for independent management of internal and external affairs. In 1931 it confirmed the new status of the colonies by means of the Statute of Westminster. Britain resigned its protectorate over Egypt in 1922 and broadened that country's independence in 1936. But in order to safeguard British investments and the supply of oil, it insisted on continued control of the Arab states—mainly Palestine, Transjordan, and Iraq—which had been founded within the area of the dissolved Turkish Empire. It also refused to withdraw from India. As a result, it became involved in a desperate struggle against Indian nationalists led by Mahatma Gandhi, who advocated passive resistance to all English authority and defiance of Western civilization. Even though Gandhi's economic precepts—based upon a reliance on traditional Indian production methods—could not survive in an industrialized world, his moral stand gained wide recognition and laid the basis for India's future independence. This objective was achieved in 1947, after his death.

All Western countries lost their privileged status and their extraterritorial rights in China. Further colonialism there was forestalled by the continued reform work of Sun Yat-sen and his party, the Kuomintang. In most colonies where European political power had to withdraw, European techniques were taken over by native forces.

NATIONAL TRENDS

Internal political developments in the Western nations after World War I were marked by the progressive introduction of democratic institutions and social legislation. Women came to take an increasingly important part in national affairs.

But the process of democratization failed to alleviate social tensions. As after the French Revolution, conflicts increased between rich and poor, between those who willingly accepted changing conditions and others who looked back longingly at former "better times." In many countries, bad feelings existed between those who had served during the war in the front lines and those who had stayed at home. Some of the latter were accused of being war profiteers. The demands of the Versailles Treaty and the triumph of communism now added fuel to internal conflicts in the West.

Britain   Reform in its empire, loss of its place as the leading financial power, and the redoubled competition, not only of the United States but also of a recovering Germany, forced Britain to make numerous internal adjustments. The Liberal party declined. For three years after 1919, Britain's wartime leader, Lloyd George, continued to preside over a coalition cabinet. But a business recession, following upon the end of hostilities and a reconversion to peacetime production, restored the Conservatives to power. Thereafter the Liberal party was eclipsed by the Labor party; in 1924 the first Labor cabinet in British history was formed. It lasted only a few months (during which time Britain formally recognized the Soviet Union) and then had to yield again to the Conservatives.

Under Liberal leadership England benefited from the general revival that began after the reparations problem had been responsibly attacked through the Dawes plan and the political climate improved through the Locarno agreements. Its trade balance and financial position improved. The government enacted social legislation to alleviate the plight of the unemployed. England modernized its industries. It achieved further political democratization in 1928 by granting equal suffrage to women. But grave problems remained to be solved: persistent unemployment, distress in some industries, and numerous acrimonious strikes, especially of coal miners, climaxing with a general strike. The Irish were dissatisfied with England's wartime promises. They received only dominion status in 1922 and especially resented the separation of Ulster from the Irish Free State. They fought desperately for complete independence. But all of these issues were overshadowed when, in 1929, a worldwide economic crisis interrupted what progress had been achieved. Together with the loosening of ties with the dominions through the Statute of Westminster, it opened a new phase in England's history.

France

Another victor of 1918, France, faced problems of a very different kind. Its people still led (as the literary critic André Siegfried had observed before 1914) a more contented life than its progressive and dynamic neighbors. Favored by tradition, character, and resources, life in France had not changed as it had in the highly industrialized countries. Its economy was more balanced and self-sufficient; its political position satisfied the nationalists after the victory of 1918. In addition, its prosperity was aided by German reparations and American debt cancellations.

Underneath the surface, however, French conditions were precarious. The prewar trend of stagnating population-growth figures remained. Politically, the individualism of the French reasserted itself, split the parties into numerous groups, and impeded nationwide cooperation. Constant changes in government prevented the passing of timely legislation needed to adapt the economic structure to modern requirements. Inflation haunted the country and increased instability; initiative was lacking. Corruption and scandals were not infrequent. In contrast to the situation in other great nations, the right of women to vote was withheld, living standards of the poor were raised but little, and class differences remained unreconciled. Thus, despite military victory, the prospects for the nation to retain its international position were substantially diminished.

Germany

Having been defeated in war, shaken by the revolution that had brought the imperial government to an end, and deprived of valuable industrial regions in the east and west, Germany faced the future under grave handicaps. At Weimar, in central Germany, a democratic constitution for the new German republic, which later became known as the Weimar Republic, was drawn up in 1919 by bourgeois and socialist liberals. It provided for parliamentary government, ministerial responsibility to the diet, equal suffrage of all citizens (including women), and guarantees of other civil rights. A socialist, Friedrich Ebert, became its first president. But the new political organization found little support or respect. Bitter partisan recriminations divided the country; Bolshevists under the leadership of the so-called Spartacists hoped to turn it into a communist state, while reactionaries sought to reestablish old monarchical forms. As in France, individualism led to a large number of splinter parties, which hindered the formation of effective governments and necessitated constantly changing coalitions. Although the civil service remained intact and government officials worked faithfully and honestly, disorder and violence marked the political scene.

A terrible and prolonged inflation resulted from the reparations demands made at Versailles, hurting even the victors themselves. It primarily ruined the liberal middle class in Germany, which would have been the force to build a sound democratic society. As a result, this middle class listened to demagogic promises of the extreme right or the extreme left. Resentment was kept alive by the Peace of Versailles with its frontier stipulations, reparations, and war-guilt clauses. Political disorders were common. On the one hand, disappointed, chauvinistic war youths, assisted by officers of the old army clique, tried to overthrow the democratic government. In 1920 they staged the Kapp Putsch, an uprising that failed. Several ministers and party leaders were assassinated, the nationalists being generally the perpetrators. In Bavaria in 1923, a small, ultranationalist group, led by an Austrian, Adolf Hitler, undertook the Bierhall Putsch, which, like the Kapp Putsch, was promptly put down.

On the other hand, leftist parties sought the destruction of the government by organizing strikes and several armed rebellions. With the help of the army, these were put down. The Treaty of Rapallo with Russia did not ensure internal stability, though it did restore Germany to its former place as a great power. It was then that inflation reached its worst form. The reparations payments could not be made; thereupon, the French and Belgians marched into the Ruhr district.

Hopes for constructive progress were reawakened only after the currency was stabilized in 1923. Reparations were reduced by the Dawes plan, a successful foreign policy was initiated by Stresemann, and foreign occupation troops were withdrawn. The Locarno Treaty brought a measure of reconciliation with the West. Even then, however, sufficient difficulties remained and nationalist extremists as well as Bolshevists exploited them by pointing to the weakness of the national economy and to the restrictions imposed at Versailles. Thus was widespread disrespect kept alive for a government that was trying to be liberal and to adapt itself to democratic forms. As long as economic conditions improved, these extremists had little chance; but when depression came in 1929, the nihilistic forces triumphed.

Russia

While England, France, Germany, and other Western countries adhered to moderately liberal democratic (and occasionally mildly socialistic) institutions, Russia set about building a communist society.

PERIOD OF WAR COMMUNISM (1919–1921)

The Soviet constitution of 1918 established a dictatorship of the proletariat; all parties except the Communist disappeared. The former ruling classes were disenfranchised. The nobility, capitalists, rich peasants, priests, and noncommunist intelligentsia were persecuted, exiled, or condemned to death. The government was put into the hands of a Central Committee of Soviets and its executive organ, the Politburo. It was supported by a new, well-trained "Red Army" and a new Bolshevik police force, which ruthlessly used terrorist methods. The state took control of all banks, industries, large businesses, and foreign trade; it thus combined political with economic power to a degree unparalleled in any Western country.

PERIOD OF THE NEP (1921–1927)

Nevertheless, owing to foreign war, civil strife, famine, and dissatisfaction among the peasants (who, unlike the industrial workers, had gained little influence in the government), communism might not have survived in Russia had Lenin not changed his tactics in 1921. A serious crisis had developed. The peasants refused to fulfill their quotas for the delivery of foodstuffs. Production came to a standstill. A contingent of sailors revolted. Faced by these problems, Lenin reintroduced, notwithstanding opposition within his own ranks, a number of capitalistic institutions. Small-scale private enterprise in trade and agriculture was once again allowed. The policy of food levies was replaced by taxation of peasants. The terror was reduced. Aid from capitalistic countries was accepted, and a stable currency was restored. Schools were reopened and pre-Revolutionary scientists were reemployed. Also, a compromise with the Orthodox Church was arranged. Lenin's new policy, known as the NEP (New Economic Policy), brought internal improvements at the very time that Russia gained external prestige through the Rapallo Treaty and won formal recognition from the leading European powers.

PERIOD OF FIRST FIVE-YEAR PLAN (1928–1932)

In July 1923, a new constitution was published. It established the Union of Socialist Soviet Republics (USSR), composed of Great Russia, Siberia, the Ukraine, and the Caucasus. Shortly thereafter, Lenin died. But his work survived, despite a bitter struggle for party leadership between his two chief co-workers, Leon Trotsky and Joseph Stalin. With the help of the Party apparatus that he controlled, Stalin, the great organizer, triumphed over Trotsky. Stalin held the view that communism had to be built on firm ground in Russia before it could be spread abroad. He rejected the individualistic tendencies of Trotsky and insisted on strict Party discipline and central direction; ideologically, he steered a middle road. Under him, the NEP (which had served well as a temporary expedient) was given up and communist planning was resumed. The first of a series of Five-Year Plans, published in 1928, provided for the central direction of all economic activities by government and Party. It stipulated production quotas for all sectors of the economy: for factories, agriculture, and individual workers. It aimed at developing the resources of the country and at improving backward regions—especially the arctic areas of Siberia. It coordinated the activities of the various industries and controlled channels of domestic and foreign distribution. Prices and wages were fixed.

The Plan promoted the collective farm, called *kolkhoz*, or "large farm." The land would belong to the state, but its activities would be managed autonomously in accordance with the Plan. Its cultivation would be attended to in common by its members, and its products sold by state or *kolkhoz* stores. Individuals retained for themselves no more than a house and garden but shared according to their work in a possible surplus of the collective. Mechanical help was rendered by government-run tractor stations.

The Plan was in many respects a success. It provided also for public education, for theaters, and for other cultural activities and led to a rapid increase in Russia's production capabilities. But its rigorous enforcement caused the population untold suffering. Especially in the country, the *kulaks* (prosperous peasants with individual holdings), whose activity had been allowed during the NEP, were sacrificed to communistic aims. Hundreds of thousands of them perished either from starvation or as the result of exile and persecution.

Under a dictatorship of the soviets, the state police were given almost unlimited power. The government exercised strict censorship of books and publications. It persecuted all who voiced critical or anticommunist opinions and undertook a continuous, all-embracing propaganda campaign. Contacts of Soviet citizens with foreign countries became almost impossible; news from the outside world hardly reached them. No one felt safe. Labor camps were erected and filled with both innocent and guilty citizens. Emigration was halted, while immigrants from the West—enthusiasts who hoped for the better society offered by communism and who intended to help build the country under the Five-Year Plan—were admitted. Betterment of living standards was to result, but for the time being it was sacrificed to the aim of building a communist society.

The United States

In the United States, World War I had left less destruction, fewer losses, less of an imprint than in Europe. Consequently, social change was less extreme. A Republican administration, which replaced the Democrats in 1921, adopted many of the policies of political and economic liberalism. The nation prospered as business expanded, national production increased rapidly, and standards of living improved. There was substantial progress in education, science, literature, and the arts. Indications of such progress included the large number of foreign students attracted to American universities, the development of inventions and technology, the organization of excellent orchestras, the founding of numerous museums, and the great variety of works of literature that gained worldwide attention. In foreign affairs, the United States, notwithstanding popular isolationist sentiments, took a more active part than ever before in contributing to the solution of world problems. A rash of political corruption and crime accompanied the "noble experiment" of national Prohibition—a constitutional amendment that outlawed alcoholic beverages; such corruption, however, failed to impede the economic and cultural progress of the nation.

But while the position of U.S. economic strength was maintained, serious social maladjustments and problems were ignored. Little heed was given to warnings about the difficulties of the farmers and the overextension of credit. Not until the stock market crash of 1929, marking the end of the era of prosperity, did the government begin to work on solutions for some of the fundamental problems confronting the United States and other Western nations.

Other Western Countries

The smaller countries of the West, with the exception of Italy, did not suffer as much as the major powers from either the war or the difficulties caused in its aftermath by revolutions, inflation, impoverishment, and social disorganization. None adopted communism. Most of them made considerable progress in the development of industrial production, educational standards, and political democracy. In some countries, however, such as Poland and Hungary, feudalistic institutions benefiting the owners of large landed estates continued to prevail; in others dictatorships prospered, as in Latin America.

In all Western nations, nationalism persisted as a dominant influence. Poland led armed aggression against its various neighbors. In Czechoslovakia, Italy, and various Balkan nations, attempts at building national industries were motivated primarily by nationalistic aspirations. Latin

America struggled against foreign economic domination; Mexico national-ized the oil companies owned by business interests in the United States. When the worldwide depression began in the late 1920s, the nationalistic trends reflected in these events created problems among the smaller nations similar to those confronting the major powers of the Western world.

Instead of creating a postwar period of stability, the Versailles Treaty led to hostility, fear, and undue hardship. Moreover, the rise of communism in Russia and civil war, which was worsened by Allied intervention, hunger, and disor-der, had a devastating effect on developments not only in the Soviet Union but in the entire West. The establishment of a dictatorship in Russia and the government's experiments there with Five-Year Plans challenged economic and political institutions in the West. Far from finding its own new order, the West saw inflation of unknown extent, labor disputes, and strikes, as well as a steady weakening of the middle class. Attempts to modify the consequences of the Versailles Treaty in conferences held in Genoa, Rapallo, and Locarno and the reduction of reparations payments proved insufficient. Failing to promote democracy, the Versailles Treaty actually hindered it. Nationalism flared up everywhere. Colonial regions attacked their masters; Ireland and the other dominions as well demanded full independence from England.

The shocks of war and the postwar period acted as a stimulus to intellec-tual developments, as witnessed by the arts, film, architecture, and education. In the field of religion, both atheistic movements and Neo-Orthodox tendencies increased; in philosophy, pragmatism dominated. The natural sciences moved into the center of Western intellectual activity. Scholars in many countries contributed new, fundamental theories and made important discoveries. This led to technical achievements in such areas as transportation and com-munications, which altered living conditions for rich and poor.

Selected Readings

Bendiner, Elmer. *A Time for Angels: The Tragicomic History of the League of Nations* (1975)

Cipolla, Carlo M., ed., *The Fontana Economic History of Europe*, 6 vols. (1973)

Craig, Gordon A. *Europe Since 1914* (1972)

de Jone, Alex. *The Weimar Chronicle: Prelude to Hitler* (1978)

Fussell, Paul. *The Great War and Modern Memory* (1975)

Gerhardie, William. *God's Fifth Column: A Biography of the Age, 1890–1940* (1981

Joll, J. *Europe Since 1870* (1976)

Keynes, John Maynard. *The Economic Consequences of the Peace* (1927)

McNeill, William H. *The Pursuit of Power: Technology, Armed Force and Society Since* A.D. (1982)

Roth, Jack J., ed., *World War I: A Turning Point in Modern History* (1967

Smith, Page *Redeeming the Time: A People's History of the 1920s and the New Deal* (1987)

Walters, F. P. *A History of the League of Nations* (1960)

22

Depression, Fascism, and War (1929–1945)

1927 Heisenberg's indeterminacy theory

1930 Young Plan for reparations adopted

      Passive resistance against England in India (Gandhi)

1931 England gives up gold standard

      England promulgates Statute of Westminster

      Austrian Kreditanstalt collapses

1932 Lausanne Reparation Conference

      Britain introduces protective tariffs

      Japanese expansion in Chinese territory

1933 Hitler becomes German chancellor

      F. D. Roosevelt becomes U. S. president; U.S.A. gives up gold standard

1934 Russia enters League of Nations

1935 Social-security acts passed in U.S.A.

1936 Purges in Russia; Stalin constitution passed

      Italy annexes Abyssinia; Rome-Berlin Axis

      Outbreak of civil war in Spain

      Germany reintroduces conscription and reoccupies the Rhineland

1937 Constitution for Ireland (Eire)

1938 Austria united with Germany

      Munich Conference ("appeasement")

      Incorporation of Sudetenland into Germany

1939 Collapse of Czechoslovakia

Italy invades Albania

Outbreak of World War II

Partition of Poland between Germany and Russia

Russia attacks Finland

1940   Germany occupies Norway, Denmark, Holland, Belgium

Incorporation of Estonia, Latvia, Lithuania into USSR

Collapse of France

1941   Germany invades Russia

Attack on Pearl Harbor by Japan; U.S.A. enters war

1942   Allied landing in Africa

1943   German defeat at Stalingrad

1944   Allied landing in Normandy, France

1945   Yalta Conference

Surrender of Germany and Japan; United Nations established

First atomic bomb (dropped by U.S.A. on Japan)

The three words—depression, fascism, *and* war,—*in this sequence, indicate a causal relationship; but they do not suffice to explain the pattern of major historical events in the 1930s. The decline of liberalism, the growing strength of nationalism, the achievements in science and technology, the failures of education, the shortsightedness of politicians and economists, the weakness of people in responsible positions, and the contradictions within human nature—all contributed to the complex events of this period. In retrospect, however, the consideration of three forces—depression, fascism, and war—to which might be added a fourth, Bolshevism, may serve as an adequate guide to analysis of the major developments.*

DEPRESSION

According to some economists, cycles of prosperity and depression are inevitable in a capitalistic society. A cycle of this kind occurred after World War I. The war boom lasted until 1919. There was a brief depression in 1920, which was followed by a long period of prosperity from which all countries (neutrals as well as those directly involved in the war) benefited. The universal prosperity engendered overconfidence in both political and in economic affairs; overoptimism and excessive speculation resulted in the production of more goods than the market could absorb. From 1925 to 1929, the gap was bridged through an expansion of credit, but when debts reached dangerous levels, banks became reluctant to make more loans. Prices dropped, production fell, and confidence was undermined.

The Crash (1929)

By 1929, a depression had begun to develop in the Western economy. New industries were created, but older ones lost in importance. Ensuing unemployment brought a chain of reactions, inasmuch as even reduced production could no longer be absorbed, and further unemployment resulted. In October of 1929 the so-called crash on the New York Stock Exchange occurred, ruining many leading business enterprises. The close relationship between domestic business and foreign trade meant that a depression in any one country (especially the United States) inevitably affected all others—not excluding communist Russia, which was compelled to accept reduced prices for its exports. In 1931 the collapse of one of the great international banks, the Kreditanstalt in Vienna, intensified the downward turn of business in all countries. Most countries gave up the gold standard. Insecurity replaced complacency.

Social Consequences of Depression

The consequences of economic disaster were felt in all areas of public and private life. Many people who had considered themselves financially secure lost their means of livelihood. Farmers, unable to find a market for their products, lost their land. Millions of factory workers were idle. Unemployment figures climbed to incredible heights in the leading industrial countries, such as the United States, Germany, and England. Even in Russia, the only large Western country that did not have an unemployment problem, the depression prevented any substantial improvement of living standards. Insecurity, demoralization, and impoverishment changed people's outlook and, in a world that seemed to be disintegrating, made them ready everywhere to seek salvation in radical corrective measures.

Political Consequences

Naturally, Western governments tried to take remedial action; in so doing, they contributed to a further weakening of liberal, laissez-faire institutions. In the United States, the Republican president Herbert Hoover introduced several farm-relief measures, and he also advocated new forms of social legislation. In 1933 the United States, during the Democrat Franklin Roosevelt's first term, devalued the dollar and instituted a program of social-security insurance. The governments of all European countries began providing subsidies for manufacturers and exporters and found it necessary to establish extensive controls over business. Tariff rates were raised and the exchange of currency was restricted. The export of gold and other funds was forbidden.

In 1931 England gave up the gold standard; as in previous emergencies, it had recourse to a national coalition cabinet, this time under a Labor party minister. In 1932 the country abandoned its free-trade policy, introducing new protective tariffs though providing "preference tariffs" for members of the empire.

In Germany, meanwhile, the government claimed almost dictatorial powers under an emergency clause of the constitution. Then, backed only by a minority against the position of a large but ideologically divided majority, it followed the example of other Western governments in exacting laws to relieve economic distress. But, also like the others, it found itself unable to solve the basic unemployment problem.

The effects of the depression were less severe in France and Italy, which were not so dependent upon highly developed industries, and in the agricultural countries of the East. Nevertheless, even in these countries, suffering was widespread and long-established political systems were imperiled as the radical parties of right or left gained adherents. Repercussions also developed in the Far East, wherever European economic methods and influence had made headway. Japan, in particular, experienced reverses owing to the loss of its foreign markets and was tempted to utilize the drastic remedies of war and territorial expansion.

International Consequences

The undermining of national economies destroyed the international balance of power, and statesmen sought in vain to restore it. The League of Nations (which, notwithstanding adverse criticisms then and since, had succeeded in settling numerous though minor international disputes and in arranging various international contracts) proved unfit for such a major task. Again, the world had to rely on traditional diplomacy. Diplomats first turned their attention to the reparations problem. As early as 1929, a new plan named after the American industrialist Owen D. Young had been drafted, which, by setting German reparations at levels pegged to the country's ability to pay, had substantially reduced the remaining balance. In 1932 the remaining reparations debts were practically canceled. Next, the former Allies held a disarmament conference in a futile attempt to economize by reducing military expenditures. Furthermore, to improve the international economic situation, Germany and Austria proposed a customs union, whereby a free central European trading area could have been created; but the plan, which had political implications, was vetoed by the victorious nations. Finally, in 1933, a general World Economic Conference was held in London to discuss concerted remedial actions. By that time, however, the various nations had initiated individual programs to deal with the crisis, and none of them was ready to accept international measures that might impede domestic relief programs. The United States, in particular, was reluctant to agree to proposed international economic ties, and the conference ended in failure. In 1934 another disarmament conference revealed a further disintegration of the international community, owing to the triumph of the fascist form of government in Germany.

FASCISM

As a political ideology, fascism had had a comparatively long history before the 1930s. Its roots lay in the economic developments and nationalistic trends of the late nineteenth and early twentieth centuries. Like socialism, fascism embraced a variety of ideas, objectives, and programs, differing in radicalism. In some of its aspects, fascism was heralded by writers hostile to the major political developments of the liberal age. Among these were sociologists such as the Italian Vilfredo Pareto, who felt that contemporary social thought was based mainly in the rational views derived from the Age of Enlightenment and that it neglected the irrational element in human behavior. With the onset of a worldwide depression, which many people attributed to the inefficiency of the democratic and capitalistic systems, fascism gained millions of adherents. Fascism appeared to offer an alternative to those who rejected democracy but who could not accept the Bolshevik doctrines of the international communist community. Demagogues would prevail over responsible political behavior. The political and economic implications of fascism made it a decisive influence in countries such as Germany and Italy, which, as a consequence of World War I, had to endure, in addition to economic difficulties, the frustration of their national ambitions.

Characteristics of Fascism

Fascism was consistent with the trend of opposition to nineteenth-century liberalism, but its opposition was far more radical than that of any other political movement except communism. The type of fascism that developed in the 1920s and 1930s relegated the individual to a minor role in society. It subordinated people entirely to the state, which was extolled as an all-embracing source of authority. The state was to become the ultimate judge of right and wrong, "right" being whatever served its interests. In fascist countries, no party but that of the fascists was to be allowed; parliamentary activity was to be reduced to a mere formality. Instead of freely elected governments, fascism would provide a single leader to whom all allegiance

304 Western Civilization from 1500

was primarily owed and who would have such authority as despots had exercised in earlier centuries. It would countenance no other loyalties. The fascists claimed the right to regulate or direct economic activities; they sought to free their country economically as well as politically from dependence upon other countries, appealing to conservatives and industrialists. They undertook to restrict civil liberties and to censor the radio, books, the cinema, and newspapers, suppressing any opinions that might encourage opposition to the leader of the nation. It was their aim to control the work of scholar and artist, whose endeavors were to be judged on the basis of utility to the nation.

In most cases fascism conflicted with religion and promoted atheism; inasmuch as it wanted to avoid any double allegiance, it sought to reduce church influence. Its moral creed was generally opposed to Christian beliefs and to many ethical concepts evolved in the West during its two thousand years of historical development. It sought to gain support from the masses—support that it needed in view of its illegitimate origin—by emphasizing the socialistic aspects of its creed. Extolling the role of laborer and peasant, the fascists promised to introduce social improvements, provide work through public projects, and raise wages. But they would not permit independent labor organizations, and they would safeguard private property rights and protect the business "leader." They considered it the task of the government to form public opinion by its most potent weapon, propaganda, and would not hesitate for this purpose to twist facts, present half-truths, and blame the ills of preceding eras on minority groups: communists, Jews, and others. Eventually, having roused chauvinistic ambitions, they would embark upon an expansionist foreign policy. In general, fascists were "men of action, not doctrinaires."

Spread of Fascism (1922–1940)

The first country to adopt fascism—indeed, the country that gave it its name—was Italy. The fascist leader Benito Mussolini established his regime in 1922. In 1923, Turkey under Mustafa Kemal, later called Atatürk, instituted a government exhibiting fascist traits. Next came Poland, in 1926, under Joseph Pilsudski; his regime (strengthened along fascist lines in 1935) was marked by more nationalistic than socialistic characteristics. In 1928, Antonio Salazar seized the government in Portugal; he established a dictatorship there in 1933. Everywhere, fascism sought, and generally gained, the support of the military. During the period 1929 to 1935, the Baltic states—Latvia, Estonia, and Lithuania—adopted some features of the fascist state. In 1929 King Alexander arbitrarily converted the parliamentary government of Yugoslavia into a personal dictatorship. Hungary began to introduce a fascist system under Gyula Gömbös in 1932 and 1933. Adolf Hitler established his regime in Germany in 1933. In Greece, Ioannis Metaxas abolished democratic institutions in 1936, and three years later Francisco Franco triumphed in Spain. These dictators permitted no opposition; their orders had to be obeyed, and their policy of aggressive nationalism prevailed. During World War II, fascist governments (usually with the help of native groups) were imposed upon several additional countries.

Fascism in Action

The regime established in Italy served as a model for other fascist states until, in the late 1930s, Hitler's Germany was accepted as a pattern.

ITALY

In Italy, fascism began in 1919 with the formation of a political party by Mussolini who, early in his career, had been a newspaperman and socialist. He opposed the liberal trend but promised his followers social improvements along noncommunistic lines; he assured them that he would put an end to social strife, establish order, and reestablish the prestige of Italy, which, he insisted, had fared badly at the hands of the Allies at Versailles. He gained support from workers, from industrialists afraid of communism, from ex-soldiers disappointed with postwar conditions, and from small-scale businessmen. Leading a number of armed bands (the so-called Black Shirts), he marched upon the government in Rome in 1922, whereupon King Victor Emmanuel III, rather than risk civil war, assigned to him the task of forming a new government. Having gained control, Mussolini abolished all parties except his own, assembled a new parliament consisting of representatives of the various economic groups (instead of representatives of political parties), and thus introduced what came to be known as a corporate state. Direction of policy was vested in the hands of the leader (il Duce); all forms of social strife, especially strikes, were outlawed; the opposition was brutally suppressed, some of its leaders being murdered; and employers and workers were called upon to work for a new order through "patriotic cooperation." The army was reorganized, programs for the drainage of swamps and for the reforestation of the denuded mountain areas were begun, and improvements were made in public services. In 1929 Mussolini signed a concordat with the papacy, which provided for recognition of a tiny sovereign state (Vatican City), compensation for the territorial losses of the Church, and designation of Catholicism as the official religion of Italy. On the whole, the population felt invigorated and hopeful; it tolerated the injustices and brutality committed by the regime and applauded Mussolini's plans for national aggrandizement. Some social legislation strengthened the regime, but it held more promise than bringing results, in particular with regard to the impoverished south.

GERMANY

The pattern set by fascism in Italy was perfected in Germany. The movement there was known as National Socialism, indicating its twofold objective. A political party, supported by force (by armed bands of Brown

Shirts), was organized by Hitler. After a first vain attempt at a putsch, or takeover, in 1923, he applied his oratorical skills and personal magnetism to gain a following. By 1932 the Nazi party had become the largest in the country, and its armed organizations were a threat to internal peace.

Seizure of Power. In 1933, after repressive constitutional measures against the Nazis had proved to be useless, Hitler was entrusted with the formation of a government. He thus achieved power "legally." With the approval and assistance of some industrialists and the demoralized segments of the middle class and the proletariat—who had suffered the consequences of Germany's defeat in 1918 and had been impoverished by inflation and depression—he substituted an authoritarian system for the national constitution. The Western powers had come too late with their support of democracy in the Weimar republic by abolishing the worst consequences of Versailles and cancelling the reparation payments. He suppressed first the Communist, then all other parties, sent his political enemies into concentration camps or had them murdered, and established himself as dictator and Fuehrer. Abandoning the left-wing tendencies apparent in the early stages of the party, he turned the resentment of the masses against the Jews, whom he pictured as the instigators of existing political and economic evils, and preached a rabid racial doctrine that was designed to appeal to the frustrated. All activities in art, science, and business had to be coordinated with party doctrines, and the "leadership principle" was extended to all areas of national life.

Legislation. Hitler attacked the unemployment problem, first by initiating public-works projects and a compulsory national labor service, then by building an armaments industry—in violation of the Versailles agreement—and, finally, by reintroducing compulsory military service. Simultaneously, he inaugurated measures to assist farmers, relieving them of their mortgage burdens and protecting inherited farms against continued indebtedness. These measures helped to revive economic life and to get the millions of disoriented unemployed off the streets; private enterprise benefited and reemployed them. Within a few years, unemployment had been replaced with a labor shortage, which forced wages to rise. A four-year plan was initiated, which mobilized all the economic forces in the country. Its financing was helped by the confiscation of property owned by Jews (and by many non-Jews, as well), who were expelled from public life and business. Steps were taken to make Germany less dependent upon foreign imports and to develop new internal resources instead; for example, many new oil wells were dug, and artificial rubber production was undertaken on a large scale. The resulting national revival—accompanied by such institutions as extra vacations through the "Strength and Joy" organization, through film festivals and sport events, including the Olympic games of 1936—impressed both Germans and foreigners, to such an extent that the injustices of the system and its neglect of the concepts embodied in Western laws and ethics were too readily overlooked. Whatever feeble opposition could be offered—by individuals, by conservative groups, by long-time staff officials of the bureaucracy, by army officers or clergymen—was defeated by defamatory propaganda and, when necessary, by violence.

SPAIN

Spain became the third great center of fascism. Unlike Germany and Italy, Spain refrained, primarily because of its internal weaknesses, from imperialistic enterprises; and again, unlike the two others, it did not combat traditional religious forces but augmented party strength through an alliance with the Catholic Church. As early as 1923, a dictatorship had been established in Spain under Miguel Primo de Rivera. He had not succeeded, however, in resolving factional strife in the country. Old ills persisted: the domineering influence of a small landowning class faced by an impoverished peasantry; the division of interests between the industrialized north and the agricultural south; the aggressiveness of both clerics and of large atheistic groups; the imposition of censorship; the agitation of monarchists opposed to fervent republicans; and the weakness of a moderating and mediating middle class.

Having failed to solve social as well as political problems, Rivera resigned in 1930. In the following year the king, potentially an effective unifying influence for the country, was forced into exile. An election put into office a republican government (at first moderately liberal, later strongly socialistic), which aroused the bitter resistance of the conservatives by passing extensive anticlerical and anticapitalistic legislation. As a result, civil war broke out in 1936. In brutality, it was perhaps unequaled by any other modern war. Foreign interventionists soon participated—communists, fascists, and volunteers from democratic countries. For years, the triangular struggle raged among these three groups, until in 1939 Franco, leader of the Falange, as the Spanish fascists came to be known, emerged victorious. He achieved internal peace by rewarding his adherents and by crushing all opponents, but, like Pilsudski—and unlike Hitler and Mussolini—he introduced few, if any, social reforms. His personal dictatorship solved few of Spain's domestic problems.

Democracies versus Fascism

Fascist doctrines and their apparent successes (particularly in the economic sphere, as in dealing with unemployment) won many adherents in the traditionally democratic countries of the West. But since these countries had not experienced the frustration of national ambitions, most people remained loyal to their well-established governments and avoided fascist experiments, despite economic difficulties and social tensions, unrest and strikes.

EUROPE

France, most of all, was in great danger. Fascists gained much ground there. In 1937 a popular-front government, which had been trying to save the country both from the rightist and from equally strong leftist extremists, was upset. The traditional forces, however, supported by much of the press, succeeded in meeting the threat and preserving most of the democratic institutions. In Holland, Norway, and other nations, fascist parties also gained influence; yet there, too, established institutions prevailed. The small fascist party in England had even fewer opportunities to make headway, for the government gradually introduced measures to improve social conditions, modernized its foreign-trade policy, and adjusted its methods of administration to contemporary needs. The English electorate, meanwhile, proved its traditional aversion to radical changes. A crisis, such as the one arising from the abdication of King Edward VIII, could be settled without disturbing the political structure. In the member nations of the Commonwealth (especially in Australia and New Zealand) the governments, opposed to all radicalism and prepared to preserve capitalism, prevented the triumph of fascism by far-reaching social legislation in the interests of the workers.

THE UNITED STATES

The influence of fascist groups in the United States was kept at a negligible level, as social and economic changes similar to those in Europe were inaugurated during the New Deal administrations of Franklin D. Roosevelt. Social-security laws were passed (such as those providing for old-age and unemployment insurance and minimum wages in industry); the gold standard was abandoned; debtors were granted a moratorium; huge government projects (e.g., the electrification of the Tennessee Valley) were undertaken; and some national planning was also attempted. Private enterprise and banking were brought under partial regulation by government, and thus a system of subsidies was used in order to influence the farmer's decisions regarding the types of crops and the acreage to be planted. Agriculture began to recover. To be sure, more radical attempts at regimentation, such as Roosevelt's proposal for "packing" (adding new judges to) the United States Supreme Court, were defeated; but even in the United States, emphasis was placed upon "leadership," and a bureaucracy dependent upon a strong central government grew rapidly. Public confidence was eventually restored, and, although a great deal of unemployment persisted, the American economy recuperated (especially, the automobile industry grew again) and standards of living of the masses improved.

Internal recovery was reflected in United States foreign policies. Despite the continued opposition of isolationists, interest and participation in European affairs increased. The Roosevelt government formally recognized the Bolshevik government in Russia; promoted closer cooperation with nonfascist nations; adopted a conciliatory attitude toward Latin American nations; proclaimed a good-neighbor policy; and settled long-standing quarrels. Through the Pan-American Union, it advanced political and economic collaboration. Thus, owing to timely action, fascism was given no chance to develop in the United States.

Communism versus Fascism

While fascism was making headway in central Europe and while a modified liberal-democratic system was being introduced in the western areas of the continent, communism increased its hold in Russia and made the appearance of any other ideology impossible.

RUSSIAN PLANNING

By 1930, the first Five-Year Plan, which was to lay the economic foundation for the new society, was well on its way toward successful completion. Production in heavy industries began to surpass the levels of tsarist Russia; the transportation system was repaired and grew rapidly, with such vast undertakings as the railway connection between Turkestan and Siberia (Turksib Railroad) and the improvement of inland waterways. Domestic commerce and foreign trade could again be expanded; the prices of consumer goods were reduced. Stability returned to the lives of the ordinary workers, and collective farming became the dominant system in agriculture. The threat of external interference receded with the strengthening of the armed forces. In 1932 a second Five-Year Plan provided for a continuation of the same domestic policies. Collectivization was continued until most private farms had disappeared, and heavy industries were given preference over those producing consumer goods.

RUSSIAN GOVERNMENT

In 1936, a new constitution was adopted for the Soviet Union. By then the nation consisted of thirteen republics, each enjoying local autonomy but subject to central political direction and central economic planning. The executive power remained in the hands of the Politburo, with Stalin at its head. Civil rights were formally extended to all Russians; thus after twenty years of discrimination, constitutional inequities directed against various "bourgeois" groups of the population were abolished. As before, only one party—the Communist—was allowed to exist and function. However, communist practice differed from theory. The Party and its functionaries exercised strict supervision over all economic and social enterprises. Promised civil rights were disregarded; dissenting voices were silenced; hundreds of thousands, possibly millions, of citizens were banished to Siberia. Workers and peasants, notwithstanding the existence of labor unions and collective-farm councils, had little chance to make their voices heard, and freedom of movement was sharply restricted. Scholars, physicians, authors, teachers, and artists who tried to act independently found their works censored and their lives imperiled. Labor camps were filled with political prisoners. One wave of purges followed another. The struggle for supreme power that had begun with Stalin and Trotsky soon engulfed all supporters of Trotsky, who had been banished in 1929. (He was assassinated in Mexico in 1940.) His adherents were brought to trial for treason and exiled or executed. By 1938 Stalin, defending himself against "right" and "left" opposition, had disposed of most of the leading Bolshevists. The terror also embraced the supreme command of the army, whose chief of staff and other high-ranking officers were executed. Purges of political opponents became an integral part of the Bolshevik system.

RUSSIAN SOCIETY

Despite sacrifices, the ideal communist society promised by the regime was slow in developing. As those who had constituted the upper classes in pre-Revolutionary times and those who had risen with the Revolution were overthrown, a constant tendency toward new class formations and elites became apparent. The Party hierarchy and officials in the state bureaucracy enjoyed numerous privileges and maintained a living standard far higher than that of the masses. In addition, intellectuals loyal to the Stalin system and an elite group of workers rose above the level of the masses. In order to speed up production, the government offered special rewards and prizes to workers who surpassed in productivity the norms demanded of them. In industry such workers were known as Stakhanovites, in honor of Aleksei Stakhanov, a miner who had shown extraordinary inventiveness and efficiency in raising production. Nevertheless, although industrial output increased rapidly, the intensive system eventually aroused dissatisfaction among ordinary workers. Nor were the recipients of the high wages greatly served, for investment possibilities were lacking and costs of luxuries were fixed so as to quickly channel the extra income back into the state treasury.

CULTURE IN THE SOVIET UNION

The Soviet government paid much attention to education. Illiteracy was practically wiped out. The emphasis was put on discipline in the schools; and training in the natural sciences, aside from political instruction in Marxism, was emphasized. As long as citizens conformed to the political demands, theater, film, music, and literature were encouraged, and some outstanding work was achieved.

WORLD WAR II

With three vigorous ideologies—fascism, remodeled democracy, and Bolshevism—competing during the 1930s, suspicion and hatred spread throughout the world. Sharpened by continued economic difficulties, they led to a rapid worsening of international relations. This happened despite the fact that the pressures of the Versailles settlement had been reduced and treaties based on equality had been made. Eventually, Germany rearmed itself and laid claim to adjoining territories. Germany's actions met with appeasement until its demands, increasing with every success, imperiled the western European powers and they decided to take up arms again. In 1939, World War II broke out.

International Tension

The first significant step on the road to war came with the withdrawal, in 1933, of Hitler's Germany from the League of Nations. In itself this action had no great effect upon the international scene, inasmuch as the League had only recently demonstrated anew its political impotence: it was unable to cope effectively with the Japanese invasion of Chinese territory and the subsequent establishment of Manchuria as a separate state subject to Japanese influence. But Hitler's exit was a psychological shock, for it highlighted the League's weaknesses and demonstrated the rebirth of extreme nationalism. His action was answered by the initiation of a policy of so-called collective security. Cooperative agreements similar to those made among the Allies prior to 1914 were negotiated. In 1935 France concluded a special defensive agreement with Russia; the Soviet Union was drawn into the League of Nations; pacts were made among Russia, France, and some of the smaller East European countries, such as Czechoslovakia and Rumania; and England assumed a friendlier attitude toward Russia. These moves were used by Germany to justify its own military preparations. Denouncing the prohibitory stipulations of the Versailles Treaty, Hitler began the full-scale rearmament of Germany in 1935 and the reintroduction of compulsory military service—pacifying England by a naval agreement that guaranteed British superiority on the seas. He then proceeded to send troops into the demilitarized Rhineland—without encountering serious opposition from the Allies, who realized that Germany would eventually have to be granted its full sovereign rights and who were divided in their political aims and in their assessment of the role of Hitler as a counterweight to Bolshevik power. Moreover, the Allies had become involved in another difficulty. In 1935 fascist Italy invaded Ethiopia and the League of Nations decreed a number of economic sanctions. Since they did not wish to offend the Italian dictator whom they regarded as a potential opponent to Hitler's expansionist schemes, neither England nor France applied the sanctions vigorously. In this way they failed to stop Mussolini and succeeded only in alienating him. He turned to Hitler, with whom he concluded an alliance in 1936, the Rome-Berlin Axis. This was supplemented by the Anti-Comintern Pact between Germany and Japan; thus, the West was once again split into two camps. The United States remained outside both camps, in a position to swing the balance of power in either direction.

Appeasement (1938)

Faced with increasing fascist aggression, the democratic countries of the West were at a disadvantage. Relying on slow parliamentary procedures, they were faced with ruthless and determined men, whose arbitrary will could at any moment be transformed into deeds. So long as they were militarily weak, Western diplomats were compelled to appease their fascist opponents and, while trying to come to terms with them, seek support from enemies of fascism outside the democratic camp. But they failed to pursue wholeheartedly the negotiations they had initiated with the only nation able to give them powerful support—the Soviet Union. Consequently, Hitler was free to resume his expansionist schemes. Early in 1938 he united Austria and Germany—a union Austrians and Germans had long desired. Austria had voted for the so-called *Anschluss* soon after the end of World War I but had been forbidden to take such action. An objective hitherto denied to Germany's democratic governments was now granted to the Nazis. Encouraged by this achievement, Hitler next demanded the incorporation of the Sudetenland, a region of western Czechoslovakia settled largely by Germans. Again, a pretext for the Nazi claim was offered: the idea that the Germans in that area had the right of self-determination. Unprepared for war, even though the Spanish civil war had served as a proving ground for weapons, the Western powers agreed to a series of conferences, and at Munich in 1938, they handed the Sudetenland over to Hitler. The Soviet Union, though affected by whatever position France and England would take, had not even been invited, and the French alliance system in the east thus collapsed.

Outbreak of War (1939)

Peace was not promoted by appeasement, for, contrary to his assertions, Hitler annexed the rest of Czechoslovakia in the following year. This time, not even the incorporation of German populations desirous of joining the Reich could be used as an argument, inasmuch as it was an alien Czech population, proud of its independence and achievements, that was forced under Nazi domination. The Western powers refused to give their sanction to this annexation and speeded up military preparations. They also revived the dragging political negotiations with Soviet Russia.

It was too late. In April 1939, Italy invaded and subjugated Albania. Germany forced Lithuania to surrender Memel and reclaimed Danzig, two areas that had been separated from Germany by the Treaty of Versailles. Next, Poland was asked to return other former German possessions but, with the backing of the Western countries, refused to do so. This time the Western powers were unwilling to make any compromises. They had become convinced of Hitler's untrustworthiness, but, more important, they had also witnessed the growing radicalism of Nazi ideology and its social implications. The extreme brutality of the Nazis was apparent in their treatment of opponents, especially the Jews, who were plundered, tortured, forced into exile, imprisoned in labor camps, and murdered.

This state-sponsored persecution was radically and perhaps prophetically demonstrated to the liberal democracies of the West in November of 1938, during the widespread rioting of Kristallnacht ("Crystal Night"), during which Jews were arrested, beaten and murdered and their shops and homes looted. (Joseph Goebbels, Hitler's minister of propaganda, assured the world that the episode was a spontaneous uprising.) Up until this time, emigration of the Jews from the Reich had been the official Nazi objective, but Kristallnacht seemed to usher in a new and more horrendous phase in the persecution.

The policy of appeasement was discarded, and no additional concessions were promised to Hitler—not even when, in August, the conclusion of a trade and nonaggression pact between Germany and the Soviet Union was suddenly announced and the pro-Western diplomat Maxim Litvinov was replaced by the anti-Western Vyacheslav Molotov as Soviet foreign minister. Thus ended all hopes for collective security. In September, German armies marched into Poland. World War II had begun.

Early Campaigns (1939–1941)

Cavalrymen were no match for armored Panzer units and dive-bombing aircraft, and Polish resistance collapsed within a few weeks. Just before the end came, Russian armies from the east marched into the country, and Poland experienced its fourth partition in modern history. This development was followed by a half-year lull (the so-called Phony War) on the Western front. Russia, however, continued its military actions, first by attacking Finland, then by incorporating and sovietizing the Baltic states. The Finns put up a surprisingly long and successful resistance but eventually had to submit and cede some of their eastern territories.

The Finnish-Russian campaign had scarcely ended when hostilities were resumed in the West. In April 1940, German forces attacked neutral Norway, Denmark, Holland, and Belgium. Aided by native fascists, the so-called quislings (named after the chief fascist in Norway), they quickly forced these countries to surrender. Hitler then turned on France, whose government was weakened by indecision, confusion, and corruption, and whose general staff were overconfident about France's main defense system along the western border, the so-called Maginot Line. This Maginot defensive system of massive concrete bunkers and static gun emplacements had been built on the basis of experiences in World War I, but it proved inadequate to cope with new techniques of mobile warfare and aerial support. It was bypassed in the north and collapsed within a few days. The Nazis overran the entire northern coastal area of France, as well as Paris, and on June 5, 1940, France capitulated; the British auxiliary corps narrowly escaped to England.

France's catastrophe was the signal for Mussolini to enter the war: He promptly seized areas in southern France that once had been under Italian rule. A pro-German French government led by World War I hero Marshal Henri Pétain was soon organized at Vichy. Despite the collapse of France, England, however, did not yield. Under the leadership of a new prime minister, Winston Churchill, the British took effective defensive measures and continued the desperate struggle. Neither prolonged Nazi air attacks nor intensive submarine warfare could soften the island nation's resolve, nor prepare the ground for invasion.

Consequently, the Germans eventually shifted their attention southeastward, in the direction of Egypt and the Suez Canal; joined by the Italians, they opened a new front in Africa. Still another area was engulfed by war when in October 1940 Mussolini failed in an attack upon Greece and the Germans rushed to his aid. By the end of May 1941, all the Balkan countries had either surrendered or, after installing fascist governments, concluded alliances with the Axis powers.

Global War (1941–1943)

The remaining months of 1941 proved to be a turning point in the war. The first decisive event occurred in June, when Hitler, following negotiations that by November 1940 had shown steadily deteriorating relations, turned upon his Russian ally and invaded the Soviet Union. This move radically changed the balance of power, for what the negotiations of England and her allies had failed to achieve, Hitler's megalomania had brought about: a common front for the Bolshevik and democratic nations and a two-front war for Germany. Both sides were fully armed. At first the Germans enjoyed great successes against the Soviet forces. Within a few months, they reached the outskirts of Leningrad, Moscow, and Sevastopol, and they conquered the industrially valuable Don basin and the rich agricultural lands of the Ukraine. But they failed to capture Moscow; instead, heavy losses and severe winter weather forced them to retreat. Just then, the second decisive event took place.

In the Far East and the Pacific Ocean, Japanese imperial ambitions had consistently been thwarted by England and the United States, both of whom were firmly established in the area. Negotiations to resolve their differences accomplished nothing, and Japan decided to seize the initiative with a lightning and daring move. On December 7, 1941, the American naval base at Pearl Harbor in the Hawaiian Islands was attacked by Japanese aircraft; concerted ground, air, and naval assaults upon a number of American and British island possessions followed.

Although not specifically bound by any treaty agreements with Japan, Hitler promptly declared war on the United States, thus committing the enormous physical resources of the self-proclaimed "arsenal of democracy" to the conflict in Europe.

From the beginning, the American people had been on the side of the Allies. Disregarding strict neutrality, they had supported England, and supplies and arms had been shipped across the Atlantic under a lend-lease plan. Moreover, the United States had introduced peacetime conscription, which paved the way for eventual military intervention. Hatred of Hitler's Germany became more and more inflamed as the Nazis disregarded all international treaties and moral precepts, attacked neutral nations, impressed labor from conquered countries into their war industries, looted art depositories, established everywhere their concentration camps for political opponents, and began on the continent a fearful extermination campaign against the Jews.

In the course of Hitler's Final Solution to the Jewish "problem," horrible numbers of Jews perished in gas chambers and camps that sprang up throughout occupied Europe, particularly in the east. Massacres had occurred before in modern history: Armenians in the Turkish Empire were slaughtered in 1915, and Stalin's collectivization program during the 1930s was responsible for uncounted masses of victims. The Holocaust remains unique, however, for the number of victims and the systematic application of science and technology to the task of mass genocide, as well as for the ideological obsession that accompanied the destruction of European Jewry. The full details of the Holocaust only became evident after the liberation of Europe.

When America became an active belligerent on the Anglo-Russian side, the fate of the Axis powers was sealed. Japan conquered much of the Chinese coast, overwhelmed French Indochina and "impregnable" British Singapore, invaded Burma and Dutch Indonesia, and drove the Americans out of the Philippines. Germany penetrated still deeper into Russia, reached the Caucasus and Volga, took an enormous toll on Allied shipping with its submarines, and, together with Italy, conquered North Africa up to the Egyptian border. But the ultimate objective—to win the war—was not achieved.

Defeat of Italy, Germany, and Japan (1943–1945)

Early in 1943, Germany's military reversals began. At Stalingrad, the Nazis suffered a terrible defeat, as an entire army surrendered to the Russians. In Africa, the Germans and Italians had to retreat before invading Allied armies, and by May 1943, all Axis forces had been either driven out of Africa or captured. The submarine menace had been overcome through speedy production of replacement shipping in America and the development of new defensive devices. Continuous heavy bombardment of German cities brought ruin to that country, which had previously been almost untouched by direct action. Japan's unchecked drive was halted. In July 1943, the Allies invaded Italy; Mussolini's government fell, and thus the first fascist regime disappeared. Italy was accepted as an additional ally.

In June 1944, the long-planned invasion of Hitler's "Fortress Europe," which the Soviets had long demanded but which had always been delayed, began as American and Allied troops landed in Normandy and quickly drove the German forces back. By September they had reached the frontier and begun their invasion of the German homeland itself. Rather than submit to the Allied demand for unconditional surrender, and notwithstanding a last attempt by determined German resistance fighters to get rid of Hitler, German soldiers obeyed the order of the Nazi leaders to fight to the bitter end. The most desperate resistance was put up against the Russians, who, having liberated their own and neighboring countries from the Nazis, had crossed the German borders from the east. Only when American and Russian troops had joined in the center of Germany and when Berlin was in flames did Hitler take his own life, and only then did the country capitulate.

The Allies promptly turned their full force against Japan. The Japanese had already lost most of their previous conquests and been forced into a steady retreat on land and sea. Their fate was sealed when, in August 1945, the Americans dropped an atomic bomb (the first one ever used in war) on Hiroshima, destroying the town, and shortly thereafter launched another such attack on Nagasaki. Simultaneously, the Russians entered the war against Japan, and the country was forced to surrender.

End of World War II

No peace treaty was concluded at the end of the war because the disagreements among the Allies multiplied during the last year of hostilities. In fact, they agreed unanimously on only one point: to destroy the power of Germany and Japan.

OCCUPATION AND CONFERENCES

Germany and Japan were occupied and governed by the victors. In Japan, this procedure was comparatively easy, for, though deprived of all overseas possessions, it retained its home territory intact, and the United States took charge of the administration. The situation was different in Germany, which was divided into four zones of occupation. Millions of inhabitants were driven out of their homes, and countless people perished. Workers were abducted, factories were dismantled, and production was brought to an almost complete standstill. A terrible famine resulted, and a cold winter added to the misery. Moral laws were ignored on all sides. No constructive plans for Germany's future existed, since the victors (Russia, England, and the United States) had failed to provide for them. In a conference at Teheran, in 1943, they had been concerned mainly with the conduct of the war. Early in 1945, when victory was in sight, they had planned in a second conference, held at Yalta, the division and occupation of Germany and a drastic reduction in its economic, industrial, and military power. During the summer of 1945, after Germany's capitulation, when a third conference was held at Potsdam, the task of determining a common future peace policy should have been undertaken. But the Potsdam meeting disclosed fundamental disagreements between the democratic West and the communist East. Russia had quickly established a communist regime in eastern Germany, such as had already been established in Poland, Hungary, Rumania—in fact, wherever Soviet Russia maintained occupation troops. On the other hand, the Western Allies sought liberal-democratic forms of government, such as had been reestablished in Italy and France where General de Gaulle took over the reins of government. During the war, he had from outside of France proved to be an unflinching leader of the resistance movement and a staunch defender of French independence vis-à-vis the Allies.

THE UNITED NATIONS

Nor did the founding of a new world organization, the United Nations, further cooperation. The United Nations was created in order to provide an international forum comparable to the defunct League of Nations and to organize humanitarian agencies concerned with economics, agriculture, health, and education. But, like the League, it received no military or police force. Although control over the organization was vested in a Security Council and a General Assembly, the three principal victors in the war—England, Russia, and the United States—as well as France and China, were each given a veto power over decisions in the Council—a power subsequently often used.

New Beginnings

The two world wars differed fundamentally in their causes, conduct, and consequences. In 1914, nations had been trapped in the nets of their diplomacy and had backed into the war. But World War II had been unilaterally provoked by the fascist countries. Ideological differences had been slight before World War I; they played a major role in the World War II era. Warfare was much more savage during the later conflict than the earlier one. Women and children of victors and vanquished alike were engulfed by the holocaust. Civilians and soldiers were equally involved, and little mercy was shown to prisoners by either side. Whole population groups were murdered. After the war many statesmen, industrialists, military leaders, and other citizens in the defeated countries (including those who were helpless tools as well as those who had wittingly perpetrated atrocities) were tried and punished as criminals, as well as large numbers of collaborators in France and other allied countries.

Nevertheless, World War II did not constitute so sharp a break in the course of history. The war of 1914 shattered the social and cultural patterns of the nineteenth century, a society based upon the ideas of enlightenment and dedicated to the aims of national freedom and progress under a capitalistic system dominated by the bourgeoisie. World War II brought no such social change. As part of the adjustment to the emerging new world, it left fewer gulfs and (except among some of the smaller countries) fewer permanent resentments. Moreover, it left Europe, if not all of Western civilization, weaker and with a deeper feeling of interdependence than had existed during the period after the Treaty of Versailles.

Ten years after World War I and following the disruptions brought on by the Versailles Treaty, a worldwide depression set in. It led to fearful suffering for millions of people and forced upon the victors adjustments in their economic demands. But the adjustments came too late. The depression contributed to the expansion of fascism from Italy to many parts of the continent, including Germany, where the National Socialists (Nazis) gained control. The Nazis immediately began rearming their country and eliminating all opponents. By so doing and by passing further social legislation, they succeeded in abolishing unemployment and thereby gained the support of businessmen as well as workers. Protective social legislation was passed also in the United States, and it too started on the road to recovery. The communist world was less affected by the depression. Under a dictatorship that freely used police power, purges, and labor camps, the Soviets carried out the collectivization of agriculture and built up their industries. They too managed to strengthen their economy.

Depression and fascism led, however, to war: first to civil war in Spain, then to a colonial war started by Italy, and finally—notwithstanding attempts at appeasing the dictators—to World War II. War brought early military victories to the fascist powers. In the process, terrible new crimes were committed. The military position was reversed in 1941 when Germany attacked the Soviet Union and the United States entered the war. The fascist powers were defeated. After the United States exploded the first atomic bomb, Japan also fell. Italy, which had deserted its allies, was accepted as a "democracy" by the Western nations. Japan was stripped of both its early conquests and its military establishment. Germany was completely subdued, divided, occupied by the victors, and stripped of a quarter of its territory. A new international organization, the United Nations, was established by the victors.

Selected Readings

Arendt, Hannah. *The Origins of Totalitarianism* (1958)
Carsten, F. L. *The Rise of Fascism* (1967)
Ellis John. *Brute Force: Allied Strategy and Tactics in the Second World War* (1990)
Gilbert, Felix. *The End of the European Era, 1890 to the Present* (1970)
Keegan, John. *The Second World War* (1989)
Kindleberger, Charles P. *The World in Depression, 1929–1939* (1973)
Marrus, Michael R. *The Holocaust in History* (1987)
Robertson, E. M. *The Origins of the Second World War* (1976)
Smith, Denis Mack. *Mussolini* (1983)

Taylor, A. J. P. *The Second World War* (1976)

Thomas, H. *The Spanish Civil War* (1961)

Thomas, Hugh. *Armed Truce: The Beginnings of the Cold War, 1945–1946* (1986)

Thorne, Christopher. *Allies of a Kind: The United States, Britain and the War Against Japan, 1941–1945* (1978)

Toland, John. *Adolf Hitler* (1976)

von Rauch, Georg. *A History of Soviet Russia* (1972)

Waite, Robert G. L. *The Psychopathic God: Adolf Hitler* (1977)

23

The Postwar Era (1947–1967)

1947	Marshall Plan for economic rehabilitation of Europe
	India becomes independent from the British and is divided
1948	Berlin blockade
	State of Israel founded
	Independence of Ireland
1949	Triumph of communists in China
	Establishment of a West German republic
1950	Outbreak of Korean War
	Schuman Plan for European steel and coal production
1953	Death of Stalin
1955	Germany enters NATO
1956	Suez Canal nationalized by Egypt; abortive invasion by England, France, Israel
1957	First earth satellite (*Sputnik*) launched
1961	Construction of Berlin Wall
1962	Independence of Algeria
1966–1975	Vietnam War
1967	Israeli-Arab War; defeat of Arabs (UAR)

In Western civilization three trends, which had developed to some extent after World War I, rapidly gained headway after World War II. These trends were the use of mechanization in production and in everyday living; the increasing equalization of social classes; and the decline of Europe's power and prestige in international affairs. Human society—though still divided into classes, into nations, and into "two worlds" with opposing ideologies—was moving in the direction of one interrelated, interdependent world.

INTELLECTUAL AND CULTURAL DEVELOPMENTS

Too short a time has elapsed since World War II to justify broad generalizations about postwar intellectual trends. Yet a few facts are apparent. The West has devoted itself increasingly to science and technology and has achieved remarkable progress in these fields. There has been a growing realization that—contrary to the hopes of the ages of Enlightenment and Liberalism—"progress," though undeniable in material achievements, does not necessarily encompass the moral side of humanity. Preoccupation with personal "security" has acted as a check on daring original thinking and has led to a measure of conservatism and the desire for conformity. This has been true for the communist as well as the democratic nations of the world, both of which have sought to maintain the status quo regardless of its manifold shortcomings.

Science

Wars have always stimulated science and technology. Danger has always forced people to develop tools and processes that could save their lives and preserve their freedom. Insights into the mechanics of nature gained during war have furthered the progress of science in times of peace. World War II was no exception. Radar, rockets, and atomic fission were developed for military purposes in the period 1939 to 1945. They afterward became important for peacetime use. Aviation in particular was greatly advanced during the war. Whereas in 1927 Lindbergh had made the lonely first transatlantic flight to Paris, twenty-five years later, when the war was over, tens of millions of passengers were crossing continents and oceans by airplane each year. Countries of vast expanse and poor transportation systems, like Brazil, could now plan to skip the "railroad age" and immediately enter the "air age."

In the fields of chemistry and nuclear physics, discoveries made under pressure of war by both victors and vanquished were exploited to serve new peaceful purposes. With the help of newly discovered vaccines and drugs, the effects of many diseases—pneumonia, tuberculosis, and infantile paralysis—could be diminished. Nations increasingly put their faith in scientists to solve their problems. The Soviet Union trained scientists by the hundred thousand, and the United States showed an unaccustomed appreciation of pure science and mathematics (fields in which the country had long relied upon European work). Wartime experiences had an effect on production methods. Automation—that is, the mechanization of industrial processes that had previously required supervision by human hands and minds—was introduced in large enterprises. Machines were being used to replace technical, clerical, and even scientific personnel.

Religion and Philosophy

After World War II the memory of the horrors and uncertainties of war had the apparent effect of impelling humanity to intensify its search for security and comfort. Fearful of the dangers inherent in the growing mastery of natural forces—the development of atomic weapons, for instance—and disturbed by the use of such subtle physiological and psychological weapons as propaganda, indoctrination, and mental persuasion, many people turned anew to the consolations of religion. The consequent religious renaissance brought about a renewed emphasis on dogma, as seen in the spread of Neo-Orthodox beliefs. This led to the acceptance of long-submerged ecumenical ideas promoting cooperation among the various faiths, and it caused a revival of religious experience in the Soviet Union, where the government eased its hostility toward church organizations and tolerated the extension of their activities. The revival embraced the older generation as well as younger people who had been brought up in a materialistic atmosphere.

In the face of invigorated religious trends and the growing realization of "uncertainty" in many of the conclusions at which the scientific community arrived, the positivist tradition lost some of its appeal. Logical positivism (or logical empiricism) continued to promote its faith in science as the only dependable source of knowledge and as an effective basis for solving social problems. It encountered increased competition from existentialism, however, which constituted a major new philosophical influence after World War II. Fearful of the dehumanizing effect of the Modern Age, existentialists affirmed the importance of the individual. They insisted that humans are not just "objects" to be described scientifically; they are "existing subjects." People gain authentic existence and knowledge of themselves through exercising their freedom. Existentialists emphasized the fact that each human being must realize and then resolutely face the inherent perils and predicaments of life.

Education

In accordance with postwar political and scientific demands, new goals were set for education. A basic objective was to develop the character of children along lines accepted by society. They were to become "well adjusted"—to a communist, democratic, or fascist society, depending upon the system in which they grew up. Society and its needs were stressed, as opposed to individualism and its demands. Therefore the equalization of educational opportunity and aims was necessary.

All governments, national and local, took a larger part than ever before in the conduct of educating. They claimed more of children's time, directed education toward natural and "social" (or politico-economic) sciences, and to an increasing extent replaced the family and other educational agencies. National governments sponsored extensive programs of adult education and even assumed the task of "re-educating" entire nations. To promote their ideologies and policies, governments particularly in the West also carried on a large-scale exchange of students and scholars.

Literature and Fine Arts

In literature and the fine arts, generalizations about the merits of what has been created in the post–World War II period may well be premature. World War I had marked the end of an age in Western civilization. Authors and artists in the 1920s had entered upon a new age and had used great artistic and social problems as their themes. New issues of like dimensions did not appear in the 1940s or 1950s. Nor did artisans face a challenge such as preceding postwar periods had posed. Solid work was done by humanistic scholars, who whoever were inclined to turn their attention less to the aesthetic side of their fields and more to historical and social aspects. Increasing numbers of painters, musicians, and architects achieved much, but, to a large extent, Western people lived on their great cultural heritage, which they cultivated with care.

ECONOMIC, SOCIAL, AND POLITICAL DEVELOPMENTS

The dominating issue on the international stage was the rivalry between the United States and the Soviet Union. This rivalry was reflected first in the failure to reach a German settlement, next in a struggle over communist penetration of other European nations, and eventually in the struggle over influence in the Far East, the Middle East, and Africa. It embraced political, economic, cultural, and military issues. Its intensity varied with temporary conditions, as well as with long-range developments, over which the rivals themselves had no control. Thus it depended upon factors such as the rapidly rising population figures in Europe and in overseas areas. Unemployment along prewar lines did not reappear, despite the population surge and despite the fact that within a decade consumer goods were, at least in the Western countries, once more abundant. Soon production totals surpassed, even in the defeated nations, the highest prewar figures, making possible an improvement of prewar living standards. Whether because of a better understanding of economic processes or of more extensive state planning, a prolonged period of economic growth began.

Postwar Economic Situation

It had been the plan of the victors to provide for the rebuilding of their own national economies and for the permanent economic subjugation of Germany. This plan was initiated by the dismantling of German industries; by the expropriation of German ships, freight cars, locomotives, and other rolling stock; by the seizure of its patents and production secrets; and by the forced recruitment of scientists as well as laborers and prisoners into the service of the victors. For more than a year after the cessation of hostilities, this additional source of suffering affected Germany, without appropriate benefit to the victors, most of whom had to continue enforcing sharp austerity measures. At this juncture, a drastic change occurred in the relationship between the victorious and the defeated nations.

REBUILDING THE WESTERN ECONOMY

By 1947 it had become clear that the intense struggle between the communist East and the democratic West required a new approach to the task of rebuilding the Western economy. The United States took the initiative. Still during the war, it had outlined programs in various conferences at Dumbarton Oaks and Bretton Woods; subsequently, an International Monetary Fund and International Bank for Reconstruction were founded, and preparations were made for the reduction of tariff barriers. The trend toward replacing national by international regulations grew stronger. Moreover, the nation had quickly "returned to normalcy" after the war. Rationing had been abolished, farm incomes had risen, a measure of controlled inflation had led to an increase in prices and wages, and a feeling of confidence and, with it, new incentives for further production and broader employment had been created. Successful reconversion of production facilities made it possible for the United States to propose in 1947 the Marshall Plan—named after the American secretary of state—which made financial aid available to European countries. Ideological, humanitarian, and economic purposes were simultaneously served thereby. England and France received most of the aid. Less impoverished peoples should fall prey to communist doctrines, however, help was extended also to other Western nations, including former enemies. This program enabled almost all the European democracies to rebuild their production apparatuses within a decade. By the mid-1950s, their economies flourished as never before. Germany, though deprived of the industries in its eastern zones, through an effort that later became known as *Wirtschaftswunder* (economic miracle) nevertheless regained its position as the leading industrial power of Europe. Italy was also put on the road toward economic recovery and stability.

REBUILDING THE EASTERN ECONOMY

In the East, Russia took the lead. New Five-Year Plans were drafted and coordinated with the industrial plans of regions controlled directly or indirectly by the Soviet Union. Important new centers of industry in Siberia, which had been built with the labor of Stalin's purge victims and then during the war, when factories were moved east, proved now to be a major asset. Production in heavy industries increased rapidly. Within less than a decade, the Soviet Union attained the rank of second-largest industrial power in the world, being surpassed only by the United States. It was thereby enabled to export surplus goods and to make investments abroad. However, since hard and long labor was needed to create the production apparatus, little could be done to develop the industries manufacturing goods for civilian consumption. Consequently, standards of living remained at a low level. In agriculture, productivity did not increase sufficiently; new experiments with collective farms, which were combined into larger units, did not bring the desired results.

The Political Situation

Political readjustment came more slowly than economic recovery. No final war settlement was achieved, no all-inclusive peace treaty negotiated.

EASTERN EUROPE

Russia enlarged its territories by incorporating parts of Finland, Poland, Germany, and Rumania. The formerly independent Baltic states, left at Yalta and Potsdam in Soviet hands, were forced to remain within the jurisdiction of the USSR. Bolshevik governments were established in Poland and in occupied Balkan countries, and all were bound closely to Russia. Eastern Germany was assigned to Polish administration, and its inhabitants were being driven out while Poles were settled there. In 1945 Czechoslovakia was reconstituted under a democratic government (her borders approximately those of 1937), and the Germans living there were likewise brutally expelled. The democratic government was, however, overthrown in 1948 and replaced by a communist regime closely allied to the Soviet Union. A special role in world affairs was played by Yugoslavia under the communist Tito, who during the war had directed the fight against the Nazis and insisted on independent policies. "Titoism" revealed tensions and dissensions among the communist powers. Tito rejected the right of the Soviet Union to dictate policies to other communist nations—notwithstanding the fact that Marxism had preached the identity of the interests of the workers in all countries and the Soviet Union had previously been considered the leader and spokesman of true Marxism.

CENTRAL AND WESTERN EUROPE

In the center of Europe, Germany—except for Polish-occupied territories—was divided: first into four zones, later into two. The latter zones became, for the time being, separate German states, a Western and an Eastern republic, both of which within a decade achieved virtual sovereignty, though each remained politically affiliated with its original occupying powers. This enforced duality reflected a continued shrinkage of the area of Western civilization and tradition, and it symbolized the division of the world into Eastern communist and Western democratic areas. Austria was reestablished as a small, and eventually independent, nation—a neutral buffer between East and West. Italy regained most of its former European territories but had to accord a measure of autonomy to the German population under its control, as well as to Sicily.

The other Western countries underwent no drastic territorial changes. Belgium, the Netherlands, and Luxembourg combined in a common customs area (Benelux) to obtain mutually beneficial trade advantages. Western Germany, France, and Benelux, with the blessing of the United States, formed a "coal and steel community," which provided for predetermined production quotas, a common market, and the elimination of tariff barriers for these products. Plans for a broader customs union, possibly including Great Britain, were formulated.

A "Council of Europe," constituting a consultative assembly of the western European nations, was established in Strasbourg, at the very border between Germany and France. A bank to ease mutual convertibility of European funds and currencies was founded. Plans were made by the member states for cooperative atomic research and exploitation of atomic energy. Even though a unified military force, as once considered, was not organized, a military alliance joining the United States and England to the Continent was concluded in 1949. This alliance, (the North Atlantic Treaty Organization, or NATO) had a central headquarters and an American supreme commander. As a whole, the idea of European unity made considerable progress. Cultural contacts and exchanges were augmented by political cooperation.

AMERICA

In America the political impact of World War II was felt much more than that of World War I. A spirit of isolationism did not return to the United States, as it did after 1918. Instead, the country took a leading role in almost all international decisions. Not only European countries but also former European colonies came to be of concern. The members of the British Empire, especially Canada and Australia, oriented themselves increasingly toward America. Economically backward countries appealed to the United States and received aid designed to prevent them from turning to communist

Russia. Military bases were installed in France, England, Germany, Spain, Turkey, and other European countries, as well as in Asia and the Arctic and Antarctic. New treaties were made with Latin American nations, which were granted financial aid for economic development. Extensive programs for the exchange of teachers and students were inaugurated, and the unprecedented scale of travel of Americans abroad helped to establish numerous relationships with the Western nations.

COLONIAL AREAS

World War II accelerated the decline of colonialism. After Japan's defeat, China gained control over most of its former territories, including Western-held Shanghai and Russian-dominated Manchuria. Indochina rebelled against and eventually defeated France, which lost more than half of its former colony; a full end to French rule came in 1954. Rebellious Indonesia separated from Holland and became an independent state. The United States granted independence to the Philippines; England gave statehood to the Gold Coast in Africa. India finally succeeded in bringing Gandhi's fight for freedom to a successful conclusion and abolished British rule. Though staying formally within the Commonwealth, it built a republic that envisioned neutrality in the East-West struggle.

Iran quarreled with the European powers over the possession and management of its oil industries and forced substantial concessions upon the Western owners. Arab states likewise asserted their independence in the conduct of their foreign policies and obtained a greater share in the profits from their oil. The people of Cyprus rose against England, as did native tribes in Africa. Egypt forced the British to withdraw their military forces from the Suez Canal and nationalized the Canal Company in 1956. This led to a Franco-British invasion, which, owing to American and Russian opposition, miscarried. Within a few months, the invading forces had to be withdrawn, and Egypt gained its objective. A particularly bloody struggle occurred in France's North African possessions when the Arabs in Tunisia and Algeria rebelled. Tunisia gained especially far-reaching concessions and subsequently its independence; France lost Algeria in 1961.

The struggle was sharpened by the fact that in 1948 a Jewish state, Israel, had been established in Palestine. As early as 1916, such a state had been promised to the Jews by the English. After Hitler's persecutions and World War II had demonstrated the urgency of finding a refuge for Jews, the pledge was finally honored. The establishment of Israel roused bitter resentment among all Arabs. Intermittent border clashes threatened the peace of the entire West.

On the whole, the revolt of Asia and the culturally advanced areas of Africa was the result of the successful Westernization of former colonial regions. European ideologies of democracy and communism, European sciences, medicine, and technology, European habits, dress, and living modes, and European-born nationalism had penetrated to all parts of the world. The time was approaching when the masters were no longer needed. The division of the Western world into democratic and communist segments gave the former colonies the opportunity to assert their independence. Eventually, there were more than 150 member states of the United Nations instead of the original fifty.

Governmental Institutions and Ideologies

No new political ideology was developed as a result of World War II. Fascism in its extreme forms was abolished, though not entirely eradicated. Fascist regimes continued to function in countries such as Spain. Fascism was even introduced in a few other countries (such as Argentina, where Juan Perón held power until 1955). Fascist principles also found their way into some of the democratic countries: In France and even in the United States, there was some fear that certain fascist tendencies might gain headway.

Communism persevered in most of eastern Europe. In Russia, where the enforcement of communist doctrines had to be relaxed during the war (so that it would not interfere with the war effort), the government resumed the drastic application of its socialistic policies. Devaluation of the currency deprived people who had accumulated profits of their gains. Land that the peasants had taken from collective farms and used for private gardens had to be returned. Writers and scientists were compelled to follow strictly the party line.

But outside of the Soviet Union, communism after the end of World War II did not win the allegiance of Europe, despite the widespread impoverishment and Russia's prestige as one of the principal victors. Except for Czechoslovakia, European countries did not establish a communist government unless they were occupied by Russian military forces. Only in Asia, notably in China, did communism spread under native leadership.

Democracy continued to be the predominant form of government in the Western countries. Democratic types of government were reintroduced in West Germany and Italy. Most democratic institutions, however, were affected by socialist ideas. In the United States, social reforms that had been assailed as "creeping socialism" in the 1930s were now accepted as a matter of course in the postwar period. Labor unions grew in influence, and employers had to make ever-increasing concessions to their workers.

In England, the Labor party, which came to power immediately after the war, socialized the steel and coal industries, nationalized the railways, and introduced a most comprehensive public health program. Subsequent conservative governments could not abandon all the new programs of socialization and reform, although they did prevent the nationalization of the steel industry. In West Germany, where a strong democratic government took office, socialists constituted the largest opposition group in the diet. Workers in the great coal and steel industries gained the right to share with the owners in the functions of management.

In France and Italy, democratic governments remained in control, but they faced grave difficulties, owing to the opposition of socialists who followed a communist line on many issues. The French and Italian communists, instead of functioning as a loyal opposition within a democratic system, attempted to disrupt the governments and to swing their countries into the Soviet orbit. In the smaller Western nations—Scandinavia, the Netherlands, and Austria—moderate socialist trends prevailed. Here government seemed to be working toward the eventual consummation of many socialist ideals within a capitalist society.

The United Nations

Persistent nationalism and the ideological conflict between East and West prevented substantial progress toward a world government. As the League of Nations had done after World War I, the United Nations provided an international forum for world opinion, and its subagencies accomplished a great deal in certain fields, such as economic affairs and education. In the political sphere, however, it fell far short of its goals. The veto power of a few large nations forestalled decisions on various important issues. Two of the five great nations—Russia and France—at one time or another resorted to boycotts. A third one, China, found itself represented by men who belonged to a regime ousted from China proper and holding no more than Formosa (Taiwan) and a few smaller islands. Neither West nor East Germany, despite their economic importance, became a member of the world organization. Small countries such as Holland and Israel refused to obey certain decisions of the United Nations. Disarmament issues, especially those involving atomic weapons, could not be agreed upon in the United Nations forum. As before, diplomatic action outside the United Nations was necessary to handle all important questions. Thus traditional patterns for international negotiations were perpetuated.

Postwar Crises

Under such circumstances, numerous international crises developed. A first major difficulty arose in 1948, when the Russians cut off the city of Berlin from land contact with the West. Supplies and personnel were transported to and from the city by air until the Soviet blockade was given up.

In 1950 a new major crisis arose when communists in North Korea invaded South Korea, which had been under American control. This time war resulted. Various members of the United Nations, including the United States, participated on the South Korean side, while North Korea had the material and economic support of Russia and active military help from Communist China. This conflict, entailing heavy casualties on both sides, led to an uneasy truce, whereby the country was divided into two sections: a communist state and a Western-supported one.

Hardly had hostilities ended than a similar war developed in French Indochina, which led to a parallel result: The North became communist and separate; the South gained considerable independence from France but remained in the Western camp.

In the meantime, crises developed in other regions: in Iran, over its decision to nationalize the foreign oil companies there; in the Middle East, over the Suez Canal and the conflict between Syria and Israel; and in North Africa over the question of freedom from French dominion. Behind all these issues loomed the greater struggle: the "cold" war between the Western democracies, under American leadership, and the Eastern communist nations, under Russian leadership. Both sides built their military potential and acquired vast stocks of atomic bombs and weapons. While they avoided an open break, they waged a bitter struggle over the allegiance of the "neutral" areas, such as India, Iran, and the Arab states, and of the colonies, where Russia had become a factor by aiding indigenous national movements.

Coexistence and New Conflict

Stalin died in 1953. During his administration, he had concentrated upon the reconstruction of the Soviet Union so that it became the second greatest industrial power of the world, and he had with an iron hand preserved the communist institutions of the nation. He had imposed his will on scholars, scientists, artists, and the masses of the Russian people. Under his regime, Soviet scientists made enormous advances, including discoveries in the fields of atomic energy and guided missiles. But owing to his arbitrariness and dictatorial ways, he had alienated even close collaborators. Owing to his ruthlessness and guile, he had forfeited the confidence of his European allies and aroused misgivings among even the communists of other nations.

Stalin's death therefore marked a turning point—especially since dissension among his political heirs introduced a further element of weakness into the position of the Soviet Union. Promptly, the Russian policy of the cold war was modified. Friendly words were addressed to the West. Amnesties were proclaimed in Russia, and travel restrictions were eased. A meeting between Eastern and Western statesmen at Geneva in 1955 seemed to herald an era of "peaceful coexistence." The cold war proved not to have ended but to have entered a new stage, however, when Stalin's successors had consolidated their position, after their sudden denunciation of Stalin's personal dictatorship. Practical concessions were few. Although the Soviet Union agreed to a peace with Austria and established diplomatic relations with West Germany, no progress was made in regard to the crucial problem of German reunification. Soviet disagreements with Tito's Yugoslavia were temporarily settled, but Soviet control of its satellites was not yielded, despite revolts in East Germany, Poland, and Hungary. Western nations were invited to establish closer ties with the communist world, especially in the economic field. Nevertheless, opposition to their policies was invariably encouraged.

Still, on the positive side, open hostilities were avoided. In 1956, the cause of world peace was imperiled by events such as Anglo-French aggression in Egypt and the brutal Russian suppression of a revolt in Hungary. Other crises occurred in the following years. In 1958, the overthrow of the monarchy in the Arab state of Iraq threatened the political and economic position of the Western powers in the Middle East and the safety of their oil interests there. Uprisings in the African Congo followed upon the withdrawal of the Belgians in 1960 and the establishment of an independent nation there. Communists attacked Laos in 1961. Indian aggression took place in Portuguese Goa. In particular, the Soviet Union persistently refused to agree to supervised reduction of atomic armaments and attempted to force the Western powers to give up their position in Berlin. In 1961, the communists built a wall through the center of Berlin with the purpose of further hindering East-West contacts and preventing Germans living in the eastern parts of the country from fleeing to the West and depriving their economy of competent workers.

The United Nations, challenged in its undertakings by its own members, lost more and more of its prestige and usefulness. Atomic testing was resumed in 1962, and new dissensions arose from continued Soviet demands with regard to Berlin, from simmering warfare in Laos and Vietnam, and ultimately from Soviet arms deliveries to Cuba. Only Western firmness in the face of this last challenge and the subsequent Soviet withdrawal, quickened perhaps by fears of a growing rift within the communist world between China and the Soviet Union, led to a certain easing of the international tension and, in 1963, to a tentative agreement on suspension of testing of atomic weapons and to an increase in East-West trade.

NEW CHALLENGES

By the mid-1960s many of the hopes held by the generation that had fought the two world wars were not realized, although in some ways progress in that direction had been made. As always in the course of human affairs, the changes that had been brought about had created a new situation, in which old solutions no longer served. New problems, too, had arisen, which demanded a new response and a fresh start.

**A Young
Generation**

By the middle sixties, a generation had grown up that had lived through neither depression nor World War II. The old issue of capitalist-communist ideological rivalry had lost much of its meaning for this generation. Russian communism had become more liberal, capitalistic, and ultranationalistic, Western capitalism more socialistic and authoritarian. The Soviet hold on its satellite countries had weakened, while United States leadership was challenged by France under President de Gaulle, as well as subsequently by Germany, England, and, despite the economic and military aid given to them, by Asian and African nations.

These political issues faced by the young generation were enhanced by economic and cultural changes. By 1967 the "economic miracles" of the postwar period had apparently come to an end; rivalries over markets, problems of inflation and stability of currencies (especially the dollar and the pound), and struggles over tariffs reappeared. Subtly, power had begun to slip from the hands of leaders and their bureaucracies into those of small groups of scientifically trained experts—the technologists and economists who advised governments. A barrage of propaganda and advertising, seeking to hammer in ideas or sell goods, sought in vain to convince a new generation of the desirability of the status quo. Witnessing persisting social, national, and racial inequalities, continuing war preparations, and the depersonalization of society through technological advances, the young generation began to challenge prevailing morality, reject hypocrisy, and attack materialism and pragmatism.

Demography

The outstanding event of the post–World War II period was the enormous population increase—not only in countries where, until then, lack of medical knowledge and care had checked population growth, but also among the highly developed countries. Once more the question posed by Malthus at the end of the eighteenth century—whether population increases would outstrip the available food supply—was raised. To meet the issue, a twofold attack was begun. To serve immediate needs, new scientific methods for improving agriculture were developed; food grown in advanced countries was distributed to hungry populations; and technical knowledge was disseminated so that disadvantaged countries would be able to increase their own production. To provide a long-term solution, steps were taken to control birth rates, which were especially high in Latin America. Even governments and churches, traditionally opposed to such measures, began to support controls, reflecting thereby a change in fundamental Western attitudes. A decrease in the birth rate, at least in the advanced countries, was noted by 1966.

Science

Scientific progress made enormous advances. Physics, biology, chemistry, medicine, and astronomy, while revealing undreamed-of complexities, also brought discoveries that involve increasingly difficult scientific and ethical problems. The discovery of the genetic code (DNA) by Crick and Watson in 1960 had revolutionary consequences in many areas in addition to medicine and biogenetics, for it created problems that could threaten human survival. New and hazardous chemical products were developed for use in agriculture. Traditional products were replaced in the textile and building industries. Space travel opened possibilities for studies that could not be done successfully on earth, for weather forcasting, and for a better understanding of origin, shape, and conditions in the universe. Most of the discoveries could also be put to use for the perfection of destructive weaponry. Borderlines between these fields were difficult to draw. Scientific thinking also permeated social fields such as economics, psychology, history, and philosophy. A fundamental approach to quantification, often relying on mathematical studies and the help of statistical methods and computer sciences, was applied to these subjects. New machinery speeded up the process of obtaining solutions to problems and made obsolete the work of even skilled personnel. Computers became part of daily life, and computer science part of school curricula.

Economy

The effect of technological evolution was felt when dealing with daily practical problems, as well as when considering long-term cultural trends. Production methods were as much affected as general social conditions.

INDUSTRY

A steady growth of industrial productivity occurred. In competition with each other, the Soviet Union and the West helped spread industrialization—with all its consequences—to the underdeveloped countries. In continental Europe, owing to mutual assistance and cooperation, the Treaty of Rome had in 1957 created a Common Market of seven leading industrial nations, and these Common Market countries showed high rates of economic growth, at least for a decade; this stimulated ideas of a Common Market organization in Latin America as well. The unemployment of prewar years was replaced by an employment shortage in many trades—especially in areas of technological services. Significantly, this occurred despite the progress of automation in industry; apparently it was made possible by state economic planning, which did not reject deficit financing and which did provide for constant and coordinated economic growth in the sectors of production, wages, and prices.

Social security was steadily extended. While this policy heightened the dangers of monetary inflation, currency regulations diminished and tariffs were lowered. These developments were accompanied by general prosperity and a rapid rise in living standards in Western Europe and the United States. In the Soviet Union, challenged not only by Western skills but also by Communist China, which by 1965 had succeeded in producing its own atomic weapons, special attention was paid to the rapid refinement of industrial processes. Marked advances in space technology enabled the Soviet Union to launch the first space satellite (*Sputnik*) in 1957; in 1961 they were the first to put a human being into orbit around the earth; and in 1966 they achieved a "soft" missile landing on the moon. Yet, notwithstanding all achievements, living standards were not correspondingly improved, owing to the inefficiency of the entire system. Other countries, notably the United States, were also making great strides in space exploration.

AGRICULTURE

Outwardly less spectacular but equally fundamental were the changes in agriculture. Agricultural organization, whether of the nature of collective farms in communist-ruled areas or individually owned farms in the West, moved toward consolidation of landholdings and the abolishment of small farms. The peasantry as a class began to merge with the middle class. Production was influenced, if not directed, by government policies, price supports, setting of standards, international agreements, and mechanization in all sectors. In the West, these measures brought overproduction despite a rapid population increase, and only the distribution of surplus products to underdeveloped parts of the world remained a serious challenge.

Education

Changed, sophisticated production methods and the resulting social transformation necessitated radical adjustments in education. The demand for unskilled laborers, who had made up the proletariat, declined; their children swelled the ranks of the middle class, since office workers were needed to operate the vast bureaucracies, as were technicians. For all these positions, training was required. Compulsory education was therefore extended. Universities, often teaching specialized knowledge, had to adjust to the influx of overwhelming numbers of students. For the few creative thinkers, the establishment of additional institutes became ever more urgent. The results were rewarding. Medical advances lengthened life expectancies, and many diseases were successfully treated. Studies of genetics and astronomy, of the weather and of human behavior patterns, were promoted, and economic and historical scholarship profited thereby. An intellectual approach, often using mathematical methods, helped solve formerly unsolvable problems. Engineering benefited especially. An expanded media—a superabundance of paperback books and pictorial magazines, films, radio, and television—spread knowledge and entertainment, and scientific journals proliferated.

Individualism

In a world so dependent on intricate scientific methods and technology and so subject to mass production and mass domination, the individual encountered ever greater difficulties in maintaining individuality and escaping the pressures of society with its set of values and tastes. Workers in factories, on the land, in the universities, and in research were dependent on others and had to pool their knowledge or skills, and much individual effort was absorbed by collective projects. Even the creative arts—architecture, literature, music—were affected. Tastes tended toward equalization; mass-communication media—newspapers, films, and television—set the tone. Sociological aspects rather than problems of the individual fascinated the writer and the historian. Theater and musical concerts, as well as other artistic or scientific programs, usually funded by public and private support, envisaged "educational" effects upon the masses. Urban living and urbanization, whether in cities or suburbs, or in settlements erected uniformly by builders, contributed to the equalization trends, as did government policies in capitalist as well as communist countries. Perhaps as a reaction, abstract tendencies in painting and music, early medieval and Byzantine studies in history, Zen and other Oriental religions, gained the interest of those who tried to remain outside the collective pattern. And even though, in the mid-60s, a certain rejection of abstract art became noticeable, the protest was continued by a younger generation that—in a certain parallel to the *jeunesse dorée* of Revolutionary France—insisted on defying tradition in sexual behavior, dress, and taste.

Nationalism

Not only the individual man or woman but also the individual nation found itself exposed to the impact of new attitudes and economic forces.

TRENDS TOWARD INTERNATIONAL ORGANIZATION

While nationalism (in the sense in which it had developed in the Western world) was still increasing in areas where earlier colonial domination had hindered its growth, it began to wane in some respects among Western nations. The emphasis on national boundaries and on closed national economic units disappeared—as seen in the coordination of foreign policies, the pooling of armed forces (witness NATO and the Warsaw Pact), the partial disappearance of economic borders and customs barriers, mutual currency policies, the institution of common scientific projects, the easing of passport regulations, and increased tourism and exchange of labor forces. The division of Germany, the disintegration of the British Empire (in 1961 a dominion, South Africa, and in 1965 a colony, Rhodesia, left the Commonwealth), and the separation of Algeria from France in 1962 did not disturb the core of these leading nations, as would have happened only a few decades earlier. The European Common Market, under French-German leadership, became, despite attacks, a working reality. Communist Eastern Europe, through an emphasis on interdependence among its members, likewise contributed its share to the progressive decline of an older type of nationalism. Even such an institution as the Catholic Church felt the impact of the more cosmopolitan trends. In an ecumenical council convened by Pope John XXIII in 1961 and held in the Vatican (Vatican II) which lasted until 1965, rules were passed designed to "update" Church life, adjust to modern patterns, and ease long-existing antagonisms between Catholics and other Christian churches, as well as Eastern religions, Jews, and Arabs.

TRENDS TOWARD REVIVAL OF NATIONALISM

As the two world wars receded further into history, an opposite movement reappeared. In France, where a fifth republic with vast powers for its president, de Gaulle, was instituted in 1958, nationalism resurged. Appealing to the old concepts of "national sovereignty," de Gaulle insisted on completely independent rights for his country and did not hesitate to weaken such cooperative institutions as the Common Market or NATO, which the Western world had created in response to the bitter lesson of the world wars. Struggling England tried to keep alive ideas of its "special" position and was hesitant to enter a European community in which it could play no privileged role. Italy, ignoring its fascist past, applauded nationalist aims.

In the communist orbit, Yugoslavia under Tito pursued policies of national self-interest; by 1966 Rumania, Bulgaria, Poland, and Hungary also began to assert their national interests and to struggle for emancipation from Soviet domination. In defeated Germany, surrounded by increasingly nationalistic sentiments, national consciousness was ever more strongly reaffirmed despite the resolute support of all forms of European and transatlantic cooperation. The United States was no less concerned with the national question: its bitter war in Vietnam, fought against native socialist forces supported by communist China, involved to some extent national prestige and honor. By 1966, the Vietnam War constituted, indeed, the foremost international problem. Nationalism contributed also to the rift between the socialist worlds of Russia and China, and it threatened the peace in India, Pakistan, Indonesia, Malaysia, the Arab states, and in various parts of Africa.

Democracy

The meaning of the term "democracy" changed. Communist countries used the word in a sense entirely opposed to that in Western countries; the latter, while holding on to the theories of the Age of Enlightenment, gave democracy in practice an entirely new content. Democratic forms taken over from Anglo-Saxon countries—with free elections and powerful popular representative assemblies, with systems of checks and balances protecting the "rights of man," including the right of private property—were maintained in the West and the countries adhering to Western ideas. Democratic forms belittling these concepts and stressing a classless society, subordination of the individual to the common good, economic equality, and the conduct of affairs by a government and single party organization representative of the interests of all the workers in society were continued in the East and its dependencies.

But everywhere, "leadership," if not in the extreme form of Nazi patterns, was extolled. In Russia, the leadership principle predominated at least until 1964, during Nikita Khrushchev's premiership, which followed a two-year struggle for power after Stalin's death. In Germany, Chancellor Konrad Adenauer, who worked within a democratic framework, provided vigorous and capable leadership from 1954 to 1964. Between 1958 and 1969, France was led by Charles de Gaulle, under a constitution that gave large powers to the president. The United States, where racial unrest threatened the traditional democratic fabric, looked to steadily enhanced authority, influence, and direction by its presidents. In Cuba, a communist-supported leader, Fidel Castro, made himself the spokesman of democratic and national forces. Leadership rather than liberal democratic patterns was accepted also by new African nations, while army dictatorships either survived, or were reintroduced, in Brazil and some Central American nations. Threatened by totalitarian patterns, a changed democracy struggled to preserve for the individual those fundamental freedoms for which Western civilization had striven for centuries.

The aftermath of World War II brought great advances in the natural sciences. The discovery of the genetic code (DNA) and discoveries in medicine, space exploration, cosmology, chemistry, and biology opened possibilities for fundamental developments. The world thus had the potential for vastly improving the quality of life, as well as destroying it utterly. Special attention was paid to education. Emphasis was placed less on the development of outstanding individuals than on an awareness of the individual's responsibilities as a member of society.

The economies of all countries improved rapidly, owing to American generosity and cooperation and the determination of the European nations to strengthen their common interests through a Common Market. Governmental influence and interference increased everywhere. Recognizing that the interdependence of nations and people was steadily developing, various international organizations were founded to promote trade and cooperation in international questions.

Nevertheless, nationalism remained strong. Ethnic conflicts brought warfare and persecution. Uprisings occurred in former colonies and dominions until these gained full independence. In America as well, nationalism lost little ground, even though it subsided somewhat in Europe. It showed itself in the struggle between the communist East and the largely democratic, capitalistic West. The "cold war" that resulted did not lead, however, to open military action, even though outside of Europe numerous local wars occurred in which Western and Eastern countries interfered.

Attempts to reach a state of peaceful coexistence between East and West failed. Both sides continued to stockpile nuclear as well as conventional weapons. A new crisis occurred when the communists built a wall dividing Berlin and a fortified border stretching from the Baltic Sea to the Adriatic, which made East-West personal contacts almost impossible.

Selected Readings

Grosser, Alfred. *The Western Alliance: European-American Relations Since 1945* (1982)

Jordan, Robert S., et al. *Europe in the Balance* (1986)

Kirchner, Walther. *History of Russia* (1991)

Kolko, G., and J. Kolko. *The Limits of Power* (1972)

Lafeber, W. *America, Russia, and the Cold War* (1982)

24

A World in Transition

1968	Students' and civil rights disorders
	Soviet invasion and occupation of Czechoslovakia
1969	Nuclear Non-Proliferation Treaty
	First manned landing on the moon
1973	Israeli-Arab war
	Oil crisis
1974	Withdrawal of Portugal from its African colonies
1975	Referendum in Britain confirms Britain's entry into Common Market
	Franco, last fascist dictator, dies
	Helsinki Conference; rejection of force in order to achieve territorial changes
	Communists win Vietnam War; country united; U.S. troops withdrawn
1978	European Parliament created in Strasbourg
	Camp David meeting; Israelis return Sinai Peninsula to Egypt
1979	Labor unrest in Poland (Lech Walesa)
	Afghanistan-Soviet Friendship Pact; Soviet troops dispatched to Afghanistan
1981	Socialist party gains presidency in France
1982	Falkland War
1983	American invasion of Grenada
1984	Recession in West ends; inflation lightened

*S*hortly after World War I, Oswald Spengler stated in his famous work The Decline of the West *that Western civilization had outlived its allotted time and was now facing dissolution—to be succeeded by a new, fresh civilization.*

Twenty years later, in his Study of History, *Arnold Toynbee agreed with some of Spengler's views but suggested that a religious resurgence revitalizing the latent strength of its culture could prolong the life of Western civilization so that its early end was not inevitable. Another twenty years later, Karl Jaspers, dealing with the same question in his* Origin and Goal of History, *concluded that even though a dangerous transition period must be anticipated, a new order—not necessarily a "Western" but a "world" civilization—would evolve. World unity was necessary and, Jaspers felt, was coming, as wars and revolutions became less and less feasible under the impact of scientific and technological developments. In a united world, humankind's soul and spirit, its aspirations and institutions, would be changed. A world civilization such as Jaspers envisioned still seems far off. Yet some general trends in that direction, distinctly Western in origin, seem to be evolving.*

INTERNATIONAL POLITICS

From the mid-1960s on, the outstanding feature of the international scene was the increasing restraint that communist and other nations of the Western world, wary of nuclear war, exercised whenever an occasion for confrontation arose. The danger spots had by then shifted from Europe to Asia and Africa. But no issue brought a military clash between the two strongest military powers, the USSR and the United States. The two superpowers confined themselves to a war of words and propaganda, in the national news media of both countries and during meetings of the United Nations. Thus the racial question in South Africa and Rhodesia, where the white population sought to maintain dominance, remained a localized issue. Struggles between ethnic and political groups or tribes in central Africa—Ethiopia (where in 1974 the emperor was deposed and supplanted by a military dictatorship), for example, or Bangladesh—did not bring military interference by the great powers. Nor did decolonization, carried on by the Netherlands in the West Indies (1973) and Portugal in Africa (1974), nor the further retreat of England from its naval bases abroad. Indeed, since 1969, some slight progress has been made in negotiations for restraining the arms race, improving the exchange of information, and expanding East-West travel, trade, and scientific collaboration. Only two areas constituted a real threat to peace: Southeast Asia and the Middle East.

Southeast Asia   Beginning in the late 1950s, after the French withdrawal from Southeast Asia, the United States allowed itself to be drawn into intervention in

Vietnam to prevent a communist takeover; by the mid-1960s, full-fledged military support was being given to the noncommunist South. The tenacity of the Vietcong, combined with bitter disagreements among the American people regarding the country's war aims and policies, led to a military stalemate. After years of suffering by the Vietnamese people and the involvement of neighboring Cambodia and Laos, peace negotiations, concluded early in 1973, led to no more than a ceasefire agreement and the continuance of two separate states, North and South Vietnam. Since neither side respected the peace terms, war broke out anew in 1975. Despite continued United States support, South Vietnamese resistance collapsed, and by May of 1975, the South had been conquered by the North. In the meantime, a coalition government that included communists had already been established in Laos, and Cambodia too fell to the communists.

The Middle East   The situation in the Middle East constituted a still graver threat to world peace, but diplomacy and restraint once again prevented a direct confrontation of the superpowers. In June 1967, Egyptian provocations led to the outbreak of the Six-Day War, the third such conflict waged by Israel against its Arab neighbors. The extent of their military success surprised even the Israelis themselves: Aside from the capture of old Jerusalem, the Israelis were able to establish important buffer zones on the Golan Heights, the West Bank, and the Gaza Strip. A prolonged period of tension, broken by sporadic outbursts of fighting, followed. A full-scale Arab attack on Israel led to some initial successes, before the Israelis stabilized the front and began to prepare for retaliation. Fearing an expansion of the war, the Soviet Union and the United States interceded, and buffer zones under United Nations supervision were established.

In the meantime, an entirely new situation had arisen, owing to a change in the economic scene. In order to gain consideration from the West, the Arabs undertook to use their economic strength, which rested on their oil resources. They tripled their price for oil, and the economies of the industrial nations seemed thereby threatened.

INTERNATIONAL ECONOMY

In the course of the 1960s and the 1970s, socioeconomic patterns underwent a worldwide change that involved the most disparate economic systems. National and ideological boundaries began to lose their economic significance. Other issues came to assume greater importance. These crucial issues included population growth and starvation in Asia and Africa, pollution and exhaustion of natural resources, migrations of workers from underdeveloped countries into the foremost industrial states, and the rise and influence of multinational firms whose enterprises were carried on beyond national boundaries and beyond the reach of national legislation. This development demanded additional types of international regulations concerning not only the old political issues and the new technical ones (such as pollution and the waste of natural resources) but also problems of lawlessness, hijacking, kidnapping, and drug abuse on a global scale.

The Monetary System

Under the impact of economic change, the monetary system in place since the end of World War II broke down. Unable to maintain its convertibility into gold, the United States devalued the dollar, and a substitute currency standard had to be sought. All exchange rates were repeatedly revised, and interest rates climbed. By 1974, inflation and rising unemployment beset most Western economies and endangered the security of the Western peoples. Economic growth slackened.

East-West Economic Relations

Despite monetary problems, international trade increased. Trade between communist and Western democratic countries especially accelerated in an atmosphere of political "détente." From 1969 on—and more especially after 1973—the Soviet Union and the nations allied to it in a common-market arrangement called Comecon showed more flexibility in their economic policies. They increased imports and exports, asked for credit, accorded industrial concessions, agreed to a measure of scientific cooperation, and hired the services of Western experts. With the help of the West and Japan, plans were made for huge developments to exploit natural gas and oil resources in Siberia and to lay pipelines from there to the seas. Although the West continued to rely on individual, capitalist initiative and the less market-oriented East on socialist planning, a new economic mechanism was at work everywhere. A measure of economic "convergence" developed.

Energy Crisis

It was in the face of such economic developments that the Arab oil-producing countries created a crisis. They drastically raised the price for their oil (other countries did likewise for other commodities, including wheat, soybeans, bauxite, sugar, and gold), placing a temporary embargo on oil deliveries to countries supporting Israel. The economy of the great industrial nations was thereby threatened. Simultaneously, Iran, Libya, and Morocco speeded up their nationalization of oil resources. However, through restraint and careful negotiations, as well as by exploiting East-West rivalry, the oil-producing countries succeeded in avoiding a military response from the West. In an attempt to adjust to the situation, the industrial nations adopted the course of moderation advocated by the European consumer nations. They began to change their wasteful habits and to concentrate on developing their own sources of energy: solar and nuclear, natural gas under the seas, coal, and so on. Better distribution, which could eventually benefit the under-developed countries, was thereby initiated. These nations, at least to the extent that they possess valuable natural resources, thus began to gain a fairer share in the wealth of nations. They could use it to industrialize, build schools, introduce social reforms, and enter an age of modernization along Western lines.

NATIONAL POLICIES

Despite the increasing interdependence of all parts of the globe, national interests remained prevalent. Independence and power remained the goals of each nation. The political union of the European Economic Community (the Common Market) thus made hardly any progress. Indeed, local autonomy movements—such as in Britain's Scotland, France's Brittany, Italy's Sicily, Yugoslavia's Croatia, the Soviet Union's Ukraine, and Spain's Basque country—gained in significance.

Germany

Somewhat contrary to the general trend was the policy of Germany, which sacrificed national goals to the cause of international détente. In 1969, the rule of the Christian Democratic party under Konrad Adenauer and his heirs in West Germany (the Federal Republic) was replaced by a coalition led by the Social Democrats, under Willy Brandt. In August 1970, the Federal Republic signed a treaty with the Soviet Union recognizing the territorial changes imposed by the Allies after World War II. West Germany sub-sequently regulated its relationship with other East European countries, recognized East Germany as a separate state—the German Democratic Republic—and agreed to the status for Berlin arranged by the victors. Moreover, the country joined the United Nations simultaneously with East Germany. Internally, the Federal Republic continued to rebuild its economy, which was largely based on exports. Under pressure of vigorous radical movements, it introduced further social reforms and expanded its educational facilities. Brandt resigned in 1974, following the disclosure of a spy scandal involving a member of his staff. He was succeeded by Helmut Schmidt.

England

Beset by determined labor-union demands and numerous strikes, England found itself in a deteriorating economic situation. The Labor party under Harold Wilson returned to power in 1974. Living conditions in Britain on the whole improved, and scientific work maintained high standards. Two other problems, however, disturbed English developments. First, England's entry into the European Common Market aroused widespread internal opposition because it implied an increased involvement, politically and economically, with European partners. Second, a new round of civil strife and unrest began in Ireland in 1969. At stake was the unification of the entire island under the leadership of the independent Catholic South—an outcome feared by the Protestant North, which formed part of Britain. No solution was worked out.

Cyprus

As in Ireland, violent nationalism was a driving force at the other end of Europe, on Cyprus, where Greeks and Turks lived together in an uneasy relationship. Provoked by a Greek military putsch, Turkey sent troops and demanded the division of the island into two autonomous parts. The struggle not only endangered peace between Greece and Turkey but also led to the collapse of the military dictatorship in Greece, its replacement by a more democratic regime, government crises in Turkey, and the possibility of a split in the NATO forces. A measure of order was precariously restored in 1974.

Other European Countries

The year 1974, whether by coincidence or as a sign of general uncertainties, witnessed government changes in many Western countries, in addition to Germany and England. In France, General de Gaulle's regime had come to an end in 1969, and "Gaullism," with its nationalistic accent, was somewhat modified under his successors. Governments changed hands in Luxembourg, Belgium, Italy, and Portugal (where the long time dictator Salazar had died in 1970), with the socialists generally gaining ground.

Economic difficulties and other problems beset most countries. For example, student unrest in France led to often violent riots in 1969; the issue of divorce laws disturbed Catholic Italy in the 1970s; and activists finally achieved voting rights for women in Switzerland. As the younger generation began to organize and assert its power, the voting age was lowered in many countries. The unrest and dissatisfaction with social and economic shortcomings indicated less a breakdown in Western ways and institutions than a change in attitudes that was to bring reform rather than revolution. In spite of difficulties, living standards almost everywhere improved. An egalitarian trend was noticeable in education and daily life, and social services, directed by an ever-increasing state bureaucracy, were extended.

United States

More than any other Western nation, the United States was affected by the attitudes of the generation born since World War II. The country was internally beset by grave problems, including racial strife, which resolute legislation envisaging racial equality tried to mitigate. Other issues included women's rights, moral and sexual standards, prison reform, antiwar legislation, and demands for improved social-welfare benefits. Economic uncertainties aggravated the situation. During 1974, inflation reached a level unequaled since the war, as did unemployment by 1975. Respect for the Constitution, law and order, and traditional values of American society diminished. Corruption penetrated many layers of society, and confidence in government was shaken as never before as a result of the Watergate scandal. In the course of an investigation into the break-in at Democratic campaign headquarters during the 1972 election, it was revealed that President Richard Nixon had lied to the American people. To avoid impeachment proceedings, he resigned in 1974, the first president to do so; his vice-president, Spiro Agnew, had already been forced to resign because of allegations stemming from an unrelated incident.

While détente with the Soviet Union relieved external pressures, diplomatic ties with China brought only meager results. The failure in Vietnam, the costs of that war in lives and money, and its moral implications upset traditional complacency and convictions. United States diplomatic efforts to settle the Middle East question failed, and cooperation with European allies and Latin America proved insufficient. As in Europe, however, a readiness to introduce reforms prevented serious rifts. Except for the effects of lawlessness, living standards improved until the inflation of the 1970s, and by 1975 the economic climate had changed for the better. As a whole, the standing of the country was not seriously affected, and its power remained unchallenged.

Latin America

The Latin American nations were also faced with inflation and other economic disruptions, especially with population pressures, but in some respects their progress was remarkable. In many regions, modern factories were created, trade flourished, and social progress was observed. Politically, a measure of stability was gained, though under military dictatorships. In 1973, Argentina called back Juan Perön, who had been in exile since 1955. A socialist government in Chile under Salvador Allende (1970–1973), intent on social reform, came to a premature end with a rightist revolt. Only in Cuba did a communist regime continue to flourish.

The Soviet Union

While many of the problems besetting other Western countries left undisturbed those Eastern European nations under communist rule that could preserve strict order, other equally grave issues emerged. Progress in meeting shortages of capital, consumer goods, and housing was slow, and labor productivity was insufficient. Oppression of dissenting groups persisted, and freedom of movement remained limited. Public criticism of the system, while occasionally possible through private publications, remained risky. Under the impact of new technology, however, the relationship between state and society changed. Dissatisfaction increased, as was seen in growing conflicts between the political bureaucracy and the industrial managers. A new Soviet

Five-Year Plan, announced in April 1971, provided for maintenance of previous goals rather than adaptation to new conditions. Still, increased collaboration and trade with the capitalist West could not be avoided. This meant not merely the exchange of goods but also joint ventures and other business arrangements. Capitalist and communist came into close and prolonged contact, which brought about the introduction and infiltration of unwanted ideas. This situation created dissensions between the Soviet leadership under Leonid Brezhnev and other members of the Politburo. Yet in view of the advantages gained by détente, the communist successes in Southeast Asia (and to an extent, Portugal), and the misgivings about China's growing world role, the Soviets continued on the path of coexistence that had been decided upon for their external relations.

East-Central Europe

In the smaller, communist-dominated Eastern European states, progress toward modernization was rapid. East Germany, harshly controlled, could do nothing to challenge Soviet might; but in 1970 the Poles rioted and succeeded in replacing the old leadership with a somewhat more flexible one. Romanians and Hungarians emancipated themselves somewhat from too close Russian supervision, adopted strongly nationalistic policies, liberalized their internal systems, and increasingly cooperated with the West. A serious clash occurred in Czechoslovakia in 1968, however, when the Czechs installed a more liberal government under Alexander Dubček. Soviet troops were called in, "for the sake of socialism and the protection of socialist countries." They removed Dubček and once more imposed strict Soviet control.

CULTURAL TRENDS

Student unrest, self-assertion of a new generation, and challenges to traditional standards opened new directions in creative thought. A good deal of intellectual effort was directed toward science and technology, as great strides continued to be made in these fields. Aside from improved industrial processes based on enormous research efforts, achievements were made in outer-space exploration and medical technology. Space walks by astronauts became almost commonplace, and a landing on the moon—seen by millions live, on television—was achieved in 1969. The first transplant of a human heart was performed in South Africa in 1967, and other vital organs such as kidneys were also successfully transplanted. The laser beam became an important tool in surgery. Numerous studies going beyond those of Freud were undertaken to probe the human psyche. Cosmology, aided by radar instruments and far-reaching satellites, brought significant new working theories concerning the extent and nature of the universe. Most important was the discovery of a new nuclear particle that held the promise of making possible the formulation of a long-searched-for general field theory.

Writers like the French Albert Camus, the Swiss Friedrich Dürrenmatt, and the Russian Aleksandr Solzhenitsyn found a wide audience. Existentialism, as proposed by Jean-Paul Sartre and Martin Heidegger, lost some of its appeal. In music, Benjamin Britten held a foremost place, but in line with the mechanization of the age, the most conspicuous innovation came with the advent of electronic music—i.e. music composed by new, often mathematical techniques of composition for electronic sound equipment.

A reforming liberal movement asserted itself within the Christian churches, and some Eastern mysticism inspired Westerners struggling for a firm faith. But as in other areas of life, conservative institutionalism proved stronger. The Second Vatican Council, begun with high hopes under Pope John XXIII, came to little under his successor. Many questions of the Modern Age received no creative answer, and arrangements for coexistence between the Catholic Church and the communist countries were achieved more on the basis of expediency than conviction. Nor did the Protestant churches or other religious (or even worldly) faiths witness a spiritual revival.

CRISIS OF CONFIDENCE

In November 1975, Francisco Franco died in Spain. With his death, the last fascist dictatorship disappeared in Europe—about half a century after fascism had gotten its start in Italy. And with the death of China's revolutionary hero Mao Tse-tung in September 1976, the greatest challenger to the Soviet Union's leadership of the communist world passed from the scene. He left an unhealed breach in the communist front, emphasized by the vigor of various socialistic, communistic, and anarchistic movements separately pursuing, often within a narrow nationalist framework, the path to socialism.

Political Scene   The new age following World War II was an age characterized by increasing uneasiness. No lasting solutions were worked out for the great political issues: for European unity (although England finally joined the Common Market in 1975); for East-West cooperation (which, if anything, declined somewhat); for tensions between developed and developing nations; for the Israeli and Egyptian-Arab conflicts (despite the peace efforts of the Egyptian president Anwar Sadat in 1977–1978); for the Greek-Turkish strife over Cyprus; or the internal racial divisions in South Africa, which increasingly involved the policies of the West. The two great powers, the Soviet Union and the United States, had in the meantime lost some of their preeminence. Despite their military strength, they could no longer impose their will as they had before—not even in their own spheres of influence. International terrorism, aimed at the negative objectives of discrediting and undermining existing political patterns rather than constructive social objectives, became a major problem. Perhaps the most positive aspect of the late 1970s rested on the continued general realization that, under the atomic weapons threat, another world war could offer no solution to international problems. War, therefore, contrary to Clausewitz's dictum, could no longer be considered a means to promote national aims and to decide conflicts. Still, arms control made limited progress. Only isolated problems could be adjusted: In 1978, the United States announced that it would relinquish control of the Panama Canal by the year 2000, for instance.

Economic Scene

In both capitalistic and socialistic nations, material living standards continued to improve, despite economic difficulties. Working hours were reduced and, owing to computer techniques, work was lightened. Social services were broadened. A barrage of propaganda and advertisements through all public media sought to create, especially in the United States, ever new "needs" for ever new products, whereby the economy was to keep expanding and profiting. Often, the truly needy were not those to benefit.

In the process, almost all Western nations accumulated excessive public debts, speeded up inflation, and steadily enlarged their political apparatus and their bureaucracies (which often failed, however, to maintain standards of integrity). New currency troubles arose, and the dollar, especially, faced a major decline in international value. In the eastern parts of Europe, unrest increased as the Soviet Union insisted upon economic integration among the member states of the Comecon; restrictions on the freedom of movement of the inhabitants of these countries were maintained, meanwhile. In many parts, doubt was voiced about the advantages of continuous industrial growth in the face of slowing birth rates, of environmental consequences, of potential shortages in safe energy supplies, and of the costs of social services.

Cultural Scene

In the late seventies, the Western world's attention continued to center on the natural sciences and technology. Research in astronomy, engineering, chemistry, and nuclear physics brought about new practical advances. Especially impressive were the achievements in bioengineering, genetic research, recombinant DNA (which offered also threatening perspectives), and medicine, in the diagnosis and prevention of some major diseases.

NEW CHALLENGES

By 1978 the effects of the Western way of life had spread so far in the economic, technological, and political arenas that it became almost impossible to restrict the term "Western civilization" to the West. Japan exemplified many aspects of that civilization. China, India (both of which had independently manufactured their own atomic bombs), the Arab states, and even newly formed African states were forced, for the sake of self-preservation, to adopt the civilization of the West, with its scientific as well as its ideological biases. Whether desired or not, a convergence occurred that included tastes, building styles, dress, habits, and even forms of music and literature, as well as economic conditions, political systems, and thought patterns. Differences faded, and democratic institutions were reshaped under both capitalist and communist systems. General issues of population growth, space, environment, technology, bureaucracy, interdependence, and humanitarianism gradually began to overshadow in importance the narrower perspectives of national policies and political ideologies. These issues became a common matter of survival, and a growing awareness of their importance constituted the promise of the future.

SOCIAL SCENE

With new production methods, computers, and robots, a fundamental shift occurred in social relationships and class structure. The traditional "proletariat" diminished in size and influence. Increasingly, it merged with the middle class and adopted middle-class standards. On the other hand, the modern state, which—conservative objections notwithstanding—had to assume ever more tasks and provide so many social and economic regulations, had to extend the bureaucracy. In conjunction with technicians working for the state, these groups constituted an ever more weighty element in the social structure.

Moreover, the migration of mostly poor people from less developed countries to highly industrialized ones and also of refugees from the East altered the social composition of the populations. France, Switzerland, Germany, the United States, England, Holland, and others were affected and faced problems about human rights, social services, and political prerogatives of the newcomers. In view of, on the one hand, the services which the immigrants offered and, on the other, the burdens and difficulties which their acculturation caused, ways to integrate them had to be found, but a solution was nowhere satisfactorily worked out.

For centuries, philosophers had been predicting the decline of the West. Terrible wars ravaged Europe. Still, the West remained strong. In the 1980s, conservatism in politics was once more in the ascendancy. Yet the radical changes in attitudes and human and national values, which had been advocated in the late 1960s and 1970s and had attacked many of the traditional moral concepts, could not entirely destroy the basic themes of Western civilization.

The last of the fascist dictators died and, injustices and ills in the capitalist world notwithstanding, democratic institutions continued to dominate in the West. Despite persistent nationalism, international cooperation as begun after World War II continued to make progress. Communism was in retreat. It failed to achieve social justice and improve living standards. The conservative forces in the Soviet Union avoided the risk of abandoning the traditional patterns.

A number of wars occurred not in Europe but in non-Western regions; where Western nations became involved, they often did not prevail. The excellence of their weaponry was of little avail, since its full weight could not be used. Thus the power of the so-called superpowers diminished.

In the cultural field, every year brought new advances in the natural sciences. Philosophers, writers, and artists followed many new and interesting courses. Some of them were, however, passing fashions, which appealed mainly to a restricted intellectual audience, but were quickly replaced by others.

Selected Readings

Barnet, Richard J. *The Alliance* (1983)
Löwenthal, Richard. *Social Change and Cultural Crisis* (1984)
Luxenburg, Norman. *Europe Since World War II* (1979)
Postan, Michael M. *An Economic History of Western Europe, 1945–1964* (1967)

25

Glasnost and Perestroika

1985 Gorbachev becomes secretary general of the Soviet Union

1986 Chernobyl atomic disaster

1987 Soviets offer disarmament proposals

1988 European Nations Conference: "Single European Market irreversible"

1989 Conference of Nations on "Human Rights"

Hungary introduces "multi-party" government

Berlin Wall dismantled

United States invades Panama

1990 Iraq annexes Kuwait

Soviets complete withdrawal from Afghanistan

German Federal Republic and German Democratic Republic become one nation

Communist governments in Czechoslovakia, Poland, Rumania, Hungary, and Bulgaria resign

1991 War against Iraq

Gorbachev resigns presidency of the USSR

1992 Dissolution of USSR; establishment of a Commonwealth

Political stagnation came to an end in 1985. Fresh initiatives came from the USSR, where Mikhail Gorbachev, a younger member of the communist hierarchy, was elected to the post of secretary general of the Party. His program of glasnost *("openness") introduced the disintegration of the Yalta agreements and a change in the traditional East-West confrontational posture. His program of* perestroika *("restructuring") envisioned the transformation of the Soviet economy. The West was unprepared, but it had to follow the Soviet lead, notwithstanding the fact that it was not strength but economic and political weakness that had prompted the reversal of Soviet policy.*

THE INTERNATIONAL SCENE

Glasnost and Western Policies

The opening of barriers to the outside world began in Hungary, with the consent of the Soviet government. The eagerness with which citizens took advantage of travel opportunities to the West and access to Western information speeded up the process of glasnost. A grave nuclear disaster in the Ukraine at Chernobyl (1986), only seven years after a nuclear accident in the United States at Three Mile Island (1979), demonstrated to what extent dangers in one country could engulf others.

GERMANY

The decisive breakthrough on the road to reunification came in 1989 when, taking advantage of glasnost, East German citizens, demonstrating peaceably, breached the Berlin Wall, which for almost three decades had separated them from their relatives in the western parts of Germany. Thus, they challenged their communist rulers, who were forced to back down. One barrier after another fell. Free movement back and forth between East and West was reintroduced. These events in Germany stunned the Western world, especially when it became clear that the Soviets were willing to stand aside and let Germany remain a member of NATO and the EEC.

The events in Germany paralleled liberation movements in Czechoslovakia, Hungary, Bulgaria, and Rumania. Everywhere the communist rulers were being removed. The reunification of Germany was completed by a national referendum in October of 1990.

This fundamental change which Gorbachev's glasnost had achieved in the existing balance of power had worldwide repercussions. In particular, it led to significant reductions in armaments and occupation troops, not only in Central Europe but also in non-European countries, such as Angola. Self-determination and autonomy movements everywhere were given new hope.

UNITED STATES

Glasnost necessitated a reversal of American foreign policy and a shift from confrontation to peaceful cooperation, far beyond the European arena. The perception of Third World struggles as "an extension of the cold war" had to be discarded. Still, Washington continued to hold as its leading principle the policy of "keeping governments in power that would not challenge U.S. policies." The United States supported the government of President Ferdinand Marcos in the Philippines until he was ousted in 1986. It indirectly involved itself in the internal struggles in Nicaragua and El Salvador. In 1989 it invaded Panama and helped overthrow the formerly friendly government of Manuel Noriega. It thus sought to reassert its power and leadership.

In 1990, a graver test came in the Middle East, when Iraq invaded neighboring Kuwait and seized this oil-rich country. An embargo on all shipments to and from Iraq was declared, and a large American military force, which included some troops from allied nations, was dispatched to the Persian Gulf. With the economic sanctions not bringing quick results, the United States sought permission from the United Nations to use military force. The brief war for the liberation of Kuwait began in early 1991 and ended successfully after causing terrible human losses to the Iraquis.

USSR

Glasnost obviously had its greatest impact on the USSR itself. Access to information from abroad was no longer forbidden to its citizens; travel abroad became easier. In foreign affairs, aside from changing its German policies, the Soviet Union tolerated the abolition of the dominating communist governments in its satellite states and the virtual dissolution of the Warsaw Pact. The Soviets completed the evacuation of Afghanistan, thereby eliminating a point of dissension, especially with the United States. Gradually they reduced their troops stationed in Central Europe; they engaged in negotiations with the European powers and the United States concerning common action in other areas of the globe where local struggles threatened peaceful developments. When the war in Iraq broke out in 1991, they refrained from military intervention but participated in the efforts to persuade Iraq to leave Kuwait.

Perestroika and the Western Economy

Just as glasnost had consequences not only for the Soviet Union but everywhere, so did perestroika.

USSR

During the years between 1985 and 1990, notwithstanding pockets of poverty and ignorance in Western Europe and the United States, living standards in these areas were high. But those in the USSR deteriorated. Severe drought conditions had contributed to the economic problems in the years 1979 to 1981, but the organization of the Soviet economy remained largely at fault. Gorbachev attacked the problem by seeking to bring about what his predecessors since Khrushchev had envisioned but not achieved. He reduced the number of central agencies directing the economy and put more responsibility as well as greater authority into the hands of industrial and agricultural units. Where discipline and obedience were formerly demanded, a measure of pluralism would now be allowed.

ECONOMIC AIMS

In 1988, steps were taken to enlarge the private sector of the economy. Peasants could use more of the available land for growing crops for private consumption and for sale. Small businesses could be founded, as long as they did not employ external help. Newspapers and books could give expression to dissenting opinions. Also the government permitted the Orthodox Church wider activities; Gorbachev even visited the pope in Rome.

But the ownership of land as well as industries remained in the hands of the state; central planning was maintained. No unifying ideology was devised that could inspire and also satisfy people trained along old Soviet lines, who preferred security to Western-type freedoms. Within the confines of socialist ownership and control, no method was found to create the open-market arrangements and free competition that the West had found useful in raising its living standards.

In 1990, Gorbachev was elected president; additional executive authority was given him. A popularly elected legislature was instituted, and the monopoly of the Communist Party was dissolved. A 500-day plan was worked out to integrate the Soviet Union into the world economy by permitting joint ventures with foreign enterprise. In the future, a measure of private ownership of land and various types of ownership in industry were to be allowed. The convertibility of the Russian currency was envisioned. For this purpose, an exchange of the existing currency into new bills took place in 1991 under harsh conditions, which created much discontent, the more so as all changes needed time to bring about the desired results. In the meantime, the economy deteriorated further. Food in the cities became still scarcer. Price increases followed. Large parts of the population had to rely on the black market, which flourished.

OPPOSITION

Dissatisfaction on the side of devoted communists as well as opponents of the system and a feeling of insecurity followed. It brought a widening gap between reformers and conservatives and a tightening of the reins by Gorbachev. Fears prevailed that with the replacement of some of the reformers in the government by old-line communists, as had happened late in 1990 and early 1991, private ownership could eventually encounter renewed persecutions.

Independence movements in several of the Soviet Union's constituent republics added to Gorbachev's problems. In the Baltic countries as well as in the Caucasus, in Asian regions and the Ukraine, and even in the republic of Russia itself, autonomy and independence were demanded. Where action in this direction was undertaken, the government did not permit it. In a few instances it used force. The 500-day plan did not, however, exclude the possibility of reforming the Union in an orderly way into a federation of sovereign states and allowing some republics to withdraw from the Union.

REACTION

At the beginning of 1991, the policy of perestroika, as opposed to that of glasnost, had brought insufficient results. The conservative forces in the country sought to reassert themselves. But when they attempted to regain power through a coup in the middle of 1991, they failed and the opposition under the president of the Russian republic, Boris Yeltsin, triumphed. The reform work was now speeded up and in December 1991 Gorbachev resigned from his office. This signified the dissolution of the Soviet Union. Practically all member republics of the Union declared their independence. A "Commonwealth" was proposed by Yeltsin and others to take its place, and in the economic sphere communism was to be replaced by a freer, market-oriented economy—largely in private hands.

The execution of this plan met, however, with grave obstacles. The problems of borders, of new ethnic disagreements, of the possession of military weapons, of finance and debts (notwithstanding the help extended by European countries), and of foreign relations were overwhelming and results remained in doubt.

The United States

Perestroika and German unification opened up opportunities to United States industries and service enterprises. But by 1990, the dollar had fallen to an all-time low. With military expenditures rising dramatically, national indebtedness had risen to an all-time high. Third World countries could not repay their debts. Foreign industrial competition, especially by Japan and, to a lesser degree, other Asian nations, threatened American industries, which failed to keep up with technical advances. Once a creditor nation, the United States had become a debtor nation. Industrial productivity lagged.

Yet, after a brief recession (1982–1984), inflation and unemployment were kept in check; credits could be extended wherever new markets opened. General living standards, notwithstanding pockets of poverty and rapidly increasing homelessness and crime in some urban centers, remained high. Achievements in the natural sciences, and especially in medicine, were outstanding. Gains were made in the struggle for integration of its black population; for the full achievement of women's equal rights; for an end to hatred toward, and discrimination against homosexual men and women; for prison reform; and for civil rights at home and abroad.

Europe

Events in the USSR and the United States reinforced the role played by Europeans in world affairs. The opening of Eastern Europe did not interfere with the maintenance of close ties with the United States, nor did the determination of the Continental powers to strengthen European unity.

England, too, adjusted to the emerging pattern and its need to cooperate with the Continental powers. Somewhat reluctantly, it yielded in 1990 with regard to the establishment of a common monetary unit.

Economic conditions in Europe were satisfactory, allowing for higher standards of living, even in less industrially advanced nations, such as Spain and Portugal. However, unemployment was high. A fair system of social security helped to mitigate its consequences in most countries. Special problems were caused by the integration of formerly communist countries into the Western economy, by the stream of immigrants from Eastern Europe and also from Asia and Africa, and by the breakup of Yugoslavia, where bitter internal warfare raged. The usual inefficiency of communist industry necessitated huge foreign investments in production centers and factories and for the improvement of environmental conditions.

Culturally, the implementation of glasnost and perestroika did not bring new departures or new achievements—not even in the USSR. Prevailing trends in the arts, in religious affairs, and in science persisted.

The great events and significant trends in 1990 included (1) the reunification of Germany and, to an extent, Western Europe itself; (2) the reduction of national ambitions among the technically developed nations and the decline of the superpowers; (3) the continued increase of world population and the steady Westernization of all nations under the impact of technology; and (4) further realization of the need for determined environmental improvement and the accelerated progress of the natural sciences, especially medicine. All this is perhaps evidence that a new period in Western civilization, sometimes labeled "postmodern," has indeed dawned. In this new world, neither war nor money hold out the promise of solving major problems. Even from a geographical point of view, a new age had begun. If the Mediterranean area circumscribed what historians call "ancient" history, Europe the "medieval" world, and the entire planet "modern" times, then it may be that expansion into air and space justifies the view that a new age is beginning. Only future historians will be able to tell whether Western civilization has retained its place in this new world.

Selected Readings

Berdyaev, Nicholas. *The Meaning of History* (1949)
Bloch, Marc. *The Historian's Craft* (1962)
Burckhardt, Jacob. *Force and Freedom* (1943)
Carr, Edward H. *What Is History?* (1962)
Muller, Herbert J. *The Uses of the Past* (1952)

Appendix

Table 1
Some Memorable Statesmen

	France	England	Germany	Russia	Italy	USA (Presidents)
XVII Century	Sully Richelieu Mazarin Colbert	Cromwell				
XVIII Century	Turgot	Walpole Pitt the Elder		Potemkin		Washington
XIX Century	Talleyrand	Pitt the Younger Palmerston Disraeli Gladstone	Metternich Bismarck	Witte	Cavour	Jefferson Jackson Lincoln
XX Century	Clemenceau Briand De Gaulle	Lloyd George Churchill	Stresemann Hitler Adenauer	Lenin Stalin Khrushchev Gorbachev	Mussolini	Wilson F.D. Roosevelt J. F. Kennedy

Table 2
Some Memorable Thinkers and Artists

Century	Philosophy	Religion	Art	Music	Literature	Social Science	Natural Science	Exploration
XVI Century		Luther Ignatius of Loyola Calvin	Leonardo da Vinci Raphael Michelangelo Dürer Holbein Titian Brueghel El Greco	Palestrina	Erasmus Shakespeare	Machiavelli	Copernicus Galileo	Magellan Cortez Pizarro
XVII Century	Descartes Spinoza Pascal Leibnitz		Rubens Valesquez Vandyke Vermeer Franz Hals Rembrandt	Monteverdi	Corneille Racine Molière Milton	Locke	Kepler Newton	
XVIII Century	Hume Kant	Wesley	Gainsborough	Bach Handel Gluck Rameau Corelli Haydn Mozart	Pope Lessing Goethe Schiller Wordsworth	Montesquieu Voltaire Rousseau Malthus	Halley Boerhaeve Franklin Linnaeus Priestley Boyle Lavoisier Laplace	Bering Cook
XIX Century	Hegel Fichte Comte Schopenhauer Nietzsche	Pius IX	Goya Manet Monet Renoir van Gogh	Beethoven Schubert Chopin Rossini Musorgski Wagner Verdi	Hugo Balzac Dickens Pushkin Dostoevsky Tolstoy Ibsen	Bentham Mill Proudhon Karl Marx	Lyell Helmholtz Darwin Pasteur Mendel Pavlov Roentgen Curie	Nansen
XX Century	Bergson Dewey	John XXIII	Picasso Klee	Strauss Sibelius Prokofiev Schönberg	Shaw Mann Joyce Gide	Lenin	Planck Einstein Freud Heisenberg Watson-Crick	Amundsen (*Sputnik*)

Index

OTHER BOOKS IN THE HARPERCOLLINS COLLEGE OUTLINE SERIES

ART
History of Art 0-06-467131-3
Introduction to Art 0-06-467122-4

BUSINESS
Business Calculus 0-06-467136-4
Business Communications 0-06-467155-0
Introduction to Business 0-06-467104-6
Introduction to Management 0-06-467127-5
Introduction to Marketing 0-06-467130-5

CHEMISTRY
College Chemistry 0-06-467120-8
Organic Chemistry 0-06-467126-7

COMPUTERS
Computers and Information Processing 0-06-467176-3
Introduction to Computer Science and Programming
    0-06-467145-3
Understanding Computers 0-06-467163-1

ECONOMICS
Introduction to Economics 0-06-467113-5
Managerial Economics 0-06-467172-0

ENGLISH LANGUAGE AND LITERATURE
English Grammar 0-06-467109-7
English Literature From 1785 0-06-467150-X
English Literature To 1785 0-06-467114-3
Persuasive Writing 0-06-467175-5

FOREIGN LANGUAGE
French Grammar 0-06-467128-3
German Grammar 0-06-467159-3
Spanish Grammar 0-06-467129-1
Wheelock's Latin Grammar 0-06-467177-1
Workbook for Wheelock's Latin Grammar
    0-06-467171-2

HISTORY
Ancient History 0-06-467119-4
British History 0-06-467110-0
Modern European History 0-06-467112-7
Russian History 0-06-467117-8
20th Century United States History 0-06-467132-1
United States History From 1865 0-06-467100-3
United States History to 1877 0-06-467111-9
Western Civilization From 1500 0-06-467102-X

Western Civilization To 1500 0-06-467101-1
World History From 1500 0-06-467138-0
World History to 1648 0-06-467123-2

MATHEMATICS
Advanced Calculus 0-06-467139-9
Advanced Math for Engineers and Scientists
    0-06-467151-8
Applied Complex Variables 0-06-467152-6
Basic Mathematics 0-06-467143-7
Calculus with Analytic Geometry 0-06-467161-5
College Algebra 0-06-467140-2
Elementary Algebra 0-06-467118-6
Finite Mathematics with Calculus 0-06-467164-X
Intermediate Algebra 0-06-467137-2
Introduction to Calculus 0-06-467125-9
Introduction to Statistics 0-06-467134-8
Ordinary Differential Equations 0-06-467133-X
Precalculus Mathematics: Functions & Graphs
    0-06-467165-8
Survey of Mathematics 0-06-467135-6

MUSIC
Harmony and Voice Leading 0-06-467148-8
History of Western Music 0-06-467107-7
Introduction to Music 0-06-467108-9
Music Theory 0-06-467168-2

PHILOSOPHY
Ethics 0-06-467166-6
History of Philosophy 0-06-467142-9
Introduction to Philosophy 0-06-467124-0

POLITICAL SCIENCE
The Constitution of the United States 0-06-467105-4
Introduction to Government 0-06-467156-9

PSYCHOLOGY
Abnormal Psychology 0-06-467121-6
Child Development 0-06-467149-6
Introduction to Psychology 0-06-467103-8
Personality: Theories and Processes 0-06-467115-1
Social Psychology 0-06-467157-7

SOCIOLOGY
Introduction to Sociology 0-06-467106-2
Marriage and the Family 0-06-467147-X

Available at your local bookstore or directly from HarperCollins at 1-800-331-3761.